Linear and Non-Linear Financial Econometrics - Theory and Practice

Edited by Mehmet Kenan Terzioğlu and Gordana Djurovic

Published in London, United Kingdom

IntechOpen

Supporting open minds since 2005

Linear and Non-Linear Financial Econometrics - Theory and Practice
http://dx.doi.org/10.5772/intechopen.88099
Edited by Mehmet Kenan Terzioğlu and Gordana Djurovic

Assistant to the Editors: Martin M. Bojaj

Contributors
Tumellano Sebehela, Katlego Kola, Gerasimos Rompotis, Gordana Djurovic, Martin M. Bojaj, Hopestone Chavula, Bodo Herzog, Shaopeng Zhong, David Olayungbo, Muhammad Jawad, Munazza Naz Naz, Claudio Elórtegui-Gómez, Hanns De La Fuente-Mella, Mauricio Alvarado Martínez, Matías Guajardo Calderón, Riaan De Jongh, Helgard Raubenheimer, Mentje Gericke, Thobeka Ncanywa, Ombeswa Ralarala, Bakhita Hamdow Braima, Verda Davasligil Atmaca, Burcu Mestav, Raed Alzghool, Tuğba Dayıoğlu, Yılmaz Aydın, Süreyya Dal, Mustafa Çakir

First published in London, United Kingdom, 2021 by IntechOpen
IntechOpen is the global imprint of INTECHOPEN LIMITED, registered in England and Wales, registration number: 11086078, 5 Princes Gate Court, London, SW7 2QJ, United Kingdom
Printed in Croatia

British Library Cataloguing-in-Publication Data
A catalogue record for this book is available from the British Library

Additional hard and PDF copies can be obtained from orders@intechopen.com

Linear and Non-Linear Financial Econometrics - Theory and Practice
Edited by Mehmet Kenan Terzioğlu and Gordana Djurovic
p. cm.
Print ISBN 978-1-83962-486-5
Online ISBN 978-1-83962-487-2
eBook (PDF) ISBN 978-1-83962-488-9

Meet the editors

Mehmet Kenan Terzioğlu received his MSc. degree in Actuarial Sciences from Hacettepe University. He studied at Tilburg University in the Department of Econometrics and Operations between 2008 and 2009 while working in the Department of Actuarial Sciences at Hacettepe University between 2006 and 2009 as a Research Assistant. He worked as a Risk Analyst Assistant (Assistant Specialist) in Ziraat Bank Risk Management Department and got his Ph.D. degree in Econometrics from the Department of Econometrics at Gazi University. Since 2018, he has been working as an Associate Professor in the Econometrics Department at Trakya University. He takes part in the management team of the Risk Management and Corporate Sustainability Application and Research Center at Trakya University.

Gordana Djurovic is a Full Professor in the Faculty of Economics, University of Montenegro, Podgorica, where she teaches economic development, environmental economics, international economic relations, regional economy, and the EU Enlargement Policy. Her area of expertise is sustainable development. Prof. Djurovic was Deputy Prime Minister and Minister for European Integration in the Montenegrin Government (2004-2010) when she was the chief negotiator for SAA negotiation. She has authored twenty books and chapters in books related to sustainable economic development and the EU integration process and more than 70 scientific papers (https://www.ucg.ac.me/objava/blog/18163/objava/1). She is a Jean Monnet Professor, President of the Montenegrin Pan-European Union (MPEU), and member of the International PEU Presidency. She is a member of the Committee for Economy, Anthropology, and Demography of the Montenegrin Economy of Science.

Contents

Preface

The effect of globalization and easy access to technology initiated the transformation to an information-oriented society. This transformation means that complete and satisfactory statistical results, which can only be achieved through appropriate methods, are now a necessity. Additionally, the emergence of specialized branches led to a movement away from the stereotypical patterns and the development of new patterns that are more in line with the current economic and financial structure. Financial markets, which do not get stuck only in theoretical structure and develop in practice, play an important role in the sustainable growth of the economy. The starting point of the financial models is the uncertainty faced by investors that include the uncertainty in the behavior of and thus the uncertainty in market prices. Therefore, the existence of financial econometrics is based on uncertainty. The structure and effect of fluctuations are determined using econometrics theory in the modeling and estimation process of uncertainties in financial models. The development of econometrics that makes use of data, statistical inference methods, and structural or descriptive modeling to solve financial and economic problems has been paralleled by the increasing variety and complexity of financial products. Efforts to measure fluctuations in terms of time, dimension, and turning/breaking points in the context of financial developments and the desire to have the best return in financial market practices with the minimum loss can be counted as some of the reasons why econometrics theory develops from linear to nonlinear models. Financial market mechanisms can be better explained by the development of models in the domains of martingales and non-linear time series, the use of parametric and non-parametric estimation methods, the use of diffusion equations, and an approximation for pricing and derivatives. Gaining the ability to build and develop a model based on events/problems experienced in life is important both in terms of solving the problems and evaluating the new models/methods in the field of application. With this in mind, the models are established on real problems with the aim of developing new models and/or achieving policy proposals through appropriate analyses that would be beneficial in solving problems.

This book aims to introduce the mathematical/statistical and econometrical underpinnings of the main tools used in empirical economics and empirical finance in an effort to bridge the gap between analytic, closed-form methods, and numerical methods and also outline the econometrics models readily applicable to financial markets using linear and nonlinear approaches. The main topics are organized to gain a profound and detailed understanding of theory and methods and to understand the interplay between interrelated field techniques and modeling assumptions both for theoretical and practical applications.

Dr. Mehmet Kenan Terzioğlu
Associate Professor,
Trakya University,
Faculty of Economics and Administrative Sciences,
Econometrics Department,
Balkan Campus, Edirne, Turkey

Gordana Djurovic
University of Montenegro,
Montenegro

Chapter 1

Modeling Inflation Dynamics with Fractional Brownian Motions and Lévy Processes

Bodo Herzog

Abstract

The article studies a novel approach of inflation modeling in economics. We utilize a stochastic differential equation (SDE) of the form $dX_t = a(X,t)dt + b(X,t)dB_t^H$, where dB_t^H is a fractional Brownian motion in order to model inflationary dynamics. Standard economic models do not capture the stochastic nature of inflation in the Eurozone. Thus, we develop a new stochastic approach and take into consideration fractional Brownian motions as well as Lévy processes. The benefits of those stochastic processes are the modeling of interdependence and jumps, which is equally confirmed by empirical inflation data. The article defines and introduces the rules for stochastic and fractional processes and elucidates the stochastic simulation output.

Keywords: inflation, dynamics, modeling, stochastic differential equation, fractional Brownian motion, Lévy process, jump-diffusion

1. Introduction

Modeling inflation dynamics is a tricky topic, particularly in the Eurozone. The determinants of inflation are multifaced, including interest rates, GDP growth, supply and demand of goods and services, exchange rates, etc. Moreover, inflation is somehow persistent over time, such as the low inflation rates in the recent years. In order to model the empirical pattern of inflation, we need a stochastic model with a mean-reversion property as well as time-dependent increments. Both features are mathematically difficult to design because all basic stochastic processes, such as a standard Brownian motion have time-independent increments and it is not mean-reverting.

We propose a novel approach by utilizing a fractional Brownian motion (fBm) and a Lévy process. Both stochastic concepts are relatively new in economic applications. Yet, recent discoveries about fBm's in mathematics already unravel striking insights to economics and finance, such as the modeling of inflation dynamics. We model inflation dynamics by a stochastic process, X_t. Before discussing the mathematical details, we provide a brief summary of the relationship across the different stochastic processes (**Figure 1**).

Each of the three stochastic processes have special properties. Interestingly, the overlap of the three stochastic processes gives a subset of new processes with highly interesting and uncommon properties. In this article, we study the subset of a

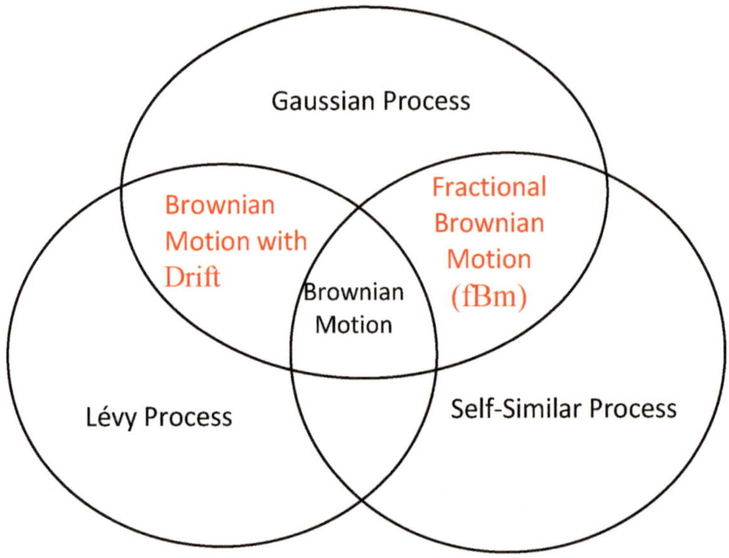

Figure 1.
Overview and Relation of Stochastic Processes. Source: B Herzog (2020).

fractional Brownian motion (fBm) and a Brownian motion with drift as a subclass of Lévy processes in general. Furthermore, for the first-time, we combine both types of stochastic processes in one model.

The standard Brownian motion is a Gaussian process with independent and stationary increments. However, a fBm is a Gaussian process but does not have independent increments. Similarly, a Brownian motion with drift is a subset of a Lévy process and a Gaussian process. This group of processes belongs to infinitely divisible distributions. We exhibit the relationships and properties between the different types of stochastic processes in order to model the inflation dynamics of the Eurozone.

Let us start with some preliminaries about stochastic processes in general. One can imagine a stochastic process as a sequence of random variables over time, t. Let (Ω, F, P) be a filtered probability space and $X = \{X_t : t > 0\}$ be a stochastic process on the probability space. The filtration $F = \{F_t : t > 0\}$ is an increasing flow of information and P is defined as a standard probability measure [1].

Furthermore, we need the idea of a stochastic differential equation (SDE) [2]. A non-linear stochastic differential equation for the inflation process, X_t, has the form:

$$dX_t = a(X,t)dt + b(X,t)dB_t^H, \tag{1}$$

where $a(X,t)dt$ is called the trend-term and $b(X,t)dB_t^H$ the diffusion-term contingent of a fractional Brownian motion, dB_t^H. The details of fractional Brownian motions with different "Hurst-Indices," $H\epsilon(0,1)$, will be discussed in more detail in Section 2. However, if we choose $H = \frac{1}{2}$, the fBm, $B_t^{1/2}$, turns into an ordinary Brownian Motion discovered by Robert Brown in 1827 [1, 3].

The origin and idea of fractional processes or fractional calculus is likewise of interest in general. Indeed, fractional calculus is a subfield in mathematics, which deals with integrals and derivatives of arbitrary order. Fractional calculus is both an old and new field at the same time. It is an old topic since some issues have been discovered by Leibniz and Euler. In fact, the idea of generalizing the notion of a derivative to non-integer order, in particular $d^{1/2}$, is already in the correspondence of Leibniz with Bernoulli and L'Hospital. Laplace, Fourier, Abel and recently up to Riesz Feller and Mishura [4] contributed to the development of fractional calculus as it is of today.

The interest to fractional calculus has to do with its relationship to dynamics and stochastic processes in general. In the past decade, the field of fractional calculus is growing anew due to new discoveries in mathematics and theoretical physics. The first book on fraction calculus is by [5]. Considerable interest in fractional calculus has been stimulated by the many applications in different fields of sciences, such as physics, biology, engineering, economics and finance.

Now, let us compute a fractional derivative of a concrete example: What is the semi-derivative of $\frac{d^{1/2}x^0}{dx^{1/2}} = \frac{d^{1/2}1}{dx^{1/2}}$? This example is a semi-derivative or half-derivative of a constant. From standard calculus, we know that the derivative of a constant is zero. Yet, the half-derivative is not zero as we will see soon. In general, you can compute fractional derivatives by the following formula:

$$D^m x^p = \frac{\Gamma(1+p)}{\Gamma(1+p-m)} x^{p-m}, \tag{2}$$

where Γ (x) is the Gamma function. Similarly, you can compute the fractional derivatives and fractional integrals by the Riemann-Liouville formula. For simplification, we do not introduce the Riemann-Liouville calculus here. The interested reader is referred to [5]. For $m = \frac{1}{2}$ and $p = 0$, we obtain from Eq. (2)

$$D^{\frac{1}{2}} x^0 = \frac{\Gamma(1+0)}{\Gamma\left(1+0-\frac{1}{2}\right)} x^{0-\frac{1}{2}} = \frac{1}{\sqrt{\pi x}}. \tag{3}$$

The result is perhaps the most remarkable result in this brief discussion of fractional calculus. It cannot be embraced too much and deserves a special place in the hall of fame in fractional calculus. Note, the semi-derivative of a constant is surprisingly dependent on π and on the variable x. Indeed, this result is utilized repeatedly in fractional calculus in order to simplify solutions.

The chapter is organized as follows: Section 2 studies the modeling with fractional Brownian motions. We introduce the concept by defining a fractional Brownian motion in more detail. Section 3 defines a Lévy process and relates it to a Brownian motion. Finally, in Section 4, we start the simulation exercise. We study the stylized facts of inflation rates in the Eurozone from 1997 to 2020. Subsequently, we specify a stochastic differential equation with a fractional Brownian motion and a Lévy process and run several numerical simulations. Section 5 concludes the chapter.

2. Inflation modeling with fractional Brownian motion (fBm)

In this section, we define a "fractional Brownian Motion" (fBm). First of all, a fBm is not a (semi-)martingale. Thus, Ito's calculus does not apply anymore. Consequently, the lack of the martingale property has major implications in stochastic calculus. Indeed, one have to develop – similar to Ito's Lemma – completely new stochastic integration and differentiation rules for fractional Brownian motions.

We define an ordinary Brownian motion as a special case of a fractional Brownian motion. Indeed, Mandelbrot and van Ness [6] defined a fractional Brownian motion, B_t^H, as a Brownian motion together with a Hurst-Index, $H\epsilon(0, 1)$, in the exponent. The parameter H is a moving average of the past increments dB_t^H weighted by the kernel $(t-s)^{H-1/2}$. Consequently, fractional Brownian motions have the feature that increments are interdependent. The latter property is known as self-similarity, which displace an invariance of the stochastic process with respect to changes of time scale. Almost all other stochastic processes, such as the ordinary Brownian motion or Lévy process have time-independent increments (at least almost surely). They create the famous class of Markov processes.

Empirically, however, there is evidence that economic and particularly financial time-series have a spectral density with a sharp peak. Additionally, we observe the phenomena of extremely long interdependence of certain trends over time in economics and finance. This presence of interdependence between past increments, directly speaks for the modeling with fractional Brownian motions. A standard Brownian motion is defined by the following properties:

1. B_t is almost surely continuous; $B_{t=0} = 0$;

2. The increments $B_t - B_s$ for $t > s$ have mean zero and variance $t - s$;

3. The increments $B_t - B_s$ are independent over time and stationary.

Indeed, we know that the variance of the increment is of $Var[B_t - B_s] = \mathbb{E}\left[(B_t - B_s)^2\right] = \mathbb{E}\left[dB_t^2\right]$. Likewise, the standard deviation is: $\sigma = \sqrt{Var[B_t - B_s]} = \sqrt{dB_t^2} \sim dt^{1/2}$. This is often referred to as the $t^{1/2}$-law. Now, we are ready to define a fractional Brownian motion:

Definition "Fractional Brownian Motion (fBm)." *Let the Hurst-Index, H, be $0 < H < 1$, then we call B_t^H a fractional Brownian Motion with parameter H, such as*

$$B_{t=0}^H = B_0$$

and;

$$B_t^H - B_0^H = \frac{1}{\Gamma(H+\frac{1}{2})}\left[\int_{-\infty}^{0}\left[(t-s)^{H-\frac{1}{2}} - (-s)^{H-\frac{1}{2}}\right]dB_t + \int_0^t (t-s)^{H-\frac{1}{2}}dB_t\right].$$

Part two of the definition is the so-called Weyl fractional integral. Equivalently, you can use the more intuitive Riemann-Liouville fractional integral, defined by

$$B_t^H - B_0^H = \frac{1}{\Gamma(H+\frac{1}{2})}\int_0^t (t-s)^{H-\frac{1}{2}}dB_s \tag{4}$$

where $\Gamma(H+\frac{1}{2})$ is the Gamma function. The rules about fractional integration and fractional differentiation are discussed in detail in [5]. It trivially follows that for $H = 1/2$, we obtain the ordinary Brownian Motion, B_t. For other values of H, such as $0 < H < 1/2$ and $1/2 < H < 1$ the fractional Brownian Motion B_t^H is a fractional derivative or integral. Note, if $0 < H < 1/2$ we say it has the property of counter persistent or short memory. This is associated with negative correlation. Vice versa for $1/2 < H < 1$, we say it is persistent. This is associated with positive correlation. Thus, modeling with fractional Brownian motions display the property of short- and long-term memory, a property very common in economic and financial time-series.

There exists an alternative definition of a fractional Brownian motion:

Proposition. *Let the Hurst-Index, H, be* $0 < H < 1$*, and* B_t^H *be fractional Brownian motion. The covariance of a fractional Brownian motion is*

$$Cov\left(B_t^H, B_s^H\right) = \frac{1}{2}\left[t^{2H} + s^{2H} - (t-s)^{2H}\right].$$

Proof. To prove that the covariance for a fractional Brownian motion is correct, we remind the reader that the variance of a fractional Brownian motion is defined as $Var[B_t - B_s] = (t-s)^{2H}$. Note, for $H = 1/2$ the variance simplifies to the variance of ordinary Brownian motion. Thus, the covariance can be rewritten as

$$\begin{aligned} Cov(B_t, B_s) &= \mathbb{E}\left[B_t^H B_s^H\right] = \frac{1}{2}\left[\mathbb{E}\left[\left(B_t^H\right)^2\right] + \mathbb{E}\left[\left(B_s^H\right)^2\right] - \mathbb{E}\left[\left(B_t^H - B_s^H\right)^2\right]\right] \\ &= \frac{1}{2}\left[t^{2H} + s^{2H} - |t-s|^{2H}\right]. \end{aligned}$$

A trivial corollary is that if $H = 1/2$, we obtain for the covariance $Cov(B_t, B_s) = \min[t, s]$, the result of a standard Brownian motion. Similarly, by trivial computation, you can show that the increments of a fBm have mean zero and variance of $|t-s|^{2H}$. Finally, you can demonstrate that two non-overlapping increments of fractional Brownian motions have the property that they are not independent. In fact, they are interdependent!

In summary, a fBm has novel properties following empirical observations in economics, yet different to ordinary stochastic processes. Indeed, a fBm has stationary and interdependent increments. Additionally, a fBm is H-self similar, meaning that $B_{at}^H = a^H B_t^H$.

The rules of fractional integration and fractional differentiation are more sophisticated than the Ito-stochastic calculus. Details about those rules are in [4]. In the remaining part of this section, we demonstrate the empirical patterns of a fractional Brownian motion for different Hurst-Indices over time (**Figure 2**).

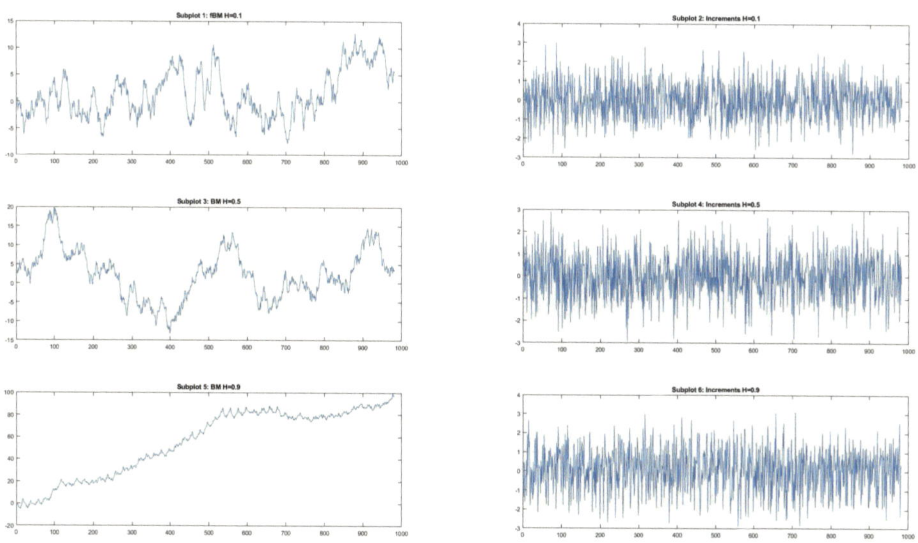

Figure 2.
Simulation of fBm for different Hurst-Index. H = 0.1 *(top panel),* H = 0.5 *(middle panel),* H = 0.9 *(bottom panel). Source: B Herzog (2020).*

For H = 0.1, we obtain in the top-panel a time-series with short-term memory (**Figure 2**). Contrary in the bottom panel (H = 0.9), we observe a strong interdependence or a non-stationary stochastic process. This process reflects long-term memory. The middle panel (H = 0.5) denotes a standard Brownian motion. It is interesting that a fractional Brownian motion is a generalization of a standard Brownian motion. **Figure 2** summarizes the different empirical patterns in relationship to the H-Index.

3. Inflation modeling with Lévy processes

On first encounter, a Poisson process and a Brownian motion seem to be considerably different. Firstly, a Brownian motion has continuous paths whereas a Poisson process does not. Secondly, a Poisson process is a non-decreasing process and thus has paths of bounded variation over finite time horizons, whereas a Brownian motion does not have monotone paths. In fact, the Brownian motion has unbounded variation over finite time horizons.

Yet, both stochastic processes have a lot in common. Both processes are right continuous with left limits (so-called càdlàg). Consequently, we use these common properties to define a general class of stochastic processes, which are so-called Lévy processes. The class of Lévy processes is rather rich, and the Brownian motion or Poisson process are two prominent subcases.

In general, Lévy processes play a major role in several fields of sciences, such as physics, engineering, economics and mathematical finance. Lévy processes are becoming fashionable to describe the observed reality of financial markets more accurately than models based on a Brownian motion alone. Lévy processes result in a more realistic modeling because it captures the empirical reality of jump-diffusions. Indeed, asset prices have jumps and spikes and thus risk managers have to consider Lévy processes in order to hedge the risks appropriately. Similarly, the pattern of implied volatility or incomplete markets is reliant to Lévy processes too.

3.1 Introduction to Lévy processes

The term Lévy process honors the work of the French mathematician Paul Lévy in the 1940s. He pioneered the understanding and characterization of stochastic processes with stationary and independent increments.

Definition 'Lévy Process." *A process* $X = \{X_t : t > 0\}$ *defined on a probability space* (Ω, F, P) *is said to be a Lévy process if it possesses the following properties:*

$$P(X_0 = 0) = 1.$$

1. The paths of X are P-almost surely right continuous with left limits. Mathematically, X is stochastically continuous for every $0 < t < T$ and $\varepsilon > 0$ such as $log_{s \to t} P(X_t - X_s > \varepsilon) = 0$.

2. For $0 < s < t$, the increments $X_t - X_s$ are stationary and equal in distribution to X_{t-s}, i.e. the increment have the same distribution whenever time elapses.

3. For $0 < s < t$, the increment $X_t - X_s$ is independent of $\{X_u : u > s\}$ or we say the increment is independent of filtration F_s.

The definition does not immediately make visible the richness of the class of Lévy processes. One simple Lévy process is a Brownian motion with drift. Other examples of Lévy processes are the Poisson process. Or a Brownian motion combined with a compound Poisson process. The last process is labeled a jump-process because it exhibits random jumps.

In order to identify Lévy processes, we use the property of infinitely divisible distributions. As soon as you can show that a process belongs to the class of infinitely divisible distributions, you immediately say that this process is a Lévy process. Indeed, there is an intimate relationship of Lévy processes to infinitely divisible distributions in general.

Definition "Infinitely divisible distribution." *A real-valued random variable X has an infinitely divisible distribution if for each* $n = 1, 2, \ldots$ *there exist a sequence of independent, identical distributed random variables* $X_{1,n}, X_{2,n}, \ldots X_{n,n}$, *such that*

$$X := X_{1,n} + X_{2,n} + \ldots + X_{n,n}$$

the process X has the same distribution as the processes of $X_{1,n}, X_{2,n}, \ldots X_{n,n}$.

One way to establish whether a given random variable has an infinitely divisible distribution is via the study of the exponent of the characteristic function. This idea is summarized by the rather sophisticated concept of the Lévy-Khintchine formula (e.g. in [7]).

3.2 A Brownian motion is a Lévy process

In this subsection, we briefly show that a Brownian motion is a Lévy process. Suppose a Gaussian random variable with distribution $X \sim N(\mu, \sigma^2)$ and the characteristic function of $\phi_{X_t}(t) = e^{i\mu - \frac{1}{2}t^2\sigma^2}$. We know that the increments of a Brownian motion follow a Gaussian process. By the characteristic function, we show that the increments of the Brownian motion are stationary and independent. Thus it stratifies the Lévy process properties:

$$\phi^n_{X_t} = e^{\left(\frac{i\mu}{n} - \frac{1}{2}\frac{t^2\sigma^2}{n}\right)^n} \tag{5}$$

$$\phi_{X_{t+s}} = \phi_{X_t} * \phi_{X_s}. \tag{6}$$

Eq. (5) demonstrates that the Brownian motion is an infinitely divisible distribution. Eq. (6) shows that the Brownian motion has independent and stationary increments. Thus, we find that the random variable X is Lévy by computing the sum of n-random variables $X = X^n_1 + \ldots + X^n_i + \ldots + X^n_n$ with each $X^n_i \sim N\left(\frac{\mu}{n}, \frac{\sigma^2}{n}\right)$. Therefore, we obtain $X \sim N(\mu, \sigma^2)$ and $X^n_1 \sim N\left(\frac{\mu}{n}, \frac{\sigma^2}{n}\right)$. Hence, the Brownian motion is infinitely divisible by n and it consists of independent, identical distributed (i.i.d) increments. Consequently, a Brownian motion satisfies the properties of a Lévy process.

Remark. Markov processes are the best-known family of stochastic processes in mathematical probability theory. Informally, a Markov process has the property that the future behavior of the process depends on the past only. One can show that Lévy processes are related to Markov processes and even simplify the theory significantly. The link between both stochastic processes is so-called random-stopping times. One can show that a random-stopping time on a Lévy process has the Markov property. Consequently, Lévy processes concern many aspects of probability theory and its applications.

4. Numerical simulation

In this section, we simulate different fractional Brownian motions and Lévy processes. The simulation reveals different new patterns of inflation dynamics. Our model is calibrated to the monthly frequency of the past inflation dynamics in the Eurozone from 1997 to 2020.

The simulation follows a mean-reverting stochastic differential equation driven by a fractional Brownian motion and a Lévy process. Suppose X_t denotes the inflation process over time t. We model the inflation dynamics by a stochastic differential equation of the form

$$dX_t = (\alpha - \beta * X_t)dt + \sigma dB_t^H + N(\mu, \gamma)dN(\lambda) \tag{7}$$

where α and β are the mean-reversion trends and σ denotes the volatility coming from the fractional Brownian motion, B_t^H. The parameter H reflects the Hurst-Index of the fractional Brownian motion. The last term is a jump-process modelled by a Poisson process, $N(\mu, \gamma)$, with parameters μ and γ. The jump-frequency is of λ.

The numerical simulation is computed over 1000 time steps and over 1000 different stochastic processes. The Eurozone inflation data are downloaded from the ECB Statistical Data Warehouse. We calibrate the model to the aggregate inflation dynamics of the Eurozone (**Figures 3** and **4**).

Figure 3 represents the Harmonized Index of Consumer Price (HICP) of the Eurozone on monthly frequency from 1997 to 2020. One clearly sees the sharp drop in inflation rates during the global financial crisis of 2008–2009. Subsequently inflation rebounded, however, afterwards with low inflation rates, partly deflation, in the years of 2013–2016. In recent years, inflation rates were in the range of 1.0–2.0%. Thus, the inflation rate in the Eurozone is following Article 127 TFEU and the definition of price-stability by the European Central Bank [8]: "… inflation rates below, but close to 2% over the medium term."

Based on the inflation data, we compute the histogram of Eurozone inflation rates in **Figure 4**. The distribution displays particularly a right-skewedness. Indeed, the mean is of 1.66, the median of 1.80 and the modus is of 2.10. Moreover, the standard deviation is of 0.77, the variance of 0.60, the skewness of -0.22 and the kurtosis of -0.06 is almost zero. These parameters characterize the Eurozone's inflation rate properties over time.

Next, we choose the following parameters in our stochastic differential equation (Eq. (7)): $\alpha = 1.7$, $\beta = 1.0$, $\sigma = 0.4$, $\mu = -2.0$, $\gamma = 0.5$, $\lambda = 0.01$ and $H = 0.2$. We run the simulation model for 1000-time steps. **Figure 5** represents the result of one simulation, where the mean is of 1.60, the median of 1.73, the variance of 0.81 and

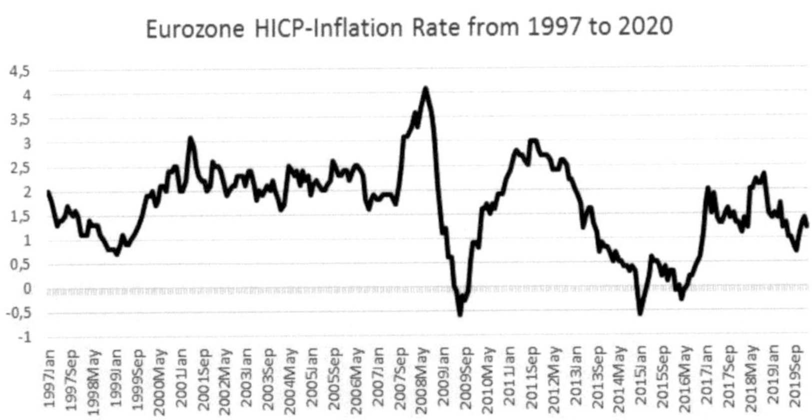

Figure 3.
Eurozone HICP-Inflation Rate. Data from ECB Data Warehouse. Source: B Herzog (2020).

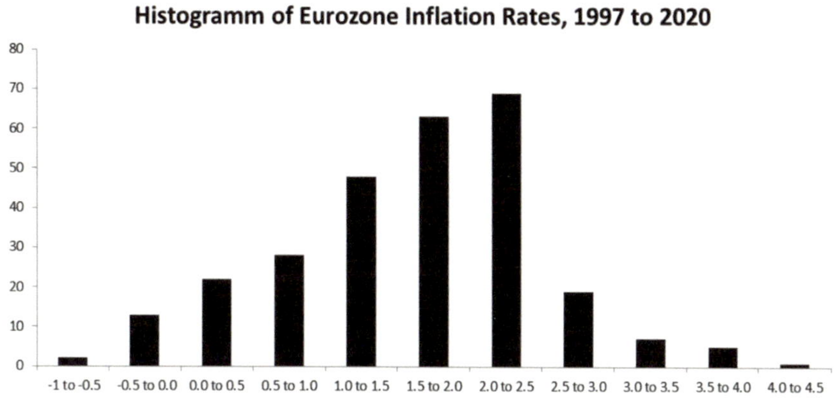

Figure 4.
Histogram of Eurozone Inflation Rates. Data from ECB Data Warehouse. Source: B Herzog (2020).

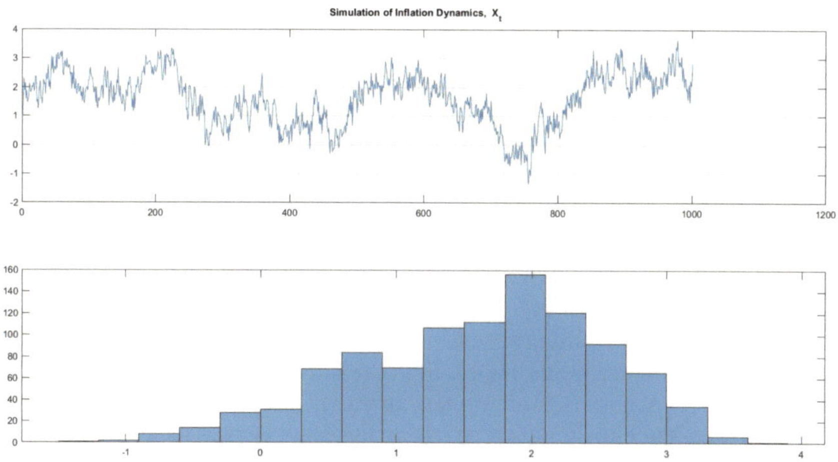

Figure 5.
Simulation of Inflation Dynamics according to equation (7). Top panel denotes the inflation rate and bottom panel the histogram. Source: B Herzog (2020).

the skewness of -0.42. This demonstrates that the simulation is following the distribution properties of inflation data, particularly the right-skewedness.

It turns out that the simulation replicates the distributional properties quite well, except for the kurtosis. Nonetheless, we clearly see in the bottom panel of **Figure 5** that the distribution is right-skewed with more tail events on the left-hand side.

If we run the same model with the Gaussian assumption, by using a standard Brownian motion, $H = 0.5$, we obtain a somewhat different result. The mean is of 0.94, the median of 0.85, the variance of 1.23, the skewness of 0.45 and the kurtosis of 2.64. This distribution is not right-skewed and has higher variance than the stylized facts. Hence, we conclude that a fractional Brownian motion with a Lévy process provide a better approach in order to model the inflation dynamics of the Eurozone.

Finally, we discuss the results of the simulation exercise with 1000 runs. In this simulation, we have specified our stochastic differential equation (Eq. (7)) as follows: $\alpha = 1.7, \beta = 0, \sigma = 0.3, \mu = -2.0, \gamma = 0.1, \lambda = 0.00$ and $H = 0.2$. **Figure 6** represents in the top-panel the stochastic paths of all stochastic processes and in the bottom-panel the respective histogram. The numerical simulation yields a mean and median of approximately 1.7, a variance of 1.4 and negative skewness of -1.71.

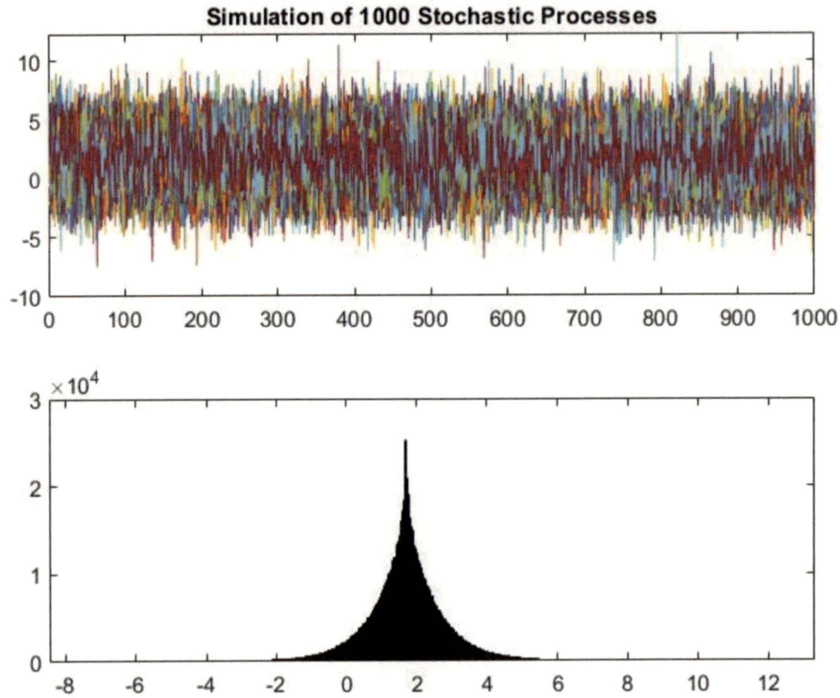

Figure 6.
Simulation of equation (7) with calibrated parameters. Top panel denotes all inflation processes and bottom panel the histogram. Source: B Herzog (2020).

Last but not least, by running several simulations we find that inflation dynamics is with high likelihood in a range of $[-2, 5]$ in the Eurozone. Hence, even with severe positive or negative shocks the inflationary process is stable and anchored around the target level of 2%. Finally, in a scenario analysis, we set the mean-reverting level to the target rate of 4% as proposed by Blanchard et al. [9]. We find inflation dynamics is more volatile and still face deflationary levels during severe negative shocks. In that regard, a higher inflation target does not eliminate deflation events as with the target level of 2% today. Of course, the buffer towards deflation is greater if the inflation target is 4%. But economically, we proclaim that a higher inflation target creates a higher volatility and de-anchor inflation expectations subsequently. Consequently, increasing the inflation target is not free of any risk due to growing uncertainty about inflation expectations and price-stability in general.

5. Conclusion

This article models the inflation dynamics of the Eurozone with a novel approach. We utilize a stochastic differential equation driven by fractional Brownian motions and a Lévy process. Empirical inflation data show that the distribution is right-skewed. Thus, any standard approach using the normality assumption in econometrics fails. Therefore, we propose the use of fractional Brownian motions and Lévy processes in order to model time-dependence and jumps. Those processes cover short- and long-term phenomena, which is a prerequisite for empirical distributions.

We find that our modeling and numerical simulation provide good results to the calibrated inflation data. Inflation dynamics of the Eurozone is according to 1000

DOI: http://dx.doi.org/10.5772/intechopen.92292

runs of our simulation stable and strongly anchored at the 2.0% inflation target. Even in the worst negative or positive shock, inflation numbers do not reach levels persistently below 0 or above 4%.

That said, the stable and low inflation rates of the Eurozone are highly contingent of the inflation target defined by the European Central Bank. Currently, inflation expectations are well anchored below the 2% level. Yet, our model simulation demonstrates that proposals to increase the inflation target, such as by Blanchard et al. [9], are highly risky because it leads to a de-anchoring of inflation. In the end, you might have higher volatility and the risk of de-anchored inflation expectations. The latter can create a strong upward bias in inflation rates out of the control of a central bank.

Acknowledgements

I thank the RRI for supporting my research. Moreover, I thank all conference participants for valuable comments and feedback to a preliminary version of this in-book article. Moreover, I thank the two anonymous referees for excellent comments and suggestions. All this improved the in-book article. All remaining errors remain my own responsibility.

Conflict of interest

There is no external funding and no conflict of interest for this research article.

Author details

Bodo Herzog[1,2,3]

1 ESB Business School, Reutlingen University, Reutlingen, Germany

2 RRI Reutlingen Research Institute, Reutlingen, Germany

3 IFE Institute of Finance and Economics, Reutlingen, Germany

*Address all correspondence to: bodo.herzog@reutlingen-university.de

References

[1] Karatzas I, Shreve SE. Brownian Motion and Stochastic Calculus. 2nd ed. Berlin, New York: Springer; 1991

[2] Oksendal B. Stochastic Differential Equations. 6nd ed. Berlin, New York: Springer; 2007

[3] Oksana B et al. Fractional Brownian Motion. 1st ed. New Jersey: Wiley; 2019

[4] Mishura Y. Stochastic Calculus for Fractional Brownian Motion and Related Processes. 1st ed. Berlin, New York: Springer; 2008

[5] Oldham KB, Spanier J. The Fractional Calculus. 2nd ed. Berlin, New York: Springer; 2002

[6] Mandelbrot BB, van Ness JW. Fractional Brownian motions, fractional noises and applications. SIAM Review. 1968;**10**(4):422-437

[7] Sato K-I. Lévy Processes and Infinitely Divisible Distributions. Revised Edition. Cambridge: Cambridge Press; 2013

[8] European Central Bank (ECB). 2020. Available from: https://www.ecb.europa.eu/home/html/index.en.html

[9] Blanchard O. et al. Rethinking Macroeconomic Policy. IMF Staff Position Note, SPN/10/03; 12 February 2012

Chapter 2

Construction of Forward-Looking Distributions Using Limited Historical Data and Scenario Assessments

Riaan de Jongh, Helgard Raubenheimer and Mentje Gericke

Abstract

Financial institutions are concerned about various forms of risk that might impact them. The management of these institutions has to demonstrate to shareholders and regulators that they manage these risks in a pro-active way. Often the main risks are caused by excessive claims on insurance policies or losses that occur due to defaults on loan payments or by operations failing. In an attempt to quantify these risks, the estimation of extreme quantiles of loss distributions is of interest. Since financial companies have limited historical data available in order to estimate these extreme quantiles, they often use scenario assessments by experts to augment the historical data by providing a forward-looking view. In this chapter, we will provide an exposition of statistical methods that may be used to combine historical data and scenario assessments in order to estimate extreme quantiles. In particular, we will illustrate their use by means of practical examples. This method has been implemented by major international banks and based on what we have learnt in the process, we include some practical suggestions for implementing the recommended method.

Keywords: operational risk, loss distribution approach, aggregate loss distribution, historical data, measures of agreement, scenario assessments

1. Introduction

Financial institutions need to carefully manage financial losses. For example, the claims made against short-term insurance policies need to be analysed in order to enable an insurance company to determine the reserves needed to meet their obligations and to determine the adequacy of their pricing strategies. Similarly, banks are required in terms of regulation to set aside risk capital to absorb unexpected losses that may occur. Of course, financial institutions are more interested in the total amount of claims or the aggregate loss occurring over one year in the future, than the individual claims or losses. For this reason, their focus will be on what may happen in the year ahead rather than what has happened in the past. Popular modelling methods involve the construction of annual aggregate claim or loss distributions using the so-called loss distribution approach (LDA) or random sums

IntechOpen

method. Such a distribution is assumed to be an adequate reflection of the past but need to be forward looking in the sense that anticipated future losses are taken into account. The constructed distribution may then be used to answer questions like 'What aggregate loss level will be exceeded only once in c years?' or 'What is the expected annual aggregate loss level?' or 'If we want to guard ourselves against a one in a thousand-year aggregate loss, how much capital should we hold next year?' The aggregate loss distribution and its quantiles will provide answers to these questions and it is therefore paramount that this distribution is modelled and estimated as accurately as possible. Often it is the extreme quantiles of this distribution that is of interest.

Under Basel II's advanced measurement approach, banks may use their own internal models to calculate their operational risk capital, and the LDA is known to be a popular method for this. A bank must be able to demonstrate that their approach captures potentially severe 'tail' events and they must hold capital to protect them against a one-in-a-thousand-year aggregate loss. To determine this capital amount, the 99.9% Value-at-Risk (VaR) of the aggregate distribution is calculated [1]. In order to estimate a one-in-a-thousand-year loss, one would hope that at least a thousand years of historical data is available. However, in reality only between five and ten years of internal data is available and scenario assessments by experts are often used to augment the historical data and to provide a forward-looking view.

The much anticipated implementation of Basel III will require banks to calculate operational risk capital on a new standardised approach, which is simple, risk-sensitive and comparable between different banks [2]. Although the more sophisticated internal models described above will no longer be allowed in determining minimum regulatory capital, these models will remain relevant for the determination of economic capital and decision making within banks and other financial institutions. It is also suggested that LDA models would form an integral part of the supervisory review of a bank's internal operational risk management process [3]. For this reason, we believe the LDA remains relevant and will continue to be studied and improved on.

In this chapter we provide an exposition of statistical methods that may be used to estimate VaR using historical data in combination with quantile assessments by experts. The proposed approach has been discussed and studied elsewhere (see [4]), but specifically in the context of operational risk and economic capital estimation. In this chapter we concentrate on the estimation of the VaR of the aggregate loss or claims distribution and strive to make the approach more accessible to a wider audience. Also, based on the implementation done for major banks, we include some practical guidelines for the use and implementation of the method in practice. In the next section we discuss two approaches, Monte Carlo and Single Loss Approximation, that may be used for the approximation of VaR assuming known distributions and parameters. Then, in the third section (Historical data and scenario modelling), we will discuss the available sources of data and formulate the scenario approach and how these may be created and assessed by experts. This is followed, in section four (Estimating VaR), by the estimation of VaR using three modelling approaches. In the fifth section (Implementation recommendations) some guidelines on the implementation of the preferred approach are given. Some concluding remarks are made in the last section.

2. Approximating VaR

Let the random variable N denotes the annual number of loss events and that N is distributed according to a Poisson distribution with parameter lambda, i.e.$N \sim Poi(\lambda)$. Note that one could use other frequency distributions like the negative binomial, but we found that the Poisson is by far the most popular in practice since it fits the data well. Furthermore, assume that the random variables $X_1, \dots, X_N$ denote the loss severities of these loss events and that they are independently and identically distributed according to a severity distribution T, i.e. $X_1, \dots, X_N \sim iid\ T$. Then the annual aggregate loss is $A = \sum_{n=1}^{N} X_n$ and the distribution of A is the aggregate loss distribution, which is a compound Poisson distribution that depends on λ and T and is denoted by $CoP(T, \lambda)$. Of course, in practice we do not know T and λ and have to estimate it. First we have to decide on a model for T, which can be a class of distributions $F(x, \theta)$. Then θ and λ have to be estimated using statistical estimates.

The compound Poisson distribution $CoP(T, \lambda)$ and its VaR are difficult to calculate analytically so that in practice Monte Carlo (MC) simulation is often used. This is done by generating N according to the assumed frequency distribution and then by generating $X_1, \dots, X_N$ independent and identically distributed according to the true severity distribution T and calculating $A = \sum_{n=1}^{N} X_n$. The previous process is repeated I times independently to obtain $A_i, i = 1, 2, \dots, I$ and then the 99.9% VaR is approximated by $A_{([0.999 * I]+1)}$ where $A_{(i)}$ denotes the i-th order statistic and $[k]$ the largest integer contained in k. Note that three input items are required to perform this, namely the number of repetitions I as well as the frequency and loss severity distributions. The number of repetitions determines the accuracy of the approximation and the larger it is, the higher its accuracy. In order to illustrate the Monte Carlo approximation method, we assume that the Burr is the true underlying severity distribution and we use six parameter sets corresponding to an extreme value index (EVI) of 0.33, 0.83, 1.0, 1.33, 1.85 and 2.35 as indicated in **Table 1** below. See Appendix A for a discussion of the characteristics of this distribution and its properties. We take the number of repetitions as $I = 1\,000\,000$ and repeat the calculation of VaR 1000 times. The 90% band containing the VaR values are shown in **Figure 1** below. Here the lower (upper) bound has been determined as the 5% (95%) percentile of the 1000 VaR values, divided by its median, and by subtracting 1. In mathematical terms the 90% band is defined as $\left[\frac{VaR_{(51)}}{Median(VaR_1, \dots, VaR_{1000})} - 1, \frac{VaR_{(951)}}{Median(VaR_1, \dots, VaR_{1000})} - 1\right]$, where $VaR_{(k)}$ denotes the k-th order statistic. From **Figure 1** it is clear that the spread, as measured by the 90% band, declines with increasing lambda, but increases with increasing EVI.

In principle, infinitely many repetitions are required to get the exact true VaR. The large number of simulation repetitions involved in the MC approaches above motivates the use of other numerical methods such as Panjer recursion, methods based on fast Fourier transforms [5] and the single loss approximation (SLA) method (see e.g. [6]). For a detailed comparison of numerical approximation

η	α	τ	*EVI*
1.00	5.00	0.60	0.33
1.00	2.00	0.60	0.83
1.00	1.00	1.00	1.00
1.00	1.50	0.50	1.33
1.00	0.30	1.80	1.85
1.00	0.17	2.50	2.35

Table 1.
Parameter sets of Burr distribution.

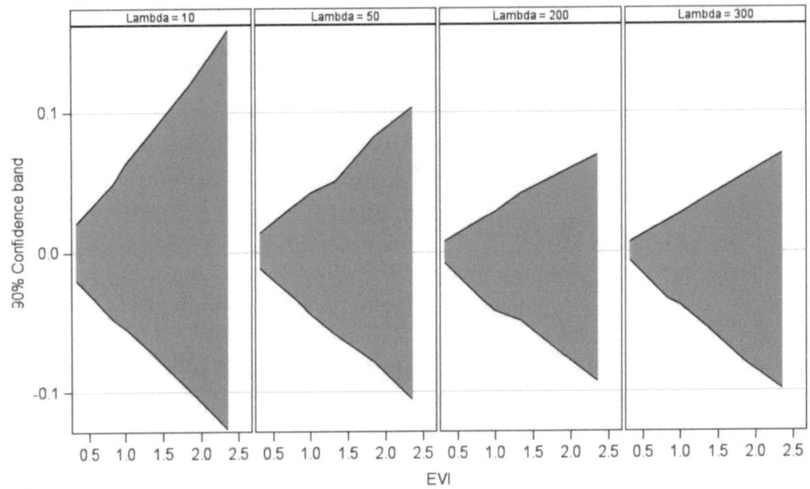

Figure 1.
Variation obtained in the VaR estimates for different values of EVI and frequency.

methods, the interested reader is referred to [7]. The SLA has become very popular in the financial industry due to its simplicity and can be stated as follows: If T is the true underlying severity distribution function of the individual losses and λ the true annual frequency then the $100(1-\gamma)\%$ VaR of the compound loss distribution may be approximated by $T^{-1}(1-\gamma/\lambda)$ or, as modified by [8] for large λ, by $T^{-1}(1-\gamma/\lambda)+\lambda\mu$, where μ is the finite mean of the true underlying severity distribution. The first order approximation by [6]

$$CoP^{-1}(1-\gamma) \approx T^{-1}(1-\gamma/\lambda), \tag{1}$$

states that the $100(1-\gamma)\%$ VaR of the aggregate loss distribution may be approximated by the $100(1-\gamma/\lambda)\%$ VaR of the severity distribution, if the latter is part of the sub-exponential class of distributions. This follows from a theorem from extreme value theory (EVT) which states that $P\left(A=\sum_{n=1}^{N} X_n > x\right) \approx P(max\{X_1, \dots, X_N\} > x)$ as $x \to \infty$ (see e.g. [9]). The result is quite remarkable in that a quantile of the aggregate loss distribution may be approximated by a more extreme quantile (if $\lambda > 1$) of the underlying severity distribution. EVT is all about modelling extremal events and is especially concerned about modelling the tail of a distribution (see e.g. [10]), i.e. that part of the distribution we are most interested in. Bearing this in mind we might consider modelling the body and tail of the severity distribution separately as follows.

Let q be a quantile of the severity distribution T. We use q as a threshold that splice T in such a way that the interval below q is the expected part and the interval above q the unexpected part of the severity distribution. Define two distribution functions

$$T_e(x) = T(x)/T(q) \text{ for } x \leq q \text{ and}$$
$$T_u(x) = [T(x) - T(q)]/[1 - T(q)] \text{ for } x > q, \tag{2}$$

i.e. $T_e(x)$ is the conditional distribution function of a random loss $X \sim T$ given that $X \leq q$ and $T_u(x)$ is the conditional distribution function given that $X > q$.

Note that we then have the identity

$$T(x) = T(q)T_e(x) + [1 - T(q)]T_u(x) \text{ for all } x. \tag{3}$$

This identity represents $T(x)$ as a mixture of the two conditional distributions. Instead of modelling $T(x)$ with a class of distributions $F(x,\theta)$ we may now consider modelling $T_e(x)$ with $F_e(x,\theta)$ and $T_u(x)$, with $F_u(x,\theta)$. Borrowing from EVT a popular choice for $F_u(x,\theta)$ could be the generalised Pareto distribution (GPD), whilst a host of choices are available for $F_e(x,\theta)$, the obvious being the empirical distribution. Note that the Pickands-Balkema-de Haan limit theorem (see e.g. [11]), states that the conditional tail of all distributions in the domain of attraction of the Generalised Extreme Value distribution (GEV), tends to a GPD distribution. The distributions in the domain of attraction of the GEV are a wide class of distributions, which includes most distributions of interest to us. Although one could consider alternative distributions to the GPD for modelling the tail of a severity distribution, this theorem, and the limiting conditions that we are interested in, suggest that the GPD is a good choice. In the fourth section (Estimating VaR) we will discuss this in more detail.

3. Historical data and scenario modelling

It is practice in operational risk management to use different data sources for modelling future losses. Banks have been collecting their own data, but realistically, most banks only have between five and ten years of reliable loss data. To address this shortcoming, loss data from external sources and scenario data can be used by banks in addition to their own internal loss data and controls [12]. Certain external loss databases exist, including publicly available data, insurance data and consortium data. The process of incorporating data from external sources requires due consideration because of biases in the external data. One method of combining operational losses collected from various banks of different sizes and loss reporting thresholds, is discussed in [13]. In the remainder of our discussion we will only refer to historical data, which may be a combination of internal and external loss data.

Three types of scenario assessments are also suggested to improve the estimation of the severity distribution, namely the individual scenario approach, the interval approach, and the percentile approach. In the remainder of the chapter we discuss the percentile approach as we believe it is the most practical of the existing approaches available in the literature [4]. That being said, it should be noted that probability assessments by experts are notoriously difficult and unreliable as discussed in [14]. We mentioned previously that it is often an extreme quantile of the aggregate loss distribution that is of interest. In the case of operational risk, the regulator requires that the one-in-a-thousand-year quantile of this distribution be estimated, in other words the aggregate loss level that will be exceeded once in a thousand years. Considering that banks' only have limited historical data available, i.e. maximum of ten years of internal data, the estimation of such a quantile, using historical data only, is a near impossible task. So modellers have suggested the use of scenarios and experts' assessments thereof.

We advocate the use of the so-called 1-in-c year scenario approach as discussed in [4]. In the 1-in-c years scenario approach, the experts are asked to answer the question: 'What loss level q_c is expected to be exceeded once every c years?'. Popular choices for c vary between 5 and 100 and often 3 values for c are used. As an example, the bank alluded to at the start of this chapter, used $c = 7, 20$ and 100 and motivated the first choice as the number of years of reliable historical data available to them. In this case the largest loss in the historical data may serve as a guide for choosing q_7 since this loss level has been reached once in 7 years. If the experts judge that the future will be better than the past, they may want to provide a lower assessment for q_7 than the largest loss experienced so far. If they foresee deterioration, they may judge that a higher assessment is more appropriate. The other choices of c are selected in order to obtain a scenario spread within the range that one can expect reasonable improvement in accuracy from the experts' inputs. Of course, the choice of $c = 100$ may be questionable because judgements on a 1-in-100 years loss level are likely to fall outside many of the experts' experience. In the banking environment, they may also take additional guidance from external data of similar banks which in effect amplifies the number of years for which historical data are available. It is argued that this is an essential input into scenario analysis [12]. Of course requiring that the other banks are similar to the bank in question may be a difficult issue and the scaling of external data in an effort to make it comparable to the bank's own internal data raises further problems (see e.g. [15]). We will not dwell on this issue here and henceforth assume that we do have the 1-in-c years scenario assessments for a range of c-values, but have to keep in mind that subjective elements may have affected the reliability of the assessments.

If the annual loss frequency is $Poi(\lambda)$ distributed and the true underlying severity distribution is T, and if the experts are of oracle quality in the sense of actually knowing λ and T, then the assessments provided should be

$$q_c = T^{-1}\left(1 - \frac{1}{c\lambda}\right). \tag{4}$$

To see this, let N_c denote the number of loss events experienced in c years and let M_c denote the number of these that are actually greater than q_c. Then $N_c \sim Poi(c\lambda)$ and the conditional distribution of M_c given N_c is binomial with parameters N_c and $1 - p_c = P(X \geq q_c) = 1 - T(q_c)$ with $X \sim T$ and $p_c = T(q_c) = 1 - \frac{1}{c\lambda}$. Therefore $EM_c = E[E(M_c|N_c)] = E[N_c(1 - p_c)] = c\lambda(1 - T(q_c))$. Requiring that $EM_c = 1$, yields (4).

As illustration of the complexity of the experts' task, take $\lambda = 50$ then $q_7 = T^{-1}(0.99714)$, $q_{20} = T^{-1}(0.999)$ and $q_{100} = T^{-1}(0.9998)$ which implies that the quantiles that have to be estimated are very extreme.

Returning to the SLA i.e. $CoP^{-1}(1 - \gamma) \approx T^{-1}(1 - \gamma/\lambda)$, and by taking $\gamma = 0.001$, which implies $c = 1000$, we could ask the oracle the question 'What loss level q_{1000} is expected to be exceeded once every 1000 years?'. The oracle will then produce an answer that can be used directly as an approximation for the 99.9% VaR of the aggregate loss distribution. Of course, the experts we are dealing with are not of oracle quality.

In the light of the above arguments one has to take in consideration: (a) the SLA gives only an approximation to the VaR we are trying to estimate, and (b) experts are very unlikely to have the experience or the information at their disposal to assess a 1-in-1000 year event reliably. One can realistically only expect them to assess events occurring more frequently such as once in 30 years.

Returning to the oracle's answer in (4), the expert has to consider both the true severity distribution and the annual frequency when an assessment is provided. In order to simplify the task of the expert, consider the mixed model in (3) discussed in the previous section. This model will assist us in formulating an easier question for the expert to answer. Note that the oracle's answer to the question in the previous setting can be stated as $T(q_c) = 1 - \frac{1}{c\lambda}$ (from (4)) and therefore depends on the annual frequency. However using the definition of T_u and taking $q = q_b, b < c$; it follows that $T_u(q_c) = 1 - \frac{b}{c}$ which does not depend on the annual frequency. This fact that $q_c = T^{-1}(1 - \frac{1}{c\lambda}) = T_u^{-1}(1 - \frac{b}{c})$ has interesting suggestions about the formulation of the basic question of the 1-in-c years approach. For example, if we take $b = 1$ then q_1 would be the experts' answer to the question 'What loss level is expected to be exceeded once annually?'. Unless we are dealing with only rare loss events, a reasonably accurate assessment of q_1 should be possible. Then $T_u(q_c) = 1 - 1/c$ or $1 - T_u(q_c) = 1/c$. Keeping in mind the conditional probability meaning of T_u this tells us that q_c would be the answer to the question: 'Amongst those losses that are larger than q_1, what level is expected to be exceeded only once in c years?'. Conditioning on the losses larger than q_1 has the effect that the annual frequency of all losses drops out of consideration when an answer is sought. In the remainder of the chapter we will assume that this question is posed to the experts to make their assessments.

4. Estimating VaR

Suppose we have available a years of historical loss data $x_1, x_2, \ldots, x_K$ and scenario assessments $\tilde{q}_7, \tilde{q}_{20}$ and $\tilde{q}_{100}$ provided by the experts. In the previous sections two modelling options have been suggested for modelling the true severity distribution T and a third will follow below. The estimation of the 99.9% VaR of the aggregate loss distribution is of interest and we will consider three approaches to estimate it, namely the naïve approach, the GPD approach and Venter's approach. The naïve approach will make use of historical data only, the GPD approach (which is based on the mixed model formulation) and Venter's approach will make use of both historical data and scenario assessments. Below we demonstrate that, as far as estimating VaR is concerned, that Venter's approach is preferred to the GPD and naïve approaches.

4.1 Naïve approach

Assume that we have available only historical data and that we collected the loss severities of a total of K loss events spread over a years and denote these observed or historical losses by $x_1, \ldots, x_K$. Then the annual frequency is estimated by $\hat{\lambda} = K/a$. Let $F(x; \theta)$ denote a suitable family of distributions to model the true loss severity distribution T. The fitted distribution is denoted by $F(x; \hat{\theta})$, with $\hat{\theta}$ denoting the (maximum likelihood) estimate of the parameter(s) θ. In order to estimate VaR a small adjustment of the Monte Carlo approximation approach, discussed earlier, is necessary.

4.1.1 Naïve VaR estimation algorithm

i. Generate N from the Poisson distribution with parameter $\hat{\lambda}$;

ii. Generate $X_1, \ldots, X_N \sim iid\ F(x; \hat{\theta})$ calculate $A = \sum_{n=1}^{N} X_n$;

iii. Repeat i and ii I times independently to obtain $A_i, i = 1, 2, \ldots, I$. Then the 99.9% VaR is estimated by $A_{([0.999 * I]+1)}$ where $A_{(i)}$ denotes the i-th order statistic and $[k]$ the largest integer contained in k.

4.1.2 Remarks

The estimation of VaR using the above-mentioned naïve approach has been discussed in several books and papers (see e.g. [11]). [16] stated that heavy-tailed data sets are hard to model and require much caution when interpreting the resulting VaR estimates. For example, a single extreme loss can cause drastic changes in the estimate of the means and variances of severity distributions even if a large amount of loss data is available. Annual aggregate losses will typically be driven by the value of the most extreme losses and the high quantiles of the aggregate annual loss distribution are primarily determined by the high quantiles of the severity distributions containing the extreme losses. Two different severity distributions for modelling the individual losses may both fit the data well in terms of goodness-of-fit statistics yet may provide capital estimates which may differ by billions. Certain deficiencies of the naïve estimation approach, in particular, the estimation of the severity distribution and the subsequent estimation of an extreme VaR of the aggregate loss distribution, are highlighted in [15].

In **Figure 2** below we used the naïve approach to illustrate the effect of some of the above-mentioned claims. In **Figure 2(a)** we assumed a Burr distribution, i.e. T_Burr(1, 0.6, 2), as our true underlying severity distribution. In the top panel we show the distribution function and in the middle the log of 1 minus the distribution

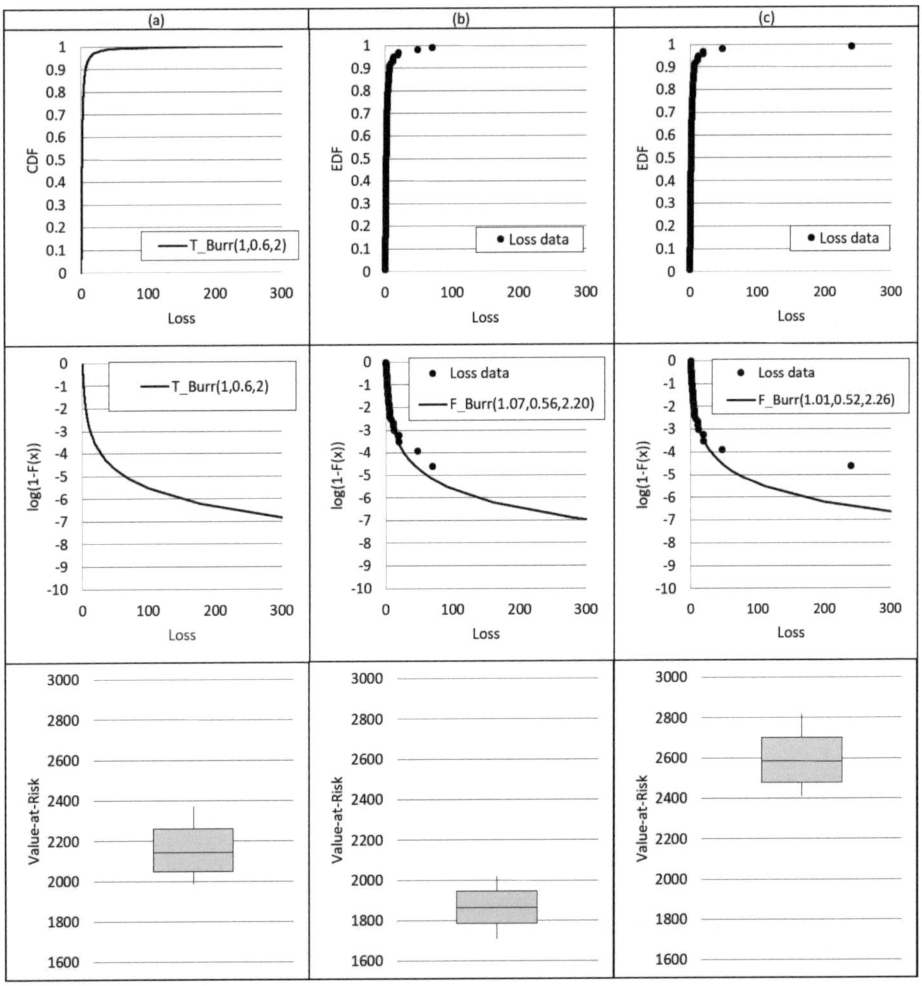

Figure 2.
Illustration of the effects of VaR estimation using the naïve approach. (a) True Burr distribution, T_Burr(1, 0.6, 2), (b) simulated observations from the T_Burr(1, 0.6, 2) distribution with fitted distribution F_Burr (1.07, 0.56, 2.2), (c) augmented simulated observations with fitted distribution F_Burr(1.01, 0.52, 2.26).

function. This gives us more accentuated view of the tail of the distribution. Then in the bottom panel the Monte Carlo results of the VaR approximations are given by means of a box plot using the 5% and 95% percentiles for the box. As before, one million simulations were used to approximate VaR and the VaR calculations were repeated a 1000 times. In **Figure 2(b)** we assume $\lambda = 10, a = 10$ and generated 100 observations from the T_Burr(1, 0.6, 2) distribution. The observations generated is plotted in the top panel and in the middle panel the fitted distribution and the maximum likelihood estimates of the parameters are depicted as F_Burr(1.07, 0.56, 2.2). In the bottom panel the results of the VaR estimates using the naïve approach is provided. Note how the distribution of the VaR estimates differ from those obtained using the true underlying severity distribution. Of course, sampling error is present, and the generation of another sample will result in a different box plot. Let us illustrate this by studying the effect of extreme observations. In order to do this, we moved the maximum value further into the tail of the distribution and repeat the fitting process. The data set is depicted in the top panel of **Figure 2(c)** and the fitted distribution in the middle as F_Burr(1.01, 0.52, 2.26). Again, the resulting VaR estimates are shown in the bottom panel. In this case the introduction of the extreme loss has a profound boosting effect on the resulting VaR estimates.

In practice, and due to imprecise loss definitions, risk managers may incorrectly group two losses into one extreme loss that has a profound boosting effect on VaR estimates. In the light of this, it is important that the manager is aware of the process generating the data and the importance of clear definitions of loss events.

4.2 The GPD approach

This modelling approach is based on the mixed model formulation (3). As before, we have available a years of historical loss data $x_1, x_2, \dots, x_K$ and scenario assessments $\tilde{q}_7, \tilde{q}_{20}$ and $\tilde{q}_{100}$. Then the annual frequency λ can again be estimated as $\hat{\lambda} = K/a$. Next b and the threshold $q = q_b$ must be specified. One possibility is to take b as the smallest of the scenario c-year multiples and to estimate q_b as the corresponding smallest of the scenario assessments $\tilde{q}_b$ provided by the experts, in this case $\tilde{q}_7$. $T_e(x)$ can be estimated by fitting a parametric family $F_e(x, \theta)$ (such as the Burr) to the data $x_1, x_2, \dots, x_K$ or by calculating the empirical distribution and then conditioning it to the interval $(0, \tilde{q}_b]$. Either of these estimates is a reasonable choice especially if K is large and the parametric family is well chosen. Whichever estimate we use, denote it by $\tilde{F}_e(x)$. For the sake of future notational consistency, we shall also put tildes on all estimates of distribution functions which involve use of the scenario assessments.

Next, $F_u(x)$ can be modelled by the $GPD(x; \sigma, \xi, q_b)$ distribution. See Appendix A for the characteristics of this distribution. For ease of explanation, suppose we have actual scenario assessments $\tilde{q}_7, \tilde{q}_{20}$ and $\tilde{q}_{100}$ and thus take $b = 7$ and estimate q_b by $\tilde{q}_7$. Substituting these scenario assessments into $F_u(q_c) = 1 - \frac{b}{c}$; with $b = 7$, $c = 20, 100$ yields two equations.

$$F_u(\tilde{q}_{20}) = GPD(\tilde{q}_{20}; \sigma, \xi, \tilde{q}_7) = 0.65 \text{ and } F_u(\tilde{q}_{100}) = GPD(\tilde{q}_{100}; \sigma, \xi, \tilde{q}_7) = 0.93 \quad (5)$$

that can be solved to obtain estimates $\tilde{\sigma}$ and $\tilde{\xi}$ of the parameters σ and ξ in the GPD that are based on the scenario assessments. Some algebra shows that a solution exists only if $\frac{\tilde{q}_{100} - \tilde{q}_7}{\tilde{q}_{20} - \tilde{q}_7} > 2.533$. This fact should be borne in mind when the experts do their assessments.

With more than three scenario assessments, fitting techniques can be based on (5) which links the quantiles of the GPD to the scenario assessments. An example would be to minimise $\sum_c \left|GPD\left(\tilde{q}_c; \sigma, \xi, \tilde{q}_7\right) - (1 - b/c)\right|$. Other possibilities include a weighted version of the sum of deviations in this expression or deviation measures comparing the GPD quantiles directly to the q_c assessments. Whichever route we follow, we denote the final estimate of $F_u(x)$ by $\tilde{F}_u(x)$. All these ingredients can now be substituted into (3) to yield the estimate $\tilde{F}(x)$ of $T(x)$, namely

$$\hat{\lambda}\tilde{F}(x) = \left(\hat{\lambda} - \frac{1}{7}\right)\tilde{F}_e(x) + \frac{1}{7}\tilde{F}_u(x). \tag{6}$$

Returning now to practical use of Eq. (6), the algorithm below summarises the integration of the historical data with the 1-in-c years scenarios following the MC approach.

4.2.1 GPD VaR estimation algorithm

i. Generate $N_e \sim Poi\left(\hat{\lambda} - \frac{1}{7}\right)$ and $N_u \sim Poi\left(\frac{1}{7}\right)$;

ii. Generate $X_1, \ldots, X_{N_e} \sim$ iid $\tilde{F}_e$ and $X_{N_e+1}, \ldots, X_{N_e+N_u} \sim$ iid $\tilde{F}_u$ and calculate $A = \sum_{n=1}^{N} X_n$ where $N = N_u + N_e$. Using the identity above it easily follows that A is distributed as a random sum of N i.i.d. losses from $\tilde{F}$.

iii. Repeat i and ii I times independently to obtain $A_i, i = 1, 2, \ldots, I$ and estimate the 99.9% VaR by the corresponding empirical quantile of these A_i's as before.

4.2.2 Remarks

When using the GPD 1-in-c years integration approach to model the severity distribution, we realised that the 99.9% VaR of the aggregate distribution is almost exclusively determined by the scenario assessments and their reliability greatly affects the reliability of the VaR estimate. The SLA supports this conclusion. As noted above, the SLA implies that we need to estimate $q_{1000} = T^{-1}\left(1 - \frac{1}{1000\lambda}\right)$ and its estimate would be $\hat{q}_{1000} = GPD^{-1}\left(\frac{\left(1-\frac{1}{1000\hat{\lambda}}\right)}{1-\left(1-\frac{1}{7\hat{\lambda}}\right)}, \tilde{\sigma}, \tilde{\xi}, \tilde{q}_b\right)$. Therefore 99.9% VaR largely depends on the GPD fitted with the scenario assessments. In **Figure 3** below we depict the VaR estimation results by fitting $\tilde{F}_e$ assuming a Burr distribution and $\tilde{F}_u$ assuming a GPD. The top panel in **Figure 3(a)** depicts the tail behaviour of the true severity distribution which is assumed as a Burr and denoted as T_Burr(1,0.6,2). Using the VaR approximation technique discussed in the second section (Approximating VaR) and assuming $\lambda = 10$, $I = 1\,000\,000$ and 1000 repetitions, the VaR approximations are depicted in the bottom panel in the form of a box plot as before. Assuming that we were supplied with quantile assessments by the oracle we use the two samples discussed in **Figure 2** and apply the GDP approach. The results are displayed in **Figure 3(b)** and **(c)** below.

The GPD fit to the oracle quantiles produce similar box plots, which in turn is very similar to the box plot of the VaR approximations. Clearly the fitted Burr has little effect on the VaR estimates. The VaR estimates obtained through the GPD approach is clearly dominated by the oracle quantiles. Of course, if the assessments

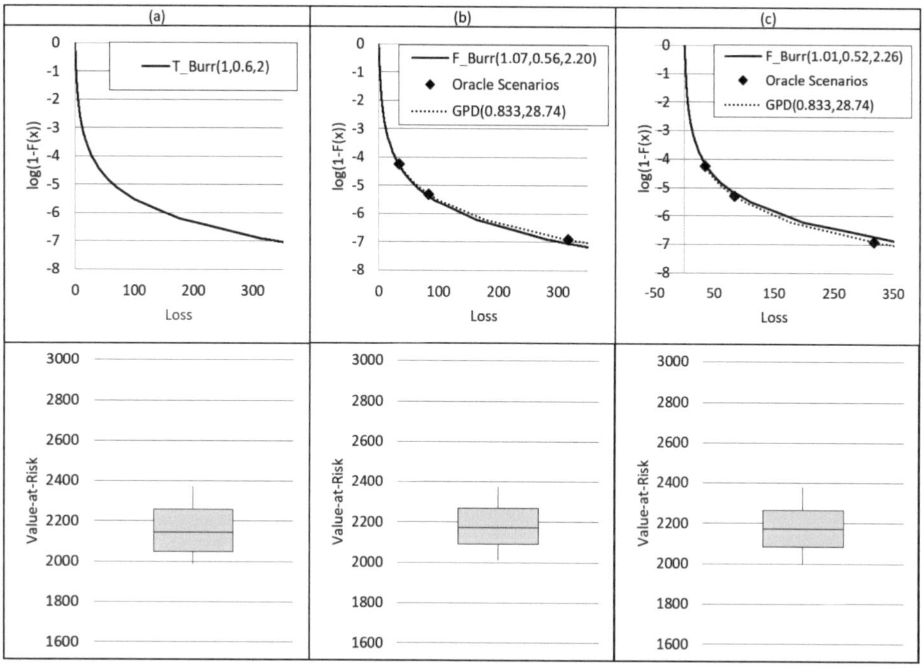

Figure 3.
Illustration of VaR estimates obtained from a GPD fit on the oracle quantiles. (a) True Burr distribution, T_Burr(1, 0.6, 2), (b) fitted distribution F_Burr(1.07, 0.56, 2.2) on simulated data, (c) fitted distribution F_Burr(1.01, 0.52, 2.26) on augmented simulated data.

are supplied by experts and not oracles the results would differ significantly. This is illustrated when we compare the GPD with Venter's approach.

The challenge is therefore to find a way of integrating the historical data and scenario assessments such that both sets of information are adequately utilised in the process. In particular, it would be beneficial to have measures indicating whether the experts' scenario assessments are in line with the observed historical data, and if not, to require them to produce reasons why their assessments are so different. Below we describe Venter's estimation method that will meet these aims.

4.3 Venter's approach

A colleague, Hennie Venter suggested that, given the quantiles q_7, q_{20}, q_{100}; one may write the distribution function T as follows:

$$T(x) = \begin{cases} \frac{p_7}{T(q_7)} T(x) & \textit{for } \ x \le q_7 \\ p_7 + \frac{p_{20} - p_7}{T(q_{20}) - T(q_7)} [T(x) - T(q_7)] & \textit{for } \ q_7 < x \le q_{20} \\ p_{20} + \frac{p_{100} - p_{20}}{T(q_{100}) - T(q_{20})} [T(x) - T(q_{20})] & \textit{for } \ q_{20} < x \le q_{100} \\ p_{100} + \frac{1 - p_{100}}{1 - T(q_{100})} [T(x) - T(q_{100})] & \textit{for } \ q_{100} < x < \infty. \end{cases} \tag{7}$$

Again$T(q_c) = p_c = 1 - \frac{1}{c\lambda}$ and it should be clear that the expressions on the right reduces to $T(x)$. Also, the definition of $T(x)$ could easily be extended for more quantiles. Given the previous discussion we can model $T(x)$ by $F(x, \theta)$ and estimate it by $F(x, \hat{\theta})$ using the historical data and maximum likelihood and estimate the annual frequency by $\hat{\lambda} = K/a$. Given scenario assessments $\tilde{q}_7, \tilde{q}_{20}$ and $\tilde{q}_{100}$, then $T(q_c)$ can be estimated by $F(\tilde{q}_c, \hat{\theta})$ and p_c by $\hat{p}_c = 1 - \frac{1}{c\hat{\lambda}}$. The estimated ratios are then defined by

$$R(7) = \frac{\hat{p}_7}{F(\tilde{q}_7;\hat{\theta})}, R(7,20) = \frac{\hat{p}_{20} - \hat{p}_7}{F(\tilde{q}_{20};\hat{\theta}) - F(\tilde{q}_7;\hat{\theta})},$$

$$R(20,100) = \frac{\hat{p}_{100} - \hat{p}_{20}}{F(\tilde{q}_{100};\hat{\theta}) - F(\tilde{q}_{20};\hat{\theta})} \text{ and } R(100) = \frac{1 - \hat{p}_{100}}{1 - F(\tilde{q}_{100};\hat{\theta})} \tag{8}$$

Notice that if our estimates were actually exactly equal to what they are estimating, these ratios would all be equal to 1. For example, we would then have $R(7) = p_7/T(q_7) = 1$ by (4), and similarly for the others. Our new method is to estimate the true severity distribution function T by an adjusted form of $F(x, \hat{\theta})$, then Hennie's distribution $\tilde{H}$ is defined as follows (see de Jongh et al. 2015):

$$\tilde{H}(x) = \begin{cases} R(7)F(x;\hat{\theta}) & \textit{for } x \leq \tilde{q}_7 \\ \hat{p}_7 + R(7,20)\left[F(x;\hat{\theta}) - F(\tilde{q}_7;\hat{\theta})\right] & \textit{for } \tilde{q}_7 < x \leq \tilde{q}_{20} \\ \hat{p}_{20} + R(20,100)\left[F(x;\hat{\theta}) - F(\tilde{q}_{20};\hat{\theta})\right] & \textit{for } \tilde{q}_{20} < x \leq \tilde{q}_{100} \\ \hat{p}_{100} + R(100)\left[F(x;\hat{\theta}) - F(\tilde{q}_{100};\hat{\theta})\right] & \textit{for } \tilde{q}_{100} < x < \infty. \end{cases} \tag{9}$$

Notice again that this estimate is consistent in the sense that it actually reduces to T if all estimators are exactly equal to what they are estimating.

Also note that $\tilde{H}(\tilde{q}_7) = \hat{p}_7$, $\tilde{H}(\tilde{q}_{20}) = \hat{p}_{20}$ and $\tilde{H}(\tilde{q}_{100}) = \hat{p}_{100}$, i.e. the equivalents of $T(q_c) = p_c$ hold for the scenario assessments when estimates are substituted for the true unknowns. Hence at the estimation level the scenario assessments are consistent with the probability requirements expressed. Thus, this new estimated severity distribution estimate $\tilde{H}$ 'believes' the scenario quantile information, but follows the distribution fitted on the historical data to the left of, within and to the right of the scenario intervals. The ratios $R(7), R(7,20)$, $R(20,100)$ and $R(100)$ in (9) can be viewed as measures of agreement between the historical data and the scenario assessments and could be useful for assessing their validities and qualities. The steps required to estimate VaR using this method are as follows:

4.3.1 Venter's VaR estimation algorithm

i. Generate $N \sim Poi(\hat{\lambda})$;

ii. Generate $X_1, \ldots, X_N \sim$ iid $\tilde{H}$ and calculate $A = \sum_{n=1}^{N} X_n$;

iii. Repeat i and ii I times independently to obtain $A_i, i = 1, 2, \ldots, I$ and estimate the 99.9% VaR by the corresponding empirical quantile of these A_i's as before.

4.3.2 Remarks

The SLA again sheds some light on this method. As noted above the SLA implies that we need to estimate $q_{1000} = T^{-1}(1 - \frac{1}{1000\lambda})$ and its estimate would be

$\hat{q}_{1000} = \tilde{H}^{-1}\left(1 - \frac{1}{1000\hat{\lambda}}\right) = \tilde{H}^{-1}(\hat{p}_{1000})$. Some algebra shows that the equation $F(\hat{q}_{1000}; \hat{\theta}) = F(\tilde{q}_{100}; \hat{\theta}) + (\hat{p}_{1000} - \hat{p}_{100})/R(100)$ needs to be solved for $\hat{q}_{1000}$. Depending on the choice of the family of distributions $F(x, \theta)$, this may be easy (e.g. when we use the Burr family for which we have an explicit expression for its quantile function). This clearly shows that a combination of the historical data and scenario assessments is involved, and not exclusively the latter. In as much as the SLA provides an approximate to the actual VaR of the aggregate loss distribution, we may expect the same to hold for Venter's approach.

In order to illustrate the properties of this approach we assume that the true underlying severity distribution is the Burr(1.0, 0.6, 2) as before. We then construct a 'false' severity distribution as the fitted distribution to the distorted sample depicted in **Figure 2(c)**, i.e. the Burr(1.00,0.52,2.26). We refer to the true severity distribution as Burr_1 and the false one Burr_2. In **Figure 4(a)** the box plots of the VaR approximations of the two distributions are given (using the same input for the MC simulations). We then illustrate the performance of the GPD and Venter approach in two cases. The first case assumes that the correct (oracle) quantiles of Burr_1 are supplied, but that the loss data are distributed according to the false distribution Burr_2. In the second case, the quantiles of the false severity distribution are supplied, but the loss data follows the true severity distribution. The box plots of the VaR estimates are given in **Figure 4(b)** for case 1 and **Figure 4(c)** for case 2.

The behaviour of the GPD approach is as expected and the box plots corresponds to the quantiles supplied. Clearly the quantiles and not the loss data dictates the results. On the other hand, the Venter approach is affected by both the loss data and quantiles supplied. In the example studied here it seems as if the method is more affected by the quantiles than by the data. This role of the data relative to the quantiles changes positively the more loss data are supplied.

4.4 GPD and Venter model comparison

In this section we conduct a simulation study to investigate the effect on the two approaches by perturbing the quantiles of the true underlying severity distributions. We assume the six parameters sets of **Table 1** as the true underlying severity distributions and then perturb the quantiles in the following way. For each simulation run, choose three perturbation factors u_7, u_{20} and u_{100} independently and uniformly distributed over the interval $[1 - \epsilon, 1 + \epsilon]$ and then take $\tilde{q}_7 = u_7 q_7, \tilde{q}_{20} = u_{20} q_{20}$ and $\tilde{q}_{100} = u_{100} q_{100}$ but truncate these so that the final values are increasing,

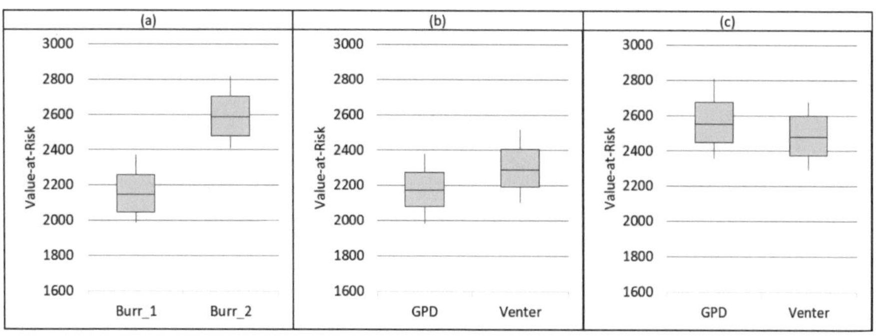

Figure 4.
Comparison of VaR results for the GPD and Venter approaches. (a) Naïve approach with correct (T_Burr(1, 0.6, 2)), and false data (F_Burr(1.01, 0.52, 2.26)), (b) Case 1 with correct quantiles and false data, (c) Case 2 with false quantiles and correct data.

i.e. $\tilde{q}_7 \leq \tilde{q}_{20} \leq \tilde{q}_{100}$. Here the fraction ϵ expresses the size or extent of the possible deviations (or mistakes) inherent in the scenario assessments. If $\epsilon = 0$ then the assessments are completely correct (within the simulation context) and the experts are in effect oracles. In practice, choosing $\epsilon > 0$ is more realistic, but how large the choice should be is not clear and we therefore vary ϵ over a range of values. We chose the values 0, 0.1, 0.2, 0.3 and 0.4 for this purpose in the results below. Choosing the perturbation factors to be uniformly distributed over the interval $[1-\epsilon, 1+\epsilon]$ implies that on average they have the value 1, i.e. the scenario assessments are about unbiased. This may not be realistic and other choices are possible, e.g. we could mimic a pessimistic scenario maker by taking the perturbations to be distributed on the interval $[1, 1+\epsilon]$ and an optimistic scenario maker by taking them on the interval $[1-\epsilon, 1]$.

For each combination of parameters of the assumed true underlying Poisson frequency and Burr severity distributions and for each choice of the perturbation size parameter ϵ the following steps are followed:

i. Use the VaR approximation algorithm in the second section to determine the 99.9% VaR for the Burr Type XII with the current choice of parameters. Note that the value obtained here approximately equals the true 99.9% VaR. We refer to this value as the approximately true (AT) VaR.

ii. Generate a data set of historical losses, i.e. generate $K \sim Poi(7\lambda)$ and then generate $x_1, x_2, \ldots, x_K \sim iid$ Burr Type XII with the current choice of parameters. Here the family $F(x, \theta)$ is chosen as the Burr Type XII but it is refitted to the generated historical data to estimate the parameters as required.

iii. Add to the historical losses three scenarios $\tilde{q}_7, \tilde{q}_{20}, \tilde{q}_{100}$ generated by the quantile perturbation scheme explained above. Estimate the 99.9% VaR using the GPD approach.

iv. Using the historical losses and the three scenarios of item iii), calculate the severity distribution estimate $\tilde{H}$ and apply Venter's approach to estimate the 99.9% VaR.

v. Repeat items i–iv 1000 times and then summarise and compare the resulting VaR estimates.

Because we are generally dealing with positively skewed data here, we shall use the median as the principal summary measure. Denote the median of the 1000 AT values by MedAT. Then we construct 90% VaR bands as before for the 1000 repeated GPD and Venter VaR estimates, i.e. $\left[\frac{VaR_{(51)}}{\text{MedAT}} - 1, \frac{VaR_{(951)}}{\text{MedAT}} - 1\right]$. The results are given in **Figure 5**. Note that light grey represents the GPD band and dark grey the Venter band, whilst the overlap between the two bands are even darker.

From **Figure 5**, we make the following observations:

For small frequencies ($\lambda \leq 10$) the GPD approach outperforms the Venter approach, except for short tailed severity distributions and higher quantile perturbations. When the annual frequency is high ($\lambda \geq 50$) and for moderate to high quantile perturbations ($\epsilon \geq 0.2$) the Venter approach is superior, and more so for higher λ and ϵ. Even for small quantile perturbations ($\epsilon = 0.1$) and high annual frequencies ($\lambda \geq 50$) the Venter approach performs reasonable when compared to the GPD.

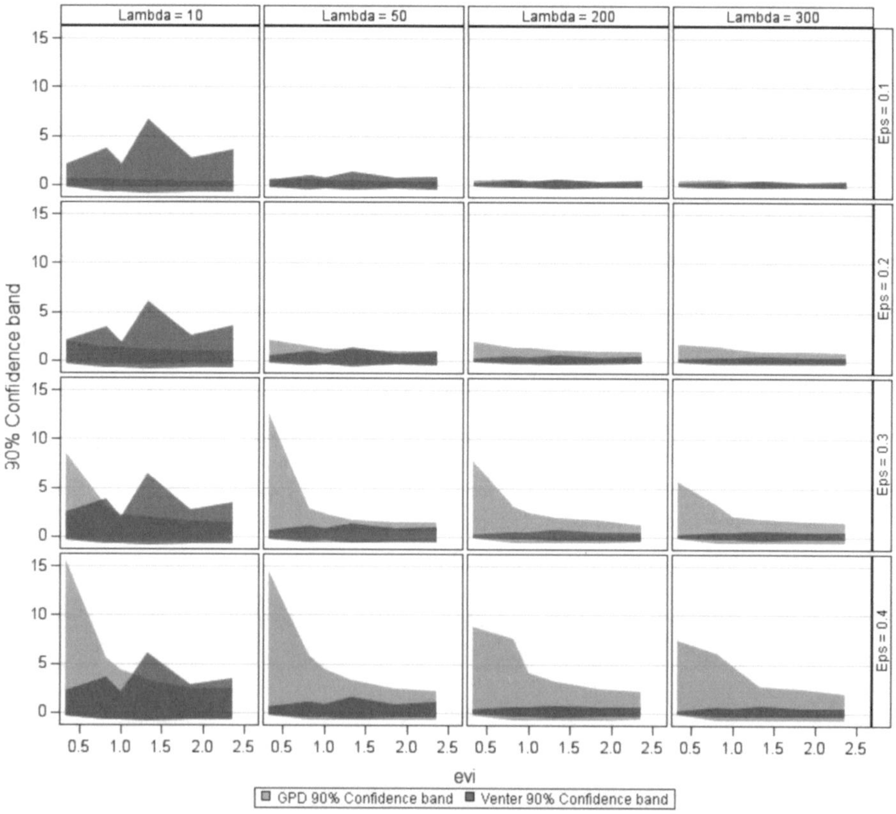

Figure 5.
VaR bands for different Burr parameter sets and frequency combinations.

The above information suggest that provided enough loss data is available the Venter approach is the best choice to work.

5. Implementation recommendations

As stated in the introduction to this chapter, Venter's method has been implemented by major international banks and approved by the local regulator. Based on this experience, we can share the following implementation guidelines:

i. Study the loss data carefully with respect to the procedures used to collect the data. Focus should be on the largest losses and one has to establish whether these losses were recorded and classified correctly according to the definitions used.

ii. Experts should be presented with an estimate of q_1 (based on the loss data) and then should answer the question 'Amongst those losses that are larger than q_1 what level is expected to be exceeded only once in c years?' where $c = 7, 20, 100$.

iii. The assessments by the expert should be checked with the condition $\frac{\tilde{q}_{100} - \tilde{q}_7}{\tilde{q}_{20} - \tilde{q}_7} > 2.533$. This bring realism as far as the ratios between the assessments are concerned.

iv. The loss data may be fitted by a wide class of severity distributions. We used SAS PROC SEVERITY in order to identify the five best fitting distributions.

v. Calculate the ratios $R(7), R(7,20)$, $R(20,100)$ and $R(100)$ of the best fitting distributions obtained above and then select the best distribution based on the ratios. Although this is a subjective selection it will lead to more realistic choices.

vi. For the best fitting distribution, present the ratios that deviate significantly from one to the experts for possible re-assessment. If new assessments are provided, repeat guidelines iii to v once or twice.

vii. Different data sources should be considered. The approaches discussed above assumes one unified dataset for the historical data source. In practice different datasets are included for example internal, external and mixed where the latter is scaled. Estimates of q_1 and q_7 based on these different datasets should inform the scenario process.

viii. Guideline vi may also be repeated on appropriate mixed (scaled) data sets to select the best distribution type.

6. Some further practical considerations

Data Scaling. It is practice in operational risk management to use different data sources for modelling future losses. Banks have been collecting their own data, but realistically, most banks only have between five and ten years of reliable loss data. To address this shortcoming, loss data from external sources can be used by banks in addition to their own internal loss data and controls. External loss data comprises operational risk losses experienced by third parties, including publicly available data, insurance data and consortium data. [16] investigate whether the size of operational risk losses is correlated with geographical region and firm size. They use a quantile matching algorithm to address statistical issues that arise when estimating loss scaling models when subjecting the data to a loss reporting threshold. [13] uses regression analysis based on the GAMLSS (generalised additive models for location scale and shape) framework to model the scaling properties. The severity of operational losses using the extreme value theory is used to account for the reporting bias of the external data losses.

No historical data available. In the event of having insufficient historical data available, the GPD approach as discussed above may be used. $T_e(x)$ in (2) can be estimated by a right truncated distribution, e.g. scaled beta, Pareto type II, etc. fitted to an expected loss scenario and q_7. In this case the expert should also provide a scenario for the expected loss $EL = E\left[T|X \le q_7\right]$. $T_u(x)$ can be estimated by a GPD distribution as discussed in the GPD approach.

Aggregation. To capture dependencies of potential operational risk losses across business lines or event types, the notion of copulas may be used (see [15]). Such dependencies may result from business cycles, bank-specific factors, or cross-dependence of large events. Banks employing more granular modelling approaches may incorporate a dependence structure, using copulas to aggregate operational risk losses across business lines and/or event types for which separate operational risk models are used.

7. Conclusion

In this chapter, we motivated the use of Venter's approach whereby the severity distribution may be estimated using historical data and experts' scenario assessments jointly. The way in which historical data and scenario assessments are integrated incorporates measures of agreement between these data sources, which can be used to evaluate the quality of both. This method has been implemented by major international banks and we included guidelines for its practical implementation. As far as future research is concerned, we are investigating the effectiveness of using the ratios in assisting the experts with their assessments. Also, we are testing the effect of replacing q_{100} with q_{50} in the assessment process.

A. Appendix A

A.1 The generalised Pareto distribution (GPD)

The GPD given by

$$GPD(x;\sigma,\xi,q_b) = \begin{cases} 1-\left[1+\frac{\xi}{\sigma}\left(x-q_b\right)\right]^{\frac{-1}{\xi}} & \xi>0 \\ 1-\ \exp\left(-\dfrac{x-q_b}{\sigma}\right) & \xi=0, \end{cases} \tag{10}$$

with $x \geq q_b$, thus taking q_b as the so-called EVT threshold and with σ and ξ respectively scale and shape parameters. Note the Extreme Value Index (EVI) of the GPD distribution is given by $EVI = \xi$ and that heavy-tailed distributions have a positive EVI and larger EVI implies heavier tails. This follows (also) from the fact that for positive EVI the GPD distribution belongs to the Pareto-type class of distributions, having a distribution function of the form $1-F(x) = x^{-1/\xi}\ell_F(x)$, with $\ell_F(x)$ a slowly varying function at infinity (see e.g. Embrechts et al., 1997). For Pareto-type, when the EVI > 1, the expected value does not exist, and when EVI > 0.5, the variance is infinite. Note also that the GPD distribution is regularly varying with index $-1/\xi$ and therefore belongs to the class of sub-exponential distributions. Note that the γ-th quantile of the GPD is $q(\gamma) = GPD^{-1}(\gamma,\sigma,\xi,q_b) = \left(q_b + \frac{\sigma\left((1-\gamma)^{-\xi}-1\right)}{\xi}\right)$ when $\xi \neq 0$ and $GPD^{-1}(\gamma,\sigma,\xi,q_b) = q_b - \sigma \ln(1-\gamma)$ when $= 0$.

A.2 The Burr distribution

The three parameter Burr type XII distribution function

$$B(x;\eta,\tau,\alpha) = 1-\left(1+(x/\eta)^{\tau}\right)^{-\alpha}, \text{for } x>0 \tag{11}$$

with parameters $\eta, \tau, \alpha > 0$ (see e.g. [10]). Here η is a scale parameter and τ and α shape parameters. Note the EVI of the Burr distribution is given by $EVI = \zeta = 1/\tau\alpha$ and that heavy-tailed distributions have a positive EVI and larger EVI implies heavier tails. This follows (also) from the fact that for positive EVI the Burr distribution belongs to the Pareto-type class of distributions, having a distribution function of the form $1-F(x) = x^{-1/\zeta}\ell_F(x)$, with $\ell_F(x)$ a slowly varying function at infinity (see e.g. [9]). For Pareto-type, when the EVI > 1, the expected value does not exist, and when EVI > 0.5, the variance is infinite. Note also that the Burr distribution is regularly varying with index $-\tau\alpha$and therefore belongs to the class of sub-exponential distributions. Note that the γ-th quantile of the Burr distribution is $q(\gamma) = B^{-1}(\gamma;\eta,\tau,\alpha) = \eta\left((1-\gamma)^{-1/\alpha}-1\right)^{1/\tau}$.

Other declarations

The authors acknowledge grants received from the National Research Foundation, the Department of Science and Technology and the Department of Trade and Industry. Any opinions, findings and conclusions or recommendations expressed in this material are those of the authors, and therefore the National Research Foundation does not accept any liability in regard to them.

Author details

Riaan de Jongh*, Helgard Raubenheimer and Mentje Gericke
Centre for Business Mathematics and Informatics, North-West University, Potchefstroom, South Africa

*Address all correspondence to: riaan.dejongh@nwu.ac.za

References

[1] Basel Committee on Banking Supervision. OPE Calculation of RWA for Operational Risk—OPE30 Advance Measurement Approach. 2019. Available from: https://www.bis.org/basel_framework/chapter/OPE/30.htm

[2] Basel Committee on Banking Supervision. Basel III: Finalising Post-Crisis Reforms. 2017. Available from: https://www.bis.org/bcbs/publ/d424.htm

[3] Prudential Regulation Authority, The PRA's Methodologies for Setting Pillar 2 Capital. Bank of England. 2020. Available from: https://www.bankofengland.co.uk/-/media/boe/files/prudential-regulation/statement-of-policy/2020/the-pras-methodologies-for-setting-pillar-2a-capital-update-february-2020.pdf

[4] De Jongh P, De Wet T, Raubenheimer H, Venter J. Combining scenario and historical data in the loss distribution approach: A new procedure that incorporates measures of agreement between scenarios and historical data. The Journal of Operational Risk. 2015;**10**(1):45-76. DOI: 10.21314/JOP.2015.160

[5] Panjer H. Operational Risk: Modeling Analytics. Chichester: Wiley; 2006. p. 448

[6] Böcker K, Klüppelberg C. Operational VaR: A closed-form approximation. Risk Magazine. 2005;**18**(12):90-93

[7] De Jongh P, De Wet T, Panman K, Raubenheimer H. A simulation comparison of quantile approximation techniques for compound distributions popular in operational risk. The Journal of Operational Risk. 2016;**11**(1):23-48. DOI: 10.21314/JOP.2016.171

[8] Degen M. The calculation of minimum regulatory capital using single-loss approximations. The Journal of Operational Risk. 2010;**5**(4):3-17. DOI: 10.21314/JOP.2010.084

[9] Embrechts P, Kluppelberg C, Mikosch T. Modelling Extremal Events for Insurance and Finance. Berlin, Heidelberg: Springer; 1997

[10] Beirlant J, Goegebeur Y, Segers J, Teugel J. Statistics of Extremes: Theory and Applications. New Jersey: John Wiley and Sons; 2004

[11] McNeil A, Frey R, Embrechts P. Quantitative Risk Management: Concepts, Techniques and Tools. Revised Edition. Princeton and Oxford: Princeton University Press; 2015

[12] Basel Committee on Banking Supervision. Operational Risk: Supervisory Guidelines for the Advanced Measurement Approaches. Report 196. 2011. Available from: https://www.bis.org/publ/bcbs196.htm

[13] Ganegoda A, Evans J. A scaling model for severity of operational losses using generalized additive models for location scale and shape (GAMLSS). Annals of Actuarial Science. 2013;**7**(1):61-100. DOI: 10.1017/S1748499512000267

[14] Kahneman D, Slovic P, Tversky A. Judgement under Uncertainty: Heuristics and Biases. New York: Cambridge University Press; 1982

[15] Embrechts P, Hofert M. Practices and issues in operational risk modelling under Basel II. Lithuanian Mathematical Journal. 2011;**51**(2):180-193

[16] Cope E, Labbi A. Operational loss scaling by exposure indicators: Evidence from the ORX database. The Journal of Operational Risk. 2008;**3**(4):25-45. DOI: 10.21314/JOP.2008.051

Chapter 3

Bayesian Analysis of Additive Factor Volatility Models with Heavy-Tailed Distributions with Specific Reference to S&P 500 and SSEC Indices

Verda Davasligil Atmaca and Burcu Mestav

Abstract

The distribution of the financial return series is unsuitable for normal distribution. The distribution of financial series is heavier than the normal distribution. In addition, parameter estimates obtained in the presence of outliers are unreliable. Therefore, models that allow heavy-tailed distribution should be preferred for modelling high kurtosis. Accordingly, univariate and multivariate stochastic volatility models, which allow heavy-tailed distribution, have been proposed to model time-varying volatility. One of the multivariate stochastic volatility (MSVOL) model structures is factor-MSVOL model. The aim of this study is to investigate the convenience of Bayesian estimation of additive factor-MSVOL (AFactor-MSVOL) models with normal, heavy-tailed Student-t and Slash distributions via financial return series. In this study, AFactor-MSVOL models that allow normal, Student-t, and Slash heavy-tailed distributions were estimated in the analysis of return series of S&P 500 and SSEC indices. The normal, Student-t, and Slash distributions were assigned to the error distributions as the prior distributions and full conditional distributions were obtained by using Gibbs sampling. Model comparisons were made by using DIC. Student-t and Slash distributions were shown as alternatives of normal AFactor-MSVOL model.

Keywords: Bayesian analysis, heavy-tailed, financial markets, stochastic volatility models, MCMC

1. Introduction

In recent years, multivariate time series analysis has become an in important research field due to the positive improvements in both methodological and analytical computations. Based on these developments, it has been possible to assess the estimations of parameters in the models of multidimensional and complex time series. Parallelly with these developments, it has been a necessity to model datasets that have simultaneous and frequently changing together. Besides the increase of dataset dimensions, multidimensional volatility models have gained importance in respect of both economic and econometric parameter estimations due to the temporal fluctuations and changes. The information provided by the correlation structures of multidimensional volatility models has contributed a lot especially in optimal portfolio management, risk management, asset allocation and financial decisions. Moreover; as the volatility between different assets and markets can move together, multivariate analysis contributes statistical efficiency [1].

GARCH and stochastic volatility (SVOL) models, which are widely used in the estimation of volatility, are developed, analysed, and applied within the frame of multivariate the analysis. While multivariate GARCH (MGARCH) models are widely used, MSVOL models are often used in recent years. In his study [2], juxtaposed the most important studies on analysis and development of these models by comparing univariate and multivariate GARCH and SVOL models.

MSVOL models vary in different structures. These structures can be sorted as alternative specifications such as asymmetric models, factor models, time-varying correlation models and matrix exponential transformation, Cholesky decomposition, Wishart autoregressive models [1]. The reason for the limited use of MSVOL is the problems faced in the method of estimation in these models. The most important one among these problems is the problem of high dimension in multivariate analysis and this problem has been eased by using latent factor structures.

Factor-MSVOL models are divided into two groups according to how the factors involved in the mean equation. The first of these structures is additive Factor-MSVOL (AFactor-MSVOL) in which the factors are added summatively and the second one is multiplicative Factor-MSVOL in which the factors are added multiplicatively [3].

AFactor-MSVOL models are firstly offered by Harvey et al. [4]. Afterward, it was developed by [5–9]. The basic idea is taken from factor multivariate ARCH models; additionally, it is a more general state of factor decomposition of covariance structures in multivariate analysis. Returns are divided into two additive components. The first component involves a limited number of factors. The factors capture the information related to the pricing of the whole assets. The other component is the term of an error on the model and it captures the specific information of the asset [1].

Factor-MSVOL models derive from the field of financial econometrics. These models are often preferred to define the terms uncertainty and risk correctly. Asset allocation and asset pricing can be given as an example here. Additionally, it is also used in the arbitrage pricing theory and financial asset pricing model [10]. In comparison with other multivariate stochastic volatility models, Factor-MSVOL models can be estimated with lesser parameters. In this respect, they are parsimonious models in terms of parameters [11]. Factor models both reduce the number of parameters and allow the changing variance structure, it considerably explains the correlation.

Factor-MSVOL models aim to combine a plain, flexible, and robust structure. Like classical factor models, these models are easier in respect of degrading high-dimensioned observation area into low-dimensioned orthogonal latent factor area [10]. Moreover; in the long term data, it is assessed with lesser deviation thanks to its being robust in case of unusual observations.

This study aims to model parameter estimations concerning AFactor-MSVOL models with normal distribution, Student-t distribution, Slash distribution assigned on the error within based on the Bayesian approach. For this purpose; S&P500 (Standard & Poor's 500) and SSEC (Shanghai Compound Index) index daily return series, involving the period between 10.20.2014 and 10.17.2019, were used. Among the models, the error was scaled out by normal, Gamma, and Beta distributions; the first one is AFactor-MSVOL-NOR model with normal distribution, the second one is AFactor-MSVOL-St model with Student-t distribution, and the last one is AFactor-MSVOL-Sl robust model with Slash distribution. Estimated AFactor-MSVOL models are bivariate and one-factor structure. Usage of Student-t and Slash distributions, while handling skewness and kurtosis features of returns, enabled a flexible approach as an alternative of normal distribution.

2. Model

Latent factor models prove the notion that high-dimensioned systems are just led by some random resources. Some factors are controlled by these random resources and these factors explain the interaction among the observations. Moreover; latent factor models are an efficient way of estimation of a dynamic covariance matrix. These models enable a decrease in the number of unknown parameters [12].

This model has several attractive features, including parsimony of the parameter space and the ability to capture the common features in asset returns and volatilities. Basic idea of Factor-MSVOL models was taken from multivariate ARCH models. In these models, returns are divided into two additive components. The first component has few factors that capture information about the pricing of all assets, while the other component is the error term that captures asset-specific information.

2.1 Multiplicative Factor-MSVOL model

Stochastic discount Factor-MSVOL, which is also called as multiplicative Factor-MSVOL model, was offered by [13]. He offered Bayesian analysis of structured dynamic factor models. Returns are divided into two multiplicative components in one-factor multiplicative model. As shown below, the first of these components is scalar common factor and the other one is idiosyncratic error vector:

$$y_t = \exp(h_t/2)\varepsilon_t, \qquad \varepsilon_t \overset{iid}{\sim} N(0, \Sigma_\varepsilon) \tag{1}$$

$$h_{t+1} = \mu + \phi(h_t - \mu) + \eta_t \qquad \eta_t \overset{iid}{\sim} N(0, 1) \tag{2}$$

The first one Σ_ε is accepted as 1 for identification. Compared to the MSVOL model, this model involves lesser parameters and it eases calculation. Different from AFactor-MSVOL model, correlation does not change according to time. Additionally, correlation in log-volatility is always equal to 1. The cross dependence among the returns derives from the dependency in ε_t.

In [14] developed the one-factor model as k-factor. In their studies, [14] researched both the persistence amount of daily stock returns and the factors affecting common persistence components in volatility. In this study, the one-factor multiplicative MSVOL model is expanded as k-factor.

2.2 Additive Factor-MSVOL model

The Factor-MSVOL model is one of the MSVOL approaches allowing the change of implicitly conditioned correlation matrix in time and producing time-varying correlation. Factor models and factors follow a stochastic volatility process. A kind of Factor-SVOL model that does not allow time-varying correlations was offered by [13]. On the other hand, Harvey et al. [4] introduced a common factor in the linearized state-space version of the basic MSVOL model. In this context, the most basic MSVOL model specification is by:

$$y_{it} = \varepsilon_{it}(\exp\{h_{it}\})^{1/2}\; i = 1, \ldots, N\; t = 1, \ldots, T \tag{3}$$

y_{it} refers to the observation values in t period of i serial. $\varepsilon_t = (\varepsilon_{1t}, \ldots, \varepsilon_{Nt})'$ is the error vector which shows normal distribution with Σ_ε covariance matrix and 0 mean. Diagonal elements of Σ_ε covariance matrix are unity and off-diagonal elements are defined as ρ_{ij}. Variance of this model is produced by AR(1) process:

$$h_{\mathrm{it}} = \gamma_i + \varphi h_{it-1} + \eta_{it}\, i = 1, \ldots, N \tag{4}$$

Here, $\eta_t = (\eta_{1t}, \ldots, \eta_{Nt})'$ with 0 mean and multivariate of $\sum_\eta$ matrix is normal. This model, Eq. (4), $N \times 1\, h_t$, can be generalised as multivariate AR(1) and even ARMA process. If we handle the multivariate random walk model of $\boldsymbol{h_t}$, which is its special case:

$$w_t = -1.27i + h_t + \xi_t \tag{5}$$

$$h_t = h_{t-1} + \eta_t \tag{6}$$

w_t and ξ_t elements are $N \times 1$ vectors in case $w_{it} = \log y_{it}^2$ and $\xi_{\mathrm{t}} = \log \varepsilon_{it}^2 + 1.27\; i = 1, \ldots, N$. i is $N \times 1$ vector which is composed of unit values.

Common factors can be included in multivariate stochastic variance models; they are unobservable components of time series models. In [4] modelled with a multivariate random walk by considering the persistence in volatility. According to this, Eq. (4) is by:

$$w_t = -1.27i + \theta h_t + \overline{h} + \xi_t, \tag{7}$$

$$h_t = h_{t-1} + \eta_t$$
$$Var(\eta_t) = \sum\nolimits_\eta \tag{8}$$

As θ k$\leq$N, $N \times k$ parameter matrix, h_t and $\eta_{\mathbf{t}}$ $k \times 1$ vectors, Σ_η $k \times k$ positively defined matrix, $\overline{h}$ is an $N \times 1$ vector in which the first k elements are zeros and the last $N - k$ elements are unbounded, Harvey et al. [4] estimated this model with QML method. Common factors are transformed as $\theta^* = \theta R'$ and $h_t^* = Rh_{\mathbf{t}}$ to evaluate the factor loading [4].

Following the model offered by [15], another kind of MSVOL factor model was handled by [8] as below:

$$y_t = Bf_t + V_t^{1/2}\varepsilon_t \varepsilon_{\mathrm{t}} \sim \mathrm{N_p}(0, \mathrm{I}) \tag{9}$$

$$f_t = D_t^{1/2}\gamma_t\gamma_t \sim N_q(0, I) \tag{10}$$

$$h_{t+1} = \mu + \Phi(h_t - \mu) + \eta_t\eta_t \sim N_{p+q}\left(0, \sum\nolimits_{\eta\eta}\right) \tag{11}$$

$$\mathbf{V_t} = diag(\exp(h_{1t}), \ldots, \exp(h_{pt})) \tag{12}$$

$$\mathbf{D_t} = diag(\exp(h_{p+1,t}), \ldots, \exp(h_{p+q,t})) \tag{13}$$

$$\Phi = diag\left(\varphi_1, \ldots, \varphi_{p+q}\right) \tag{14}$$

$$\Sigma_{\eta\eta} = diag\left(\sigma_{1,\eta\eta}, \ldots, \sigma_{p+q,\eta\eta}\right) \tag{15}$$

$$\Phi = diag\left(\varphi_1, \ldots, \varphi_{p+q}\right) \tag{16}$$

$$\Sigma_{\eta\eta} = diag\left(\sigma_{1,\eta\eta}, \ldots, \sigma_{p+q,\eta\eta}\right) \tag{17}$$

and $h_t = \left(h_{1t}, \ldots, h_{pt}, h_{p+1,t,\ldots,}h_{p+q,t}\right)$.

B is a $p \times q$ matrix of factor loadings. For $i < j, i \leq j\ b_{ij} = 0$, for $i \leq q b_{ii} = 1$, and all remaining elements are unconstrained. Therefore, each of the factors and errors in this model develops according to SVOL models. Similar to this model, except the fact that V_t does not change in time under restriction, another model was handled in [6] and [16]. In [6] estimated their models with Markov Chain Monte Carlo (MCMC) method. On the other hand, [16] showed how to assess MLE with the Efficient Importance Sampling method. Presented by [17], a more generalised version of these models allows spikes in observation equations and the errors are distributed by heavy-tailed-t [18].

In [3] showed that additive factor models are by both time-varying volatility and correlations. In this context, they offered two varieties one-Factor SVOL model and they showed that the correlation between two return series is related to the volatility of the factor. According to this, logarithmic returns observed in t period are expressed as $\mathbf{y}_t = \left(y_{1t}, y_{2t}\right)'$. Additionally, when it is showed as $\boldsymbol{\varepsilon}_t = (\varepsilon_{1t}, \varepsilon_{2t})'$, $\boldsymbol{\eta}_t = (\eta_{1t}, \eta_{2t})'$, $\boldsymbol{\mu}_t = (\mu_{1t}, \mu_{2t})'$ and $\boldsymbol{h}_t = (h_{1,t}, h_{2,t})'$, two varieties one-Factor MSVOL models are such as below:

$$\mathbf{y}_t = Df_t + \boldsymbol{\varepsilon}_t \boldsymbol{\varepsilon}_t \overset{iid}{\sim} \mathrm{N}\left(\mathbf{0}, \mathrm{diag}\left(\sigma_{\varepsilon 1}^2, \sigma_{\varepsilon 2}^2\right)\right) \tag{18}$$

$$h_{t+1} = \mu + \varphi(h_t\text{-}\mu) + \sigma_\eta \eta_t, \eta_t \overset{iid}{\sim} \mathrm{N}(0, 1) \tag{19}$$

and $h_0 = 0$. This model is offered by [5, 6]. The first component that takes place in return equation involves a small number of factors which includes the information related to the pricing of the whole assets. The second term is error term peculiar to equation; it involves specific information of the asset. A Factor-MSVOL model allows high kurtosis and volatility cluster. It also enables cross dependency in both returns and volatility. $\mathrm{h_t}$ represents the log-volatility of the common factor $(\mathrm{f_t})$ which takes place in A Factor-MSVOL model. The conditional correlation between y_{1t} and y_{2t} is as below:

$$\frac{d\,exp\,(h_t)}{\sqrt{\left(exp\,(h_t) + \sigma_{\varepsilon 1}^2\right)\left(d^2\,exp\,(h_t) + \sigma_{\varepsilon 2}^2\right)}} \tag{20}$$

$$= \frac{d}{\sqrt{1 + \sigma_{\varepsilon 1}^2\,exp\,(-h_t)\left(d^2 + \sigma_{\varepsilon 2}^2\,exp\,(-h_t)\right)}} \tag{21}$$

$\sigma_{\varepsilon 1}^2 = \sigma_{\varepsilon 2}^2 = 0$ is not, so correlation coefficient changes in time. Correlation dynamics is dependent on the dynamics of $\mathrm{h_t}$; likewise, the correlation is an increasing function of $\mathrm{h_t}$. It refers that the correlation will be high as much as the common factor volatility is high.

Offered by [3], specification of two varieties one-factor AFactor-MSVOL model, which allows heavy-tailed distribution, is as below:

$$\mathbf{y}_t = Df_t + \boldsymbol{\varepsilon}_t \boldsymbol{\varepsilon}_t \overset{iid}{\sim} \mathrm{t}\left(\mathbf{0}, \mathrm{diag}\left(\sigma^2_{\varepsilon 1}, \sigma^2_{\varepsilon 2}\right), \mathbf{v}\right) \tag{22}$$

$$f_t = exp\ (h_t/2)u_t, u_t \overset{iid}{\sim} \mathrm{t}(0, 1, \omega), \tag{23}$$

$$h_{t+1} = \mu + \varphi(h_t\text{-}\mu) + \sigma_\eta \eta_t, \eta_t \overset{iid}{\sim} \mathrm{N}(0, 1) \tag{24}$$

$h_0 = \mu$, $\mathbf{v} = (v_1, v_2)'$. In this model, heavy-tailed Studentt distribution is used for return shocks. The conditional correlation between y_{1t} and y_{2t} is as below:

$$\frac{d}{\sqrt{1 + \frac{\omega}{v_1}\sigma^2_{\varepsilon 1} exp\ (-h_t)\left(d^2 + \frac{\omega}{v_2}\sigma^2_{\varepsilon 2} exp\ (-h_t)\right)}} \tag{25}$$

In addition to these models, AFactor-MSVOL-Sl model in which error distribution is scaled with Slash distribution is defined as:

The error for the AFactor-MSVOL-Sl model is shown as Slash distribution $(\varepsilon_t|v_t) \sim slash\left(0, \sum_\varepsilon, v\right)$ with $\sigma^2_{\varepsilon_t} \sim beta(\alpha, \beta)$ prior distribution.

$$\mathbf{y}_t = Df_t + \boldsymbol{\varepsilon}_t, \boldsymbol{\varepsilon}_t \sim \mathrm{slash}\left(\mathbf{0}, \mathrm{diag}\left(\sigma^2_{\varepsilon 1}, \sigma^2_{\varepsilon 2}\right), \mathbf{v}\right) \tag{26}$$

$$f_t = exp\ (h_t/2)u_t, u_t \sim \mathrm{slash}(0, 1, \omega) \tag{27}$$

$$h_{t+1} = \mu + \varphi(h_t\text{-}\mu) + \sigma_\eta \eta_t, \eta_t \overset{iid}{\sim} \mathrm{N}(0, 1) \tag{28}$$

Philipov and Glickman [19] offered high-dimensioned additive factor-MSVOL models in their studies. In this study, factor covariance matrix is led by Wishart random process. On the other hand, it is known that daily return series are leptokurtic. In context of stochastic volatility, [20] and [21] presented empirical proofs on the usage of heavy-tailed distribution in conditioned mean equation. Moreover, [22] analysed SVOL models with Student-t distribution and GED. Daily data analysis of JPY/Dollar and TOPIX were carried out by the method of MCMC. Comparison of distributions, in respect of accordance, was calculated with Bayesian factor values. It is determined that SVOL-t model assorts with both of the data compared to SVOL-normal and SVOL-GED models.

In [23] analysed new-class linear factor models. In these models, factors are latent and covariance matrix is followed with MSVOL process. Wu et al. [24] proposed dynamic correlated latent factor SVOL model structure in his studies. According to the results of analysis led by MCMC method, statistically comprehensible results were obtained for financial and economic data.

3. Empirical analysis

3.1 Dataset

This study aims to model parameter estimations concerning AFactor-MSVOL models with Student-t, Slash and normal distributions assigned to the error. For this purpose; S&P500 and SSEC index daily return series, involving the period between 10.20.2014 and 10.17.2019, were used. Among the models the error was scaled by normal, Gamma, and Beta distributions; the first one is AFactor-MSV-NOR model with normal distribution, the second one is AFactor-MSVOL-St model with Student-t distribution, and the last one is AFactor-MSVOL-Sl robust model with Slash distribution. Analyses of data were carried out with R and WinBugs programmes. Daily mean logarithmic return series were determined by:

$$Y_t = 100 \times (\log P_t - \log P_{t-1}) \tag{29}$$

$$y_t = Y_t - \frac{1}{T}\sum_{t=1}^{T} Y_t \tag{30}$$

S&P500 index is composed of stocks of the most valuable 500 companies in USA. On the other hand, SSEC has the most important and the biggest companies of China. Commercial and financial relations between the USA and China not only affect themselves but also global economy. Commercial and financial tensions between them and the anxieties on currency wars can negatively affect Asia and Europe stock markets. Therefore; index values of two grand economies such as China and USA are preferred for analyses. In **Figure 1**, time series plots for S&P500 and SSEC return series are given.

Descriptive statistic values of S&P500 and SSEC series are given in **Table 1**. S&P500 and SSEC series have negative mean returns. It seems that SSEC return series have more volatility. Moreover, both of the series are negatively skew. Kurtosis level is higher for both S&P500 and SSEC. Jarque-Bera normality test results show that series do not have a normal distribution.

In **Table 2**, Ljung-Box and ARCH-LM test results are illustrated in some lags. As Q statistics of Ljung-Box test are examined, null hypothesis that there is not auto-correlation is rejected for both of the series in 20th and 50th lags. It refers that autocorrelation exists in series. According to the ARCH test results, ARCH effect is seen in the whole series. It shows the necessity of preferring the models allowing heteroscedastic structures in the analyses of volatility in return series.

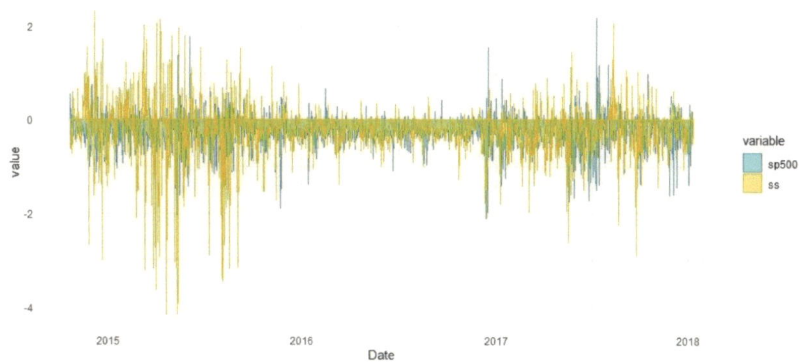

Figure 1.
Time series plots for S&P500 and SSEC returns.

	S&P500	SSEC
Sample size	1177	1177
Mean	−0.2784	−0.2862
Maximum	2.1777	2.3282
Minimum	−2.112	−4.1485
Standard deviation	0.39	0.6802
Skewness	−0.1463	−0.9852
Kurtosis	4.7226	6.0157
Jarque-Bera (possibility)	1098.0 (3.7495e-239)	1965.2 (0.0000)

Table 1.
Descriptive statistics of S&P500 and SSEC return series.

	S&P500	SSEC
Q(5)	7.0117 [0.2197]	12.8221 [0.0251]
Q(10)	16.1735 [0.0947]	20.6526 [0.0236]
Q(20)	29.5883 [0.0768]	59.9778 [0.0000]
Q(50)	71.0158 [0.0269]	115.200 [0.0000]
$Q^2(5)$	149.806 [0.0000]	262.809 [0.0000]
$Q^2(10)$	198.313 [0.0000]	323.350 [0.0000]
$Q^2(20)$	223.106 [0.0000]	575.391 [0.0000]
$Q^2(50)$	290.457 [0.0000]	937.313 [0.0000]
ARCH-LM(2)	37.195 [0.0000]	52.090 [0.0000]
ARCH-LM(5)	19.487 [0.0000]	31.799 [0.0000]
ARCH-LM(10)	11.359 [0.0000]	16.405 [0.0000]

Table 2.
Ljung-box and ARCH-LM test results.

3.2 Bayesian estimation

The most important factor, which limits the usage of Factor-MSVOL models, is difficulty in estimating the statistics, whereupon some methods were offered for estimation. In these methods, quasi maximum likelihood, simulated maximum likelihood, and Bayesian MCMC are offered as the most efficient methods. Bayesian MCMC method is very efficient against high dimension problems of the dataset [8, 9, 17].

In this study, parameter estimations are obtained by the Bayesian approach. As it is known, in parameter estimation it is supposed that the error term shows the normal distribution, but this assumption is not valid in case unusual points exist, therefore error term has a heterogeneous variance. This case is often faced in longitudinal datasets. In case unusual points exist in datasets, researchers generally prefer some strategies such as keeping the outliers, removing outliers, and recoding outliers. If keeping the outliers is chosen, the heavy-tailed distribution must be preferred rather than normal distribution. Otherwise, it causes statistical inferences.

In recent years, multidimensional analytical operations in computational science have become easier thanks to the advances in computer technology. In parallel with these advances and usage of the Bayesian approach, using more robust models in analyses has increased in the observation of unusual points. In the Bayesian approach, model parameters are random variables and it is supposed that it shows a known distribution. The Bayesian approach relies on the combination of subjective experiences of the researcher, the prior information obtained from the former studies, and the likelihood obtained from data. Posterior information is achieved from the combination with prior information. This information is defined with a known distribution function and parameter estimations are achieved from the posterior distribution.

$$\text{Posterior} \propto \text{Prior X Likelihood}$$

In the Bayesian approach, in obtained of the posterior distribution of parameters requires multidimensional integral computations in multidimensional and longitudinal datasets. This difficulty is overcome by the development of iterative methods such as MCMC. MCMC methods are based on the randomly generate parameter values from posterior distribution; thus, some analytically difficult problems are easily solved by simulation techniques. In this study, parameter estimations are obtained by Gibbs sampling which is also a MCMC method. Gibbs sampling is a method used in case posterior distribution has a closed-form and it is a kind of iterative method reproducing random values from these values. The full conditional density function is obtained by Gibbs sampling as all the unknown parameters are given and parameters are estimated with this method.

In this study, parameter estimations are obtained by modelling three different prior distributions assigned on the error term. In modelling, error term is scaled with λ variable and normal/independent (or scaled mixture) defined distributions are used. As y variable, which shows normal/independent distribution, is expressed in longitudinal model given below [25];

$$y = \mu + \frac{e}{\sqrt{\lambda}} \tag{31}$$

Here μ is a mean vector, e is error vector and have normal distribution. λ variable that takes place in the model shows different distributions according to the degrees of freedom of υ, and it is defined as random variable with positive valence. As degrees of freedom goes infinite, λ variable is 1 and the error term shows normal distribution. As λ variate shows Gamma $\left(\frac{\upsilon}{2}, \frac{\upsilon}{2}\right)$ distribution, it converges Student-t; and as λ variate shows Beta$(\upsilon, 1)$ distribution in $[0,1]$ closed interval, it converges Slash distribution.

3.3 Findings

As an addition to the AFactor-MSVOL offered by [3] and heavy-tailed AFactor-MSVOL models, bivariate one-factor AFactor-MSVOL model in which the error term is scaled with Slash distribution is estimated in the analysis.

In **Table 3**, posterior mean values of the parameters, standard errors and 95% credible intervals are shown. Using different initial values for each model, two chains are formed. Total iteration number in each chain is determined as 500,000

		AFactor-MSVOL-NOR	**AFactor-MSVOL-St**	**AFactor-MSVOL-Sl**
μ	Mean	−1.59	−1.586	−3.930
	Sd	0.2899	0.292	0.614
	%95 CI	[−2.208, −1.054]	[−2.231, −1.072]	[−5.531, −3.102]
Ø	Mean	0.9910	0.991	0.830
	Sd	0,005198	0.006	0.055
	%95 CI	[0.9788,0.9988]	[0.978, 0.999]	[0.708, 0.926]
σ_η^2	Mean	95.68	87.230	0.653
	Sd	36.89	36.339	0.076
	%95 CI	[42.81, 183.0]	[39.950,177.002]	[0.496, 0.793]
d	Mean	0.178	0.158	0.174
	Sd	0.02329	0.018	0.052
	%95 CI	[0.1335,0.2248]	[0.123,0.194]	[0.074, 0.278]
σ^2_{e1}	Mean	0.003672	0.001	0.345
	Sd	0.006022	0.007	0.042
	%95 CI	[3.984E-8, 0.0216]	[0.000,0.023]	[0.260, 0.426]
σ^2_{e2}	Mean	0.1781	0.151	0.309
	Sd	0.01054	0.011	0.037
	%95 CI	[0.1583, 0.1996]	[0.131, 0.174]	[0.242, 0.387]

		AFactor-MSVOL-NOR	AFactor-MSVOL-St	AFactor-MSVOL-Sl
v_1	Mean		8.735	8.317
	Sd		5.744	4.665
	%95 CI		[2.396, 24.190]	[3.869, 21.360]
v_2	Mean		4.372	3.652
	Sd		0.599	1.702
	%95 CI		[3.433, 5.780]	[2.418, 8.375]
ω	Mean		7.237	5.299
	Sd		1.670	4.727
	%95 CI		[5.128,11.600]	[2.027, 19.570]

Note: Parameter estimations for AFactor-MSVOL-NOR, AFactor-MSVOL-St and AFactor-MSVOL-Sl models are Rhat = 1.

Table 3.
Posterior mean values of the parameters in the AFactor-MSVOL models.

and the iteration number that must be omitted in the burn-in is 250,000. Thus, when the first burn-in period of 250,000 is omitted, a Gibbs chain of 250,000 is obtained for each parameter by means of saving each iteration value.

It is seen that for AFactor-MSVOL and AFactor-MSVOL-St models Ø parameter of posterior mean value is so close to the unit value. It refers that latent volatility had random walk behaviour. On the other hand, factor process for all the models was highly obtained. It is seen that standard deviation of posterior mean value of Ø parameter is too low. According to this, logarithmic volatility of time-varying latent components shows persistent features. Posterior mean value of Ø parameter is lower in AFactor-MSVOL-Sl model in comparison to the other models, while the posterior means of ϕ are all nearby unity and seem to propose random walk behaviour for h_t. The mean of ϕ is close to unity with a low standard deviation under all specifications, offering persistent time-varying log-volatility for latent components. Factor loading for the estimated models are determined as 0.178, 0.158, and 0.17, respectively. The overall variance-covariance is decomposed into a component which is due to the variation in the common factor and a component reflecting the variation in the idiosyncratic errors. Diebold and Nerlov [26] suggest the common factor reflects the flow of new information relevant to the pricing of all assets, upon which asset-specific shocks represented by the idiosyncratic errors are superimposed (**Figures 2**, **3** and **4**).

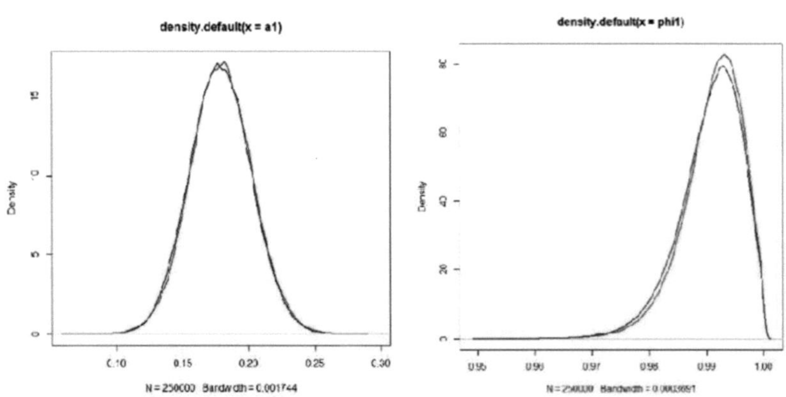

Figure 2.
Kernel density estimation of AFactor-MSVOL-NOR model μ and Ø parameters.

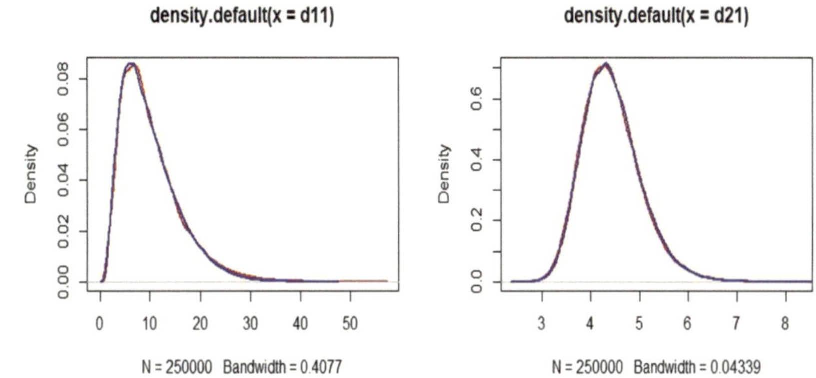

Figure 3.
Kernel density of AFactor-MSVOL-St model v_1 and v_2 parameters.

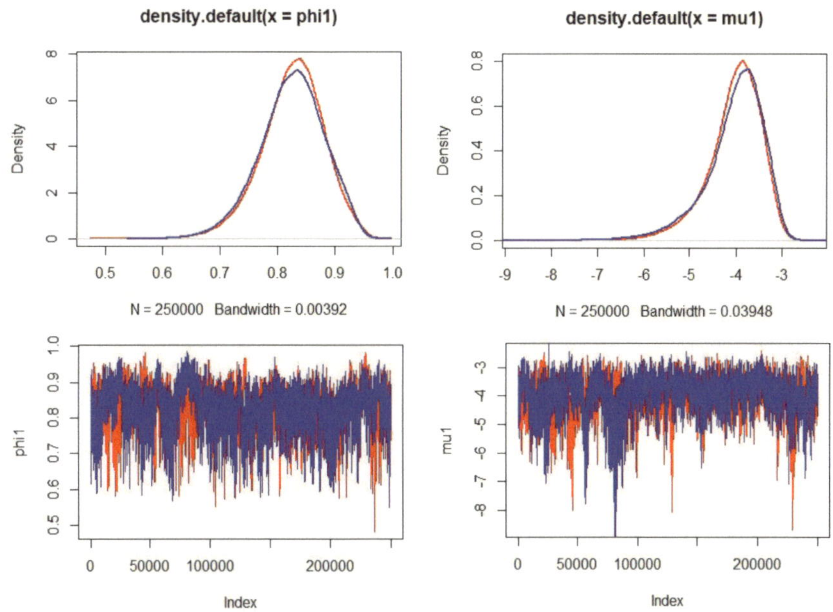

Figure 4.
Kernel density of AFactor-MSVOL-SL model μ and Ø parameters.

Gelman-Rubin statistics is an approach to determining convergence. According to it, convergence takes place in case means of variance within the chain and the variance values between the chains are equal. In this case, Gelman-Rubin statistics is about 1. In **Table 4**, Gelman-Rubin statistics of estimated models for parameter estimation take place. According to this, it is seen that all the parameters take 1 value of Gelman-Rubin statistics and convergence occurs.

	AFactor-MSVOL-NOR	AFactor-MSVOL-St	AFactor-MSVOL-Sl
μ	1.00	1.00	1.01
Ø	1.00	1.00	1.00
$\sigma_\eta{}^2$	1.02	1.00	1.00
d	1.00	1.00	1.00
$\sigma^2_{\varepsilon 1}$	1.01	1.04	1.00

	AFactor-MSVOL-NOR	AFactor-MSVOL-St	AFactor-MSVOL-Sl
$\sigma^2_{\varepsilon 2}$	1.00	1.00	1.00
v_1		1.00	1.00
v_2		1.00	1.00
ω		1.00	1.00

Table 4.
Gelman-Rubin diagnostic test.

DIC allows comparison between the models by taking into consideration the complexity of the model [27, 28]. p_d is expressed as efficient parameter number. p_d model gives the approximate value of parameter number and measures the complexity of the model. DIC can take both negative and positive values. It causes negative valorisation of both deviation and DIC. In conclusion, the model with the lowest DIC value must be chosen from alternative models [29]. In **Table 5**, DIC values of each three values are given; according to this, the model with the lowest DIC values should be chosen.

	DIC	pd
AFactor-MSVOL-NOR	3705.3	316.1
AFactor-MSVOL-St	3657.7	396.0
AFactor-MSVOL-Sl	3609.3	183.4

Table 5.
DIC values.

4. Conclusion

In financial applications, modelling the correlation structures of the returns is important because empirical analyses show that there is time-varying relation among return-on-assets. In this context, factor-MSVOL models have been preferred. Thanks to these models, volatility dynamics of financial and economic time series can be modelled with few latent factors.

In this study, parameter estimations concerning additive factor-MSVOL models were modelled with normal distribution assigned on the error, Student-t distribution, and Slash distribution in the frame of Bayesian analysis. Normal, Student-t and Slash distributions were assigned as prior distribution to the error distributions and full conditioned posterior distributions were obtained by a kind of MCMC method-Gibbs sampling. Among the criteria of model choosing, DIC is used for comparison and it showed that Student-t and Slash distributions can be used as alternative of normal AFactor-MSVOL models. Provided that the analysis results are evaluated in respect of DIC criteria and model complexity, it is seen that AFactor-MSVOL-Sl model in which the errors are scaled with Slash distribution is better than the other models. In case the error terms are modelled with Slash distribution, analysis of financial return series, which involves deviated and extreme observations, will provide more correct results. Both Student-t and Slash distributions are robust distributions. Both of the distributions better adapted to the data compared to normal distribution. Student-t distribution allows kurtosis in a larger interval for high degrees of freedom but it is possible to say that Slash distribution is more robust as it gives better parameter estimations in case there are more unusual points. Therefore; it is seen that Student-t and Slash distributions are applicable as an alternative of normal distribution in the analysis of financial return series. Moreover, it is possible to say that heavy-tailed distributions can substitute normal distribution in case deviated observation values are not present.

Acknowledgements

This study was presented at the 20th International Symposium on Econometrics, Operations Research and Statistics, 12–14 February 2016, Ankara, Turkey. (Oral presentation).

Additional classification

JEL codes: C11, C46, G19, C59, C15.

Author details

Verda Davasligil Atmaca[1*] and Burcu Mestav[2]

1 Department of Econometrics, Biga Faculty of Economics and Administrative Sciences, Çanakkale Onsekiz Mart University, Çanakkale, Turkey

2 Department of Statistics, Faculty of Arts and Sciences, Çanakkale Onsekiz Mart University, Çanakkale, Turkey

*Address all correspondence to: verdaatmaca@comu.edu.tr

References

[1] Asai M, McAller M, Yu J. Multivariate stochastic volatility: A review. Econometric Reviews. 2006;**25** (2–3):145-175

[2] McAleer M. Automated inference and learning in modeling financial volatility. Econometric Theory. 2005;**21**: 232-261

[3] Yu J, Meyer R. Multivariate stochastic volatility models: Bayesian estimation and model comparison. Econometric Reviews. 2006;**25**(2/3): 361-384. Research Collection School of Economics

[4] Harvey A, Ruiz E, Shephard N. Multivariate stochastic variance models. The Review of Economic Studies. 1994; **61**(2):247-264

[5] Jacquier E, Polson NG, Rossi PE. Models and Priors for Multivariate Stochastic Volatility. Montreal: CIRANO Working Papers; 1995. pp. 95s-918s

[6] Jacquier E, Polson NG, Rossi PE. Stochastic Volatility: Univariate and Multivariate Extensions. Montreal: CIRANO Working Paper; 1999. pp. 99s-926s

[7] Shephard N. Statistical aspects of ARCH and stochastic volatility. In: Cox DR, Hinkley DV, Barndorff-Neilsen OE, editors. Time Series Models in Econometrics, Finance and Other Fields. London: Chapman&Hall; 1996. pp. 1-67

[8] Pitt MK, Shephard N. Time-varying covariances: A factor stochastic volatility approach. In: Bayesian Statistics. Oxford: Oxford University Press; 1999. pp. 547-570

[9] Aguilar O, West M. Bayesian dynamic factor models and portfolio allocation. Journal of Business & Economic Statistics. 2000;**18**(3):338-357

[10] Kastner G, Frühwirth-Schnatter S, Lopes HF. Efficient Bayesian inference for multivariate factor stochastic volatility models. Journal of Computational and Graphical Statistics. 2017;**26**(4):905-9174

[11] Hepsağ A. Çok Değişkenli Stokastik Oynaklık Modelleri: Petrol Piyasası ile Finansal Piyasalarda İşlem Gören Sanayi Sektörü Endeksi Arasındaki Oynaklık Etkileşimi Üzerine Bir Uygulama. İstanbul: İstanbul University; 2013

[12] Hosszejni D, Kastner G: Modeling Univariate and Multivariate Stochastic Volatility in R with Stochvol and Factor Stochvol. R package vignette. Cornell University Eprint; 2019;**1906**:12123. Available from: https://CRAN.R-project.org/package= factorstochvol/vignettes/paper.pdf

[13] Quintana JM, West M. An analysis of international exchange rates using multivariate DLMs. Stat. 1987;**36**: 275-281

[14] Ray BK, Tsay RS. Long-range dependence in daily stock volatilities. Journal of Business and Economic Statistics. 2000;**18**:254-262

[15] Kim S, Shephard N, Chib S. Stochastic volatility: Likelihood inference and comparison with ARCH models. The Review of Economic Studies. 1998;**65**(3):361-393

[16] Liesenfeld R, Richard J-F. Univaria te and multivariate stochastic volatility models: Estimation and diagnostics. ournal of Empirical Finance. 2003;**4**: 505-531

[17] Chib S, Nardari F, Shephard N. Analysis of high dimensional multivariate stochastic volatility models. Journal of Econometrics. 2006;**134**:341-371

[18] Chib S, Nardari F, Shepard N. Markov chain Monte Carlo methods for

stochastic volatility models. Journal of Econometrics. 2002;**108**:281-316

[19] Philipov A, Glickman M. Factor multivariate stochastic volatility via Wishart processes. Econometric Reviews. 2006;**25**:311-334

[20] Gallant AR, Hsieh D, Tauehen G. Estimation of stochastic volatility models with diagnostics. Journal of Econometrics. 1997;**81**:159-192

[21] Geweke J. Bayesian analysis of stochastic volatility models: Comment. Journal of Business & Economic Statistics. 1994;**12**(4):397-399

[22] Watanabe T, Asai M: Stochastic Volatility Models with Heavy-Tailed Distributions: A Bayesian Analysis. Japan: Technical report, Discussion paper 2001-E-17, Institute for Monetary and Economic Studies; 2001

[23] Nardari F, Scruggs JT. Bayesian analysis of linear factor models with latent factors, multivariate stochastic volatility, and APT pricing restrictions. The Journal of Financial and Quantitative Analysis. 2007;**42**(4): 857-891

[24] Wu S-J, Ghosh SK, Ku Y-C, Bloomfield P. Dynamic correlation multivariate stochastic volatility with latent factors. Statistica Neerlandica. 2018;**72**(1):48-69

[25] Lange KL, Sinsheimer JS. Normal/ independent distributions and their applications in robust regression. Journal of Computational and Graphical Statistics. 1993;**2**:175-198

[26] Diebold FX, Nerlov M. The dynamics of exchange rate volatility: A multivariate latent factor ARCH model. Journal of Applied Econometrics. 1989; **4**:1-21

[27] Spiegelhalter DJ, Best NG, Carlin BP, Linde A. Bayesian measures of model complexity and fit. The Royal Statistical Society. 2002;**64**(4):583-639

[28] Berg A, Meyer R, Yu J. Deviance information criterion for comparing stochastic volatility models. Journal of Business and Economic Statistics. 2004; **22**(1):107-120

[29] Spiegelhalter DJ. Some DIC Slides. Cambridge: MRC Biostatistics Unit; 2006

Chapter 4

Reliability-Based Marginal Cost Pricing Problem

Shaopeng Zhong

Abstract

This chapter is concerned with first-best marginal cost pricing (MCP) in a stochastic network with both supply and travel demand uncertainty and perception errors within the travelers' route choice decision processes. To account for the travelers' perception error, moment analysis is adopted in this chapter to derive the mean and variance of total perceived travel time of the network. We then developed a Perceived Risk-Based Stochastic Network Marginal Cost Pricing (PRSN-MCP) model. Furthermore, in order to illustrate the effect of incorporating both stochastic supply and demand into the PRSN-MCP model, the calculation of the PRSN-MCP model is divided up into four scenarios under different simplifications of network uncertainties. Numerical examples are also provided to demonstrate the importance and properties of the proposed model. The main finding is that ignoring the effect of stochastic travel demand, capacity degradation, and travelers' perception error may significantly reduce the performance of the first-best MCP tolls, especially under high traveler's confidence and network congestion levels.

Keywords: marginal cost pricing, moment analysis, demand uncertainty, supply uncertainty, perception error

1. Introduction

It is well known, due to stochastic variations in both supply and demand, that travel time almost always involves a measure of uncertainty. Recently, several empirical studies on the value of time and reliability revealed that travel time reliability plays an important role in the traveler's route choice decision-making process [1–3]. With these studies as a basis, the study of travel time variability (reliability) has gradually emerged as an important topic. In this context, travel time reliability pertains to the probability that a trip can be successfully completed within a specified time interval, reflecting the uncertainty in trip journey times [4, 5]. To model the characteristics of travel time reliability, the concept of TTB is commonly used. TTB is defined as the average travel time plus extra time (for a measure of the buffer time) such that the probability of completing the trip within the TTB is no less than a predefined reliability threshold α [6]. Earlier research applied the concept of effective travel time to capture the travel time reliability [7]. Recently, [6] further proposed a stochastic mean-excess traffic equilibrium model to represent both the reliability and unreliability aspects of travel time variability and travelers' route choice perception errors.

Generally speaking, uncertainties from both the demand and supply sides of a system directly lead to recurring variability and unreliability of travel times and have an obvious impact on the traveler's route choice behavior. Supply-side sources refer to the capacity variations that can occur, due to several exogenous sources of uncertainty on the road sections or at-grade intersections concerned. These exogenous sources of uncertainty may take different forms, such as environmental conditions, traffic incidents, traffic management and control, work zones, and so on. Such stochastic link capacity degradations usually lead to non-recurrent congestion [8–10]. Demand-side sources are regarded as the travel demand fluctuations, which result from various endogenous sources. These endogenous sources can include temporal factors, special events, population characteristics, and traffic information among others. Travel demand variations usually lead to recurrent congestion [4, 11, 12].

Several stochastic traffic network (SN) modeling approaches have been proposed to represent such uncertainties. On the capacity side, [13] proposed a probabilistic approach using the concept of capacity reliability to model the uncertain characteristics of link capacities. Lo et al. [14] proposed the Probabilistic User Equilibrium (PUE) model, which takes the fact that the link capacities are subject to stochastic degradations into account. In subsequent research using the concept of Travel Time Budget (TTB), [10] further extended the PUE model to capture the route choice behaviors of travelers with heterogeneous risk aversions. On the demand side, [11] proposed a framework of the stochastic network model to represent the stochastic demand. Ref. [12] extended the TTB model and proposed a travel time reliability-based traffic assignment model to consider the effect of daily demand fluctuations. On both the demand and supply sides, [15] proposed a traffic assignment model, which considers the uncertainties of a traffic network due to adverse weather conditions. Sumalee et al. [16] proposed a stochastic network model with log-normal distributed origin–destination (OD) travel demands and link capacities. It should be noted that all of the above studies focused on the question of how to represent the travel time reliability in a traffic assignment model, but did not answer the question of how to improve the travel time reliability in a stochastic traffic network.

All the aforementioned studies discovered that travelers do indeed consider travel time variability as a risk in their route choice decisions. Nevertheless, the first-best marginal cost pricing (MCP) is commonly modeled via a deterministic approach, which assumes that both traffic supply and travel demand are known, and that the route travel times are deterministic [17]. Furthermore, travelers are assumed to know exactly the time on each available route and can always choose the least-cost routes for their trips. As indicated earlier, due to various sources of uncertainty coming from both supply-side and demand-side of road network, it is unreasonable to assume that travel times are deterministic and known perfectly by all the travelers. Though several traffic equilibrium models have been developed for environments characterized by uncertainty in the past decades, such models have not been adopted in the analysis of first-best MCP. Intuitively, the variability and unreliability of travel times caused by network uncertainties directly influence the traveler's route choice behavior, thereby negatively affecting the performance of MCP. However, there is little theoretical basis for this intuition. At least, it is not yet clear to what extent the stochastic demand and supply and the travelers' perception error affect the performance of MCP. In this context, the study of first-best MCP under an uncertain environment is a necessary and urgent theoretical task. In addition, this investigation is also practically relevant. As indicated by [18], the recent change in the Electronic Road Pricing (ERP) toll adjustment scheme in Singapore involves the consideration of the 85th-percetile traffic condition (speed) to reflect the variability of traffic conditions. This involves determining optimal tolls in a stochastic environment, where both demand and capacity are subject to uncertainty.

Although considerable research exists on congestion pricing and travel time reliability, relatively little research combines the two, especially regarding travelers' risk attitudes and/or the valuation of reliable travel [19]. Some examples of research that do combine congestion pricing and travel time reliability are included here. Li et al. [20] proposed a reliability-based optimal toll design bi-level model. On the upper level, network performance is optimized from a road authority point of view including travel time reliability, while a dynamic user-equilibrium is achieved from the viewpoint of travelers on the lower level. Boyles et al. [19] proposed a first-best congestion pricing model considering network capacity uncertainty and user valuation of travel time reliability, while [18] investigated marginal cost pricing in a stochastic traffic network in which demand uncertainty is explicitly considered. By assuming that all travelers have complete information about the road traffic condition, [18] derived an analytical function of Stochastic Network-Marginal Cost Pricing (SN-MCP) for a risk-neutral case and risk-based SN-MCP (RSN-MCP) for a risk-based case under the assumptions of lognormal demand and constant VMR across all OD pairs. Gardner et al. [21] consider the uncertainty in long-term travel demand and in day-to-day network capacity, and discuss the benefit of responsive pricing and travel information.

In the above-mentioned studies, MCP is analysis in a stochastic network, which considers either link supply uncertainty (e.g., see [19]) or stochastic travel demand (e.g., see [18]). In addition, to account for the travelers' perception error, researchers usually assume the commonly adopted Gumbel variate as the random error term and use the conventional logit-based Stochastic User Equilibrium (SUE) model. However, this approach may not reflect the travelers' perception of the random travel time exactly. Due to the variation of travel time, it is more rational to assume that the travelers' perception error is also dependent on the random perceived travel time [22]. Therefore, in order to explicitly consider both supply and demand aspects of a stochastic network and to reflect the travelers' perception error of the random travel time, this investigation extends [18] by (1) considering both the stochastic travel demand and link capacity degradation, and (2) incorporating travelers' perception error into the first-best MCP analysis.

The remainder of the chapter is organized as follows. The next section introduces the assumptions used in the analysis and presents the variational inequality (VI) formulation for different stochastic models. It also discusses the stochastic travel times under different sources of uncertainty. Then, Section 3 and Section 4

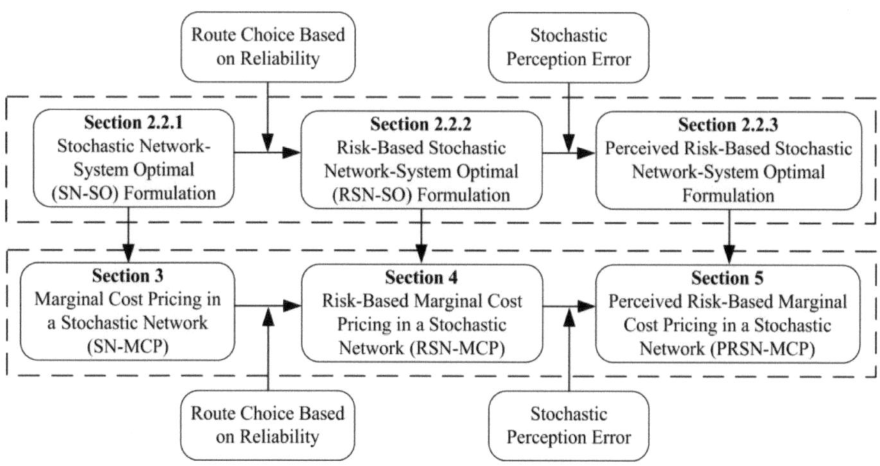

Figure 1.
Flow chart for the research process.

derive the analytical function of SN-MCP for a risk-neutral case and RSN-MCP for a risk-based case in a stochastic network with both supply and demand uncertainty, respectively. In Section 5, the analysis for the PRSN-MCP is then described under different simplifications of network uncertainties. In Section 6, numerical examples with respect to a small-scale network and a medium-scale network (Sioux Falls network) are undertaken to demonstrate the effects of the proposed models. The final section contains some concluding remarks and recommends further research. The flow chart of the process applied in this chapter is presented in **Figure 1**.

2. Framework of stochastic network model

2.1 Notations and assumptions

Consider a strongly connected network $G = (N, A)$, where N is the set of nodes and A is the set of links in the network. Let W represent the set of OD pairs in the network and the set of routes between OD pair $w \in W$ be denoted by R_w. Random variables are expressed in capital letters and lower-case letters are used for mean values of random variables or deterministic variables.

Q^w	travel demand between OD pair $w \in W$
q^w	mean travel demand between OD pair $w \in W$
ε_q^w	variance of travel demand between OD pair $w \in W$
VMR_w	variance-to-mean ratio (VMR) of the random travel demand
F_r^w	route flow on path $r \in R_w$
f_r^w	mean traffic flow on path $r \in R_w$
$\varepsilon_f^{w,r}$	variance of traffic flow on path $r \in R_w$
$\mathbf{f}$	column vector of mean route flow, where $\mathbf{f} = \{ f_r^w \}$
V_a	traffic flow on link $a \in A$
v_a	mean traffic flow on link $a \in A$
ε_v^a	variance of traffic flow on link $a \in A$
$\mathbf{v}$	column vector of mean link flow, where $\mathbf{v} = \{v_a\}$
$\delta_{a,r}^w$	link-path incidence parameter; 1 if link a on path r, zero otherwise
TT	total travel time of the system, where $TT = \sum_{a \in A} V_a T_a$
VoR	relative weight assigned to the travel time budget, that is, value of reliability
T_r^w	travel time on path $r \in R_w$
t_r^w	mean travel time on path $r \in R_w$
$\varepsilon_t^{w,r}$	variance of travel time on path $r \in R_w$
T_a	travel time on link a
t_a	mean travel time on link a
ε_t^a	variance of travel time on link $a \in A$
$\tilde{T}_r^w$	perceived travel time on path $r \in R_w$
$\tilde{t}_r^w$	mean perceived travel time on path $r \in R_w$
$\tilde{\varepsilon}_t^{w,r}$	variance of perceived travel time on path $r \in R_w$
$\tilde{T}_a$	perceived travel time on link a

$\tilde{t}_a$	mean perceived travel time on link a
$\tilde{\varepsilon}_t^a$	variance of perceived travel time on link $a \in A$
$\tilde{T}\tilde{T}$	total perceived travel time of the system, where $\tilde{T}\tilde{T} = \sum_{a \in A} V_a \tilde{T}_a$
t_a^0	free-flow travel time on link $a \in A$
C_a	capacity of link $a \in A$
	design capacity (upper bound) of link $a \in A$
	degree of worst-degraded capacity for link $a \in A$
y_a	parameter, where $y_a = \sqrt{1 + VMR/v_a}$
$\varepsilon_a\|_{T_a}$	travelers' perception error on link $a \in A$
$N(\chi, \varpi^2)$	perception error distribution of traveler, in this chapter $N(\chi, \varpi^2)$ follows a normal distribution with predefined and deterministic mean χ and variance ϖ^2

Before proceeding with the analysis, some assumptions are made to allow for the closed-form formulation/calculation of the PRSN-MCP model.

A1. The travel demand Q^w between each OD pair is assumed to be an independent random variable with a mean of $q^w$and variance of ε_q^w, while VMR_w is the variance-to-mean ratio (VMR) of the random travel demand in which $VMR_w = \varepsilon_q^w / q^w$. Stochastic demand is further assumed to follow a lognormal distribution, which is a nonnegative, asymmetrical distribution. This has been adopted in the literature as a more realistic approximation of the stochastic travel demand, as opposed to the more commonly used normal distribution [18, 23].

A2. The route flow F_r^w, and link flow V_a are also assumed to be independent random variables that follow the same statistical distribution as OD demand. The *VMRs* of route flows are equal to those of the corresponding OD demand.

A3. The *VMRs* of travel demand are assumed to be the same for all OD pairs in order to derive the closed-form formulation of the PRSN-MCP model.

A4. The capacity degradation random variable C_a is independent of the traffic flow v_a on it and follows a uniform distribution with the design capacity $\bar{c}_a$of the link as its upper bound and the worst-degraded capacity as its lower bound (the lower bound would be a fraction θ_a of the design capacity).

2.2 VI formulation for different stochastic network models

2.2.1 Stochastic network-system optimal (SN-SO) formulation

According to the Assumption A1 and A2, the OD travel demand, route flow F_r^w, and link flow V_a are random variables, which consequently induce the random route/link travel times. As such, we have the following flow conservation relationships among them

$$Q^w = \sum\nolimits_{r \in R_w} F_r^w, w \in W \tag{1}$$

$$V_a = \sum\nolimits_{w \in W} \sum\nolimits_{r \in R_w} \delta_{a,r}^w F_r^w, \forall a \in A \tag{2}$$

$$F_r^w \geq 0, w \in W, r \in R_w \tag{3}$$

where Eq. (1) is the travel demand conservation constraint, Eq. (2) is a definitional constraint that sums up all route flows that pass through a given link a, and Eq. (3) is a non-negativity constraint on the route flows. Let $\Delta = \left[\delta_{a,r}^{w}\right]$ denote the route-link incidence matrix, $\delta_{a,r}^{w} = 1$ if route r traverses link a, and $\delta_{a,r}^{w} = 0$ otherwise. Let f_{r}^{w}, v_a denote the mean route flow and link flow, respectively. From Eqs. (1) ~ (3), these route and link flows satisfy the following conservation conditions:

$$q^{w} = \sum\nolimits_{r \in R_w} f_{r}^{w}, w \in W \tag{4}$$

$$v_a = \sum\nolimits_{w \in W} \sum\nolimits_{r \in R_w} \delta_{a,r}^{w} f_{r}^{w}, \forall a \in A \tag{5}$$

$$f_{r}^{w} \geq 0, w \in W, r \in R_w \tag{6}$$

Let $\varepsilon_{f}^{w,r}, \varepsilon_{v}^{a}$ be the variance of route flow and link flow, respectively. Then from the Assumption A1 and A2, we have

$$\sum\nolimits_{r \in R_w} \varepsilon_{f}^{w,r} = \sum\nolimits_{r \in R_w} f_{r}^{w} VMR_w = q^{w} VMR_w = \varepsilon_{q}^{w}, w \in W \tag{7}$$

$$\begin{aligned} \varepsilon_{v}^{a} &= \sum\nolimits_{w \in W} \sum\nolimits_{r \in R_w} \left(\delta_{a,r}^{w}\right)^{2} \varepsilon_{f}^{w,r} = \sum\nolimits_{w \in W} \sum\nolimits_{r \in R_w} \delta_{a,r}^{w} \varepsilon_{f}^{w,r} \\ &= \sum\nolimits_{w \in W} \sum\nolimits_{r \in R_w} \delta_{a,r}^{w} f_{r}^{w} VMR_w \end{aligned} \tag{8}$$

From Eqs. (7) and (8), we know that the variances of both route flow and link flow can be determined by the means of route flows. Furthermore, the route and link flow distribution can be derived through known travel demand distributions. Next, we discuss the VI formulation for the SN-SO model. In this section, we consider all the travelers to be risk-neutral. That is, travelers are not sensitive to the travel time variations and they do not need to budget the safety margin for their trips. The system optimal assignment under the stochastic network (SN-SO) aims to minimize the expected total travel time. The VI formulation for the SN-SO model can be obtained by finding $\mathbf{v}^* \in \Omega_{\mathbf{v}}$ such that for any $\mathbf{v} \in \Omega_{\mathbf{v}}$,

$$(\mathbf{v} - \mathbf{v}^*)^{\mathrm{T}} \nabla_{\mathbf{v}} E[TT^*] \geq 0 \tag{9}$$

where $\nabla_{\mathbf{v}} E[TT^*] = \left\{\partial E\left[\sum_{a \in A} V_{a}^{*} T_{a}^{*}\right] / \partial v_{a}^{*}\right\}$, $\Omega_{\mathbf{v}} = \left\{\mathbf{v} | \mathbf{v} = \Delta \mathbf{f}, \mathbf{f} \geq 0; q^{w} = \sum_{r \in R_w} f_{r}^{w}, w \in W\right\}$. $\mathbf{v}$ and $\mathbf{f}$ are the column vector of mean link and route flow, respectively. T_a represents the travel time on link a. TT is the total travel time of the system, where $TT = \sum_{a \in A} V_a T_a$.

2.2.2 Risk-based SN-SO (RSN-SO) formulation

Up to this point, we have presented the risk-neutral case. However, several empirical studies reveal that travel time reliability plays an important role in the traveler's route choice decision process [1–3]. In this section, we consider the risk-based (averse or prone) case in which travelers are assumed to consider both the mean travel time and travel time variability in their route decision-making process. Researchers have used the Travel Time Budget (TTB) to represent travelers' risk-based travel behavior. Mathematically, the TTB associated with route r, b_{r}^{w}, is expressed as

$$b_{r}^{w} = E\left[T_{r}^{w}\right] + VoR \cdot \varepsilon_{t}^{w,r}, w \in W, r \in R_w \tag{10}$$

where $\varepsilon_t^{w,r}$ is the variance of route travel time, which represents the travel time reliability (TTR) of that route, is the route travel time, and *VoR* is the relative weight assigned to the TTR, that is, value of reliability. Similarly, let ε_t^a be the variance of the link travel time, the TTB associated with link a, b_a, which can be described by

$$b_a = E[T_a] + VoR \cdot \varepsilon_t^a, a \in A \tag{11}$$

Based on the assumption of independent travel time on each link, we can infer the following relationship between route travel time variance and link travel time variance as shown below:

$$\varepsilon_t^{w,r} = \sum\nolimits_{a\in A} \delta_{a,r}^w \varepsilon_t^a, w \in W, r \in R_w \tag{12}$$

From Eqs. (10) $\sim$ (12), the TTB of route and link satisfy the following conservation conditions:

$$\begin{aligned} b_r^w &= E\left[T_r^w\right] + VoR \cdot \varepsilon_t^{w,r} = \sum\nolimits_{a\in A} \delta_{a,r}^w E[T_a] + VoR \cdot \sum\nolimits_{a\in A} \delta_{a,r}^w \varepsilon_t^a \\ &= \sum\nolimits_{a\in A} \delta_{a,r}^w b_a, w \in W, r \in R_w \end{aligned} \tag{13}$$

Let $U[TT] = E[TT] + VoR \cdot Var[TT]$. With Eq. (13), the VI formulation for the link-based RSN-SO model can be expressed as

$$(\mathbf{v} - \mathbf{v}^*)^{\mathrm{T}} \nabla_{\mathbf{v}} U[TT^*] \geq 0 \tag{14}$$

where $\nabla_{\mathbf{v}} U[TT^*] = \left\{\partial E\left[\sum_{a\in A} V_a^* T_a^*\right]/\partial v_a^* + VoR \cdot \partial Var\left[\sum_{a\in A} V_a^* T_a^*\right]/\partial v_a^*\right\}$.

2.2.3 Perceived RSN-SO formulation

In the previous subsections, we consider that travelers can always choose the route with the minimum TTB; the resulting model is called a deterministic traffic assignment model. The main assumption underlying this kind of model is that travelers have full information about travel conditions, that is, they have perfect information about travel time and its variability. In this subsection, we relax this unreasonable assumption and include travelers' perception errors in their route choice process. The perceived TTB associated with route $r, \tilde{b}_r^w$ is described as

$$\tilde{b}_r^w = E\left[\tilde{T}_r^w\right] + VoR \cdot \tilde{\varepsilon}_t^{w,r}, w \in W, r \in R_w \tag{15}$$

where $\tilde{\varepsilon}_t^{w,r}$ is the variance of the perceived route travel time, and $\tilde{T}_r^w$ is the perceived route travel time. Similarly, let $\tilde{\varepsilon}_t^a$ be the variance of perceived link travel time, and $\tilde{T}_a$ be the perceived link travel time. The perceived TTB associated with link $a, \tilde{b}_a$ can be described by

$$\tilde{b}_a = E\left[\tilde{T}_a\right] + VoR \cdot \tilde{\varepsilon}_t^a, a \in A \tag{16}$$

Based on the assumption of independent travel time on each link, we can infer the following relationship between variances of perceived route travel time and perceived link travel time as follows:

$$\tilde{\varepsilon}_t^{w,r} = \sum_{a \in A} \delta_{a,r}^w \tilde{\varepsilon}_t^a, w \in W, r \in R_w \tag{17}$$

From Eqs. (15) $\sim$ (17), the perceived TTB of the route and link satisfy the following conservation conditions

$$\begin{aligned} \tilde{b}_r^w &= E\left[\tilde{T}_r^w\right] + VoR \cdot \tilde{\varepsilon}_t^{w,r} = \sum_{a \in A} \delta_{a,r}^w E\left[\tilde{T}_a\right] + VoR \cdot \sum_{a \in A} \delta_{a,r}^w \tilde{\varepsilon}_t^a \\ &= \sum_{a \in A} \delta_{a,r}^w \tilde{b}_a, w \in W, r \in R_w \end{aligned} \tag{18}$$

Let $\tilde{T}\tilde{T}$ represent the total perceived travel time of the system, where $\tilde{T}\tilde{T} = \sum_{a \in A} V_a \tilde{T}_a$, and let $U\left[\tilde{T}\tilde{T}\right] = E\left[\tilde{T}\tilde{T}\right] + VoR \cdot Var\left[\tilde{T}\tilde{T}\right]$. With Eq. (18), the VI formulation for the link-based perceived RSN-SO model can be expressed as

$$(\mathbf{v} - \mathbf{v}^*)^{\mathrm{T}} \nabla_{\mathbf{v}} U\left[\tilde{T}\tilde{T}^*\right] \geq 0 \tag{19}$$

where $\nabla_{\mathbf{v}} U\left[\tilde{T}\tilde{T}^*\right] = \left\{\partial E\left[\sum_{a \in A} V_a^* \tilde{T}_a^*\right] / \partial v_a^* + VoR \cdot \partial Var\left[\sum_{a \in A} V_a^* \tilde{T}_a^*\right] / \partial v_a^*\right\}$.

2.3 Stochastic travel times under different sources of uncertainty

Next, we will review the commonly adopted stochastic network models and their associated corresponding derivations of stochastic travel time in the literature in order to clarify the derivation of our proposed modeling approach.

The link travel time function is assumed to be the Bureau of Public Roads (BPR) function, $T_a = t_a^0(1 + \beta(V_a/C_a)^n), \forall a \in A$, where T_a, t_a^0, C_a, V_a are the travel time, free-flow travel time, capacity, and traffic flow on link a. β and n are the deterministic parameters.

2.3.1 Capacity degradation

As has been discussed in Section 1, link capacities are subject to stochastic degradations to different degrees in the forms of traffic incidents, traffic management and control, work zones, and others. These constitute one of the main sources of travel time variability. To model the characteristics of stochastic link capacity degradation, [14] proposed the Probabilistic User Equilibrium (PUE) model. By assuming the capacity degradation random variable is independent of the traffic flow on it and follows a uniform distribution with the design capacity of the link as its upper bound and the worst-degraded capacity as its lower bound (the lower bound to be a fraction of the design capacity), they derived the mean and variance of T_a as follows:

$$E[T_a] = t_a^0 + \beta t_a^0 v_a^n \frac{(1 - \theta_a^{1-n})}{\bar{c}_a^n (1 - \theta_a)(1 - n)} \tag{20}$$

$$Var[T_a] = \beta^2 \left(t_a^0\right)^2 v_a^{2n} \left\{ \frac{(1 - \theta_a^{1-2n})}{\bar{c}_a^{2n}(1 - \theta_a)(1 - 2n)} - \left[\frac{(1 - \theta_a^{1-n})}{\bar{c}_a^n (1 - \theta_a)(1 - n)}\right]^2 \right\} \tag{21}$$

They further indicated that the uniform distribution assumption can be relaxed with respect to other probability distributions via the Mellin transform technique [14].

2.3.2 Demand fluctuation

Another main source of travel time variability, to be discussed in this section, is the stochastic travel demand. Several types of probability distributions of OD travel demand have been adopted by researchers to simulate the travel demand fluctuation, such as normal distribution [12], lognormal distribution [23], and Poisson distribution [11]. As indicated in Assumption A1, we use the lognormal distribution in this study, which is more realistic than the commonly adopted normal distribution. The probability density function of the lognormal distribution is given below

$$f(x|\mu,\sigma) = \frac{1}{x\sigma\sqrt{2\pi}} \exp\left(\frac{-(\ln x - \mu)^2}{2\sigma^2}\right), \forall x > 0 \tag{22}$$

where x is the random variable, μ and σ are the distribution parameters, and the mean and variance of x are $E[x] = e^{\mu+\sigma^2/2}$ and $\mathrm{Var}[x] = e^{2\mu+\sigma^2/2}\left(e^{\sigma^2} - 1\right)$. Based on the Assumption A1 and A2, with lognormal OD demand, the link flows also follow a lognormal distribution

$$V_a \sim LN\left(\mu_v^a, \sigma_v^a\right), \forall a \in A \tag{23}$$

where $\mu_v^a = \ln(v_a) - \frac{1}{2}\ln\left(1 + \frac{\varepsilon_v^a}{(v_a)^2}\right), \left(\sigma_v^a\right)^2 = \ln\left(1 + \frac{\varepsilon_v^a}{(v_a)^2}\right)$. v_a, ε_v^a are the mean and variance of link flow on link $a \in A$. All of the moments of a lognormal random variable exist and are given as follows:

$$E[X^s] = \exp\left(s\mu + s^2\sigma^2/2\right) \tag{24}$$

where $E[X^s]$ is the sth moment of X. With Eq. (8) and A3, we have

$$\varepsilon_v^a = \sum_{w\in W}\sum_{r\in R_w}\left(\delta_{a,r}^w\right)^2\varepsilon_f^{w,r} = VMR\cdot\sum_{w\in W}\sum_{r\in R_w}\delta_{a,r}^w f_r^w = VMR\cdot v_a, a \in A \tag{25}$$

Let $y_a = \sqrt{1 + VMR/v_a}$. Then, by using Eqs. (23) ~ (25) and performing some derivations according to [18], we can obtain

$$E\left[V_a^n\right] = \exp\left(n\mu_v^a + n^2\left(\sigma_v^a\right)^2/2\right) = v_a^n\left(\sqrt{1 + VMR/v_a}\right)^{n^2-n} = v_a^n y_a^{n^2-n} \tag{26}$$

$$Var\left[V_a^n\right] = E\left[V_a^{2n}\right] - \left(E\left[V_a^n\right]\right)^2 = v_a^{2n} y_a^{4n^2-2n} - v_a^{2n} y_a^{2n^2-2n} \tag{27}$$

Using the BPR function of link travel time, we can derive the mean and variance of the link travel time as follows:

$$E[T_a] = t_a^0 + \frac{\beta t_a^0}{C_a^n}\left(v_a^n y_a^{n^2-n}\right) \tag{28}$$

$$Var[T_a] = \frac{\beta^2\left(t_a^0\right)^2}{C_a^{2n}}\left[v_a^{2n} y_a^{4n^2-2n} - \left(v_a^n y_a^{n^2-n}\right)^2\right] \tag{29}$$

2.3.3 Both link capacity and demand variation

From the above analysis and under the Assumption A4, we can easily derive the mean and variance of the link travel time in the case of both link capacity and demand variation as follows:

$$E[T_a] = t_a^0 + \beta t_a^0 \frac{(1-\theta_a^{1-n})}{\overline{c}_a^n(1-\theta_a)(1-n)} \left(v_a^n y_a^{n^2-n}\right) \tag{30}$$

$$Var[T_a] = \beta^2 \left(t_a^0\right)^2 \left\{ \frac{(1-\theta_a^{1-2n})}{\overline{c}_a^{2n}(1-\theta_a)(1-2n)} \left(v_a^{2n} y_a^{4n^2-2n}\right) - \left[\frac{(1-\theta_a^{1-n})}{\overline{c}_a^n(1-\theta_a)(1-n)} \left(v_a^n y_a^{n^2-n}\right) \right]^2 \right\} \tag{31}$$

3. Marginal cost pricing in a stochastic network (SN-MCP) with both supply and demand uncertainty

3.1 Analysis of SN-MCP

In this section, we discuss the SN-MCP in the risk-neutral case. The MCP in the stochastic network aims to minimize the expected total travel time. Sumalee and Xu [18] investigated the relationship between the Stochastic Network-User Equilibrium (SN-UE) and Stochastic Network-System Optimal (SN-SO) models and established the first-marginal cost toll scheme for the SN model. They classified the marginal cost toll in the stochastic network into three forms. The first one is referred to as original marginal cost pricing, which takes the form of $E[V_a] \cdot dt(E[V_a])/dE[V_a]$; the second one is referred to as average marginal cost pricing, which takes the form of $E[V_a] \cdot dE[T_a(V_a)]/dE[V_a]$; and the third one is referred to as Stochastic Network-Marginal Cost Pricing (SN-MCP), which takes the form of $\partial E\left[\sum_{a \in A} V_a T_a\right]/\partial v_a - E[T_a]$. They further indicate that only the SN-MCP can make the traffic network achieve the optimal pattern.

Let, then, the real gap between the marginal social and marginal private costs in a stochastic network be represented by

$$\text{SN} - \text{MCP} = \partial E\left[\sum\nolimits_{a \in A} V_a T_a\right] / \partial v_a - E[T_a] = \partial E[TT]/\partial v_a - E[T_a] \tag{32}$$

3.2 Calculation of SN-MCP

In this study, we attempt to compute the value of SN-MCP in the case of both link capacity and demand variation. To achieve this goal, we need to calculate $\partial E\left[\sum_{a \in A} V_a T_a\right]/\partial v_a$ and $E[T_a]$, respectively. In considering the stochasticity of both link capacity and demand, $E[T_a]$ should be determined by Eq. (30). The expected total travel time is expressed as

$$\begin{aligned} E[TT] &= E\left[\sum\nolimits_{a \in A} V_a T_a\right] = \sum\nolimits_{a \in A} \left\{ t_a^0 E[V_a] + \beta t_a^0 E\left[V_a^{n+1}\right] E\left[\frac{1}{C_a^n}\right] \right\} \\ &= \sum\nolimits_{a \in A} \left\{ t_a^0 v_a + \beta t_a^0 \frac{(1-\theta_a^{1-n})}{\overline{c}_a^n(1-\theta_a)(1-n)} \left(v_a^{n+1} y_a^{n^2+n}\right) \right\} \end{aligned} \tag{33}$$

Differentiating Eq. (33) with respect to the mean link flow v_a yields

$$\frac{\partial E[TT]}{\partial v_a} = t_a^0 + \beta t_a^0 \frac{\left(1-\theta_a^{1-n}\right)}{\bar{c}_a^n(1-\theta_a)(1-n)} \left[\frac{n v_a^{n-1}\left(1-y_a^2\right)}{2y_a^2} + 1\right] \left[(n+1) v_a y_a^{n^2+n}\right] \tag{34}$$

By substituting Eqs. (30) and (34) into Eq. (32), the value of SN-MCP in case of Stochastic Supply and Stochastic demand (SS-SD) can be determined as follows:

$$\begin{aligned} \mathrm{SN-MCP} &= \frac{\partial E[TT]}{\partial v_a} - E[T_a] \\ &= \beta t_a^0 \frac{\left(1-\theta_a^{1-n}\right)}{\bar{c}_a^n(1-\theta_a)(1-n)} v_a^n y_a^{n^2-n} \left\{\left[(n+1)y_a^{2n} + \frac{(n^2+n)}{2} y_a^{2n-2}\left(1-y_a^2\right)\right] - 1\right\} \end{aligned} \tag{35}$$

Note that if we neglect the degradation of link capacity, Eq. (35) degenerates into the classical SN-MCP model proposed by [18], which considers only the stochastic travel demand. Furthermore, they pointed out that the SN-MCP toll is guaranteed to be positive when $y_a \leq 1.4$. This conclusion is also applicable in the SN-MCP proposed in this section.

4. Risk-based MCP (RSN-MCP) in a stochastic network

4.1 Analysis of risk-based SN-MCP

In the previous section, we know that the Stochastic Network-User Equilibrium (SN-UE) flow pattern can be driven toward a SN-SO flow pattern by charging a toll equal to the SN-MCP. Meanwhile, the expected total travel time can be minimized. In this section, we consider the risk-based (averse or prone) case. The objective function of the RSN-MCP model is to minimize the weighted sum of the mean and the variance of the total travel time, not simply to minimize the expected total travel time. Therefore, the RSN-MCP toll can be determined as

$$\mathrm{RSN-MCP} = \{\partial E[TT]/\partial v_a - E[T_a]\} + VoR \cdot \{\partial Var[TT]/\partial v_a - Var[T_a]\} \tag{36}$$

4.2 Calculation of RSN-MCP

In this section, we discuss the most complete and realistic situation in which travelers consider both stochastic fluctuations in supply (or link capacity) and demand in their route choice decision-making process. From Eqs. (32) and (36), we can see that the difference between SN-MCP and RSN-MCP is the term in the second parentheses of Eq. (36). This second term reflects the congestion toll on travel time reliability due to travelers' risk-based behavior. Let us now turn our attention to $\partial Var[TT]/\partial v_a$. The variance of the total travel time is described by

$$\begin{aligned} Var[TT] &= E\left[TT^2\right] - (E[TT])^2 \\ &= \sum_{a\in A}\left\{\left(t_a^0\right)^2 \cdot Var[V_a] + \left(\beta t_a^0\right)^2 \frac{Var\left[V_a^{n+1}\right]}{Var\left[C_a^n\right]} + 2\beta\left(t_a^0\right)^2 \frac{\left\{E\left[V_a^{n+2}\right] - E\left[V_a^{n+1}\right]E[V_a]\right\}}{E\left[C_a^n\right]}\right\} \\ &= \sum_{a\in A}\left\{\begin{aligned} &\left(t_a^0\right)^2 \cdot VMR \cdot v_a + \left(\beta t_a^0\right)^2 \left\{\frac{\left(1-\theta_a^{1-2n}\right)}{\bar{c}_a^{2n}(1-\theta_a)(1-2n)} v_a^{2n} y_a^{4n^2+6n+2} - \left[\frac{\left(1-\theta_a^{1-n}\right)}{\bar{c}_a^n(1-\theta_a)(1-n)} v_a^{n+1} y_a^{n^2+n}\right]^2\right\} \\ &+2\beta\left(t_a^0\right)^2 \frac{\left(1-\theta_a^{1-n}\right)}{\bar{c}_a^n(1-\theta_a)(1-n)} v_a^{n+2} y_a^{n^2+n}\left(y_a^{2n+2}-1\right) \end{aligned}\right\} \end{aligned} \tag{37}$$

Differentiating Eq. (37) with respect to the mean link flow yields

$$\frac{\partial Var[TT]}{\partial v_a} = \left(t_a^0\right)^2 \cdot VMR + \left(\beta t_a^0\right)^2 \left\{ \begin{array}{l} \dfrac{\left(1-\theta_a^{1-2n}\right)}{\bar{c}_a^{2n}(1-\theta_a)(1-2n)} \left\{ v_a^{2n} y_a^{4n^2+6n} \left[(2n+2)v_a - \left(2n^2+n-1\right) \cdot VMR\right] \right\} \\ -\left(\frac{\left(1-\theta_a^{1-n}\right)}{\bar{c}_a^{n}(1-\theta_a)(1-n)} \right)^2 \left\{ v_a^{2n} y_a^{2n^2+2n-2} \left[(2n+2)v_a - \left(n^2-n-2\right) \cdot VMR\right] \right\} \end{array} \right\}$$
$$+2\beta\left(t_a^0\right)^2 \frac{\left(1-\theta_a^{1-n}\right)}{\bar{c}_a^{n}(1-\theta_a)(1-n)} \left\{ \begin{array}{l} \left\{ v_a^n y_a^{n^2+3n} \left[(n+2)v_a - \dfrac{\left(n^2+n-2\right)}{2} \cdot VMR \right] \right\} \\ -\left\{ v_a^n y_a^{n^2+n-2} \left[(n+2)v_a - \dfrac{\left(n^2-n-4\right)}{2} \cdot VMR \right] \right\} \end{array} \right\} \tag{38}$$

By substituting Eqs. (31), (35), and (38) into Eq. (36), the value of RSN-MCP in case of SS-SD can be determined. In the same way, by neglecting the degradation of link capacity, the RSN-MCP in case of SS-SD degenerates into the classical RSN-MCP model proposed by [18], which considers only the stochastic travel demand.

5. Formulation of perceived RSN-MCP (PRSN-MCP)

5.1 Model incorporating the travelers' perception error

Up to this point, we have studied the SN-MCP model and RSN-MCP model based on the assumption that all the travelers have perfect knowledge about the network condition. However, in real life, due to the limitations of their own condition, travelers' perception errors have to be incorporated into their route choice decision process. In view of this, it is necessary to investigate the RSN-MCP model with travelers' perception errors. In order to develop such a model, we need to make some additional assumptions on the perception error as follows:

A5. The perception error distribution of an individual traveler for a segment of road with unit travel time equals $N(\chi, \varpi^2)$, where $N(\chi, \varpi^2)$ represents a normal distribution with predefined and deterministic mean χ and variance ϖ^2.

A6. Traveler's perception errors are independent for nonoverlapping route segments.

A7. Traveler's perception errors are mutually independent over the population of travelers.

In order to compute the value of PSN-MCP of each link in the stochastic network, we need to derive the perceived link travel time, based on moment analysis. According to Assumption A5, the perception error for unit travel time, denoted by $\varepsilon|_{t=1}$, is a sample from. Besides, travel time on link a is the sum of independent unit travel times (see Assumption A6). Therefore, the conditional perception error for link with deterministic travel time t_a^0 is normally distributed as

$$\varepsilon_a|_{T_a=t_a^0} \sim N\left(\chi t_a^0, \varpi^2 t_a^0\right) \tag{39}$$

with conditional moment generating function (MGF)

$$M_{\varepsilon_a|_{T_a=t_a^0}}(s) = \exp\left(\chi t_a^0 s + \frac{\varpi^2 t_a^0 s^2}{2}\right) = \exp\left[s t_a^0\left(\chi + \frac{\varpi^2 s}{2}\right)\right] \tag{40}$$

where s is a real number. Following [22], the MGF of the perceived travel time $\tilde{T}_a$ of link for an individual traveler can be derived as follows:

$$\begin{aligned} M_{\tilde{T}_a}(s) &= E\left[\exp\left(s\tilde{T}_a\right)\right] \\ &= E[\exp s(T_a + \varepsilon_a)] \\ &= E\left\{\exp\left(sT_a\right)E_{\varepsilon_a|T_a}\left[\exp\left(s\varepsilon_a|_{T_a}\right)\right]\right\} \\ &= E_{T_a}\left\{\exp\left(sT_a\right)M_{\varepsilon_a|T_a}(s)\right\} \end{aligned} \tag{41}$$

where $E_x[]$ denotes the expectation with respect to random variable x. Substituting Eq. (40) in Eq. (41), we can get

$$\begin{aligned} M_{\tilde{T}_a}(s) &= E_{T_a}\left\{\exp\left[sT_a\left(1+\chi+\frac{\varpi^2 s}{2}\right)\right]\right\} \\ &= M_{T_a}\left[s\left(1+\chi+\frac{\varpi^2 s}{2}\right)\right] \end{aligned} \tag{42}$$

From the first derivative of the equation above and evaluating at $s = 0$, we can obtain the first moment of the perceived travel time distribution

$$E\left[\tilde{T}_a\right] = (1+\chi)E[T_a] \tag{43}$$

where $E[T_a]$ denotes the mean of the random travel time. Likewise, the second-order moment is derived from the second derivative evaluated at

$$E\left[\left(\tilde{T}_a\right)^2\right] = (1+\chi)^2 E\left[\left(T_a\right)^2\right] + \varpi^2 E[T_a] \tag{44}$$

The variance of the perceived travel time can be expressed as follows:

$$Var\left[\tilde{T}_a\right] = E\left[\left(\tilde{T}_a\right)^2\right] - E\left[\tilde{T}_a\right]^2 = (1+\chi)^2 Var[T_a] + \varpi^2 E[T_a] \tag{45}$$

Using these equations, we can analyze the RSN-MCP model with travelers' perception errors. When taking travelers' perception error into consideration, the objective function of the PRSN-MCP model is to minimize the weighted sum of the mean and the variance of the total perceived travel time. Thus, the PRSN-MCP toll can be given by

$$\text{PRSN}-\text{MCP} = \left\{\partial E\left[\tilde{T}\tilde{T}\right]/\partial v_a - E\left[\tilde{T}_a\right]\right\} + VoR\cdot\left\{\partial Var\left[\tilde{T}\tilde{T}\right]/\partial v_a - Var\left[\tilde{T}_a\right]\right\} \tag{46}$$

where $\tilde{T}\tilde{T} = \sum_{a\in A} V_a \tilde{T}_a$.

According to Eq. (46), it is clear that the value of PRSN-MCP can be determined as long as $\partial E\left[\tilde{T}\tilde{T}\right]/\partial v_a, E\left[\tilde{T}_a\right], \partial Var\left[\tilde{T}\tilde{T}\right]/\partial v_a$, and $Var\left[\tilde{T}_a\right]$ are known. From the conditional moment analysis above, we have already obtained $E\left[\tilde{T}_a\right]$ and $Var\left[\tilde{T}_a\right]$. Moreover, based on the moment analysis, we can derive the mean and variance of $\tilde{T}\tilde{T}$ (see Appendix for the derivations). Substituting Eqs. (43), (45), (A2), and (A4) into Eq. (46) and performing some derivation, we have

$$\begin{aligned} \text{PRSN}-\text{MCP} &= (1+\chi)\{\partial E[TT]/\partial v_a - E[T_a]\} \\ &+ VoR\cdot\left\{(1+\chi)^2\{\partial Var[TT]/\partial v_a - Var[T_a]\} + \varpi^2\left\{\partial E\left[V_a^2 T_a\right]/\partial v_a - E[T_a]\right\}\right\} \end{aligned} \tag{47}$$

5.2 Calculation of PRSN-MCP

In order to illustrate the importance of incorporating both stochastic supply and demand into the proposed PRSN-MCP model, the calculation of PRSN-MCP can be separated into four scenarios based on (1) network uncertainty caused by the stochasticity of travel demand; and (2) network uncertainty induced by the stochastic supply (link capacity). Case A is the most complete situation in which both stochastic link capacity and travel demand are considered. In contrast to Case A, which describes the "true" behaviors of travelers, Case D is the simplest case, neglecting the stochasticity of traffic network. Case B and C ignore, respectively, the effect of stochastic demand and link capacity.

5.2.1 Case a: stochastic supply, stochastic demand (SS-SD)

To begin, we discuss the most complete and realistic case in which the travelers consider both stochastic fluctuations in supply (or link capacity) and demand in their route choice decision-making process. As of now, we have already obtained the values of $\partial E[TT]/\partial v_a, E[T_a]$, $Var[T_a]$ and $\partial Var[TT]/\partial v_a$. The only value left unknown is $\partial E\left[V_a^2 T_a\right]/\partial v_a$. With Eq. (26) we can obtain

$$
\begin{aligned}
E\left[(V_a)^2 T_a\right] &= t_a^0 E[V_a]^2 + \beta t_a^0 E\left[V_a^{n+2}\right] E\left[\frac{1}{C_a^n}\right] \\
&= t_a^0 v_a^2 y_a^2 + \beta t_a^0 \frac{\left(1-\theta_a^{1-n}\right)}{\overline{c}_a^n (1-\theta_a)(1-n)} \left(v_a^{n+2} y_a^{n^2+3n+2}\right)
\end{aligned} \tag{48}
$$

Differentiating Eq. (48) with respect to the mean link flow v_a and performing some simple algebraic operations we have

$$
\begin{aligned}
\frac{\partial E\left[(V_a)^2 T_a\right]}{\partial v_a} &= 2 \cdot t_a^0 v_a y_a^2 - t_a^0 \cdot VMR + \beta t_a^0 \frac{\left(1-\theta_a^{1-n}\right)}{\overline{c}_a^n (1-\theta_a)(1-n)} \\
&\left[(n+2) v_a^{n+1} y_a^{n^2+3n+2} - \frac{n^2+3n+2}{2} \cdot VMR \cdot v_a^n y_a^{n^2+3n}\right]
\end{aligned} \tag{49}
$$

Substituting Eqs. (30), (31), (34), (38), and (49) into Eq. (47), we can obtain the value of PRSN-MCP in case of SS-SD.

5.2.2 Case B: stochastic supply, deterministic demand (SS-DD)

In Case B, the effect of stochastic demand is neglected; only the effect of stochastic link capacity is considered in modeling the travelers' route choice decision-making process. Thus, the mean and variance of T_a are given by Eqs. (20) and (21), respectively. To calculate the value of PRSN-MCP in case of stochastic supply and deterministic demand, we need to recalculate $\partial E[V_a T_a]/\partial v_a$, $\partial Var[TT]/\partial v_a$, and$\partial E\left[V_a^2 T_a\right]/\partial v_a$, respectively.

The expected total travel time can be simplified to

$$
\begin{aligned}
E[TT] = E\left[\sum_{a \in A} V_a T_a\right] &= \sum_{a \in A} \left\{ t_a^0 E[V_a] + \beta t_a^0 E\left[V_a^{n+1}\right] E\left[\frac{1}{C_a^n}\right] \right\} \\
&= \sum_{a \in A} \left\{ t_a^0 v_a + \beta t_a^0 \frac{\left(1-\theta_a^{1-n}\right)}{\overline{c}_a^n (1-\theta_a)(1-n)} v_a^{n+1} \right\}
\end{aligned} \tag{50}
$$

Differentiating Eq. (50) with respect to the mean link flow v_a yields

$$\frac{\partial E[TT]}{\partial v_a} = t_a^0 + \beta t_a^0 \frac{\left(1-\theta_a^{1-n}\right)}{\overline{c}_a^n (1-\theta_a)(1-n)}\left[(n+1)v_a^n\right] \tag{51}$$

The variance of the total travel time is described by

$$\begin{aligned} Var[TT] &= E\left[TT^2\right] - (E[TT])^2 \\ &= \sum\nolimits_{a\in A}\left\{\left(\beta t_a^0\right)^2 \frac{Var\left[V_a^{n+1}\right]}{Var\left[C_a^n\right]}\right\} \\ &= \sum\nolimits_{a\in A}\left\{\left(\beta t_a^0\right)^2 v_a^{2n+2}\left\{\frac{\left(1-\theta_a^{1-2n}\right)}{\overline{c}_a^{2n}(1-\theta_a)(1-2n)} - \left[\frac{\left(1-\theta_a^{1-n}\right)}{\overline{c}_a^n(1-\theta_a)(1-n)}\right]^2\right\}\right\} \end{aligned} \tag{52}$$

Differentiating Eq. (52) with respect to the mean link flow yields

$$\frac{\partial Var[TT]}{\partial v_a} = (2n+2)\left(\beta t_a^0\right)^2 v_a^{2n+1}\left\{\frac{\left(1-\theta_a^{1-2n}\right)}{\overline{c}_a^{2n}(1-\theta_a)(1-2n)} - \left[\frac{\left(1-\theta_a^{1-n}\right)}{\overline{c}_a^n(1-\theta_a)(1-n)}\right]^2\right\} \tag{53}$$

With Eq. (26) we have

$$E\left[(V_a)^2 T_a\right] = t_a^0 E[V_a]^2 + \beta t_a^0 E\left[V_a^{n+2}\right] E\left[\frac{1}{C_a^n}\right] = t_a^0 v_a^2 + \beta t_a^0 \frac{\left(1-\theta_a^{1-n}\right)}{\overline{c}_a^n(1-\theta_a)(1-n)} v_a^{n+2} \tag{54}$$

Differentiating Eq. (54) with respect to the mean link flow v_a we have, upon simplifying

$$\frac{\partial E\left[(V_a)^2 T_a\right]}{\partial v_a} = 2\cdot t_a^0 v_a + (n+2)\beta t_a^0 \frac{\left(1-\theta_a^{1-n}\right)}{\overline{c}_a^n(1-\theta_a)(1-n)} v_a^{n+1} \tag{55}$$

By substituting Eqs. (20), (21), (51), (53), and (55) into Eq. (47), the value of PRSN-MCP in case of SS-DD can be determined.

5.2.3 Case C: deterministic supply, stochastic demand (DS-SD)

In Case C, only the effect of stochastic travel demand is captured in modeling travelers' route choice decision process. The effect of stochastic link capacity is ignored in this case. Therefore, $E\left[1/C_a^n\right]$ and $E\left[1/C_a^{2n}\right]$ are simplified to $1/\overline{c}_a^n$ and $1/\overline{c}_a^{2n}$, respectively. Consequently, the mean and variance of T_a are given by Eqs. (28) and (29), respectively. Similar to Case B, we need to recalculate $\partial E[V_a T_a]/\partial v_a$, $\partial Var[TT]/\partial v_a$, and $\partial E\left[V_a^2 T_a\right]/\partial v_a$, respectively.

The expected total travel time is given by

$$\begin{aligned} E[TT] &= E\left[\sum\nolimits_{a\in A} V_a T_a\right] = \sum\nolimits_{a\in A}\left\{t_a^0 E[V_a] + \beta t_a^0 E\left[V_a^{n+1}\right] E\left[\frac{1}{C_a^n}\right]\right\} \\ &= \sum\nolimits_{a\in A}\left\{t_a^0 v_a + \frac{\beta t_a^0}{\overline{c}_a^n}\left(v_a^{n+1} y_a^{n^2+n}\right)\right\} \end{aligned} \tag{56}$$

Differentiating Eq. (56) with respect to the mean link flow v_a yields

$$\frac{\partial E[TT]}{\partial v_a} = t_a^0 + \frac{\beta t_a^0}{\overline{c}_a^n}\left[\frac{n v_a^{n-1}(1-y_a^2)}{2y_a^2} + 1\right]\left[(n+1)v_a y_a^{n^2+n}\right] \tag{57}$$

The variance of the total travel time is expressed as

$$\begin{aligned} Var[TT] &= E\left[TT^2\right] - (E[TT])^2 \\ &= \sum\nolimits_{a\in A}\left\{\left(t_a^0\right)^2\cdot Var[V_a] + \left(\frac{\beta t_a^0}{\overline{c}_a^n}\right)^2 Var\left[V_a^{n+1}\right] + \frac{2\beta\left(t_a^0\right)^2}{\overline{c}_a^n}\left\{E\left[V_a^{n+2}\right] - E\left[V_a^{n+1}\right]E[V_a]\right\}\right\} \\ &= \sum\nolimits_{a\in A}\left\{\left(t_a^0\right)^2\cdot VMR\cdot v_a + \left(\frac{\beta t_a^0}{\overline{c}_a^n}\right)^2\left\{v_a^{2n} y_a^{4n^2+6n+2} - \left(v_a^{n+1} y_a^{n^2+n}\right)^2\right\} + \frac{2\beta\left(t_a^0\right)^2}{\overline{c}_a^n} v_a^{n+2} y_a^{n^2+n}\left(y_a^{2n+2}-1\right)\right\} \end{aligned} \tag{58}$$

Differentiating Eq. (58) with respect to the mean link flow yields

$$\begin{aligned} \frac{\partial Var[TT]}{\partial v_a} = {} & \left(t_a^0\right)^2\cdot VMR + \left(\frac{\beta t_a^0}{\overline{c}_a^n}\right)^2\left\{\begin{array}{l} \left\{v_a^{2n} y_a^{4n^2+6n}\left[(2n+2)v_a - (2n^2+n-1)\cdot VMR\right]\right\} \\ -\left\{v_a^{2n} y_a^{2n^2+2n-2}\left[(2n+2)v_a - (n^2-n-2)\cdot VMR\right]\right\} \end{array}\right\} \\ & + \frac{2\beta\left(t_a^0\right)^2}{\overline{c}_a^n}\left\{\begin{array}{l} \left\{v_a^n y_a^{n^2+3n}\left[(n+2)v_a - \frac{(n^2+n-2)}{2}\cdot VMR\right]\right\} \\ -\left\{v_a^n y_a^{n^2+n-2}\left[(n+2)v_a - \frac{(n^2-n-4)}{2}\cdot VMR\right]\right\} \end{array}\right\} \end{aligned} \tag{59}$$

With Eq. (26) we have

$$E\left[(V_a)^2 T_a\right] = t_a^0 E[V_a]^2 + \beta t_a^0 E\left[V_a^{n+2}\right]E\left[\frac{1}{C_a^n}\right] = t_a^0 v_a^2 y_a^2 + \frac{\beta t_a^0}{\overline{c}_a^n}\left(v_a^{n+2} y_a^{n^2+3n+2}\right) \tag{60}$$

Differentiating Eq. (60) with respect to the mean link flow v_a and performing some simple algebraic operations, we have

$$\begin{aligned} \frac{\partial E\left[(V_a)^2 T_a\right]}{\partial v_a} = {} & 2\cdot t_a^0 v_a y_a^2 - t_a^0\cdot VMR \\ & + \frac{\beta t_a^0}{\overline{c}_a^n}\left[(n+2)v_a^{n+1} y_a^{n^2+3n+2} - \frac{n^2+3n+2}{2}\cdot VMR\cdot v_a^n y_a^{n^2+3n}\right] \end{aligned} \tag{61}$$

Thus the value of PRSN-MCP in case of DS-SD can be determined by substituting Eqs. (28), (29), (57), (59), and (61) into Eq. (47).

5.2.4 Case D: Deterministic supply, deterministic demand (DS-DD)

Case D degenerates into the MCP model in a deterministic traffic network, in which neither the stochastic link capacity nor stochastic travel demand is considered in travelers' route choice decision making. In this case, the variance of both $Var[TT]$ and $Var[T]$ is equal to zero, and $E[T_a] = t_a^0 + \beta t_a^0 v_a^n / C_a^n$. We only need to recalculate $\partial E[V_a T_a]/\partial v_a$, and $\partial E\left[V_a^2 T_a\right]/\partial v_a$, respectively.

The expected total travel time can be simplified to

$$\begin{aligned} E[TT] &= E\left[\sum_{a\in A} V_a T_a\right] = \sum_{a\in A}\left\{t_a^0 E[V_a] + \beta t_a^0 E\left[V_a^{n+1}\right] E\left[\frac{1}{C_a^n}\right]\right\} \\ &= \sum_{a\in A}\left\{t_a^0 v_a + \frac{\beta t_a^0 v_a^{n+1}}{\overline{c}_a^n}\right\} \end{aligned} \tag{62}$$

Then we have

$$\frac{\partial E[TT]}{\partial v_a} - E[T_a] = \left[t_a^0 + (n+1)\frac{\beta t_a^0}{\overline{c}_a^n} v_a^n\right] - \left[t_a^0 + \frac{\beta t_a^0}{\overline{c}_a^n} v_a^n\right] = \frac{n\beta t_a^0}{\overline{c}_a^n} v_a^n \tag{63}$$

From Eq. (26) we can obtain

$$E\left[(V_a)^2 T_a\right] = t_a^0 E[V_a]^2 + \beta t_a^0 E\left[V_a^{n+2}\right] E\left[\frac{1}{C_a^n}\right] = t_a^0 v_a^2 + \frac{\beta t_a^0 v_a^{n+2}}{\overline{c}_a^n} \tag{64}$$

Consequently, we have, upon simplifying

$$\frac{\partial E\left[(V_a)^2 T_a\right]}{\partial v_a} - E[T_a] = (2v_a - 1)\cdot t_a^0 - [(n+2)v_a - 1]\frac{\beta t_a^0 v_a^n}{\overline{c}_a^n} \tag{65}$$

By substituting Eqs. (63) and (65) into Eq. (47), the value of PRSN-MCP in case of DS-DD can be expressed as follows:

$$\text{PRSN} - \text{MCP} = (1+\chi)\left(\frac{n\beta t_a^0}{\overline{c}_a^n} v_a^n\right) + VoR\cdot \varpi^2\left\{(2v_a - 1)\cdot t_a^0 - [(n+2)v_a - 1]\frac{\beta t_a^0 v_a^n}{\overline{c}_a^n}\right\} \tag{66}$$

6. Numerical examples

The purpose of the numerical examples is to illustrate: (1) the effect of the *VMR* on the performance of the SN-MCP model; (2) the effect of both the demand and supply uncertainties on the performance of the PRSN-MCP model; (3) the importance of incorporating the travelers' perception error in the RSN-MCP model; and (4) the application of the proposed PRSN-MCP model in a medium-scale traffic network. The proposed models in this chapter can be solved by the method of successive averages (MSA).

6.1 Effect of the VMR on the performance of SN-MCP toll scheme

Figure 2 shows a network consisting of 14 nodes and 21 directed links. There are two OD pairs, one is from node 1 to 12, and the other one is from node 1 to14. The link travel time function is assumed to be the Bureau of Public Roads (BPR) function with the following parameters:$\beta = 0.15, n = 4$, which is, $T_a = t_a^0(1 + 0.15 (V_a/C_a)^4), \forall a \in A$. The free-flow travel time, design capacity, and degradation parameter for each link are given in **Table 1**. In order to test the effects of different demand levels, the potential mean total demand for OD pair 1 and 2 is set as $\overline{q}^1 = 3800z$ and $\overline{q}^2 = 4200z$, respectively. In $0 \le z \le 1$, z is the OD demand multiplier.

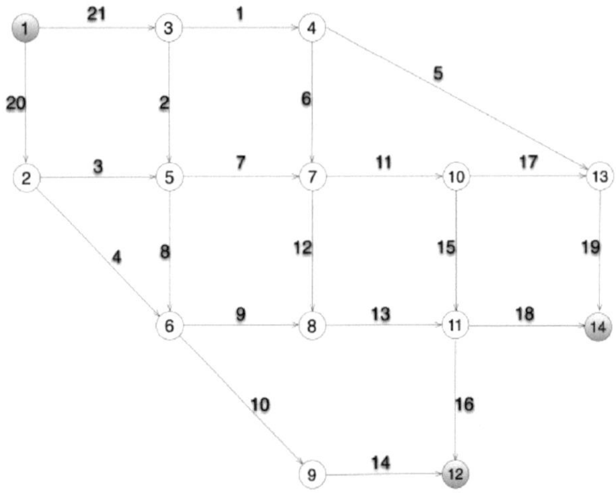

Figure 2.
Traffic network.

Link	Free-flow travel time	Design capacity	Degradation parameter θ_a	Link	Free-flow travel time	Design capacity	Degradation parameter θ_a
1	3	2000	0.95	12	3	1000	0.95
2	3	2000	0.95	13	3	2600	0.95
3	3	2000	0.95	14	3	2000	0.95
4	4.5	1800	0.95	15	3	1400	0.95
5	7.5	1200	0.95	16	3	2000	0.95
6	3	1000	0.95	17	3	800	0.95
7	3	2000	0.95	18	3	2000	0.95
8	3	1800	0.95	19	3	2000	0.95
9	3	1800	0.95	20	3	4000	0.95
10	4.5	1800	0.95	21	3	4000	0.95
11	3	2000	0.95				

Table 1.
Link parameters.

For the first example, we examine the effect of *VMR* on the performance of the SN-MCP model proposed in Section 3. All travelers are assumed to be risk-neutral (i.e., $VoR = 0$). In addition, travelers' perception errors are not considered in the first example. The relationship between the expected total perceived travel time, OD demand level, and *VMR* level under the toll free case and the SN-MCP toll scheme are shown in **Figure 3**. It can be observed that the difference of the expected total perceived travel time (i.e.,$U[TT_{\text{toll free}}] - U[TT_{\text{SN-MCP}}]$) between these two scenarios decreases with the OD demand and *VMR* levels. For example, if the demand multiplier z is 0.8 and *VMR* level is 10, $U[TT_{\text{toll free}}] - U[TT_{\text{SN-MCP}}]$ is more than 2900. However, when the demand multiplier z increases to 1 and *VMR* level increases to 50, $U[TT_{\text{toll free}}] - U[TT_{\text{SN-MCP}}]$ is less than 1633. Remember that VMR_w is the variance-to-mean ratio (*VMR*) of random travel demand. This indicates that along with the increase of travel demand variance and congestion level, the performance of the SN-MCP toll scheme decreases.

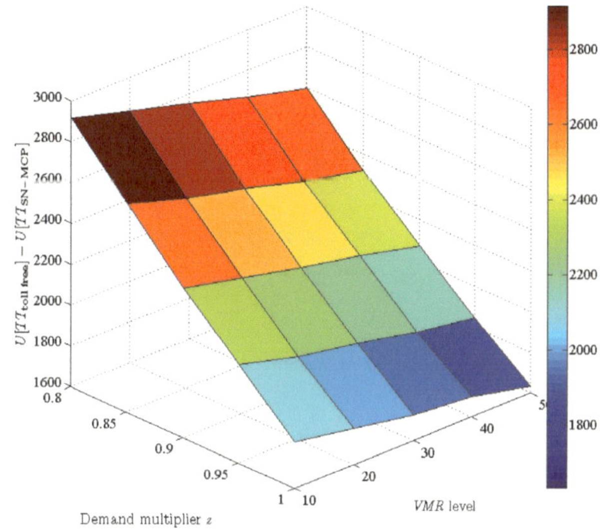

Figure 3.
Difference of the expected total perceived travel time between toll free case and SN-MCP under different OD demand multiplier z *and* VMR *levels.*

6.2 Importance of incorporating supply and demand uncertainty

6.2.1 Effect of congestion on the performance of different PRSN-MCP toll schemes.

We also use the traffic network shown in **Figure 2** in the following test, in which both supply and travel demand uncertainty and travelers' perception errors will be simulated. To demonstrate the effects of neglecting certain aspects of the stochasticity of the network, we compare the expected total perceived travel time under the four PRSN-MCP scenarios discussed in Section 5.2. These four scenarios are analyzed under different congestion levels (the OD demand multiplier z increases from 0.8 to 1 by interval 0.05). As a reminder, all the four scenarios consider the travelers' perception error, with the following differences: Case A is the most complete and realistic representation of the actual traffic flow as both stochastic fluctuations in supply (or link capacity) and demand are incorporated. In comparison, Case B and C are "incomplete cases," because they neglect certain aspects of the stochastic network. Case D is the classical MCP model in a deterministic traffic network.

In this example, we study the effect of congestion levels on the performance of different toll schemes with fixed VoR (i.e., $VoR = 0.0165$) and VMR_w (i.e., $VMR_w = 1.5$). Furthermore, we assume the perception error distribution of unit travel time follows $N(0.1, 0.2)$. **Table 2** displays the expected total perceived travel time at different congestion levels under the toll free, SS-SD, SS-DD, DS-DD, and DS-SD of the PRSN-MCP toll schemes. The results show that the expected total perceived travel time of the toll free and = other toll schemes increases as the demand multiplier z increases.

Figure 4 demonstrates the percentage improvements in the expected total perceived travel time related to **Table 2**. The "Improvement" in **Figure 4** is, in this case, the percentage of improvement in the expected total perceived travel time from the toll free case compared to the SS-SD tolls case, that is,

$$\text{Improvement} = \left(U\left[\tilde{T}\tilde{T}_{\text{toll-free}}\right] - U\left[\tilde{T}\tilde{T}_{\text{case}}\right]\right) / \left(U\left[\tilde{T}\tilde{T}_{\text{toll-free}}\right] - U\left[\tilde{T}\tilde{T}_{\text{SS-SD}}\right]\right) \times 100\% \tag{67}$$

Demand multiplier (z)	$U[\tilde{TT}]$				
	Toll free	SS-SD	SS-DD	DS-DD	DS-SD
0.8	132,261	129,158	129,171	129,184	129,300
0.85	142,651	139,878	139,908	139,928	140,084
0.9	153,870	151,438	151,474	151,502	151,695
0.95	166,113	163,979	164,033	164,072	164,283
1	179,550	177,688	177,757	177,801	177,996

Table 2.
Comparison of system performance under different modeling scenarios and OD demand multipliers.

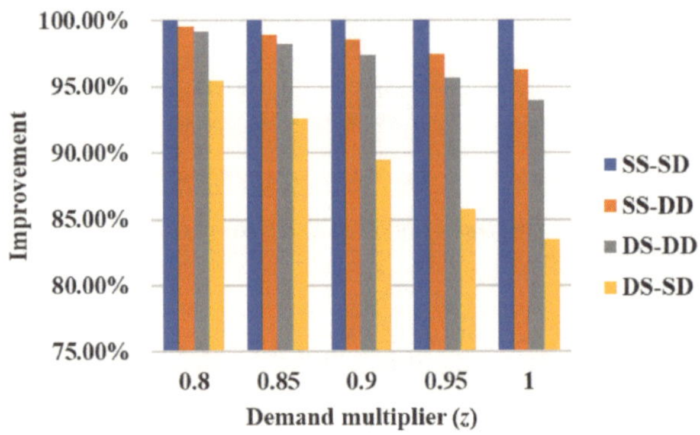

Figure 4.
Improvement in system performance under different modeling scenarios and OD demand multipliers.

From the figure above, the improvement in the expected total perceived travel time obtained by the SS-DD, DS-DD, and DS-SD tolls is lower than that obtained by the SS-SD tolls. Besides, the gap between the expected total perceived travel time under the SS-SD tolls and other toll schemes increases as z increases. When traffic is light, all toll schemes achieve similar system performances, revealing that other toll schemes do not lose too much accuracy by ignoring the stochasticity of the traffic network. However, when traffic is heavy, the differences between them become pronounced. Furthermore, for the DS-SD tolls, neglecting the stochastic link capacity makes the system performance decrease rapidly. This indicates that the toll scheme is more sensitive to the stochasticity of link capacity.

6.2.2 Effect of the VoR on the performance of different PRSN-MCP toll schemes

By assuming the levels of congestion and VMR_w are fixed (i.e., $z = 1$, $VMR_w = 1.5$), the effect of the *VoR* on the expected total perceived travel time under different toll schemes is examined in this section. In **Table 3**, the expected total perceived travel time at different *VoR* levels under the toll free, SS-SD, SS-DD, DS-DD, and DS-SD of the PRSN-MCP toll schemes are compared. The expected total perceived travel time increases with an increase in the level of the *VoR*. This is logical: when *VoR* increases, travelers need to budget a large buffer time to improve their travel time reliability.

Based on Eq. (67) and **Table 3**, we can obtain the percentage improvements in the expected total perceived travel time, as shown in **Figure 5**. It can be seen that the discrepancies between the performance of the SS-SD toll and that of other toll schemes become conspicuously larger as the *VoR* increases. This implies that the higher the travel time reliability that travelers are concerned with, the worse the

VoR	$U[\tilde{T}\tilde{T}]$				
	Toll free	**SS-SD**	**SS-DD**	**DS-DD**	**DS-SD**
0.0068	179,233	177,335	177,384	177,413	177,510
0.0085	179,291	177,394	177,445	177,491	177,620
0.0104	179,344	177,468	177,525	177,568	177,716
0.0129	179,432	177,560	177,623	177,668	177,844
0.0165	179,550	177,688	177,757	177,801	177,996

Table 3.
Comparison of system performance under different modeling scenarios and VoR *levels.*

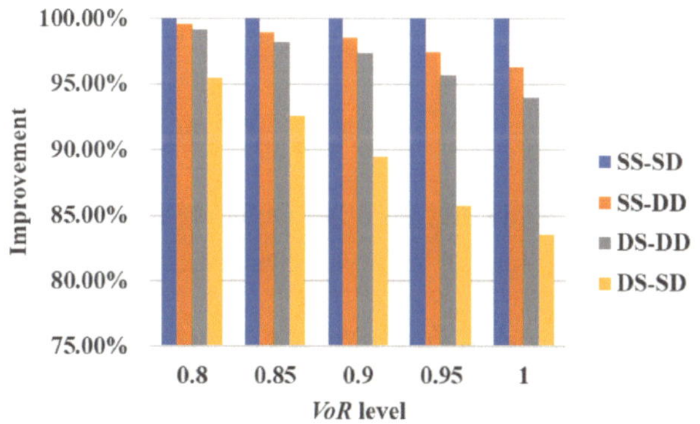

Figure 5.
Improvement in system performance under different modeling scenarios and VoR *levels.*

actual effect of other toll schemes, which ignore the effect of stochastic travel demand and link capacity.

From the above analysis, it can be concluded that the discrepancies of these simplifications depend on both the congestion and *VoR* levels. Capturing the effect of stochastic capacity degradation and stochastic travel demand is critically important.

6.3 Analysis of the essentiality of incorporating the travelers' perception error

The traffic network shown in **Figure 2** is again adopted in examining the PRSN-MCP model. By comparing the difference of the expected total perceived travel time achieved by the RSN-MCP tolls (expressed by $U[TT_{\text{SS-SD}}]$) and the PRSN-MCP tolls (denoted by $U[\tilde{T}\tilde{T}_{\text{SS-SD}}]$), we examine the effect of incorporating the traveler's perception error into the RSN-MCP tolls. In this example, both stochastic fluctuations in supply (or link capacity) and demand are considered for both toll schemes. **Figure 6** illustrates the influence of various combinations of travel demand level and *VoR* level on the difference of the expected total perceived travel time achieved by the RSN-MCP tolls and the PRSN-MCP tolls. Based on the survey results of [24], it is reasonable to assume that all the travelers are risk-averse under an uncertain environment. Therefore, we test the *VoR* level from 0.0068 to 0.0165, and the OD demand multiplier z from 0.8 to 1 with an interval of 0.05. From **Figure 6**, it is clear that $U[TT_{\text{SS-SD}}] - U[\tilde{T}\tilde{T}_{\text{SS-SD}}]$ increases as the demand level z increases. This implies that the consideration of travelers' perception error in the RSN-MCP tolls may have a more significant impact on system performance

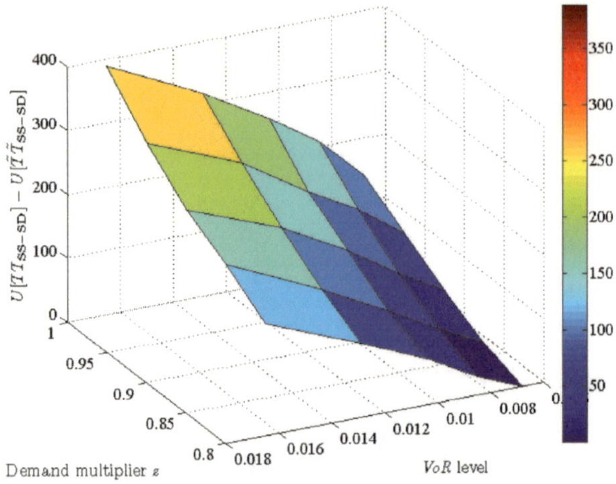

Figure 6.
Difference of the expected total perceived travel time between PRSN-MCP and RSN-MCP under different OD demand multiplier z *and* VoR *levels.*

under heavier congestion levels. On the other hand, we can see that $U[TT_{\text{SS-SD}}] - U[\tilde{T}\tilde{T}_{\text{SS-SD}}]$ is increasing while the *VoR* level increases. This is to be expected, since a higher travel time reliability requires a larger time buffer. Therefore, ignoring the travelers' perception error may significantly reduce the performance of the RSN-MCP tolls, especially when the network congestion level is heavy and travelers require a higher travel time reliability level.

6.4 Application to the Sioux Falls network in the PRSN-MCP (SS-SD) case

The final example illustrates the calculation of the PRSN-MCP (SS-SD) toll in a larger network. This example network is the well-known medium-scale Sioux Falls

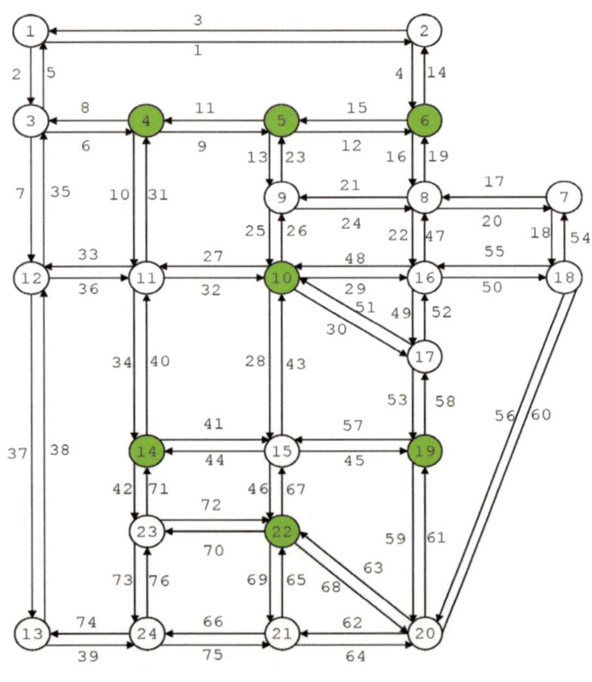

Figure 7.
Sioux Falls network.

network (see **Figure 7**), which consists of 24 nodes and 76 links. The link design capacity and link free-flow travel time can be found in [25]. Degradation parameter θ_a for each link is 0.95. In this example, we also assume $VMR_w = 1.5$, and the perception error distribution of a unit travel time follows $N(0.1, 0.2)$. Forty-two OD pairs are considered in the Sioux Falls network and the mean of the lognormal demand for all OD pairs is given in **Table 4**. The stopping tolerance criterion is set at 0.001. Convergence is achieved in 48 iterations as depicted in **Figure 8**.

In this example, we compare two scenarios. One is the toll free case, and the other one is the PRSN-MCP toll scheme. **Table 5** presents the link toll under the PRSN-MCP scenario. By levying these tolls on each link, the network becomes smooth and efficient. At the equilibrium state, the expected total perceived travel time achieved by the toll free case and PRSN-MCP toll scheme is 345,749 and 324,636, respectively. Therefore, the proposed PRSN-MCP model is an efficient method in reducing traffic congestion.

O/D	4	5	6	10	14	19	22
4		800	800	800	800	800	800
5	800		800	800	800	800	800
6	800	800		800	800	800	800
10	800	800	800		800	800	800
14	800	800	800	800		800	800
19	800	800	800	800	800		800
22	800	800	800	800	800	800	

Table 4.
Means of the stochastic demand for all OD pairs in the Sioux Falls network.

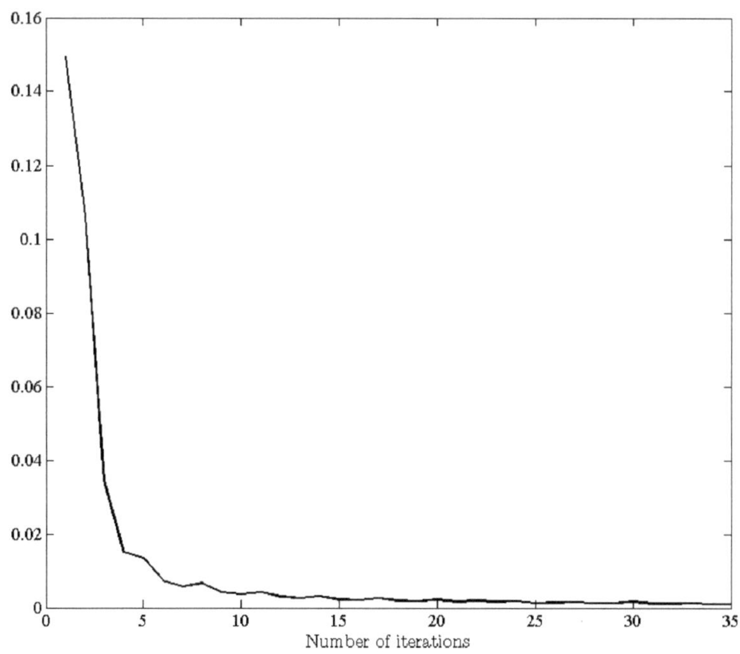

Figure 8.
Convergence of the MSA for the Sioux Falls network.

Link	Link toll	Link	Link toll	Link	Link toll	Link	Link toll
1	19.37	20	23.16	39	33.54	58	45.96
2	12.81	21	17.97	40	68.29	59	20.13
3	19.37	22	37.02	41	38.43	60	35.53
4	16.08	23	95.53	42	22.83	61	20.13
5	12.81	24	17.97	43	59.94	62	23.86
6	34.19	25	37.12	44	38.43	63	32.55
7	78.43	26	37.12	45	22.83	64	23.86
8	34.19	27	33.15	46	29.97	65	7.68
9	39.22	28	59.94	47	37.02	66	15.86
10	125.82	29	17.53	48	17.53	67	29.97
11	39.22	30	30.77	49	14.00	68	32.55
12	46.12	31	125.82	50	3.07	69	7.68
13	95.53	32	33.15	51	30.77	70	18.04
14	16.08	33	18.94	52	14.00	71	22.83
15	46.12	34	68.29	53	45.96	72	18.04
16	73.25	35	78.43	54	15.33	73	5.24
17	23.16	36	18.94	55	3.07	74	33.54
18	15.33	37	24.96	56	35.53	75	15.86
19	73.25	38	24.96	57	22.83	76	5.24

Table 5.
PRSN-MCP tolls for each link at equilibrium state.

7. Conclusions

To make pricing more efficient and effective, this chapter developed a reliability-based marginal cost pricing model. The new model explicitly accounts for both stochastic link degradation and stochastic demand of road network and perception errors within the travelers' route choice decision process. We consider that the stochastic demand follows a lognormal distribution and the capacity degradation follows a uniform distribution, and *VMR* across all OD pairs. Based on moment analysis, we derive the mean and variance of the expected total perceived travel time. After performing some derivations, we derived four analytical functions of PRSN-MCP under different simplifications of network uncertainty.

This chapter investigated possible defects associated with ignoring certain aspects of the stochastic behaviors of the network. Through numerical examples, we find that both link capacity degradation and stochastic demand play essential roles in the PRSN-MCP model, especially under high travelers' confidence level and network congestion. We further examined the effect of incorporating the travelers' perception error into the RSN-MCP tolls. The numerical example illustrates that travelers' perception errors have a significant impact on the performance of the PRSN-MCP tolls and, therefore, should not be neglected.

A. Appendix: computation of the MGF of $\tilde{T}\tilde{T}$

The MGF of $\tilde{T}\tilde{T}$can be represented as follows:

$$\begin{aligned} M_{\tilde{T}\tilde{T}}(s) &= \sum\nolimits_{a\in A} E\left[\exp\left(sV_a\tilde{T}_a\right)\right] \\ &= \sum\nolimits_{a\in A} E\{\exp\left[sV_a(T_a+\varepsilon_a)\right]\} \\ &= \sum\nolimits_{a\in A} E_{T_a}\{\exp\left(sV_aT_a\right)\exp\left(sV_a\varepsilon_a\right)\} \\ &= \sum\nolimits_{a\in A} E_{T_a}\left\{\exp\left(sV_aT_a\right)E_{\varepsilon_a|T_a}\left[\exp\left(sV_a\varepsilon_a|_{T_a}\right)\right]\right\} \\ &= \sum\nolimits_{a\in A} E_{T_a}\left\{\exp\left(sV_aT_a\right)M_{\varepsilon_a|T_a}\left(sV_a\right)\right\} \\ &= \sum\nolimits_{a\in A} E_{T_a}\{\exp\left(sV_aT_a\right)\exp\left[sV_aT_a\left(\chi+\varpi^2 sV_a/2\right)\right]\} \end{aligned} \tag{68}$$

The first-order moment is, from the first derivative evaluated at $s=0$,

$$E\left[\tilde{T}\tilde{T}\right] = \sum\nolimits_{a\in A}(1+\chi)E[V_aT_a] \tag{69}$$

Similarly, the second-order moment of $\tilde{T}\tilde{T}$ can be derived from the second derivative evaluated at$s=0$,

$$E\left[\left(\tilde{T}\tilde{T}\right)^2\right] = \sum\nolimits_{a\in A}\left\{(1+\chi)^2E\left[\left(V_aT_a\right)^2\right]+\varpi^2E\left[V_a^2T_a\right]\right\} \tag{70}$$

Then we can obtain the variance of $\tilde{T}\tilde{T}$ as follows:

$$\begin{aligned} Var\left[\tilde{T}\tilde{T}\right] &= E\left[\left(\tilde{T}\tilde{T}\right)^2\right] - E\left[\tilde{T}\tilde{T}\right]^2 \\ &= \sum\nolimits_{a\in A}\left\{(1+\chi)^2\left\{E\left[\left(V_aT_a\right)^2\right]-E[V_aT_a]^2\right\}+\varpi^2E\left[V_a^2T_a\right]\right\} \\ &= \sum\nolimits_{a\in A}\left\{(1+\chi)^2Var[TT]+\varpi^2E\left[V_a^2T_a\right]\right\} \end{aligned} \tag{71}$$

Acknowledgements

This research has been supported by the National Natural Science Foundation of China (Project No. 71701030 and 71971038), the Humanities and Social Sciences Youth Foundation of the Ministry of Education of China (Project No. 17YJCZH265), and the Fundamental Research Funds for the Central Universities of China (Project No. DUT20GJ210).

Author details

Shaopeng Zhong
Dalian University of Technology, Dalian, China

*Address all correspondence to: szhong@dlut.edu.cn

References

[1] Abdel-Aty MA, Kitamura R, Jovanis PP. Using stated preference data for studying the effect of advanced traffic information on drivers' route choice. Transportation Research Part C: Emerging Technologies. 1997;**5**:39-50

[2] Brownstone D, Small KA. Valuing time and reliability: Assessing the evidence from road pricing demonstrations. Transportation Research Part A: Policy and Practice. 2005;**39**:279-293

[3] Liu HX, Recker W, Chen A. Uncovering the contribution of travel time reliability to dynamic route choice using real-time loop data. Transportation Research Part A: Policy and Practice. 2004;**38**:435-453

[4] Asakura Y, Kashiwadani M. Road network reliability caused by daily fluctuation of traffic flow. In: Proceedings of Proceedings of the 19th PTRC Summer Annual Meeting. Brighton, England: PTRC Education and Research Services; 1991. pp. 73-84

[5] Nicholson A, Schmocker JD, Bell MGH. Assessing transport reliability: Malvolence and user knowledge. In: Proceedings of the Network Reliability of Transport: Proceedings of the 1st International Symposium on Transportation Network Reliability. Kyoto: Elsevier Science Ltd; 2003

[6] Chen A, Zhou Z. A Stochastic α-reliable mean-excess traffic equilibrium model with probabilistic travel times and perception errors. In: Lam WHK, Wong SC, Lo HK, Golden Jabilee editors. Transportation and Traffic Theory 2009. Hong Kong: Springer; 2009. pp. 117-145

[7] Uchida T, Iida Y. Risk Assignment. A New Traffic Assignment Model Considering the Risk of Travel Time Variation. Amsterdam, Berkeley, CA, USA: University of California; 1993. pp. 89-105

[8] Chen A, Yang H, Lo HK, Tang WH. Capacity reliability of a road network: An assessment methodology and numerical results. Transportation Research Part B: Methodological. 2002; **36**:225-252

[9] Chen A, Zhou Z. The α-reliable mean-excess traffic equilibrium model with stochastic travel times. Transportation Research Part B: Methodological. 2010;**44**:493-513

[10] Lo HK, Luo XW, Siu BWY. Degradable transport network: Travel time budget of travelers with heterogeneous risk aversion. Transportation Research Part B: Methodological. 2006;**40**:792-806

[11] Clark S, Watling D. Modelling network travel time reliability under stochastic demand. Transportation Research Part B: Methodological. 2005; **39**:119-140

[12] Shao H, Lam W, Tam M. A reliability-based stochastic traffic assignment model for network with multiple user classes under uncertainty in demand. Networks and Spatial Economics. 2006;**6**:173-204

[13] Chen A, Yang H, Lo HK, Tang WH. A capacity related reliability for transportation networks. Journal of Advanced Transportation. 1999;**33**: 183-200

[14] Lo HK, Tung Y-K. Network with degradable links: Capacity analysis and design. Transportation Research Part B: Methodological. 2003;**37**:345-363

[15] Lam WHK, Shao H, Sumalee A. Modeling impacts of adverse weather

conditions on a road network with uncertainties in demand and supply. Transportation Research Part B: Methodological. 2008;**42**:890-910

[16] Sumalee A, Connors RD, Luathep P. Network equilibrium under cumulative prospect theory and endogenous stochastic demand and supply. In: Lam WHK, Wong SC, Lo HK, Golden Jabilee editors. Transportation and Traffic Theory 2009. Hong Kong: Springer; 2009. pp. 19-38

[17] Yao T, Friesz TL, Wei MM, Yin Y. Congestion derivatives for a traffic bottleneck. Transportation Research Part B: Methodological. 2010;**44**: 1149-1165

[18] Sumalee A, Xu W. First-best marginal cost toll for a traffic network with stochastic demand. Transportation Research Part B: Methodological. 2011; **45**:41-59

[19] Boyles SD, Kockelman KM, Travis Waller S. Congestion pricing under operational, supply-side uncertainty. Transportation Research Part C: Emerging Technologies. 2010;**18**: 519-535

[20] Li H, Bliemer MCJ, Bovy PHL. Network reliability-based optimal toll design (Technical report). Journal of Advanced Transportation. 2008;**42**: 311-322

[21] Gardner LM, Boyles SD, Waller ST. Quantifying the benefit of responsive pricing and travel information in the stochastic congestion pricing problem. Transportation Research Part A: Policy and Practice. 2011;**45**:204-218

[22] Mirchandani P, Soroush H. Generalized traffic equilibrium with probabilistic travel times and perceptions. Transportation Science. 1987;**21**:133-152

[23] Zhou Z, Chen A. Comparative analysis of three user equilibrium models under stochastic demand. Journal of Advanced Transportation. 2008;**42**:239-263

[24] de Palma A, Picard N. Route choice decision under travel time uncertainty. Transportation Research Part A: Policy and Practice. 2005;**39**:295-324

[25] Tam M, Lam WHK. Analysis of demand for road-based transport facilities: A bi-level programming approach. Transportation Research Record. 1999;**1685**:73-80

Chapter 5

ARCH and GARCH Models: Quasi-Likelihood and Asymptotic Quasi-Likelihood Approaches

Raed Alzghool

Abstract

This chapter considers estimation of autoregressive conditional heteroscedasticity (ARCH) and the generalized autoregressive conditional heteroscedasticity (GARCH) models using quasi-likelihood (QL) and asymptotic quasi-likelihood (AQL) approaches. The QL and AQL estimation methods for the estimation of unknown parameters in ARCH and GARCH models are developed. Distribution assumptions are not required of ARCH and GARCH processes by QL method. Nevertheless, the QL technique assumes knowing the first two moments of the process. However, the AQL estimation procedure is suggested when the conditional variance of process is unknown. The AQL estimation substitutes the variance and covariance by kernel estimation in QL. Reports of simulation outcomes, numerical cases, and applications of the methods to daily exchange rate series and weekly prices' changes of crude oil are presented.

Keywords: ARCH model, GARCH model, the quasi-likelihood, asymptotic quasi-likelihood, martingale difference, daily exchange rate series, prices changes of crude oil

1. Introduction

The autoregressive conditional heteroscedasticity (ARCH(q)) process is defined by

$$y_t = \mu + \xi_t, \quad t = 1, 2, 3, \cdots, T. \tag{1}$$

and

$$\sigma_t^2 = \alpha_0 + \alpha_1 \xi_{t-1}^2 + \cdots + \alpha_q \xi_{t-q}^2 + \zeta_t, \quad t = 1, 2, 3, \cdots, T. \tag{2}$$

ξ_t are i.i.d with $E(\xi_t) = 0$ and $V(\xi_t) = \sigma_t^2$; and ζ_t are i.i.d with $E(\zeta_t) = 0$ and $V(\zeta_t) = \sigma_\zeta^2$. For estimation and applications of ARCH models, see [1–19]. Moreover, ARCH models have now become the standard textbook material in econometrics and finance as exemplified by, for example, [20–23].

The generalized autoregressive conditional heteroscedasticity (GARCH(p,q)) process y_t is defined by

$$y_t = \mu + \xi_t, \qquad t = 1, 2, 3, \cdots, T. \tag{3}$$

and

$$\sigma_t^2 = \alpha_0 + \alpha_1 \xi_{t-1}^2 + \cdots + \alpha_p \xi_{t-p}^2 + \beta_1 \sigma_{t-1}^2 + \cdots + \beta_q \sigma_{t-q}^2, \qquad t = 1, 2, 3, \cdots, T. \quad (4)$$

ξ_t are i.i.d with $E(\xi_t) = 0$ and $V(\xi_t) = \sigma_t^2$.

The GARCH model was developed by Bollersev [24] to extend the earlier work on ARCH models by Engle [1]. For estimation and applications of GARCH models, (see, [2, 3, 6–8, 10, 11, 14]). Moreover, GARCH models have now become the standard textbook material in econometrics and finance as exemplified by, for example, [20–23].

This chapter considers estimation of ARCH and GARCH models using quasi-likelihood (QL) and asymptotic quasi-likelihood (AQL) approaches. Distribution assumptions are not required of ARCH and GARCH processes by the QL method. But, the QL technique assumes knowing the first two moments of the process. However, The AQL estimation procedure is suggested when the conditional variance of process is unknown. The AQL estimation substitutes the variance and covariance by kernel estimation in QL.

This chapter is structured as follows. Section 2 introduces the QL and AQL approaches. The estimation of ARCH model using QL and AQL methods are developed in Section 3. The estimation of GARCH model using QL and AQL methods are developed in Section 4. Reports of simulation outcomes, numerical cases and applications of the methods to a daily exchange rate series, and weekly prices changes of crude oil are also presented. Summary and conclusion are given in Section 5.

2. The QLE and AQL methods

Let the observation equation be given by

$$\mathbf{y}_t = \mathbf{f}_t(\theta) + \zeta_t, \qquad t = 1, 2, 3 \cdots, T, \quad (5)$$

where ζ_t is a sequence of martingale difference with respect to $\mathcal{F}_t$, $\mathcal{F}_t$ denotes the σ-field generated by $\mathbf{y}_t, \mathbf{y}_{t-1}, \cdots, \mathbf{y}_1$ for $t \geq 1$; that is, $E(\zeta_t | \mathcal{F}_{t-1}) = E_{t-1}(\zeta_t) = 0$, where $\mathbf{f}_t(\theta)$ is an $\mathcal{F}_{t-1}$ measurable and θ is parameter vector, which belongs to an open subset $\Theta \in R^d$. Note that θ is a parameter of interest.

2.1 The QL method

For the model given by Eq. (5), assume that $E_{t-1}(\zeta_t \zeta_t') = \Sigma_t$ is known. Now, the linear class $\mathcal{G}_T$ of the estimating function (EF) can be defined by

$$\mathcal{G}_T = \left\{ \sum_{t=1}^{T} \mathbf{W}_t (\mathbf{y}_t - \mathbf{f}_t(\theta)) \right\}$$

and the quasi-likelihood estimation function (QLEF) can be defined by

$$\mathbf{G}_T^*(\theta) = \sum_{t=1}^{T} \dot{\mathbf{f}}_t(\theta) \Sigma_t^{-1} (\mathbf{y}_t - \mathbf{f}_t(\theta)) \quad (6)$$

where $\mathbf{W}_t$ is $\mathcal{F}_{t-1}$-measureable and $\dot{\mathbf{f}}_t(\theta) = \partial \mathbf{f}_t(\theta) / \partial \theta$. Then, the estimation of θ by the QL method is the solution of the QL equation $\mathbf{G}_T^*(\theta) = 0$ (see [25]).

If the sub-estimating function spaces of $\mathcal{G}_T$ are considered as follows:

$$\mathcal{G}_t = \{\mathbf{W}_t(\mathbf{y}_t - \mathbf{f}_t(\theta))\}$$

then the QLEF can be defined by

$$\mathbf{G}^*_{(t)}(\theta) = \dot{\mathbf{f}}_t(\theta)\Sigma_t^{-1}(\mathbf{y}_t - \mathbf{f}_t(\theta)) \tag{7}$$

and the estimation of θ by the QL method is the solution of the QL equation $\mathbf{G}^*_{(t)}(\theta) = 0$.

A limitation of the QL method is that the nature of Σ_t may not be obtainable. A misidentified Σ_t could result in a deceptive inference about parameter θ. In the next subsection, we will introduce the AQL method, which is basically the QL estimation assuming that the covariance matrix Σ_t is unknown.

2.2 The AQL method

The QLEF (see Eqs. (6) and (7)) relies on the information of Σ_t. Such information is not always accessible. To find the QL when $E_{t-1}(\zeta_t\zeta_t')$ is not accessible, Lin [26] proposed the AQL method.

Definition 2.2.1: *Let $\mathbf{G}^*_{T,n}$ be a sequence of the EF in $\mathcal{G}$. For all $\mathbf{G}_T \in \mathcal{G}$, if*

$$\left(E\dot{\mathbf{G}}_T\right)^{-1}(E\mathbf{G}_T\mathbf{G}_T)'\left(E\dot{\mathbf{G}}_T'\right)^{-1} - \left(E\dot{\mathbf{G}}'^{*}_{T,n}\right)^{-1}\left(E\mathbf{G}^*_{T,n}\mathbf{G}^{*\prime}_T\right)\left(E\dot{\mathbf{G}}^{*\prime}_{T,n}\right)^{-1}$$

is asymptotically nonnegative definite, $\mathbf{G}^*_{T,n}$ can be denoted as the asymptotic quasi-likelihood estimation function (AQLEF) sequence in $\mathcal{G}$, and the AQL sequence estimate $\theta_{T,n}$ by the AQL method is the solution of the AQL equation $\mathbf{G}^*_{T,n} = 0$.

Suppose, in probability, $\Sigma_{t,n}$ is converging to $E_{t-1}(\zeta_t\zeta_t')$. Then,

$$\mathbf{G}^*_{T,n}(\theta) = \sum_{t=1}^{T} \dot{\mathbf{f}}_t(\theta)\Sigma_{t,n}^{-1}(\mathbf{y}_t - \mathbf{f}_t(\theta)) \tag{8}$$

expresses an AQLEF sequence. The solution of $\mathbf{G}^*_{T,n}(\theta) = 0$ expresses the AQL sequence estimate $\{\theta^*_{T,n}\}$, which converges to θ under certain regular conditions.

In this chapter, the kernel smoothing estimator of Σ_t is suggested to find $\Sigma_{t,n}$ in the AQLEF (Eq. (8)). A wide-ranging appraisal of the Nadaray-Watson (NW) estimator-type kernel estimator is available in [27]. By using these kernel estimators, the AQL equation becomes

$$\mathbf{G}^*_{T,n}(\theta) = \sum_{t=1}^{T} \dot{\mathbf{f}}_t(\theta)\hat{\Sigma}_{t,n}^{-1}\left(\hat{\theta}^{(0)}\right)(\mathbf{y}_t - \mathbf{f}_t(\theta)) = 0. \tag{9}$$

The estimation of θ by the AQL method is the solution to Eq. (9). Iterative techniques are suggested to solve the AQL equation (Eq. (9)). Such techniques start with the ordinary least squares (OLS) estimator $\hat{\theta}^{(0)}$ and use $\hat{\Sigma}_{t,n}\left(\hat{\theta}^{(0)}\right)$ in the AQL equation (Eq. (9)) to obtain the AQL estimator $\hat{\theta}^{(1)}$. Repeat this a few times until it converges.

For estimation of unknown parameters in fanatical models by QL and AQL approaches, see [21, 28–33]. The next sections present the parameter estimation of ARCH model using the QL and AQL methods.

3. Parameter estimation of ARCH(q) model using the QL and AQL methods

In this section, we will develop the estimation of ARCH model using QL and AQL methods.

3.1 Parameter estimation of ARCH(q) model using the QL method

The ARCH(q) process is defined by

$$y_t = \mu + \xi_t, \qquad t = 1, 2, 3, \cdots, T. \tag{10}$$

and

$$\sigma_t^2 = \alpha_0 + \alpha_1 \xi_{t-1}^2 + \cdots + \alpha_q \xi_{t-q}^2 + \zeta_t, \qquad t = 1, 2, 3, \cdots, T. \tag{11}$$

ξ_t are i.i.d with $E(\xi_t) = 0$ and $V(\xi_t) = \sigma_t^2$; and ζ_t are i.i.d with $E(\zeta_t) = 0$ and $V(\zeta_t) = \sigma_\zeta^2$. For this scenario, the martingale difference is

$$\begin{pmatrix} \xi_t \\ \zeta_t \end{pmatrix} = \begin{pmatrix} y_t - \mu \\ \sigma_t^2 - \alpha_0 - \alpha_1 \xi_{t-1}^2 - \cdots - \alpha_q \xi_{t-q}^2 \end{pmatrix}.$$

The QLEF to estimate σ_t^2 is given by

$$\begin{aligned} G_{(t)}\left(\sigma_t^2\right) &= (0, 1) \begin{pmatrix} \sigma_t^2 & 0 \\ 0 & \sigma_\zeta^2 \end{pmatrix}^{-1} \begin{pmatrix} y_t - \mu \\ \sigma_t^2 - \alpha_0 - \alpha_1 \xi_{t-1}^2 - \cdots - \alpha_q \xi_{t-q}^2 \end{pmatrix} \\ &= \sigma_\zeta^{-2}\left(\sigma_t^2 - \alpha_0 - \alpha_1 \xi_{t-1}^2 - \cdots - \alpha_q \xi_{t-q}^2\right). \end{aligned} \tag{12}$$

Given $\hat{\xi}_0 = 0$, initial values $\psi_0 = \left(\mu_0, \alpha_{0_0}, \alpha_{1_0}, \cdots, \alpha_{q_0}, \sigma_{\zeta_0}^2\right)$ and $\hat{\xi}_{t-1}^2 = \left(y_{t-1} - \mu_0\right)^2$, then the QL estimation of σ_t^2 is the solution of $G_{(t)}\left(\sigma_t^2\right) = 0$:

$$\hat{\sigma}_t^2 = \alpha_0 + \alpha_1 \hat{\xi}_{t-1}^2 + \cdots + \alpha_q \hat{\xi}_{t-q}^2, \qquad t = 1, 2, 3 \cdots, T. \tag{13}$$

The QLEF, using $\{\hat{\sigma}_t^2\}$ and $\{y_t\}$, to estimate the parameters μ, α_0, α_1, $\cdots$, α_q is given by

$$G_T\left(\mu, \alpha_0, \alpha_1, \cdots, \alpha_q\right) = \sum_{t=1}^{T} \begin{pmatrix} -1 & 0 \\ 0 & -1 \\ 0 & -\xi_{t-1}^2 \\ \vdots & \vdots \\ 0 & -\xi_{t-q}^2 \end{pmatrix} \begin{pmatrix} \sigma_t^2 & 0 \\ 0 & \sigma_{\zeta_0}^2 \end{pmatrix}^{-1} \times \begin{pmatrix} y_t - \mu \\ \sigma_t^2 - \alpha_0 - \alpha_1 \xi_{t-1}^2 - \alpha_q \xi_{t-q}^2 \end{pmatrix}.$$

The QL estimate of $\mu, \alpha_0, \alpha_1, \cdots, \alpha_q$ is the solution of $G_T(\mu, \alpha_0, \alpha_1, \cdots, \alpha_q) = 0$, where $\hat{\zeta}_t = \hat{\sigma}_t^2 - \hat{\alpha}_0 - \hat{\alpha}_1\hat{\xi}_{t-1}^2 - \cdots - \hat{\alpha}_q\hat{\xi}_{t-q}^2, t = 1, 2, 3, \cdots, T$ and

$$\hat{\sigma}_\zeta^2 = \frac{\sum_{t=1}^{T}\left(\hat{\zeta}_t - \bar{\hat{\zeta}}\right)^2}{T-1} \tag{14}$$

$\hat{\psi} = \left(\hat{\mu}, \hat{\alpha}_0, \hat{\alpha}_1, \cdots, \alpha_q, \hat{\sigma}_\zeta^2\right)$ is an initial value in the iterative procedure.

3.2 Parameter estimation of ARCH(q) model using the AQL method

For ARCH(q) model given by Eqs. (10) and (11) and using the same argument listed under Eq. (11). First, to estimate σ_t^2, so the sequence of (AQLEF) is given by

$$G_{(t)}\left(\sigma_t^2\right) = (0, 1)\Sigma_{t,n}^{-1}\begin{pmatrix} y_t - \mu \\ \sigma_t^2 - \alpha_0 - \alpha_1\xi_{t-1}^2 - \cdots - \alpha_q\xi_{t-q}^2 \end{pmatrix}$$

Given $\hat{\xi}_0 = 0, \theta_0 = (\mu_0, \alpha_0, \alpha_1, \cdots, \alpha_q), \Sigma_{t,n}^{(0)} = \mathbf{I}_2$, and $\hat{\xi}_{t-1}^2 = (y_{t-1} - \mu_0)^2$, then the AQL estimation of σ_t^2 is the solution of $G_{(t)}\left(\sigma_t^2\right) = 0$, that is,

$$\hat{\sigma}_t^2 = \alpha_0 + \alpha_1\hat{\xi}_{t-1}^2 + \cdots + \alpha_q\hat{\xi}_{t-q}^2, \qquad t = 1, 2, 3\cdots, T. \tag{15}$$

Second, by kernel estimation method, we find

$$\hat{\Sigma}_{t,n}\left(\theta^{(0)}\right) = \begin{pmatrix} \hat{\sigma}_n(y_t) & \hat{\sigma}_n(y_t, \sigma_t) \\ \hat{\sigma}_n(\sigma_t, y_t) & \hat{\sigma}_n(\sigma_t) \end{pmatrix}.$$

Third, to estimate the parameters $\theta_0 = (\mu_0, \alpha_0, \alpha_1, \cdots, \alpha_q)$ using $\{\hat{\sigma}_t^2\}$ and $\{y_t\}$ and the sequence of (AQLEF):

$$G_T(\mu_0, \alpha_0, \alpha_1, \cdots, \alpha_q) = \sum_{t=1}^{T}\begin{pmatrix} -1 & 0 \\ 0 & -1 \\ 0 & -\xi_{t-1}^2 \\ \vdots & \vdots \\ 0 & -\xi_{t-q}^2 \end{pmatrix}\hat{\Sigma}_{t,n}^{-1} \times \begin{pmatrix} y_t - \mu \\ \sigma_t^2 - \alpha_0 - \alpha_1\xi_{t-1}^2 - \cdots - \alpha_q\xi_{t-q}^2 \end{pmatrix}.$$

The AQL estimate of $\theta_0 = (\mu_0, \alpha_0, \alpha_1, \cdots, \alpha_q)$ is the solution of $G_T(\theta_0) = 0$. The estimation procedure will be iteratively repeated until it converges.

3.3 Simulation studies for the ARCH(1) model

The estimation of ARCH(1) model using QL and AQL methods are considered in simulation studies. The ARCH(1) process is defined by

$$y_t = \mu + \xi_t, \qquad t = 1, 2, 3, \cdots, T. \tag{16}$$

and

$$\sigma_t^2 = \alpha_0 + \alpha_1 \xi_{t-1}^2 + \zeta_t, \qquad t = 1, 2, 3, \cdots, T. \tag{17}$$

ξ_t are i.i.d with $E(\xi_t) = 0$ and $V(\xi_t) = \sigma_t^2$; and ζ_t are i.i.d with $E(\zeta_t) = 0$ and $V(\zeta_t) = \sigma_\zeta^2$.

3.3.1 Parameter estimation of ARCH(1) model using the QL method

For ARCH(1) given by Eqs. (16) and (17), the martingale difference is

$$\begin{pmatrix} \xi_t \\ \zeta_t \end{pmatrix} = \begin{pmatrix} y_t - \mu \\ \sigma_t^2 - \alpha_0 - \alpha_1 \xi_{t-1}^2 \end{pmatrix}.$$

The QLEF to estimate σ_t^2 is given by

$$\begin{aligned} G_{(t)}\left(\sigma_t^2\right) &= (0,1)\begin{pmatrix} \sigma_t^2 & 0 \\ 0 & \sigma_\zeta^2 \end{pmatrix}^{-1} \begin{pmatrix} y_t - \mu \\ \sigma_t^2 - \alpha_0 - \alpha_1 \xi_{t-1}^2 \end{pmatrix} \\ &= \sigma_\zeta^{-2}\left(\sigma_t^2 - \alpha_0 - \alpha_1 \xi_{t-1}^2\right). \end{aligned} \tag{18}$$

Given $\hat{\xi}_0 = 0$, initial values $\psi_0 = \left(\mu_0, \alpha_{0_0}, \alpha_{1_0}, \sigma_{\zeta_0}^2\right)$ and $\hat{\xi}_{t-1}^2 = \left(y_{t-1} - \mu_0\right)^2$, then the QL estimation of σ_t^2 is the solution of $G_{(t)}\left(\sigma_t^2\right) = 0$,

$$\hat{\sigma}_t^2 = \alpha_0 + \alpha_1 \hat{\xi}_{t-1}^2, \qquad t = 1, 2, 3 \cdots, T. \tag{19}$$

To estimate the parameters μ, α_0, and α_1, using $\left\{\hat{\sigma}_t^2\right\}$ and $\left\{y_t\right\}$, the QLEF is given by

$$G_T(\mu, \alpha_0, \alpha_1) = \sum_{t=1}^{T} \begin{pmatrix} -1 & 0 \\ 0 & -1 \\ 0 & -\xi_{t-1}^2 \end{pmatrix} \begin{pmatrix} \sigma_t^2 & 0 \\ 0 & \sigma_{\zeta_0}^2 \end{pmatrix}^{-1} \begin{pmatrix} y_t - \mu \\ \sigma_t^2 - \alpha_0 - \alpha_1 \xi_{t-1}^2 \end{pmatrix}.$$

The solution of $G_T(\mu, \alpha_0, \alpha_1) = 0$ is the QL estimate of μ, α_0, and α_1. Therefore

$$\hat{\mu} = \sum_{t=1}^{T} \frac{y_t}{\hat{\sigma}_t^2} \Big/ \sum_{t=1}^{T} \frac{1}{\hat{\sigma}_t^2}. \tag{20}$$

$$\hat{\alpha}_1 = \frac{T\sum_{t=1}^{T} \hat{\sigma}_t^2 \hat{\xi}_{t-1}^2 - \sum_{t=1}^{T} \hat{\sigma}_t^2 \sum_{t=1}^{T} \hat{\xi}_{t-1}^2}{T\sum_{t=1}^{T} \hat{\xi}_{t-1}^4 - \left(\sum_{t=1}^{T} \hat{\xi}_{t-1}^2\right)^2}. \tag{21}$$

$$\hat{\alpha}_0 = \frac{\sum_{t=1}^{T} \hat{\sigma}_t^2 - \hat{\alpha}_1 \sum_{t=1}^{T} \hat{\xi}_{t-1}^2}{T}. \tag{22}$$

and let

$$\hat{\sigma}_\zeta^2 = \frac{\sum_{t=1}^{T} \left(\hat{\zeta}_t - \bar{\hat{\zeta}}\right)^2}{T-1} \tag{23}$$

where $\hat{\zeta}_t = \hat{\sigma}_t^2 - \hat{\alpha}_0 - \hat{\alpha}_1 \hat{\xi}_{t-1}^2, t = 1, 2, 3, \cdots, T.$

$\hat{\psi} = \left(\hat{\mu}, \hat{\alpha}_0, \hat{\alpha}_1, \hat{\sigma}_\zeta^2\right)$ is an initial value in the iterative procedure.

The initial values might be affected the estimation results. For extensive discussion on assigning initial values in the QL estimation procedures, see [21, 34].

3.3.2 Parameter estimation of ARCH(1) model using the AQL method

Considering the ARCH(1) model given by Eqs. (16) and (17) and using the same argument listed under Eq. (17). First, we need to estimate σ_t^2, so the sequence of (AQLEF) is given by

$$G_{(t)}\left(\sigma_t^2\right) = (0,1)\Sigma_{t,n}^{-1}\begin{pmatrix} y_t - \mu \\ \sigma_t^2 - \alpha_0 - \alpha_1\xi_{t-1}^2 \end{pmatrix}$$

Given $\hat{\xi}_0 = 0$, $\theta_0 = (\mu_0, \alpha_0, \alpha_1, \mu_0)$, $\Sigma_{t,n}^{(0)} = \mathbf{I}_2$ and $\hat{\xi}_{t-1}^2 = \left(y_{t-1} - \mu_0\right)^2$, then the AQL estimation of σ_t^2 is the solution of $G_{(t)}\left(\sigma_t^2\right) = 0$, that is,

$$\hat{\sigma}_t^2 = \alpha_0 + \alpha_1\hat{\xi}_{t-1}^2, \qquad t = 1, 2, 3\cdots, T. \tag{24}$$

Second, by kernel estimation method, we find

$$\hat{\Sigma}_{t,n}\left(\theta^{(0)}\right) = \begin{pmatrix} \hat{\sigma}_n\left(y_t\right) & \hat{\sigma}_n\left(y_t, \sigma_t\right) \\ \hat{\sigma}_n\left(\sigma_t, y_t\right) & \hat{\sigma}_n\left(\sigma_t\right) \end{pmatrix}.$$

Third, to estimate the parameters $\theta = (\mu, \alpha_0, \alpha_1)$ using $\left\{\hat{\sigma}_t^2\right\}$ and $\left\{y_t\right\}$ and the sequence of AQLEF:

$$G_T(\mu, \alpha_0, \alpha_1) = \sum_{t=1}^{T}\begin{pmatrix} -1 & 0 \\ 0 & -1 \\ 0 & -\hat{\xi}_{t-1} \end{pmatrix}\hat{\Sigma}_{t,n}^{-1}\begin{pmatrix} y_t - \mu \\ \sigma_t^2 - \alpha_0 - \alpha_1\xi_{t-1}^2 \end{pmatrix}.$$

The AQL estimate of γ, ϕ, and μ is the solution of $G_T(\mu, \alpha_0, \alpha_1) = 0$. Therefore

$$\hat{\mu} = \sum_{t=1}^{T}\frac{y_t}{\hat{\sigma}_n\left(y_t\right)} \Big/ \sum_{t=1}^{T}\frac{1}{\hat{\sigma}_n\left(y_t\right)}. \tag{25}$$

$$\hat{\alpha}_1 = \frac{\left(\sum_{t=1}^{T}\frac{\hat{\sigma}_t^2}{\hat{\sigma}_n(\sigma_t)}\right)\left(\sum_{t=1}^{T}\frac{\hat{\xi}_{t-1}^2}{\hat{\sigma}_n(\sigma_t)}\right) - \left(\sum_{t=1}^{T}\frac{1}{\hat{\sigma}_n(\sigma_t)}\right)\left(\sum_{t=1}^{T}\frac{\hat{\xi}_{t-1}^2}{\hat{\sigma}_n(\sigma_t)}\right)}{\left(\sum_{t=1}^{T}\frac{\hat{\xi}_{t-1}^2}{\hat{\sigma}_n(\sigma_t)}\right)^2 - \left(\sum_{t=1}^{T}\frac{1}{\hat{\sigma}_n(\sigma_t)}\right)\left(\sum_{t=1}^{T}\frac{\hat{\xi}_{t-1}^4}{\hat{\sigma}_n(\sigma_t)}\right)}. \tag{26}$$

$$\hat{\alpha}_0 = \frac{\left(\sum_{t=1}^{T}\frac{\hat{\sigma}_t^2}{\hat{\sigma}_n(\sigma_t)}\right) - \hat{\alpha}_1\left(\sum_{t=1}^{T}\frac{\hat{\xi}_{t-1}^2}{\hat{\sigma}_n(\sigma_t)}\right)}{\sum_{t=1}^{T}\frac{1}{\hat{\sigma}_n(\sigma_t)}}. \tag{27}$$

and let

$$\hat{\sigma}_\zeta^2 = \frac{\sum_{t=1}^{T}\left(\hat{\zeta}_t - \overline{\hat{\zeta}}\right)^2}{T-1} \tag{28}$$

The estimation procedure will be iteratively repeated until it converges.

For each parameter setting, T = 500 observations are simulated from the true model. We then replicate the experiment for 1000 times to obtain the mean and root mean squared errors (RMSE) for $\hat{\alpha}_0$, $\hat{\alpha}_1$, and $\hat{\mu}$. In **Table 1**, QL denotes the QL estimate and AQL denotes the AQL estimate.

We generated N = 1000 independent random samples of size T = 20, 40, 60, 80, and 100 from ARCH(1) model. In **Table 2**, the QL and AQL estimation methods show the property of consistency, the RMSE decreases as the sample size increases.

3.4 Empirical applications

The first data set we analyze are the daily exchange rate of $r_t = AUD/USD$ (Australian dollar/US dollar) for the period from 5/6/2010 to 5/5/2016, 1590 observations in total. The ARCH model (Eqs. (16) and (17)) is used to model $y_t = log\,(r_t) - log\,(r_{t-1})$.

We used the S + FinMetrics function archTest to carry out Lagrange multiplier (ML) test for the presence of ARCH effects in the residuals (see [35]). For r_t the p-values are significant (< 0.05 level), so reject the null hypothesis that there are no ARCH effects and we fit $\{y_t\}$ by following models:

$$y_t = \mu + \xi_t, \qquad t = 1, 2, 3, \cdots, T. \tag{29}$$

	α_0	α_1	μ	α_0	α_1	μ	α_0	α_1	μ
True	0.010	0.980	1.30	0.010	0.980	−1.30	0.010	0.980	0.030
QL	0.009	0.989	1.299	0.009	0.989	−1.30	0.009	0.989	0.029
	0.001	0.010	0.006	0.001	0.010	0.006	0.001	0.010	0.006
AQL	0.009	0.989	1.30	0.009	0.989	−1.29	0.009	0.989	0.030
	0.001	0.010	0.0003	0.002	0.009	0.0003	0.001	0.009	0.0003
True	0.050	0.950	1.30	0.050	0.950	−1.30	0.050	.950	0.030
QL	0.049	0.949	1.29	0.049	0.940	−1.30	0.049	0.94	0.029
	0.001	0.0001	0.014	0.001	0.010	0.014	0.001	0.010	0.014
AQL	0.049	0.940	1.32	0.049	0.940	−1.30	0.049	0.940	0.032
	0.001	0.010	0.018	0.001	0.010	0.018	0.001	0.01	0.001
True	0.10	0.90	1.30	0.10	0.90	−1.30	0.10	0.90	0.030
QL	0.098	0.910	1.29	0.098	0.910	−1.30	0.098	0.910	0.023
	0.002	0.010	0.019	0.002	0.010	0.020	0.002	0.010	0.029
AQL	0.098	0.910	1.31	0.098	0.910	−1.32	0.098	0.910	0.031
	0.002	0.010	0.012	0.002	0.010	0.021	0.001	0.010	0.001
True	0.1	0.90	−0.03	0.05	0.95	−0.03	0.01	0.98	−0.03
QL	0.098	0.910	−0.031	0.051	0.949	−0.030	0.009	0.990	−0.030
	0.002	0.010	0.019	0.001	0.001	0.014	0.001	0.016	0.006
AQL	0.098	0.910	−0.031	0.051	0.949	−0.031	0.009	0.990	−0.031
	0.002	0.010	0.001	0.001	0.001	0.002	0.001	0.010	0.001

Table 1.
The QL and AQL estimates and the RMSE of each estimate is stated below that estimate for ARCH model.

		α_0	α_1	μ	α_0	α_1	μ
T = 20	True	0.010	0.980	−0.030	0.05	0.950	1.3
	QL	0.009	0.990	−0.029	0.0495	0.9485	1.300
		0.0008	0.0100	0.0319	0.0005	0.0015	0.0703
	AQL	0.009	0.990	−0.031	0.0495	0.9485	1.3107
		0.0009	0.010	0.0084	0.0005	0.0015	0.0213
T = 40	QL	0.009	0.990	−0.031	0.0495	0.9485	1.3015
		0.00089	0.010	0.0223	0.0005	0.0015	0.0492
	AQL	0.009	0.990	−0.031	0.0495	0.9485	1.3113
		0.00089	0.010	0.0039	0.0005	0.0015	0.0143
T = 60	QL	0.009	0.990	−0.029	0.0495	0.9485	1.300
		0.0009	0.010	0.0180	0.0005	0.0015	0.0404
	AQL	0.009	0.990	−0.031	0.0495	0.9485	1.311
		0.0009	0.010	0.0027	0.0005	0.0015	0.0128
T = 80	QL	0.009	0.990	−0.029	0.0490	0.9485	1.300
		0.0009	0.010	0.016	0.0005	0.0015	0.0353
	AQL	0.009	0.990	−0.310	0.0495	0.9485	1.3112
		0.0009	0.010	0.0020	0.0005	0.0015	0.0119
T = 100	QL	0.009	0.990	0.0292	0.0495	0.9485	1.3017
		0.0009	0.010	0.0142	0.0005	0.0015	0.0314
	AQL	0.009	0.990	−0.031	0.0495	0.9485	1.3111
		0.0009	0.010	0.0018	0.0005	0.0015	0.0116

Table 2.
The QL and AQL estimates and the RMSE of each estimate is stated below that estimate for ARCH model with different sample size.

and

$$\sigma_t^2 = \alpha_0 + \alpha_1 \xi_{t-1}^2 + \zeta_t, \qquad t = 1, 2, 3, \cdots, T. \tag{30}$$

ξ_t are i.i.d with $E(\xi_t) = 0$ and $V(\xi_t) = \sigma_t^2$; and ζ_t are i.i.d with $E(\zeta_t) = 0$ and $V(\zeta_t) = \sigma_\zeta^2$.

The estimation of unknown parameters, $(\alpha_0, \alpha_1, \mu)$, using QL and AQL are given in **Table 3**. Conclusion can be drawn based on the standardized residuals from the fourth column in **Table 3**, which favors the QL method, gives smaller standardized residuals, better than AQL method.

	$\hat{\alpha}_0$	$\hat{\alpha}_1$	$\hat{\mu}$	$\frac{\bar{\xi}_t}{S.d(\xi_t)}$
QL	0.1300	0.8387	−0.00012	0.00013
AQL	0.0200	0.9599	−0.00111	0.1350

Table 3.
Estimation of α_0, α_1, μ for the exchange rate pound/dollar data.

4. Parameter estimation of GARCH(p,q) model using the QL and AQL methods

In this section, we developing the estimation of GARCH model using QL and AQL methods.

4.1 Parameter estimation of GARCH(p,q) model using the QL method

The GARCH(p,q) process is defined by

$$y_t = \mu + \xi_t, \qquad t = 1, 2, 3, \cdots, T. \tag{31}$$

and

$$\sigma_t^2 = \alpha_0 + \alpha_1 \xi_{t-1}^2 + \cdots + \alpha_p \xi_{t-p}^2 + \beta_1 \sigma_{t-1}^2 + \cdots + \beta_q \sigma_{t-q}^2, \qquad t = 1, 2, 3, \cdots, T. \tag{32}$$

ξ_t are i.i.d with $E(\xi_t) = 0$ and $V(\xi_t) = \sigma_t^2$; and ζ_t are i.i.d with $E(\zeta_t) = 0$ and $V(\zeta_t) = \sigma_\zeta^2$. For this scenario, the martingale difference is

$$\begin{pmatrix} \xi_t \\ \zeta_t \end{pmatrix} = \begin{pmatrix} y_t - \mu \\ \sigma_t^2 - \alpha_0 - \alpha_1 \xi_{t-1}^2 - \cdots - \alpha_p \xi_{t-p}^2 - \beta_1 \sigma_{t-1}^2 - \cdots - \beta_q \sigma_{t-q}^2 \end{pmatrix}.$$

The QLEF to estimate σ_t^2 is given by

$$\begin{aligned} G_{(t)}\left(\sigma_t^2\right) &= (0, 1) \begin{pmatrix} \sigma_t^2 & 0 \\ 0 & \sigma_\zeta^2 \end{pmatrix}^{-1} \begin{pmatrix} \xi_t \\ \zeta_t \end{pmatrix} \\ &= \sigma_\zeta^{-2}\left(\sigma_t^2 - \alpha_0 - \alpha_1 \xi_{t-1}^2 - \cdots - \alpha_p \xi_{t-p}^2 - \beta_1 \sigma_{t-1}^2 - \cdots - \beta_q \sigma_{t-q}^2\right). \end{aligned} \tag{33}$$

Given $\hat{\xi}_0 = 0$, initial values $\psi_0 = \left(\mu_0, \alpha_{0_0}, \alpha_{1_0}, \cdots, \alpha_{p_0}, \beta_{1_0}, \cdots, \beta_{q_0}, \sigma_{\zeta_0}^2\right)$, $\hat{\xi}_{t-i}^2 = \left(y_{t-i} - \mu_0\right)^2$, and $\hat{\sigma}_{t-j}^2$ are the QL estimations of σ_{t-j}^2, where i = 1, 2, ⋯, p and j = 1, 2, ⋯, q, then the QL estimation of σ_t^2 is the solation of $G_{(t)}\left(\sigma_t^2\right) = 0$,

$$\hat{\sigma}_t^2 = \alpha_0 + \alpha_1 \xi_{t-1}^2 + \cdots + \alpha_p \xi_{t-p}^2 + \beta_1 \sigma_{t-1}^2 + \cdots + \beta_q \sigma_{t-q}^2, \qquad t = 1, 2, 3 \cdots, T. \tag{34}$$

The QLEF, using $\{\hat{\sigma}_t^2\}$ and $\{y_t\}$, to estimate the parameters $\theta = \mu$, α_0, α_1, ⋯, α_q, β_1, ⋯, β_q is given by

$$G_T(\theta) = \sum_{t=1}^{T} \begin{pmatrix} -1 & 0 \\ 0 & -1 \\ 0 & -\xi_{t-1}^2 \\ \vdots & \vdots \\ 0 & -\xi_{t-p}^2 \\ 0 & -\sigma_{t-1}^2 \\ \vdots & \vdots \\ 0 & -\sigma_{t-q}^2 \end{pmatrix} \begin{pmatrix} \sigma_t^2 & 0 \\ 0 & \sigma_{\zeta_0}^2 \end{pmatrix}^{-1} \begin{pmatrix} \xi_t \\ \zeta_t \end{pmatrix}$$

The QL estimate of μ, α_0, α_1, $\cdots$, α_q, β_1, $\cdots$, β_q is the solation of $G_T(\theta) = 0$, where $\hat{\zeta}_t = \hat{\sigma}_t^2 - \hat{\alpha}_0 - \hat{\alpha}_1\hat{\xi}_{t-1}^2 - \cdots - \hat{\alpha}_p\hat{\xi}_{t-p}^2 - \hat{\beta}_1\hat{\sigma}_{t-1}^2 - \cdots - \hat{\beta}_q\hat{\sigma}_{t-q}^2, t = 1, 2, 3, \cdots, T$ and

$$\hat{\sigma}_\zeta^2 = \frac{\sum_{t=1}^{T}\left(\hat{\zeta}_t - \bar{\hat{\zeta}}\right)^2}{T-1} \tag{35}$$

$\hat{\psi} = (\hat{\mu}, \hat{\alpha}_0, \hat{\alpha}_1, \cdots, \hat{\alpha}_p, \hat{\beta}_1, \cdots, \hat{\beta}_q, \hat{\sigma}_\zeta^2)$ is an initial value in the iterative procedure.

4.2 Parameter estimation of GARCH(p,q) model using the AQL method

Considering the GARCH(p,q) model given by Eqs. (31) and (32) and using the same argument listed under Eq. (32). First, we need to estimate σ_t^2, so the sequence of (AQLEF) is given by

$$G_{(t)}\left(\sigma_t^2\right) = (0, 1)\Sigma_{t,n}^{-1}\begin{pmatrix} \xi_t \\ \zeta_t \end{pmatrix}$$

Given $\hat{\xi}_0 = 0$, $\theta_0 = \left(\mu_0, \alpha_{0_0}, \alpha_{1_0}, \cdots, \alpha_{p_0}, \beta_{1_0}, \cdots, \beta_{q_0}\right)$, $\Sigma_{t,n}^{(0)} = \mathbf{I}_2$, and $\hat{\xi}_{t-i}^2 = \left(y_{t-i} - \mu_0\right)^2$, and $\hat{\sigma}_{t-j}^2$ is the AQL estimation of σ_{t-j}^2, where i = 1, 2, $\cdots$, p and j = 1, 2, $\cdots$, q, then the AQL estimation of σ_t^2 is the solation of $G_{(t)}\left(\sigma_t^2\right) = 0$, that is,

$$\hat{\sigma}_t^2 = \alpha_0 + \alpha_1\hat{\xi}_{t-1}^2 + \cdots + \alpha_p\xi_{t-p}^2 + \beta_1\sigma_{t-1}^2 + \cdots + \beta_q\sigma_{t-q}^2, \qquad t = 1, 2, 3\cdots, T. \tag{36}$$

Second, by kernel estimation method, we find

$$\hat{\Sigma}_{t,n}\left(\theta^{(0)}\right) = \begin{pmatrix} \hat{\sigma}_n\left(y_t\right) & \hat{\sigma}_n\left(y_t, \sigma_t\right) \\ \hat{\sigma}_n\left(\sigma_t, y_t\right) & \hat{\sigma}_n\left(\sigma_t\right) \end{pmatrix}.$$

Third, to estimate the parameters $\theta_0 = \left(\mu_0, \alpha_0, \alpha_1, \cdots, \alpha_q\right)$ using $\left\{\hat{\sigma}_t^2\right\}$ and $\left\{y_t\right\}$ and the sequence of (AQLEF):

$$G_T\left(\mu_0, \alpha_0, \alpha_1, \cdots, \alpha_q\right) = \sum_{t=1}^{T}\begin{pmatrix} -1 & 0 \\ 0 & -1 \\ 0 & -\xi_{t-1}^2 \\ \vdots & \vdots \\ 0 & -\xi_{t-q}^2 \\ 0 & -\sigma_{t-1}^2 \\ \vdots & \vdots \\ 0 & -\sigma_{t-q}^2 \end{pmatrix}\hat{\Sigma}_{t,n}^{-1}\begin{pmatrix} \xi_t \\ \zeta_t \end{pmatrix}.$$

The AQL estimate of $\theta = \left(\mu, \alpha_0, \alpha_1, \cdots, \alpha_q\right)$ is the solation of $G_T(\theta) = 0$. The estimation procedure will be iteratively repeated until it converges.

4.3 Simulation studies for the GARCH(1,1) model

The estimation of GARCH(1,1) model using QL and AQL methods are considered in simulation studies. The GARCH(1,1) process is defined by

$$y_t = \mu + \xi_t, \qquad t = 1, 2, 3, \cdots, T. \tag{37}$$

and

$$\sigma_t^2 = \alpha_0 + \alpha_1 \xi_{t-1}^2 + \beta_1 \sigma_{t-1} + \zeta_t, \qquad t = 1, 2, 3, \cdots, T. \tag{38}$$

ξ_t are i.i.d with $E(\xi_t) = 0$ and $V(\xi_t) = \sigma_t^2$; and ζ_t are i.i.d with $E(\zeta_t) = 0$ and $V(\zeta_t) = \sigma_\zeta^2$.

4.3.1 Parameter estimation of GARCH(1,1) model using the QL method

For GARCH(1,1) given by Eqs. (37) and (38), the martingale difference is

$$\begin{pmatrix} \xi_t \\ \zeta_t \end{pmatrix} = \begin{pmatrix} y_t - \mu \\ \sigma_t^2 - \alpha_0 - \alpha_1 \xi_{t-1}^2 - \beta_1 \sigma_{t-1}^2 \end{pmatrix}.$$

The QLEF to estimate σ_t^2 is given by

$$\begin{aligned} G_{(t)}\left(\sigma_t^2\right) &= (0, 1) \begin{pmatrix} \sigma_t^2 & 0 \\ 0 & \sigma_\zeta^2 \end{pmatrix}^{-1} \begin{pmatrix} y_t - \mu \\ \sigma_t^2 - \alpha_0 - \alpha_1 \xi_{t-1}^2 - \beta_1 \sigma_{t-1}^2 \end{pmatrix} \\ &= \sigma_\zeta^{-2}\left(\sigma_t^2 - \alpha_0 - \alpha_1 \xi_{t-1}^2 - \beta_1 \sigma_{t-1}^2\right). \end{aligned} \tag{39}$$

Given $\hat{\xi}_0 = 0$, initial values $\psi_0 = \left(\mu_0, \alpha_{0_0}, \alpha_{1_0}, \sigma_{\zeta_0}^2\right)$, $\hat{\xi}_{t-1}^2 = \left(y_{t-1} - \mu_0\right)^2$, and $\hat{\sigma}_{t-1}^2$ is the QL estimation of σ_{t-1}^2, then the QL estimation of σ_t^2 is the solation of $G_{(t)}\left(\sigma_t^2\right) = 0$,

$$\hat{\sigma}_t^2 = \alpha_0 + \alpha_1 \hat{\xi}_{t-1}^2 + \beta_1 \hat{\sigma}_{t-1}^2, \qquad t = 1, 2, 3 \cdots, T. \tag{40}$$

To estimate the parameters μ, α_0, and α_1, using $\left\{\hat{\sigma}_t^2\right\}$ and $\left\{y_t\right\}$, the QLEF is given by

$$G_T(\mu, \alpha_0, \alpha_1, \beta_1) = \sum_{t=1}^{T} \begin{pmatrix} -1 & 0 \\ 0 & -1 \\ 0 & -\xi_{t-1}^2 \\ 0 & -\sigma_{t-1}^2 \end{pmatrix} \begin{pmatrix} \sigma_t^2 & 0 \\ 0 & \sigma_{\zeta_0}^2 \end{pmatrix}^{-1} * \begin{pmatrix} y_t - \mu \\ \sigma_t^2 - \alpha_0 - \alpha_1 \xi_{t-1}^2 - \beta_1 \sigma_{t-1}^2 \end{pmatrix}.$$

The solation of $G_T(\mu, \alpha_0, \alpha_1, \beta_1) = 0$ is the QL estimate of μ, α_0, α_1, and β_1. Therefore

$$\hat{\mu} = \sum_{t=1}^{T} \frac{y_t}{\hat{\sigma}_t^2} \Big/ \sum_{t=1}^{T} \frac{1}{\hat{\sigma}_t^2}. \tag{41}$$

$$\hat{\beta}_1 = \frac{S_{\hat{\sigma}^2_{t-1}\hat{\xi}^2_{t-1}} S_{\hat{\sigma}^2_t \hat{\xi}^2_{t-1}} - S_{\hat{\xi}^2_{t-1}\hat{\xi}^2_{t-1}} S_{\hat{\sigma}^2_t \hat{\sigma}^2_{t-1}}}{S^2_{\hat{\sigma}^2_{t-1}\hat{\xi}^2_{t-1}} - S_{\hat{\sigma}^2_{t-1}\hat{\sigma}^2_{t-1}} S_{\hat{\xi}^2_{t-1}\hat{\xi}^2_{t-1}}}. \tag{42}$$

$$\hat{\alpha}_1 = \frac{S_{\hat{\sigma}^2_t \hat{\xi}^2_{t-1}} - \hat{\beta}_1 S_{\hat{\sigma}^2_{t-1}\hat{\xi}^2_{t-1}}}{S_{\hat{\xi}^2_{t-1}\hat{\xi}^2_{t-1}}}. \tag{43}$$

$$\hat{\alpha}_0 = \frac{\sum_{t=1}^T \hat{\sigma}^2_t - \hat{\alpha}_1 \sum_{t=1}^T \hat{\xi}^2_{t-1} - \hat{\beta}_1 \sum_{t=1}^T \hat{\sigma}^2_{t-1}}{T}. \tag{44}$$

and let

$$\hat{\sigma}^2_\zeta = \frac{\sum_{t=1}^T \left(\hat{\zeta}_t - \bar{\hat{\zeta}}\right)^2}{T-1} \tag{45}$$

where

$$\hat{\zeta}_t = \hat{\sigma}^2_t - \hat{\alpha}_0 - \hat{\alpha}_1 \hat{\xi}^2_{t-1} - \hat{\beta}_1 \hat{\sigma}^2_{t-1}, \qquad t = 1, 2, 3, \cdots, T,$$

$$S_{\hat{\sigma}^2_{t-1}\hat{\xi}^2_{t-1}} = \sum_{t=1}^T \hat{\sigma}^2_{t-1}\hat{\xi}^2_{t-1} - \frac{\sum_{t=1}^T \hat{\sigma}^2_{t-1} \sum_{t=1}^T \hat{\xi}^2_{t-1}}{T},$$

$$S_{\hat{\sigma}^2_t \hat{\xi}^2_{t-1}} = \sum_{t=1}^T \hat{\sigma}^2_t \hat{\xi}^2_{t-1} - \frac{\sum_{t=1}^T \hat{\sigma}^2_t \sum_{t=1}^T \hat{\xi}^2_{t-1}}{T},$$

$$S_{\hat{\xi}^2_{t-1}\hat{\xi}^2_{t-1}} = \sum_{t=1}^T \hat{\xi}^4_{t-1} - \frac{\left(\sum_{t=1}^T \hat{\xi}^2_{t-1}\right)^2}{T},$$

$$S_{\hat{\sigma}^2_t \hat{\sigma}^2_{t-1}} = \sum_{t=1}^T \hat{\sigma}^2_t \hat{\sigma}^2_{t-1} - \frac{\sum_{t=1}^T \hat{\sigma}^2_t \sum_{t=1}^T \hat{\sigma}^2_{t-1}}{T},$$

$$S_{\hat{\sigma}^2_{t-1}\hat{\sigma}^2_{t-1}} = \sum_{t=1}^T \hat{\sigma}^4_{t-1} - \frac{\left(\sum_{t=1}^T \hat{\sigma}^2_{t-1}\right)^2}{T}.$$

$\hat{\psi} = \left(\hat{\mu}, \hat{\alpha}_0, \hat{\alpha}_1, \hat{\sigma}^2_\zeta\right)$ is an initial value in the iterative procedure.

The initial values might be affected the estimation results. For extensive discussion on assigning initial values in the QL estimation procedures, see [21, 34].

4.3.2 Parameter estimation of GARCH(1,1) model using the AQL method

Considering the GARCH(1,1) model given by Eqs. (37) and (38) and using the same argument listed under (Eq. (38)). First, we need to estimate σ^2_t, so the sequence of (AQLEF) is given by

$$G_{(t)}\left(\sigma^2_t\right) = (0, 1)\Sigma^{-1}_{t,n} \begin{pmatrix} y_t - \mu \\ \sigma^2_t - \alpha_0 - \alpha_1 \xi^2_{t-1} - \beta_1 \sigma^2_{t-1} \end{pmatrix}$$

Given $\hat{\xi}_0 = 0$, $\theta_0 = \left(\mu_0, \alpha_{0,0}, \alpha_{1,0}, \beta_{1,0}\right)$, $\Sigma^{(0)}_{t,n} = \mathbf{I}_2$, $\hat{\xi}^2_{t-1} = \left(y_{t-1} - \mu_0\right)^2$, and $\hat{\sigma}^2_{t-1}$ is the AQL estimation of σ^2_{t-1}, then the AQL estimation of σ^2_t is the solation of $G_{(t)}\left(\sigma^2_t\right) = 0$, that is,

$$\hat{\sigma}^2_t = \alpha_0 + \alpha_1 \hat{\xi}^2_{t-1} + \beta_1 \sigma^2_{t-1}, \qquad t = 1, 2, 3 \cdots, T. \tag{46}$$

Second, by kernel estimation method, we find

$$\hat{\Sigma}_{t,n}\left(\theta^{(0)}\right) = \begin{pmatrix} \hat{\sigma}_n(y_t) & 0 \\ 0 & \hat{\sigma}_n(\sigma_t) \end{pmatrix}.$$

Third, to estimate the parameters $\theta = (\mu, \alpha_0, \alpha_1, \beta_1)$ using $\{\hat{\sigma}_t^2\}$ and $\{y_t\}$ and the sequence of AQLEF:

$$G_T(\mu, \alpha_0, \alpha_1, \beta_1) = \sum_{t=1}^{T} \begin{pmatrix} -1 & 0 \\ 0 & -1 \\ 0 & -\hat{\xi}_{t-1}^2 \\ 0 & -\hat{\sigma}_{t-1}^2 \end{pmatrix} \hat{\Sigma}_{t,n}^{-1} \begin{pmatrix} y_t - \mu \\ \sigma_t^2 - \alpha_0 - \alpha_1 \xi_{t-1}^2 - \beta_1 \sigma_{t-1}^2 \end{pmatrix}.$$

The AQL estimate of μ, α_0, α_1, and β_1 is the solation of $G_T(\mu, \alpha_0, \alpha_1, \beta_1) = 0$. Therefore

$$\hat{\mu} = \sum_{t=1}^{T} \frac{y_t}{\hat{\sigma}_n(y_t)} \Big/ \sum_{t=1}^{T} \frac{1}{\hat{\sigma}_n(y_t)}. \tag{47}$$

$$\hat{\beta}_1 = \frac{SS_{\hat{\sigma}_{t-1}^2 \hat{\xi}_{t-1}^2} SS_{\hat{\sigma}_t^2 \hat{\xi}_{t-1}^2} - SS_{\hat{\xi}_{t-1}^2 \hat{\xi}_{t-1}^2} SS_{\hat{\sigma}_t^2 \hat{\sigma}_{t-1}^2}}{SS_{\hat{\sigma}_{t-1}^2 \hat{\xi}_{t-1}^2}^2 - SS_{\hat{\sigma}_{t-1}^2 \hat{\sigma}_{t-1}^2} SS_{\hat{\xi}_{t-1}^2 \hat{\xi}_{t-1}^2}}. \tag{48}$$

$$\hat{\alpha}_1 = \frac{SS_{\hat{\sigma}_t^2 \hat{\xi}_{t-1}^2} - \hat{\beta}_1 SS_{\hat{\sigma}_{t-1}^2 \hat{\xi}_{t-1}^2}}{SS_{\hat{\xi}_{t-1}^2 \hat{\xi}_{t-1}^2}}. \tag{49}$$

$$\hat{\alpha}_0 = \frac{\sum_{t=1}^{T} \frac{\hat{\sigma}_t^2}{\hat{\sigma}_n(\sigma_t)} - \hat{\alpha}_1 \sum_{t=1}^{T} \frac{\hat{\xi}_{t-1}^2}{\hat{\sigma}_n(\sigma_t)} - \hat{\beta}_1 \sum_{t=1}^{T} \frac{\hat{\sigma}_{t-1}^2}{\hat{\sigma}_n(\sigma_t)}}{\sum_{t=1}^{T} \frac{1}{\hat{\sigma}_n(\sigma_t)}}, \tag{50}$$

and let

$$\hat{\sigma}_{\zeta}^2 = \frac{\sum_{t=1}^{T} \left(\hat{\zeta}_t - \overline{\hat{\zeta}}\right)^2}{T-1} \tag{51}$$

where

$$\hat{\zeta}_t = \hat{\sigma}_t^2 - \hat{\alpha}_0 - \hat{\alpha}_1 \hat{\xi}_{t-1}^2 - \hat{\beta}_1 \hat{\sigma}_{t-1}^2, \quad t = 1, 2, 3, \cdots, T,$$

$$SS_{\hat{\sigma}_{t-1}^2 \hat{\xi}_{t-1}^2} = \left(\sum_{t=1}^{T} \frac{\hat{\sigma}_{t-1}^2 \hat{\xi}_{t-1}^2}{\hat{\sigma}_n(\sigma_t)}\right)\left(\sum_{t=1}^{T} \frac{1}{\hat{\sigma}_n(\sigma_t)}\right) - \left(\sum_{t=1}^{T} \frac{\hat{\sigma}_{t-1}^2}{\hat{\sigma}_n(\sigma_t)}\right)\left(\sum_{t=1}^{T} \frac{\hat{\xi}_{t-1}^2}{\hat{\sigma}_n(\sigma_t)}\right),$$

$$SS_{\hat{\sigma}_t^2 \hat{\xi}_{t-1}^2} = \left(\sum_{t=1}^{T} \frac{\hat{\sigma}_t^2 \hat{\xi}_{t-1}^2}{\hat{\sigma}_n(\sigma_t)}\right)\left(\sum_{t=1}^{T} \frac{1}{\hat{\sigma}_n(\sigma_t)}\right) - \left(\sum_{t=1}^{T} \frac{\hat{\sigma}_t^2}{\hat{\sigma}_n(\sigma_t)}\right)\left(\sum_{t=1}^{T} \frac{\hat{\xi}_{t-1}^2}{\hat{\sigma}_n(\sigma_t)}\right),$$

$$SS_{\hat{\xi}_{t-1}^2 \hat{\xi}_{t-1}^2} = \left(\sum_{t=1}^{T} \frac{1}{\hat{\sigma}_n(\sigma_t)}\right)\left(\sum_{t=1}^{T} \frac{\hat{\xi}_{t-1}^4}{\hat{\sigma}_n(\sigma_t)}\right) - \left(\sum_{t=1}^{T} \frac{\hat{\xi}_{t-1}^2}{\hat{\sigma}_n(\sigma_t)}\right)^2,$$

$$SS_{\hat{\sigma}_t^2 \hat{\sigma}_{t-1}^2} = \left(\sum_{t=1}^{T} \frac{1}{\hat{\sigma}_n(\sigma_t)}\right) \sum_{t=1}^{T} \frac{\hat{\sigma}_t^2 \hat{\sigma}_{t-1}^2}{\hat{\sigma}_n(\sigma_t)} - \sum_{t=1}^{T} \frac{\hat{\sigma}_t^2}{\hat{\sigma}_n(\sigma_t)} \sum_{t=1}^{T} \frac{\hat{\sigma}_{t-1}^2}{\hat{\sigma}_n(\sigma_t)},$$

$$SS_{\hat{\sigma}_{t-1}^2 \hat{\sigma}_{t-1}^2} = \left(\sum_{t=1}^{T} \frac{1}{\hat{\sigma}_n(\sigma_t)}\right)\left(\sum_{t=1}^{T} \frac{\hat{\sigma}_{t-1}^4}{\hat{\sigma}_n(\sigma_t)}\right) - \left(\sum_{t=1}^{T} \frac{\hat{\sigma}_{t-1}^2}{\hat{\sigma}_n(\sigma_t)}\right)^2.$$

	μ	α_0	α_1	β_1	μ	α_0	α_1	β_1
True	0.15	0.65	0.87	0.10	0.20	0.41	0.88	0.08
QL	0.149	0.779	0.865	0.074	0.199	0.461	0.912	0.057
	0.040	0.353	0.011	0.029	0.031	0.155	0.033	0.025
AQL	0.150	0.661	0.851	0.092	0.209	0.405	0.901	0.076
	0.001	0.012	0.019	0.009	0.010	0.006	0.021	0.004
True	−0.10	0.48	0.89	0.08	0.16	0.37	0.9	0.08
QL	−0.101	0.556	0.902	0.058	0.159	0.434	0.922	0.058
	0.034	0.212	0.014	0.024	0.030	0.189	0.024	0.025
AQL	−0.110	0.486	0.891	0.0752	0.161	0.374	0.911	0.076
	0.010	0.006	0.001	0.005	0.001	0.004	0.011	0.004
True	0.18	0.39	0.88	0.08	0.09	0.50	0.89	0.05
QL	0.179	0.447	0.892	0.058	0.089	0.538	0.898	0.036
	0.031	0.146	0.015	0.024	0.033	0.090	0.009	0.015
AQL	0.180	0.395	0.882	0.076	0.091	0.504	0.892	0.046
	0.001	0.005	0.002	0.005	0.002	0.004	0.002	0.004

Table 4.
The QL and AQL estimates and the RMSE of each estimate is stated below that estimate for GARCH model.

The estimation procedure will be iteratively repeated until it converges.

For each parameter setting, T = 500 observations are simulated from the true model. We then replicate the experiment for 1000 times to obtain the mean and root mean squared errors (RMSE) for $\hat{\alpha}_0$, $\hat{\alpha}_1$, $\hat{\beta}_1$, and $\hat{\mu}$. In **Table 4**, QL denotes the QL estimate and AQL denotes the AQL estimate.

We generated N = 1000 independent random samples of size T = 20, 40, 60, 80, and 100 from GARCH(1,1) model. In **Table 5**, The QL and AQL estimation methods show the property of consistency, and the RMSE decreases as the sample size increases.

4.4 Empirical applications

The second set of data is the weekly price changes of crude oil prices P_t. The P_t of Cushing, OK, West Texas Intermediate (US dollars per barrel) is considered for the period from 7/1/2000 to 10/6/2016, with 858 observations in total. The data are transformed into rates of change by taking the first difference of the logs. Thus, $y_t = log\,(P_t) - log\,(P_{t-1})$ and fit $\{y_t\}$ by using GARCH (1,1):

$$y_t = \mu + \xi_t, \qquad t = 1, 2, 3, \cdots, T. \tag{52}$$

and

$$\sigma_t^2 = \alpha_0 + \alpha_1 \xi_{t-1}^2 + \beta_1 \sigma_{t-1} + \zeta_t, \qquad t = 1, 2, 3, \cdots, T. \tag{53}$$

ξ_t are i.i.d with $E(\xi_t) = 0$ and $V(\xi_t) = \sigma_t^2$; and ζ_t are i.i.d with $E(\zeta_t) = 0$ and $V(\zeta_t) = \sigma_\zeta^2$.

The estimation of unknown parameters, $(\alpha_0, \alpha_1, \beta_1, \mu)$, using QL and AQL are given in **Table 6**. Conclusion can be drawn based on the standardized residuals

		μ	α_0	α_1	β_1	μ	α_0	α_1	β_1
	True	0.16	0.37	0.90	0.08	−0.10	0.48	0.89	0.08
	QL	0.17	0.42	0.89	0.07	−0.09	0.51	0.90	0.06
T = 20		0.176	0.511	0.008	0.016	0.169	0.451	0.018	0.022
	AQL	0.16	0.38	0.89	0.07	−0.10	0.47	0.90	0.07
		0.037	0.012	0.007	0.014	0.066	0.014	0.013	0.018
	QL	0.16	0.42	0.89	0.07	−0.09	0.51	0.91	0.06
		0.149	0.422	0.007	0.016	0.137	0.326	0.018	0.021
T = 40	AQL	0.16	0.38	0.89	0.07	−0.10	0.47	0.90	0.07
		0.027	0.012	0.007	0.013	0.022	0.014	0.012	0.016
	QL	0.16	0.42	0.89	0.07	−0.09	0.52	0.91	0.06
		0.121	0.289	0.007	0.018	0.119	0.307	0.018	0.021
T = 60	AQL	0.16	0.38	0.89	0.07	−0.10	0.47	0.90	0.07
		0.019	0.012	0.007	0.011	0.014	0.013	0.012	0.015
	QL	0.16	0.42	0.89	0.07	−0.10	0.51	0.90	0.06
		0.100	0.159	0.007	0.017	0.108	0.248	0.018	0.021
T = 80	AQL	0.16	0.38	0.89	0.07	−0.10	0.47	0.90	0.07
		0.012	0.012	0.007	0.011	0.012	0.013	0.012	0.015
	QL	0.16	0.42	0.89	0.07	−0.10	0.51	0.90	0.06
		0.100	0.159	0.007	0.018	0.101	0.242	0.018	0.021
T = 100	AQL	0.16	0.38	0.89	0.07	−0.10	0.47	0.90	0.07
		0.012	0.011	0.007	0.011	0.011	0.013	0.012	0.015

Table 5.
The QL and AQL estimates and the RMSE of each estimate is stated below that estimate for GARCH model with different sample size.

	$\hat{\mu}_0$	$\hat{\alpha}_0$	$\hat{\alpha}_1$	$\hat{\beta}_1$	$\frac{\bar{\hat{\xi}}_t}{S.d(\hat{\xi}_t)}$
QL	0.0008	0.566	0.912	0.0004	0.002
AQL	0.0089	0.630	0.972	0.041	0.185

Table 6.
Estimation of $\mu, \alpha_0, \alpha_1, \beta_1$ for the rates of change prices data.

from the fourth column in **Table 6**, which favors the QL method and gives smaller standardized residuals, better than AQL method.

5. Conclusions

In this chapter, two alternative approaches, QL and AQL, have been developed to estimate the parameters in ARCH and GARCH models. Parameter estimation for ARCH and GARCH models, which include nonlinear and non-Gaussian models is given. The estimations of unknown parameters are considered without any distribution assumptions concerning the processes involved, and the estimation is based on different scenarios in which the conditional covariance of the error's terms are assumed to be known or unknown. Simulation studies and empirical analysis show that our proposed estimation methods work reasonably quite well for parameter estimation of ARCH and GARCH models. It will provide a robust tool for obtaining an optimal point estimate of parameters in heteroscedastic models like ARCH and GARCH models.

This chapter focuses on models in univariate, while it is desirable to consider multivariate extensions of the proposed models.

Acknowledgements

The author would like to acknowledge the helpful comments and suggestion of the editor. This study is conducted in the King Faisal University, Saudi Arabia, during the sabbatical year of the author from the Al Balqa Applied University, Jordan.

Author details

Raed Alzghool[1,2]

1 Department of Mathematics, Faculty of Science, Al-Balqa Applied University, Salt, Jordan

2 Department of Quantitative Methods, School of Business, King Faisal University, Al-Ahsa, Saudi Arabia

*Address all correspondence to: raedalzghool@bau.edu.jo; ralzghool@kfu.edu.sa

References

[1] Engle RF. Autoregressive conditional heteroskedasticity with estimates of the variance of U.K. inflation. Econometrica. 1982;**50**:987-1008

[2] Engle RF. GARCH 101: The use of ARCH/GARCH models in applied econometrics. The Journal of Economic Perspectives. 2001;**15**:157-168

[3] Bollerslev T, Chou RY, Kroner KF. ARCH modeling in finance: A selective review of the theory and empirical evidence. Journal of Econometrics. 1992; **52**:5-59

[4] Bera A, Higgins M. ARCH models: Properties, estimation and testing. Journal of Economic Surveys. 1993;**7**: 305-366

[5] Bollerslev T, Engle RF, Nelson DB, Models ARCH. In: Engle RF, McFadden D, editors. Handbook of Econometrics. Vol. 4. Amsterdam: North-Holland; 1994. pp. 2959-3038

[6] Diebold F, Lopez J. Modeling volatility dynamics. In: Hoover K, editor. Macroeconometrics: Developments, Tensions and Prospects. Boston: Kluwer Academic Press; 1995. pp. 427-472

[7] Pagan A. The econometrics of financial markets. Journal of Empirical Finance. 1996;**3**:15-102

[8] Palm F. GARCH models of volatility. In: Rao CR, Maddala GS, editors. Handbook of Statistics. Vol. 14. Amsterdam: North-Holland; 1996. pp. 209-240

[9] Shephard N. Statistical aspects of ARCH and stochastic volatility models. In: Cox DR, Hinkley DV, Barndorff-Nielsen OE, editors. Time Series Models in Econometrics, Finance and Other Fields. London: Chapman Hall; 1996. pp. 1-67

[10] Andersen T, Bollerslev T. ARCH and GARCH models. In: Kotz S, Read CB, Banks DL, editors. Encyclopedia of Statistical Sciences. Vol. 2. New York: John Wiley and Sons; 1998

[11] Engle R, Patton A. What good is a volatility model? Quantitative Finance. 2001;**1**:237-245

[12] Degiannakis S, Xekalaki E. Autoregressive conditional heteroscedasticity (arch) models: A review. Quality Technology and Quantitative Management. 2004;**1**: 271-324

[13] Diebold F. The Nobel memorial prize for Robert F. Engle. The Scandinavian Journal of Economics. 2004;**106**:165-185

[14] Andersen T, Diebold F. Volatility and correlation forecasting. In: Granger CWJ, Elliott G, Timmermann A, editors. Handbook of Economic Forecasting. Amsterdam: North-Holland; 2006. pp. 777-878

[15] Engle RF, Gonzalez-Rivera G. Semiparametric ARCH models. Journal of Business & Economic Statistics. 1991; **9**(4):345-359

[16] Li DX, Turtle HJ. Semiparametric ARCH models: An estimating function approach. Journal of Business & Economic Statistics. 2000;**18**(2):174-186

[17] Linton O, Mammen E. Estimating semiparametric ARCH models by kernel smoothing methods. Econometrica. 2005;**73**(3):771-836

[18] Linton OB. Semiparametric and nonparametric ARCH modeling. In: Handbook of Financial Time Series. Berlin Heidelberg: Springer; 2009. pp. 157-167

[19] Su L, Ullah A, Mishra S. Nonparametric and semiparametric

volatility models: Specification, estimation, and testing. In: Handbook of Volatility Models and Their Applications. Hoboken, New Jersey, USA: John Wiley Sons, Inc.; 2012. pp. 269-291

[20] Alexander C. Market Models: A Guide to Financial Data Analysis. Chichester, UK: John Wiley and Sons, Ltd.; 2001

[21] Alzghool R. Estimation for state space models: Quasi-likelihood and asymptotic quasi-likelihood approaches [Ph.D. thesis]. Australia: School of Mathematics and Applied Statistics, University of Wollongong; 2008

[22] Enders W. Applied Econometric Time Series. Hoboken, NJ: John Wiley and Sons, Inc.; 2004

[23] Taylor S. Asset Price Dynamics and Prediction. Princeton, NJ: Princeton University Press; 2004

[24] Bollerslev T. Generalized autoregressive conditional heteroscedasticity. Journal of Econometrics. 1986;**31**(3):307-327

[25] Hedye CC. Quasi-Likelihood and Its Application: A General Approach to Optimal Parameter Estimation. New York: Springer; 1997

[26] Lin Y-X. A new kind of asymptotic quasi-score estimating function. Scandinavian Journal of Statistics. 2000; **27**:97-109

[27] Hardle W. Applied Nonparametric Regression. Cambridge: Cambridge University Press; 1991

[28] Alzghool R, Lin Y-X. Asymptotic Quasi-Likelihood Based on Kernel Smoothing for Nonlinear and Non-Gaussian State-Space Models. Lecture Notes in Engineering and Computer Science. London, UK: ICCSDE; 2007. pp. 926-932

[29] Alzghool R, Lin Y-X. Parameters estimation for SSMs: QL and AQL approaches. IAENG International Journal of Applied Mathematics. 2008; **38**:34-43

[30] Alzghool R, Lin Y-X, Chen SX. Asymptotic quasi-likelihood based on kernel smoothing for multivariate heteroskedastic models with correlation. American Journal of Mathematical and Management Sciences. 2010;**30**(1&2): 147-177

[31] Alzghool R. Estimation for stochastic volatility model: Quasi-likelihood and asymptotic quasi-likelihood approaches. Journal of King Saud University-Science. 2017;**29**: 114-118

[32] Alzghool R. Parameters estimation for GARCH (p,q) model: QL and AQL approaches. Electronic Journal of Applied Statistical Analysis (EJASA). 2017;**10**(1):180-193

[33] Alzghool R, Al-Zubi LM. Semi-parametric estimation for ARCH models. Alexandria Engineering Journal. 2018;**57**:367-373

[34] Alzghool R, Lin Y-X. Initial values in estimation procedures for state space models (SSMs). In: Proceedings of World Congress on Engineering, WCE 2011; London, UK: Newswood Limited; 2011

[35] Zivot E, Wang J. Modeling Financial Time Series with S-PLUS. New York: Springer; 2006

Chapter 6

IPO ETFs: An Alternative Way to Enter the Initial Public Offering Business

Gerasimos G. Rompotis

Abstract

This chapter focuses on the initial public offerings (IPO) ETFs, which constitute an alternative way to enter the IPO business. Short- and long-term performance of ETFs is examined vis-a-vis the performance of major market indices. Three types of returns are computed; the absolute, benchmark-adjusted, and abnormal return. Returns are computed for the initial trading day and for the first 2, 3, 4, 5, 21, and 63 trading days. Long-run returns are also calculated for the first 6, 12, 18, and 24 months of trading and for the entire history of ETFs up to October 31, 2016 from a cumulative and a buy-and-hold perspective. Risk-adjusted returns are estimated with a six-factor model. The results indicate that the average first-day return is positive but below 1%. In the long run, the cumulative absolute returns are positive during the several intervals examined, whereas the cumulative benchmark-adjusted and abnormal returns are positive only for the first 6 months of trading. These returns become negative after the first 6 months. Going further, ETFs deliver significant buy-and-hold returns over the several periods examined. Finally, the results reveal that just one out of the four IPO ETFs examined can produce a robust and statistically significant alpha.

Keywords: initial public offerings, Exchange Traded Funds, performance, risk-adjusted returns

1. Introduction

Initial public offerings (IPOs) business has diachronically been of great interest to the investing community worldwide as investors deem IPOs as a great opportunity for significant short-term and possibly long-term gains. In addition, tens of tens of academic articles have been written on this field. The main finding of the literature is that IPOs are usually underpriced as depicted in their initial returns, which are significantly positive, either in absolute terms or when compared to corresponding non-IPO stocks or relevant market indices. Underpricing refers to the significantly low offer price of IPOs relative to the close price of stocks on their first trading day. On the contrary, when long-run returns are assessed, the academic research has shown that IPOs tend to underperform their reference portfolios.

This chapter focuses on IPO Exchange Traded Funds (IPO ETFs), which constitute an alternative vehicle for investors to enter the IPO business. An IPO ETF is an exchange traded fund that focuses on stocks of companies that have recently held an initial public offering. IPO ETFs are appealing to investors because they provide them with an inexpensive and flexible tool to invest in a large pool of initial public offerings. On the contrary, investing in such a large number of IPOs individually would not be practically feasible due to the high cost of such a strategy. In addition, IPO ETFs enable robust diversification strategies against the highly volatile IPO market.

The origins of IPO ETFs go back to April 2006, when the First Trust US Equity Opportunities ETF was launched on the New York Stock Exchange (NYSE). The Renaissance IPO ETF came to the surface about 7 years later in October 2013. The Renaissance International IPO ETF followed 1 year later. The last entry in the IPO ETF market was the First Trust International IPO ETF. This fund began trading in November 2014.

In this chapter, we examine the short- and the long-term performance of IPO ETFs. In particular, we compute the absolute, benchmark-adjusted, and abnormal returns of ETFs. Abnormal returns are obtained with the usage of the market model successively against the S&P 500 Index and the S&P 600 Small Cap Index. These indices also serve as benchmarks when we calculate the benchmark-adjusted returns of ETFs. Moreover, in the short-run, returns are computed for the first trading day as well as for the first 2, 3, 4, 5, 21, and 63 trading days. At the long run, cumulative absolute, benchmark-adjusted, and abnormal returns are calculated over the first 6, 12, 18, and 24 months of trading and for the entire trading history of each ETF up to October 31, 2016. Respective buy-and-hold returns are computed too. Furthermore, risk-adjusted returns are estimated with the usage of a six-factor model, which follows the Fama and French multivariate model. Finally, a market trend analysis is performed. This analysis assesses the pricing behavior of IPO ETFs during the descending and the upward phases of the overall stock market.

The results show that IPO ETFs provide slightly positive average first-day returns given that the average initial return is positive but well below 1%. Going further, the average absolute return of IPO ETFs is positive over the first five trading days, but it is negative over the first 21 and 63 days of trading. Benchmark-adjusted returns are also positive up to 5 days when the S&P 500 Index is taken into consideration, but they are rather negative when the S&P 600 Small Cap Index is assessed. Finally, average abnormal returns are negative after the initial day of trading.

With respect to ETF long-term performance, results reveal positive cumulative absolute returns over the various periods considered, whereas the cumulative benchmark-adjusted and abnormal returns are positive only for the first 6 months of trading with the majority of returns becoming negative over the next time periods examined. In the case of buy-and-hold returns, results indicate that ETFs produce significant such returns in the long run, either when the absolute or the benchmark-adjusted returns are assessed. As far as risk-adjusted return is concerned, the regression analysis shows that just one out of the four IPO ETFs examined can produce robust and statistically significant excess return relative to market performance.

In the last step, the market trend analysis reveals that when the stock market goes down, the absolute return of IPO ETFs goes down too on about 76% of negative trading days. When market goes up, IPO ETFs go up to in a rate of about 63% of positive trading days. The opposite behavior is displayed by the benchmark-adjusted return of ETFs. This means that when the market goes down, the benchmark-adjusted returns of ETFs moves upward in a rate of about 68% of days and when market returns increase, the benchmark-adjusted performance of ETFs declines in a rate of about 65% of days. A similar one to benchmark-adjusted return's behavior is the case for abnormal returns.

To the best of our knowledge, this is the first study on IPO ETFs. Given the convenience of trading with ETFs, the low cost of investing in such products, the high liquidity of the ETF market in general and the great interest of investors and researchers in IPOs, our study should be highly welcome by the investing community and researchers. In addition, the positive initial returns and, even more importantly, the significant buy-and-hold returns revealed by our study should help investors plot profitable trading strategies. Finally, the results of the market trend performance analysis could also help investors implement strategies with mighty potential of substantial gains.

The remainder of this chapter is structured as follows. Next section provides a brief literature review on IPOs performance in the United States and other international markets. Section 3 develops the methodology used in our empirical investigation. Section 4 describes the data used in this study and provides information about the trading features of the sample's ETFs. The empirical findings of our research are presented in Section 5 and the conclusions are discussed in Section 6.

2. Literature review

Given the lack of any research papers on IPO ETFs, we will provide a brief review of the main findings of the literature concerning the short- and long-run performance of IPOs worldwide.

A plethora of papers have examined the performance of IPOs using data from the United States. In early years, several studies, such as [1–7], have accentuated that IPOs are underpriced as can be inferred by the returns on their first trading days, which are significantly positive. In the same concept, [8] estimate that during 1990–1998, US IPOs left over $27 billion of money on the table, where the money left on the table is defined as the price gain of the first trading day times the number of shares sold. The money left on the table is translated into significant underpricing of IPOs during the nineties. Furthermore, [9] report that in the 1980s, the average initial return on IPOs was 7%, whereas the average first-day IPO return doubled to almost 15% during the period 1990–1998, before jumping to 65% during the internet bubble years of 1999–2000. Finally, [10] shows that, after the bubble of 1999–2000, the average initial return of IPOs in the US over the first decade of the new century was moving around 10%.

The short-run performance of IPOs in other developed and emerging markets has attracted the interest of researchers. Loughran et al. [11] show that the move by most East Asian countries to reduce regulatory interference in the setting of offering prices resulted in less short-run underpricing in the 1990s than in the 1980s. Ritter [10] shows that in China, the second largest economy of the world, underpricing of IPOs has been severe with initial returns amounting to up to 200%. However, over the recent years, IPO underpricing in China has started to decline as a result of the changing institutional constraints. The great underpricing of Chinese IPOs is also supported by the findings of [12, 13]. In Australia, Lee et al. [14] report strong first-day returns. Significant underpricing of IPOs is reported for Canada by [15] IPOs are underpriced in Japan too as evidenced by [16]. In the UK, Levis [17] has documented a significant underpricing of the companies going public in the British stock market. The same pattern has been revealed by [18] for Italy and [19] for France. More or less, IPO underpricing is a global phenomenon. To testify this assertion, Loughran et al. [20] report comprehensive statistical evidence of strong first-day IPO returns for a sample of 52 developed and emerging capital markets, which range from 3.3% in Russia to 239.8% in Saudi Arabia.

When it comes to the long-run performance of IPOs in the United States, the main conclusion of the literature is that that the stocks of companies going public tend to be overpriced in the long run. Overpricing is depicted in the underperformance of IPOs versus similar non-IPO stocks or relevant market indices. In this respect, Ibbotson

[21] provides evidence that the initial returns and the long-run performance of IPOs were negatively related during the period 1960–1969. Ritter [7] finds that IPO stocks significantly underperform a set of comparable companies over the 3 years after going public. Rajan and Servaes [22] reveal that over a 5-year period after going public, companies' underperformance relative to the market benchmarks ranges from 17% to 47.1%. Carter et al. [23] estimate an average underperformance of US IPOs over a three-year period after the initial offering of 19.92%. Gompers and Lerner [24] examine the performance for up to 5 years after listing of nearly 3661 IPOs in the US during the period 1935–1972 and find some evidence of underperformance when event time buy-and-hold abnormal returns are used but underperformance disappears when cumulative abnormal returns are utilized.

Outside the United Sates, in Australia, How et al. [25] compare the long-run performance of companies going public that payed a dividend and similarly matched firms, which did not pay a dividend revealing strong evidence that the paying firms perform significantly better than the nonpaying firms for a period up to 5 years after the dividend initiation date. Moshirian et al. [26] indicate that in China, Hong Kong, Japan, Korea, Malaysia, and Singapore, whilst there is initial underpricing in Asian IPOs, the existence of long-run underperformance depends on the methodology used. In Japan, Kirkulak [27] reports a three-year underperformance of −18.3% for the stocks listed between 1998 and 2001. In Canada, Kooli and Suret [28] find that investors who buy stocks immediately after their listing and hold these shares for a period of 3 years will incur a loss of about 20%. When a five-year buy-and-hold strategy is considered, underperformance amounts to −26.5%. In the United Kingdom, a number of studies such as those of [17, 29–31] have documented the existence of IPOs' long-run overpricing. Other studies on European IPOs, such as those of [32–34] for Germany, [35] for Austria, [36] for Spain, [18] for Italy, and [37] for France, also reveal significant long-run overpricing of IPOs. Overpricing is evidenced by their poor long-term performance compared to the performance of relevant market indices or reference stock portfolios. Based on these findings, IPOs would not be suitable for long-term buy-and-hold trading strategies.

3. Methodology

3.1 Short-term return analysis

In this section, we assess the short-term performance of IPO ETFs. In this respect, we compute the first day or initial return of ETFs. The first-day return does not necessarily refer to the return on the launch day of ETFs but refers to the return on the first trading day with no-zero volume because an ETF may have started actual trading on the days that followed its listing on the stock exchange.

Three alternative types of initial returns are computed. The first one refers to the absolute return of ETFs, which, based on [38], is defined as the gain or the loss on a portfolio achieved over a certain period without being compared to a reference portfolio or another benchmark. First-day absolute return is computed in percentage terms using the following formula:

$$IAR_{i,t=1} = \frac{CTP_{i,t=1} - OPEN_{i,t=1}}{OPEN_{i,t=1}} \tag{1}$$

where $IAR_{i,t=1}$ refers to the percentage absolute return of the *i*th ETF on its first trading day, $CTP_{i,t=1}$ refers to the close trade price of the ETF on its first trading day and $OPEN_{i,t=1}$ refers to the open trade price of this ETF on the same day.

The second type of initial return computed is the benchmark-adjusted return of ETFs, which, following [7], is computed as the difference between the initial absolute return of the *i*th ETF and the corresponding return of the benchmark. The first-day benchmark-adjusted return of ETFs is shown in the following formula:

$$\mathrm{BAIR}_{i,t=1} = \mathrm{IR}_{i,t=1} - \mathrm{BR}_{t=1} \tag{2}$$

where $\mathrm{BAIR}_{i,t=1}$ refers to percentage benchmark-adjusted return of the *i*th ETF on its first trading day, $\mathrm{IR}_{i,t=1}$ is defined as above and $\mathrm{BR}_{t=1}$ concerns the return of the market index on ETF's first trading day.

In our estimations of benchmark-adjusted returns, we employ two alternative stock indices to serve as benchmarks. The first one is the S&P 500 Index, which consists of the 500 largest companies in terms of market capitalization listed on the NYSE or NASDAQ. The second benchmark used is the S&P 600 Small Cap Index, which covers the small-cap range of US stocks. According to [39], indices that consist mostly of small cap companies are better benchmarks when assessing the performance of smaller stocks or portfolios. The S&P 600 Small Cap Index is used because the ETFs that have been selected to be studied are rather small-cap ETFs and, consequently, a small-cap index may be a more appropriate benchmark.[1]

In order to calculate the return of the index, which will correspond to ETF's first-day return, we use formula (1) for indices too. This means that given that the trading history of the selected benchmarks is much longer than the history of the sample's ETFs, we calculate the return of indices on ETF's first trading day by subtracting the open price of the index on the day which relates to ETF's first trading day from its close price on the same day and we divide by the open price.

The third type of initial return estimated is the abnormal return obtained with the usage of the market model. In order to estimate abnormal returns of ETFs, we follow the approach of [40]. More specifically, so as to estimate the abnormal returns of ETFs, we first need to estimate the time series market model expressed in Eq. (3), via which the return of ETFs is successively regressed on the return of the selected market indices:

$$R_i = \alpha_i + \beta_i R_m + \varepsilon_i \tag{3}$$

where R_i stands for the daily return of the *i*th ETF, R_m represents the return of the market index, namely the return of the S&P 500 Index or the S&P 600 Small Cap Index. We estimate market model to obtain the alpha and beta coefficients of each ETF, which we will then use to compute abnormal returns with the following model:

---

[1] As we will explain in a following section, each IPO ETF has its own benchmark and, thus, one could wonder why we do not use each ETF's own benchmark to estimate their benchmark-adjusted performance. We do not do so, for two reasons. The first one is that the majority of ETFs worldwide and IPO ETFs in particular are passively managed and, thus, the tracking error of these funds, that is the difference in returns between ETFs and underlying indices, is expected to be low. (We will see in **Table 1** that the tracking error of the sample's ETFs is indeed low.) Therefore, a new ETF's price will also generally remain in line with the price of the underlying basket of securities and an "underpricing" pattern like that observed in IPOs of ordinary stocks is not expected to be the case. The second reason is that we try to identify whether IPO ETFs can be an alternative investing tool of investors seeking returns, which will be better than the average market returns, with the market returns being usually represented by indices such as the two used in our analysis.

$$AR_{i,t=1} = R_{i,t=1} - \hat{\alpha}_i - \hat{\beta}_i R_{m,t=1} \quad (4)$$

where $AR_{i,t=1}$ is the abnormal return of the *ith* ETF on the first trading day, computed as the difference between the actual absolute return of ETF and the expected return based on the market model on the first trading day, $\hat{\alpha}_i$ and $\hat{\beta}_i$ are the parameters obtained from the market model. The estimation window of Eq. (4) covers the entire trading history of each ETF up to October 31, 2016.

After calculating the three types of ETFs' initial return, we then compute the average short-term returns of longer periods. More specifically, we compute the average daily returns of ETFs over the first 2, 3, 4, 5, 21 (i.e., 1 month), and 63 (i.e., 3 months) of trading. Similarly to the initial returns, we first calculate the absolute return of each ETF as follows:

$$AR_{i,t} = \frac{CTP_{i,t} - CTP_{i,t-1}}{CTP_{i,t-1}} \quad (5)$$

where $AR_{i,t}$ refers to percentage absolute return of the ith ETF on day t and $CTP_{i,t}$ refers to the close trade price of the ETF on the same day. Afterward, we estimate the benchmark-adjusted and abnormal returns of ETFs using the framework described in formulas (2), (3) and (4) above.

3.2 Long-term return analysis

The long-run performance of IPO ETFs is assessed in this section. Two types of long-run performance measures are employed in the analysis; cumulative average returns and buy-and-hold returns. The cumulative average return is calculated as in [41]. More specifically, we calculate the average daily return of each ETF for each calendar month during its entire trading history excluding the launch month of ETF and starting from the month that follows the initial trading of the fund. Following [30], we do so to allow for the possibility of price support in the first few trading days. The cumulative average return starting on the first trading day of the month following the listing of the *ith* ETF and extending to T months after the listing is the summation of the average returns in each month:

$$CAR_i = \sum_{t=2}^{T} AMR_t \quad (6)$$

where CAR_i refers to the cumulative average return of the ith ETF and AMR_t is the average daily return of the fund in month t.

We note that we calculate three alternative types of cumulative returns, which are the cumulative absolute return, the cumulative benchmark-adjusted return and the cumulative abnormal return following the framework described in the previous section. Again, two benchmarks are used; the S&P 500 Index and the S&P 600 Small Cap Index. Moreover, we compute cumulative returns over the first 6 months (i.e., 126 trading days), 12 months (i.e., 252 trading days), 18 months (i.e., 378 trading days), and 24 months (i.e., 504 trading days) of the trading history of each ETF as well as over its entire trading history up to October 31, 2016.

In order to calculate the buy-and-hold return of ETFs, we assume that an investor buys ETF shares on their listing day and holds them up to a specific time interval, which, in our case, ranges from 6 months to the entire trading history of each ETF (as above). The buy-and-hold return is estimated in percentage terms using a formula similar to formula (5). The key difference between the two calculations concerns the estimation window. This means that, for instance, in the case of the first 6-month period, buy-and-hold return is computed by considering the percentage difference in the close trade prices of the *i*th ETF between the first and the 126th trading day after the month of ETF's listing on the stock exchange, in the case of the 12-month period, buy-and-hold return is computed by considering the percentage difference in the close trade price of the *i*th ETF between the first and the 252nd trading day after the month of ETF's listing, and so on. A last note is that, similarly to cumulative returns, we estimate the buy-and-hold return in its absolute, benchmark-adjusted and abnormal forms.

3.3 Risk-adjusted performance analysis

The risk-adjusted performance of IPO ETFs is evaluated in this section with the usage of an augmented Fama and French model. This model is based on the model developed by [42] to which the [43] Momentum factor, a Conservative Minus Aggressive factor and a Robust Minus Weak factor have been added. The model is shown in Eq. (7):

$$R_i - R_f = \alpha_i + \beta_{1,i}(R_m - R_f) + \beta_{2,i}SMB + \beta_{3,i}HML + \beta_{4,i}UMD + \beta_{5,i}CMA + \beta_{6,i}RMW + \varepsilon_i \tag{7}$$

where R_i and R_m are defined as above, R_f is the risk-free rate expressed by the 1-month US Treasury bill rate, SMB (Small Minus Big) is the average return on nine small cap portfolios minus the average return on nine big cap portfolios, HML (high minus low) is the average return on two value portfolios (in book-to-market equity terms) minus the average return on two growth portfolios, UMD is the average of the returns on two (big and small) high prior return portfolios minus the average of the returns on two low prior return portfolios,[2] CMA (Conservative Minus Aggressive) is the average return on two conservative portfolios minus the average return on two aggressive portfolios and RMW (Robust Minus Weak) is the average return on two robust operating profitability portfolios minus the average return on 2-weak operating profitability portfolios.[3]

In the [42] model, the size effect implies that small cap firms exhibit returns that are superior to those of large firms. Theoretical explanations for the small size effect suggest that the stocks of small firms are less liquid and trading in them generates greater transaction costs; there is also less information available on small companies and, thus, the monitoring cost of a portfolio with small stocks is generally greater than the cost of a portfolio of large firms.

The book-to-market equity ratio effect captured by the HML factor implies that the average returns on stocks with a high book-value to market-value equity ratio must be greater than the returns on stocks with a low book-value to market-value equity ratio. The high book-value firms are considered to be underpriced by the market and, therefore, they constitute appealing buy-and-hold targets, as their

---

[2] Big means that a firm is above the median market cap on the NYSE at the end of the previous day while small firms are below the median NYSE market cap.

[3] The historical daily data of the risk-free rate, the Fama and French three factors, the Carhart momentum factor, the robust minus weak factor and the conservative minus aggressive factor are available on the website of Kenneth French (http://mba.tuck.dartmouth.edu/pages/faculty/ken.french/data_library.html).

price is expected to rise later. This anomaly undermines the semi-strong form efficiency of the stock market.

The existence of momentum in asset prices is an anomaly which has not been explained sufficiently by the finance theory. The difficulty in explaining the momentum anomaly is that, as the efficient capital markets theory suggests, an increase in the price of an asset cannot be indicative of a further increase in future prices. Behavioral finance has offered some possible explanations to the existence of the momentum anomaly. In particular, investors are assumed to be irrational and, consequently, they underreact to the release of new information failing to incorporate new information in the prices of their transactions.

The Conservative Minus Aggressive and Robust Minus Weak factors correspond to the [44] investment and operating profitability factors. [44] use past investment as a proxy for the expected future investment and, based on valuation theory, they suggest that CMA implies a negative relation between the expected investment and the expected internal rate of return. Furthermore, based on the findings of [44], a negative loading is expected for the RMW factor, that is, the excess return of IPO ETFs must be affected by the profitability factor in a negative fashion.

The usage of Eq. (7) aims at capturing the market elements that can affect the performance of IPO ETFs and considering whether these funds can produce any meaningful above market returns, which will be represented by a positive and statistically significant alpha. With respect to the latter, [44] assert that if an asset pricing model fully captures expected returns, the intercept of the model should be indistinguishable from zero in a regression of an asset's excess return on the factor returns of the model.

The model is successively run for six different time periods. The first period concerns the first 21 trading days of each ETF excluding the month in which the ETF began trading on the exchange. We do so as we did when we estimated the long-run performance of ETFs above to allow for the possibility of price support in the first few trading days. This month is also excluded from all the other time intervals over which Eq. (7) is applied.

The second interval assessed concerns the first 63 trading days of each ETF. The third period examined regards the first 6 months of trading, that is, the first 126 trading days of each fund. The next period taken into consideration covers the first 12 months of trading data. In our analysis, the intervals ranging up to 1 year can be considered as a short-term investment horizon. Looking for more long run, we run the model for a period covering the first 18 and the first 24 months of each ETF's trading records. Finally, we run Eq. (7) over the entire history of each ETF so as to define the overall buy-and-hold risk-adjusted performance of ETFs.

3.4 Market trend return analysis

In the last step, we perform a "market trend" analysis of IPO ETF returns by examining how the return of ETFs responds to the decreasing or increasing swings of the overall stock market as the latter is alternatively represented by the S&P 500 Index and the S&P 600 Small Cap Index.

In our analysis, we first sort the daily returns of benchmark and then compute the number and portion of daily returns of each ETF that are negative or equal to zero and the number and portion of positive ETF daily returns during the descending path and during the ascending path of the stock market. If ETFs follow the market closely, they are expected to decline when the market declines and vice versa. Similarly to the short- and long-term performance analysis in the previous sections, we use three alternative types of returns, which are the absolute, benchmark-adjusted and abnormal return.

4. The sample

The sample of the study includes the four IPO ETFs available in the US capital market. **Table 1** presents the profiles of ETFs. Presented in the table are the ticker, name of each ETF, name of tracking index, inception date, age in years, expense ratio, average daily volume in number of traded shares, and the historical tracking error of ETFs, which is the difference in returns between ETF and benchmark based on information on historical performance of ETFs before taxes and benchmark returns from each ETF's inception up to December 31, 2015. The information on ETFs' ticker, name, benchmark, inception date, and expense ratio as well as on the historical performance of ETFs and underlying indices has been found on the websites of ETFs' managing companies.

Moreover, **Table 1** reports the trading frequency of ETFs that is calculated as the fraction of trading days with nonzero volume to the total trading history (in days) for each fund, the average intraday volatility computed as the percentage fraction of the highest minus the lowest trade price of each fund on day t to its close trade price on the same day, and the fraction of each ETF's intraday volatility to the intraday volatility of the S&P 500 Index and the S&P 600 Small Cap Index, respectively. The last ratios help assessing whether IPO ETFs are more volatile than the market or not. The time series of daily volumes, open, high, low, and close prices of ETFs and the S&P 500 Index have been found on the website of NASDAQ. The historical data of the S&P 600 Small Cap Index have been obtained from Yahoo! Finance.

Regarding the underlying assets of ETFs, we note that the first fund tracks the Renaissance US IPO Index, which reflects approximately the top 80% of newly public firms based on full market capitalization. The second ETF follows the Renaissance International IPO Index, which is a portfolio of the top 80% non-US-listed newly public companies, prior to their inclusion in global core equity portfolios. The third ETF seeks to replicate the return of the IPOX®-100 US Index. This index measures the performance of the top 100 largest, typically best performing and most liquid US IPOs during their first 1000 trading days. The last IPO ETF examined tracks the IPOX International Index, which measures the performance of the 50 largest and typically most liquid companies domiciled outside the US within the IPOX Global Composite Index during their first 1000 trading days. All the indices above are reconstituted and adjusted quarterly and companies that have been public for 2 years (in the case of the Renaissance indices) or 1000 days (in the case of the IPOX®-100 US Index and IPOX International Index) are removed.

The average age of ETFs is equal to 4.42 years with the oldest one being the First Trust US Equity Opportunities ETF, which was launched in April 2006. The rest funds are 3 years old at a maximum indicating that this niche of the ETF market is very young but possibly very prosperous. The average expense ratio is modest being equal to 0.68%. In addition, the ETFs tracking non-US-listed IPOs are more expensive than their domestically allocated peers. This cost superiority of domestic ETFs is not surprising as it has been observed in the case of the "traditional" ETFs both in and outside the US.

Moreover, **Table 1** shows that an average number of about 16,000 ETF shares are traded every day with the First Trust US Equity Opportunities ETF being the more tradable fund in the sample. The concentration of trading to the most aged fund may be the result of the advantage of this ETF in terms of information availability relative to the younger funds and may indicate that investors deem this ETF as more prosperous based on its amassed trading experience.

Going further, the average raw tracking error of the sample is equal to −0.56%. The negative sign means that the average ETF underperforms its benchmark by 56 basis points (bps). Among the four ETFs in the sample, only one outperforms its

Ticker	Name	Benchmark	Inception date	Age	Expense ratio
IPO	Renaissance IPO ETF	Renaissance US IPO Index	10/14/13	3.049	0.60%
IPOS	Renaissance International IPO ETF	Renaissance International IPO Index	10/6/2014	2.071	0.80%
FPX	First Trust US Equity Opportunities ETF	IPOX®-100 US Index	4/12/2006	10.562	0.60%
FPXI	First Trust International IPOX ETF	IPOX International Index	11/4/2014	1.992	0.70%
Mean				**4.418**	**0.68%**
Ticker	**Name**	**Benchmark**	**Volume**	**Tracking error**	**Trading freq.**
IPO	Renaissance IPO ETF	Renaissance US IPO Index	13,273	−1.12%	99.61%
IPOS	Renaissance International IPO ETF	Renaissance International IPO Index	461	0.12%	55.36%
FPX	First Trust US Equity Opportunities ETF	IPOX®-100 US Index	37,016	−0.68%	98.87%
FPXI	First Trust International IPOX ETF	IPOX International Index	14,605	−0.56%	78.64%
Mean			**16,339**	**−0.56%**	**83.12%**
Ticker	**Name**	**Benchmark**	**Intraday volatility**	**ETF Int. Vol/ S&P 500 Int. Vol**	**ETF Int. Vol/ S&P 600 Int. Vol**
IPO	Renaissance IPO ETF	Renaissance US IPO Index	1.101	1.232	0.976
IPOS	Renaissance International IPO ETF	Renaissance International IPO Index	0.486	0.568	0.515
FPX	First Trust US Equity Opportunities ETF	IPOX®-100 US Index	1.098	0.934	0.740
FPXI	First Trust International IPOX ETF	IPOX International Index	0.574	0.644	0.527
Mean			**0.815**	**0.844**	**0.689**

This table presents the profiles of IPO ETFs, which include their ticker, name, benchmark, inception date, age as at October 31, 2016, expense ratio, average daily volume, historical tracking error, i.e., difference in performance between ETF and its benchmark, since each ETF's inception up to December 31, 2015, trading frequency calculated as the fraction of trading days with nonzero volume to the total trading history (in days) for each fund, average intraday volatility calculated as the percentage fraction of the highest minus the lowest trading price of each fund on day t to its close price on the same day, and the fraction of each ETF's intraday volatility to the intraday volatility of the S&P 500 Index and the S&P 600 Small Cap Index, respectively.

Table 1.
Profiles of ETFs.

benchmark by 12 bps. As a comment on tracking error, we should point out that the literature has accentuated that tracking error is an unavoidable event for ETFs given that their returns are usually calculated free of expenses and transaction costs while index returns reflect no costs at all. In addition, other factors, such as the different time schedules between the stock exchanges on which the shares of ETFs and the underlying securities are traded, especially in the case of ETFs tracking nondomestic market indices, can hamper the effort of ETFs to efficiently replicate the performance of their benchmarks.

When it comes to trading frequency, **Table 1** reports an average term of 83%. This percentage indicates that there is a considerable amount of days on which ETFs present nil trading activity. These findings are in line with the low volumes discussed above. The next trading feature concerns the intraday volatility of ETFs, which is equal to 0.815 on average terms. Surprisingly enough, the international IPO ETFs are less volatile than their domestically allocated peers. This is a new finding as the relevant ETF literature has provided strong evidence that ETFs tracking international indices are riskier than those that track indices from the local stock market. In any case, however, both the average and the individual intraday volatility calculations are quite low showing that IPO ETFs can be a relatively safe haven for equity investors when the overall capital market is in turbulence. This claim can be verified by the ratios of ETFs' intraday volatility to those of the two Standard and Poor's indices taken into consideration. In both cases, the average ratios are below unity, whereas only one out of eight single ratios is greater than unity indicating that IPO ETFs are less volatile than the market.

5. Empirical results

5.1 Short-term return analysis

Table 2 presents the estimations of IPO ETFs' short-term performance. Specifically, the table reports the three types of initial returns, that is, the first-day absolute, benchmark-adjusted, and abnormal return along with the corresponding average returns over the first 2, 3, 4, 5, 21, and 63 trading days.

As far as absolute returns are concerned, **Table 2** shows that the average initial return of the sample is positive amounting to 29 bps. This positive mean term indicates a favorable response to the launch of these alternative investing tools on behalf of investors. However, it should be noted that, when focusing on the performance of individual funds, we can see that the absolute initial return can be either negative or positive and ranges from −0.35% for the Renaissance International IPO ETF to 1.45% for the Renaissance IPO ETF.

After the first trading day, the average absolute return of the sample remains positive up to the first 5 days and becomes negative when the 1- and 3-month periods are assessed. In addition, after the third day, average absolute return starts deteriorating. At the fund level, most of the longer-term average returns are positive for the Renaissance International IPO ETF and the First Trust US Equity Opportunities ETF, they are steadily negative for the Renaissance International IPO ETF, while returns are mixed in the case of the First Trust International IPOX ETF.

When it comes to benchmark-adjusted returns, **Table 2** reports a positive average initial return for the sample, either when the S&P 500 Index or the S&P 600 Small Cap Index is the benchmark into consideration. In addition, when the latter index is used, the average initial return of the sample is about double the respective return when the S&P 500 Index is used to compute the benchmark-adjusted returns of IPO ETFs. At the fund level, only the First Trust International IPOX ETF produces negative benchmark-adjusted return, whereas the rest of ETFs can beat the market on their first trading day.

Absolute returns										
Period	IPO	IPOS	FPX	FPXI	Mean					
t_1	1.446	−0.348	0.299	−0.250	**0.287**					
t_2	0.944	−0.184	0.175	−0.125	**0.202**					
t_3	1.103	−0.731	0.398	0.285	**0.264**					
t_4	0.714	−0.706	0.471	0.213	**0.173**					
t_5	0.604	−0.614	0.475	0.171	**0.159**					
t_{21}	0.092	−0.046	−0.072	−0.029	**−0.014**					
t_{63}	0.163	−0.021	−0.119	−0.111	**−0.022**					
Benchmark-adjusted returns										
	Benchmark: S&P 500 Index					**Benchmark: S&P 600 Small Cap Index**				
Period	**IPO**	**IPOS**	**FPX**	**FPXI**	**Mean**	**IPO**	**IPOS**	**FPX**	**FPXI**	**Mean**
t_1	0.209	1.041	0.222	−0.285	**0.297**	1.500	0.925	0.056	−0.274	**0.552**
t_2	−0.012	−0.362	0.283	−0.299	**−0.098**	0.512	−0.492	0.027	−0.308	**−0.065**
t_3	0.247	−0.162	−0.099	0.146	**0.033**	0.409	−0.155	−0.528	0.154	**−0.030**
t_4	0.070	0.008	0.048	0.127	**0.063**	0.225	−0.006	−0.483	−0.050	**−0.078**
t_5	−0.026	0.286	0.113	0.091	**0.116**	0.151	−0.005	−0.236	0.133	**0.011**
t_{21}	−0.133	−0.171	−0.085	−0.097	**−0.122**	−0.054	−0.398	−0.077	0.001	**−0.132**
t_{63}	0.029	−0.058	−0.065	−0.127	**−0.055**	0.051	−0.124	−0.009	−0.144	**−0.056**
Abnormal returns										
	Benchmark: S&P 500 Index					**Benchmark: S&P 600 Small Cap Index**				
Period	**IPO**	**IPOS**	**FPX**	**FPXI**	**Mean**	**IPO**	**IPOS**	**FPX**	**FPXI**	**Mean**
t_1	0.199	0.167	0.194	−0.236	**0.081**	1.495	0.043	0.083	−0.236	**0.346**
t_2	−0.017	−0.252	0.252	−0.183	**−0.050**	0.580	−0.275	0.028	−0.180	**0.038**
t_3	0.244	−0.521	−0.120	0.244	**−0.038**	0.516	−0.553	−0.321	0.253	**−0.026**
t_4	0.070	−0.442	0.025	0.200	**−0.037**	0.302	−0.490	−0.269	0.125	**−0.083**
t_5	−0.025	−0.281	0.089	0.161	**−0.014**	0.223	−0.425	−0.086	0.179	**−0.028**
t_{21}	−0.126	−0.095	−0.114	−0.032	**−0.092**	−0.029	−0.150	−0.114	0.008	**−0.071**
t_{63}	0.038	−0.037	−0.096	−0.087	**−0.046**	0.071	−0.050	−0.075	−0.101	**−0.039**

This table presents the return of IPO ETFs on their first trading day, i.e., the first day with positive trading volume, calculated in percentage terms as the fraction of the close trade price minus the opening trade price to the opening trade price, as well as the average absolute (daily) return over the first 2, 3, 4, 5, 21 (i.e., 1 month), and 63 (i.e., 3 months) days of each ETF's trading history. Then, the table presents the benchmark-adjusted returns of ETFs, i.e., ETF return minus benchmark return, over the same intervals using as alternative benchmarks the S&P 500 Index and the S&P 600 Small Cap Index. Finally, the table presents the abnormal returns of IPO ETFs estimated with the market model.

Table 2.
Short-term return analysis.

Furthermore, **Table 2** reports mixed results about longer-run benchmark-adjusted returns. For instance, when the 2-day period is considered and the S&P 500 Index is used as the benchmark, the returns of three ETFs are negative (two return estimates in the case of the S&P 600 Small Cap Index). In the case of the 3-day investment window, returns are mixed. In the case of the 4-day period and the S&P 500 Index, all the average returns are positive while over longer periods, whatever the benchmark may be, the majority of benchmark-adjusted returns are negative.

The abnormal returns of ETFs behave similarly to benchmark-adjusted returns. The average first-day abnormal return of the sample is positive irrespective of the index incorporated in the market model to estimate abnormal returns. In addition, the average abnormal return of the sample based on the S&P 600 Small Cap Index is more than three times the respective average return when the S&P 500 Index is taken into consideration. Scanning through the single ETF returns, we observe that three out of four funds deliver significant first-day profits, which range from 17 bps for the Renaissance International IPO ETF to 20 bps for the Renaissance IPO ETF.

At the longer-run level, abnormal returns mimic the benchmark-adjusted returns quite closely. For instance, similarly to benchmark-adjusted returns, the average 2-day abnormal returns based on the S&P 500 Index is negative for three out of four ETFs (the same ETFs as in the case of benchmark-adjusted performance). Returns over other frequencies up to 5 days are either negative or positive without allowing us to detect any specific pricing trend. However, when it comes to longer periods reaching one or 3 months, average returns become negative.

The main conclusion that can be reached by the analysis of the various types of short-term returns is that, on average, significant gains can be realized on the first trading day of IPO ETFs. However, gains diminish or even vanish when longer periods, such as 1 month or 3 months of trading, are assessed. Based on these findings, we could claim that IPO ETFs may be suitable for day traders but not for investors with a short-term horizon, which does not exceed 3 months.

5.2 Long-term return analysis

The long-run performance of ETFs is assessed in this section. The relevant estimations of cumulative and buy-and-hold returns over a 6-month, 12-month, 18-month, and 24-month period are presented in **Table 3** along with the corresponding returns over the entire trading history of ETFs. Cumulative returns are presented from an absolute, benchmark-adjusted, and abnormal perspective. On the other hand, buy-and-hold returns are reported in their absolute and benchmark-adjusted form.

We note that, as shown in **Table 1**, the Renaissance International IPO ETF is about 2 years old. This means that the total trading history of this fund coincides with the 24-month subperiod considered in our analysis. Moreover, the trading history of the First Trust International IPOX ETF is less than 2 years and, thus, we cannot compute returns over a 24-month period for this fund.

When it comes to cumulative absolute returns, the results in **Table 3** indicate that IPO ETFs can produce positive such returns. In particular, the average return over the first 6 months of trading approximates 30 bps. Average returns are also positive for the rest intervals considered as well as over the entire trading history of ETFs. In addition, except for the First Trust International IPOX ETF, the funds of the sample provide positive cumulative returns over the several time periods assessed. The First Trust International IPOX ETF presents a positive cumulative absolute return only over the first 6 months of trading.

When the cumulative benchmark-adjusted returns are considered, **Table 3** reports mixed results. For example, the average historical return (i.e., over the total trading history up to October 31, 2016) of the sample is positive when the S&P 500 Index is taken into consideration, but it becomes negative when the S&P 600 Small Cap Index is the reference portfolio. Moreover, three (two) out of four funds underperform the S&P 500 Index (the S&P 600 Small Cap Index).

In the case of cumulative abnormal returns, the results in **Table 3** indicate that the average IPO ETF underperforms the S&P 500 Index, but it performs better than the S&P 600 Small Cap Index up to 24 trading months. However, the average IPO

Cumulative absolute returns					
Period	**IPO**	**IPOS**	**FPX**	**FPXI**	**Mean**
6 months	0.292	0.564	0.186	0.143	**0.296**
12 months	0.621	0.147	0.707	−0.541	**0.233**
18 months	0.927	−0.021	1.168	−0.741	**0.333**
24 months	0.404	0.007	1.009	N/A	**0.474**
Total period	0.219	0.007	5.718	−0.478	**1.366**

Cumulative benchmark-adjusted returns										
	Benchmark: S&P 500 Index					**Benchmark: S&P 600 Small Cap Index**				
Period	**IPO**	**IPOS**	**FPX**	**FPXI**	**Mean**	**IPO**	**IPOS**	**FPX**	**FPXI**	**Mean**
6 months	−0.058	0.380	−0.106	0.027	**0.061**	0.105	0.387	0.134	−0.159	**0.117**
12 months	−0.018	−0.105	0.081	−0.626	**−0.167**	0.281	−0.067	0.315	−0.808	**−0.070**
18 months	−0.008	−0.182	0.338	−0.899	**−0.188**	0.278	−0.170	0.678	−1.073	**−0.072**
24 months	−0.486	−0.337	0.625	N/A	**−0.066**	−0.141	−0.406	1.012	N/A	**0.155**
Total period	−0.824	−0.337	2.350	−0.712	**0.119**	−0.623	−0.406	1.287	−0.925	**−0.167**

Cumulative abnormal returns										
	Benchmark: S&P 500 Index					**Benchmark: S&P 600 Small Cap Index**				
Period	**IPO**	**IPOS**	**FPX**	**FPXI**	**Mean**	**IPO**	**IPOS**	**FPX**	**FPXI**	**Mean**
6 months	0.004	0.483	−0.278	0.276	**0.121**	0.151	0.528	−0.078	0.157	**0.189**
12 months	0.107	0.029	−0.262	−0.199	**−0.081**	0.369	0.117	−0.034	−0.368	**0.021**
18 months	0.180	−0.117	−0.178	−0.244	**−0.090**	0.430	−0.013	0.128	−0.452	**0.024**
24 months	−0.229	−0.170	−0.074	N/A	**−0.158**	0.014	−0.048	0.106	N/A	**0.024**
Total period	−0.434	−0.170	−1.301	0.141	**−0.441**	−0.388	−0.048	−2.297	−0.119	**−0.713**

Buy-and-hold absolute returns					
Period	**IPO**	**IPOS**	**FPX**	**FPXI**	**Mean**
6 months	5.468	12.174	3.261	2.549	**5.863**
12 months	13.251	0.040	14.773	−11.786	**4.070**
18 months	17.409	−4.058	25.445	−15.965	**5.708**
24 months	7.241	−4.078	19.417	N/A	**7.527**
Total period	−0.246	−4.078	158.585	−11.786	**35.619**

Buy-and-hold benchmark-adjusted returns										
	Benchmark: S&P 500 Index					Benchmark: S&P 600 Small Cap Index				
Period	**IPO**	**IPOS**	**FPX**	**FPXI**	**Mean**	**IPO**	**IPOS**	**FPX**	**FPXI**	**Mean**
6 months	7.294	3.539	5.987	2.033	**4.713**	3.428	3.211	0.213	5.966	**3.204**
12 months	14.888	4.262	13.405	0.621	**8.294**	7.982	3.313	7.147	4.422	**5.716**
18 months	18.953	1.639	17.577	1.537	**9.926**	11.450	1.004	8.434	4.919	**6.452**
24 months	19.784	5.357	5.721	N/A	**10.287**	11.559	6.341	−3.974	N/A	**4.642**
Total period	21.042	5.357	62.226	2.834	**22.865**	14.830	6.341	83.129	6.763	**27.766**

This table presents the cumulative absolute returns of IPO ETFs over the first 6, 12, 18, and 24 months of their trading history as well as over their entire trading history up to October 31, 2016. Cumulative benchmark-adjusted and cumulative abnormal returns relative to the S&P 500 Index and the S&P 600 Small Cap Index, respectively, are presented too. Finally, the table presents the buy-and-hold absolute and benchmark-adjusted returns of ETFs over the several periods considered.

Table 3.
Long-term return analysis.

ETF as well as the individual funds fails to derive positive abnormal returns over their entire trading history irrespective of the market index used to estimate abnormal returns. At the fund level, three and two ETFs provide investors with a positive cumulative abnormal return against the S&P 500 Index over the 6- and 12-month period, respectively, but returns are basically negative over the rest time intervals examined. In the case, of the S&P 600 Small Cap Index, only one ETF can produce consistent cumulative abnormal returns over a 24-month investment horizon.

After discussing cumulative returns, we focus on the buy-and-hold returns of IPO ETFs. One element revealed in **Table 3** is that the average ETF derives significant buy-and-hold absolute returns, which range from 4.07% over the 12-month period to 35.62% over the entire trading history examined. Moreover, all the individual ETFs present positive buy-and-hold absolute returns over the first 6-month trading period, three funds offer positive returns during the first year of their trading, and two ETFs achieve positive returns during the 18- and 24-month periods. However, when the entire trading history of ETFs is considered, just the First Trust US Equity Opportunities ETF provides a significant positive buy-and-hold absolute return, which approximates 159%.[4]

On the question of how the buy-and-hold benchmark-adjusted returns of ETFs behave, **Table 3** reports significant such returns over the several intervals investigated. With only one exception, all the return estimates of each single ETF are positive. Moreover, the average IPO ETF produces a mean buy-and-hold benchmark-adjusted of 23 and 28% against the S&P 500 Index and S&P 600 Small Cap Index, respectively, over the whole trading history of ETFs up to October 31, 2016. At the fund level, the First Trust US Equity Opportunities ETF is the most profitable ETF in the sample. The historical buy-and-hold benchmark-adjusted return of this fund amounts to 62 and 83% in the case of the S&P 500 Index and the S&P 600 Small Cap Index, respectively.[5]

Overall, the analysis of long-run performance reveals that IPO ETFs can be suitable investment choices for investors looking for substantial long-term profits from entering the IPO business. More importantly, the findings on buy-and-hold benchmark-adjusted returns indicate that IPO ETFs can beat the overall stock market over shorter or longer periods. This pattern should be highly welcome by investors who always seek for alternative investment tools to perform above the market.

[4] The rest ETFs present significantly negative buy-and-hold absolute returns. However, the magnitude of the positive return of the First Trust US Equity Opportunities ETF is that big so that the average historical buy-and-hold absolute return of the sample be equal to 36%.

[5] A comment that can be made with respect to the First Trust US Equity Opportunities ETF significantly outperforming its peers (in the case of the S&P 500 Index, the mean benchmark-adjusted outperformance of this fund over other ETFs in the sample is equal to 45.81% whereas, in the case of the S&P 600 Small Cap Index, average outperformance approximates 67%), concerns the age of this ETF. In particular, as we have seen in the previous sections, this ETF was the pioneer in the IPO ETF business and has more than 10 years of trading records. The performance superiority of the oldest fund in the sample over its younger peers from a buy-and-hold benchmark-adjusted perspective resembles the long-run performance advantage of the companies going public after several years of operation as private non-listed firms. The findings of several studies such as those of [23, 45–47] provide strong evidence of a positive relationship between a firm's age and its long-run performance. Obviously, an ETF has no operating history before its inception on a stock exchange. That said, after inception, the trading experience accumulated to an ETF seems to be a decisive factor that can affect its performance. In our study, the very small size of the sample (just four funds) does not allow running a cross-sectional regression of ETFs' long-run performance on their age to obtain statistical support of our assertion about the return of aged ETFs against their young counterparts.

5.3 Risk-adjusted performance analysis

The results of the six-factor regression model are provided in **Table 4**. The table includes the alpha coefficient along with the estimates of the explanatory variables of the model. Probabilities on the statistical significance of estimates are provided too along with R-squared on the sufficiency of the model to explain the performance of IPO ETFs. Finally, the results are presented for each ETF over the several estimation windows considered and against the two different market indices employed in our analysis.

When it comes to excess performance, **Table 4** shows that most of the average alpha estimates over the several subperiods examined are positive either when the S&P 500 Index is the benchmark in the model or the S&P 600 Small Cap Index is used as a proxy for the market return. However, at the fund level, most of the individual alphas are insignificant both in statistical and economic terms. Based on this element, we conclude that IPO ETFs fail to deliver any above market return. However, this conclusion does not apply to the First Trust US Equity Opportunities ETF. Over the 6-month estimation window or longer, the alpha estimates of this fund are positive and statistically significant at the 10% or better indicating that this ETF can beat the market. We remind that this ETF is the oldest among the funds in the sample. Thus, the assertion about the positive relationship between the age of IPO ETFs and their long-run performance is verified by the results of regression analysis.

With respect to systematic risk, the beta estimates presented in **Table 4** are all positive with the majority of them being significant at the 5% or better. Moreover, a wide fluctuation in betas is observed among the various subperiods examined. However, in each single period as well as over the entire trading history of each ETF, there is a convergence in betas obtained from using the two alternative market benchmarks. At the sample level, the average beta coefficients are below unity indicating that IPO ETFs are more conservative than the market. Conservativeness implies that investors choosing IPO ETFs are relatively protected during declining paths of the overall stock market. This finding is in line with the ratios of ETFs' intraday volatility to that of benchmarks in **Table 1**, where we saw that ETFs are less volatile than the market indices. Therefore, our assertion about IPO ETFs standing as a relative safe haven for equity investors during turbulent markets is verified by the estimations of systematic risk via regression analysis.

Going further, when the S&P 500 Index represents the stock market in the model, the effect of the size factor on the performance of ETFs seems to be significant only in the case of the Renaissance IPO ETF and the First Trust US Equity Opportunities ETF. For these funds, the coefficients of the SMB factor are constantly positive, while most of them are significant at the 10% or better. The positive and significant effect of the size factor on the performance of at least two ETFs in the sample is in line with our expectations given that, according to Fama and French (2015), the SMB slopes are strongly positive for small stocks (and slightly negative for big stocks), and that the ETFs examined are indeed small cap or even very small cap.[6] When the S&P 600 Small Cap Index is used as the market

[6] Based on the definition of "small capitalization" offered by Investopedia, a small cap firm is a company with a capitalization of between $300 million and $2 billion (http://www.investopedia.com/terms/s/small-cap.asp). As of 5 January, 2017, the ETFs in our sample have a minimum of Net Assets of $1.9 million in the case of the Renaissance International IPO ETF and a maximum of assets of $633.6 million in the case of the First Trust US Equity Opportunities ETF (according to information found on the website of ETFs' managing companies). Based on these figures, it is obvious that the ETFs in the sample stand as small cap portfolios and, consequently, the positive sign of the SMB estimates for at least two funds is a reasonable finding.

Benchmark: S&P 500 Index								
1 month	**Alpha**	**Beta**	**SMB**	**HML**	**UMD**	**CMA**	**RMW**	**R_2**
IPO	−0.090	1.085[a]	0.002	−0.671	0.260	−2.190[a]	0.441	0.850
IPOS	0.153	0.304	−0.589	−1.828	−0.474	−0.366	−0.385	0.206
FPX	0.153	0.639[a]	0.095[a]	−1.025[b]	0.415[c]	−0.440	0.307	0.795
FPXI	−0.117	1.184[a]	0.100	−0.157	0.006	−0.334	0.709	0.608
Mean	**0.025**	**0.803**	**−0.098**	**−0.920**	**0.052**	**−0.833**	**0.268**	**0.615**
3 months	**Alpha**	**Beta**	**SMB**	**HML**	**UMD**	**CMA**	**RMW**	**R_2**
IPO	0.087	0.799[a]	0.095	−0.116	0.464[a]	−1.600[a]	−0.139[a]	0.688
IPOS	0.029	0.436[a]	0.230	−0.609	−0.066	0.154	−0.050	0.184
FPX	0.042	0.879[a]	0.222	−0.130	0.377[a]	−0.093	−0.696[a]	0.878
FPXI	−0.148[c]	0.200	−0.174	−0.253	−0.120	0.284	0.105	0.082
Mean	**0.002**	**0.579**	**0.093**	**−0.277**	**0.164**	**−0.314**	**−0.195**	**0.458**
6 months	**Alpha**	**Beta**	**SMB**	**HML**	**UMD**	**CMA**	**RMW**	**R_2**
IPO	0.044	0.755[a]	0.209[c]	−0.155	0.487[a]	−0.613[b]	−0.445[b]	0.813
IPOS	0.084	0.291[a]	0.064	−0.105	−0.074	−0.050	−0.214	0.132
FPX	0.087[a]	0.949[a]	0.472[a]	−0.155	0.168[b]	−0.538[a]	−0.621[a]	0.870
FPXI	−0.040	0.287[b]	0.097	−0.389	−0.162	−0.138	0.234	0.039
Mean	**0.044**	**0.570**	**0.211**	**−0.201**	**0.105**	**−0.335**	**−0.262**	**0.463**
12 months	**Alpha**	**Beta**	**SMB**	**HML**	**UMD**	**CMA**	**RMW**	**R_2**
IPO	0.003	0.831[a]	0.117	−0.278[b]	0.205[b]	−0.874[a]	−0.749[a]	0.808
IPOS	0.042	0.405[a]	0.000	−0.516[b]	−0.160	0.485	−0.235	0.065
FPX	0.047[b]	0.902[a]	0.436[a]	−0.175	0.207[a]	−0.367[a]	−0.502[a]	0.862
FPXI	−0.048	0.403[a]	−0.063	−0.538[a]	−0.240[a]	0.441[c]	0.174	0.164
Mean	**0.011**	**0.635**	**0.122**	**−0.377**	**0.003**	**−0.078**	**−0.328**	**0.475**
18 months	**Alpha**	**Beta**	**SMB**	**HML**	**UMD**	**CMA**	**RMW**	**R2**
IPO	0.001	0.869[a]	0.215[a]	−0.185[c]	0.042	−1.008[a]	−0.547[a]	0.738
IPOS	0.021	0.330[a]	−0.096	−0.225	−0.107	−0.073	−0.477[b]	0.064
FPX	0.037[c]	0.908[a]	0.490[a]	−0.047	0.224[a]	−0.293[a]	−0.423[a]	0.850
FPXI	−0.066	0.406[a]	−0.039	−0.159	−0.144	−0.061	−0.028	0.202
Mean	**−0.002**	**0.628**	**0.143**	**−0.154**	**0.004**	**−0.359**	**−0.369**	**0.464**
24 months	**Alpha**	**Beta**	**SMB**	**HML**	**UMD**	**CMA**	**RMW**	**R_2**
IPO	−0.017	0.893[a]	0.364[a]	−0.307[a]	−0.101[b]	−0.576[a]	−0.486[a]	0.742
IPOS	−0.003	0.309[a]	−0.023	−0.129	−0.118[c]	−0.128	−0.409[b]	0.070
FPX	0.037[c]	0.949[a]	0.402[a]	−0.124[c]	0.188[a]	−0.480[a]	−0.516[a]	0.830
FPXI	N/A	N/A	N/A	N/A	N/A	N/A	N/A	N/A
Mean	**0.005**	**0.717**	**0.248**	**−0.187**	**−0.010**	**−0.395**	**−0.470**	**0.547**
Total period	**Alpha**	**Beta**	**SMB**	**HML**	**UMD**	**CMA**	**RMW**	**R_2**
IPO	−0.017	0.900[a]	0.443[a]	−0.150[b]	−0.121[a]	−0.596[a]	−0.440[a]	0.728
IPOS	−0.003	0.309[a]	−0.023	−0.129	−0.118[c]	−0.128	−0.409[b]	0.070
FPX	0.021[a]	0.962[a]	0.279[a]	−0.179[a]	0.053[a]	−0.346[a]	−0.245[a]	0.698

			Benchmark: S&P 500 Index					
24 months	**Alpha**	**Beta**	**SMB**	**HML**	**UMD**	**CMA**	**RMW**	**R_2**
FPXI	−0.031	0.507[a]	0.020	−0.098	−0.132[b]	0.105	−0.158	0.267
Mean	**−0.008**	**0.669**	**0.180**	**−0.139**	**−0.080**	**−0.241**	**−0.313**	**0.441**
			Benchmark: S&P 600 Small Cap Index					
1 month	**Alpha**	**Beta**	**SMB**	**HML**	**UMD**	**CMA**	**RMW**	**R_2**
IPO	−0.022	1.003[a]	−0.918[a]	−0.521	0.246	−2.693[a]	0.512	0.791
IPOS	0.195	0.270	−0.753	−1.596	−0.343	−0.185	−0.350	0.205
FPX	0.125[a]	0.631[a]	−0.335	−0.910[b]	0.423	0.019	0.400	0.722
FPXI	−0.096[a]	0.862[b]	−0.868[c]	−0.410	−0.078	−0.519	0.364	0.559
Mean	**0.050**	**0.691**	**−0.718**	**−0.859**	**0.062**	**−0.845**	**0.232**	**0.569**
3 months	**Alpha**	**Beta**	**SMB**	**HML**	**UMD**	**CMA**	**RMW**	**R_2**
IPO	0.078	0.893[a]	−0.822[b]	−0.393	0.351	−1.309[a]	−0.603	0.694
IPOS	0.010	0.441[a]	−0.322[c]	−0.834[b]	−0.076	0.361	−0.301	0.207
FPX	0.025	0.783[a]	−0.434[b]	−0.021	0.360[a]	−0.157	−0.860[a]	0.875
FPXI	−0.154[b]	0.215[b]	−0.413[b]	−0.310	−0.111	0.330	0.052	0.088
Mean	**−0.010**	**0.583**	**−0.498**	**−0.389**	**0.131**	**−0.194**	**−0.428**	**0.466**
6 months	**Alpha**	**Beta**	**SMB**	**HML**	**UMD**	**CMA**	**RMW**	**R_2**
IPO	0.042	0.749[a]	−0.610[a]	−0.324	0.534[a]	−0.550[c]	−0.534[b]	0.816
IPOS	0.084	0.284[a]	−0.229	−0.143	−0.069	−0.073	−0.279	0.131
FPX	0.058[a]	0.845[a]	−0.323[b]	−0.181	0.288[a]	−0.235	−0.613[a]	0.861
FPXI	−0.047	0.272[b]	−0.162	−0.396	−0.158	−0.173	0.205	0.037
Mean	**0.034**	**0.537**	**−0.331**	**−0.261**	**0.149**	**−0.258**	**−0.305**	**0.461**
12 months	**Alpha**	**Beta**	**SMB**	**HML**	**UMD**	**CMA**	**RMW**	**R_2**
IPO	0.004	0.782[a]	−0.706[a]	−0.463[a]	0.249[a]	−0.798[a]	−0.869[a]	0.797
IPOS	0.033	0.416[a]	−0.421[a]	−0.626[b]	−0.187[c]	0.518	−0.280	0.068
FPX	0.047[a]	0.857[a]	−0.394[a]	−0.226[c]	0.269[a]	−0.250[b]	−0.584[a]	0.850
FPXI	−0.071	0.382[a]	−0.285[b]	−0.547[a]	−0.234[a]	0.042	0.282	0.169
Mean	**0.003**	**0.609**	**−0.451**	**−0.465**	**0.025**	**−0.122**	**−0.363**	**0.471**
18 months	**Alpha**	**Beta**	**SMB**	**HML**	**UMD**	**CMA**	**RMW**	**R_2**
IPO	0.002	0.827[a]	−0.649[a]	−0.359[a]	0.041	−0.944[a]	−0.720[a]	0.731
IPOS	0.015	0.331[a]	−0.433[a]	−0.301	−0.132[b]	−0.046	−0.520[a]	0.065
FPX	0.031	0.877[a]	−0.383[a]	−0.092	0.259[a]	−0.219[a]	−0.463[a]	0.833
FPXI	−0.077	0.404[a]	−0.447[a]	−0.248[b]	−0.187[a]	−0.067	−0.087	0.206
Mean	**−0.007**	**0.610**	**−0.478**	**−0.250**	**−0.005**	**−0.319**	**−0.448**	**0.459**
24 months	**Alpha**	**Beta**	**SMB**	**HML**	**UMD**	**CMA**	**RMW**	**R_2**
IPO	−0.020	0.859[a]	−0.521[a]	−0.504[a]	−0.170[a]	−0.572[a]	−0.641[a]	0.729
IPOS	−0.007	0.304[a]	−0.331[a]	−0.200	−0.147[b]	−0.112	−0.454[a]	0.069
FPX	0.031	0.919[a]	−0.505[a]	−0.184[b]	0.192[a]	−0.414[a]	−0.543[a]	0.816
FPXI	N/A	N/A	N/A	N/A	N/A	N/A	N/A	N/A
Mean	**0.002**	**0.694**	**−0.453**	**−0.296**	**−0.042**	**−0.366**	**−0.546**	**0.538**

Benchmark: S&P 600 Small Cap Index								
24 month	**Alpha**	**Beta**	**SMB**	**HML**	**UMD**	**CMA**	**RMW**	**R_2**
Total period	**Alpha**	**Beta**	**SMB**	**HML**	**UMD**	**CMA**	**RMW**	**R_2**
IPO	−0.019	0.853[a]	−0.431[a]	−0.335[a]	−0.203[a]	−0.591[a]	−0.606[a]	0.714
IPOS	−0.007	0.304[a]	−0.331[a]	−0.200	−0.147[b]	−0.112	−0.454[b]	0.069
FPX	0.023[a]	0.912[a]	−0.630[a]	−0.301[a]	0.013	−0.352[a]	−0.372[a]	0.681
FPXI	−0.037	0.497[a]	−0.484[a]	−0.219[c]	−0.184[a]	0.132	−0.240	0.272
Mean	**0.002**	**0.694**	**−0.453**	**−0.296**	**−0.042**	**−0.366**	**−0.546**	**0.538**

This table presents the results of a six-factor performance regression model. The daily excess return of IPO ETFs is successively regressed on the excess return of the S&P 500 Index or the S&P 600 Small Cap Index, and the Fama&French SMB (small minus big) factor, the Fama&French HML (high minus low book-to-price ratio) factor, the Carhart UMD (momentum) factor, the Fama&French CMA (conservative minus aggressive) factor, and the Fama&French RMW (robust minus weak) factor. The model is run over the first month, 3 months, 6 months, 12 months, 18 months, and 24 months of each ETF's trading history excluding the month of each ETF's launch on the stock exchange. The model is also run over the entire trading history of each ETF up to October 31, 2016 also excluding the month of each ETF's launch on the stock exchange.
[a]*indicates statistical significance at 1% level.*
[b]*indicates statistical significance at 5% level.*
[c]*indicates statistical significance at 10% level.*

Table 4.
Risk-adjusted performance analysis.

portfolio, the results about the SMB factor are opposite to those just discussed. All the individual estimates are negative with the majority of them being statistically significant. This pattern was not expected but it could possibly be considered by the correlation of the SMB factor with the S&P 600 Small Cap Index.[7] This means that the effect of the size factor may be expressed by the positive slope of the market index.[8]

On the impact of the value factor on performance of IPO ETFs, the relevant estimates of the HML variable are all negative with most of them being statistically significant at the 10% or better, especially when the 12-month or longer estimation windows are considered. This finding applies to both versions of the model, namely either when the S&P 500 Index or the S&P 600 Small Cap Index is used. Based on Fama and French [44], the strongly negative slope of the HML factor indicates that IPO ETFs may be deemed as to resemble low B/M (i.e., book-to-market) growth stock portfolios. This is true given that the stocks that comprise the underlying indices of IPO ETFs are usually small cap companies that go public with strong perceived potential for significant growth in the future.

The next variable considered is the momentum factor of Carhart. The majority of the relevant sample average estimates are positive, especially in the short-run, namely over periods up to 12 months. In the long run, the average momentum coefficients are negative. A negative sample average is obtained when the entire trading history of each ETFs is taken into consideration when running the performance regression model. At the fund level, when the first version of the model is assessed (i.e., the one with the S&P 500 Index), about half of the momentum

[7] We have computed an average correlation between the SMB and the S&P 600 Small Cap Index of 0.55 over the various time intervals that correspond to the trading history of each ETFs under examination.

[8] To verify that the results reported with the usage of the S&P 600 Small Cap Index are not spurious, we run performance regressions after detracting the SMB variable from the model. The results obtained do not differ significantly from those reported in **Table 4**.

estimates up to the 18-month investment window are positive and statistically significant. After this period, only the First Trust US Equity Opportunities ETF presents a stable positive relationship with the momentum factor, whereas the rest three ETFs are negatively related to this factor. This is also the case when the S&P 600 Small Cap Index is the reference market portfolio in the model. The main conclusion reached though analyzing the results about the momentum factor is that IPO ETFs follow the trends of the overall stock market in the short-run, but in the long-run, the pricing behavior of that products can deviate from the market.

When it comes to the Conservative Minus Aggressive factor, the results indicate a rather negative impact on IPO ETF performance. The majority of CMA estimates are negative when the S&P 500 Index is the market portfolio in the model. Moreover, 12 out 27 single CMA estimates are statistically significant. More or less, the same results are obtained when we use the S&P 600 Small Cap Index in regressions. The negative sign of the CMA variable is in accordance with our expectations for a negative relationship between the performance of IPO ETFs and the CMA factor based on the suggestions of Fama and French [44] about a negative relationship between expected investment and expected rate of return.

Finally, as far as the impact of Robust Minus Weak factor on performance of IPO ETFs is concerned, the results in **Table 4** reveal a negative such effect. In both versions of the model, the majority of the relevant RMW estimates are negative and statistically significant (15 and 14 out of 27 individual estimates in the case of the S&P 500 Index and the S&P 600 Small Cap Index, respectively). This finding is in accordance with our expectations about a negative relationship between the performance of ETFs and RMW. According to Fama and French [44], the combination of negative CMA and RMW slopes in the performance regression model (as is the case in our analysis) indicates that the returns of IPO ETFs resemble the returns of those firms that invest a lot despite their low profitability.

5.4 Market trend return analysis

The outcomes of the market trend return analysis are provided in **Table 5**. The results are presented for absolute, benchmark-adjusted and abnormal returns over the descending and ascending paths of the S&P 500 Index and the S&P 600 Small Cap Index, respectively. For each single ETF and over each market path, the number and percentage of days with negative (or zero) and positive returns are displayed along with the corresponding average negative and positive returns.

To begin with, when the S&P 500 Index declines, the average IPO ETFs declines too on 75.31% of the corresponding trading days. The average absolute return on these negative days amounts to −86 bps. During the negative days of the S&P 500 Index, ETFs present an average positive absolute return on 24.69% of negative trading days. When the market goes up, IPO ETFs move upward too on 62.08% of the respective positive days delivering an average return of 102 bps. Moreover, during the positive path of the S&P 500 Index, ETFs move opposite to the market on 37.92% of days. When we use the S&P 600 Small Cap Index as a proxy for the stock market return, we obtain similar results.

The main conclusion that can be drawn from the discussion of absolute returns is that IPO ETFs are quite but not absolutely aligned to the overall stock market. The fact that when the market moves downward, IPO ETFs have more than 20% probability of moving against the market indicates that IPO ETFs can possibly be useful hedging tools during turbulent stock markets. However, the significant number of negative return days (i.e., 37.92%) when the stock market moves upward should be borne in mind when planning investment strategies with IPO ETFs.

Taking the analysis a little further, the results on the benchmark-adjusted returns are very interesting. More specifically, during the negative days of the stock market, the benchmark-adjusted returns decline too but only on 36.51% (28.26%) of the respective trading days in the case of the S&P 500 Index (S&P 600 Small Cap Index). The opposite trend is presented when the market ascends, namely the benchmark-adjusted ETF returns decline by a rate of 61.32% (or 68.19%) trading days depending on the index used to represent the stock market. The outcomes obtained on benchmark-adjusted returns verify that IPO ETFs can be used as hedging tools over the negative paths of the stock market; however, hedging efficiency is in question when equity prices increase.

When it comes to abnormal returns, we can in see in **Table 5** that they behave qualitatively equal to benchmark-adjusted returns. In particular, they move against the negative markets on 58.86% of the corresponding negative trading days, whereas when the pricing in the market are positive, IPO ETFs have a 57.08%

Absolute returns						
Descending S&P 500 Index						
	No of neg.	**% of neg.**	**Average**	**No of pos.**	**% of pos.**	**Average**
IPO	260	71.04%	−1.103	106	28.96%	0.426
IPOS	202	77.69%	−0.564	58	22.31%	0.855
FPX	958	78.52%	−1.103	262	21.48%	0.451
FPXI	185	74.00%	−0.685	65	26.00%	0.570
Mean	**401**	**75.31%**	**−0.864**	**123**	**24.69%**	**0.576**
Ascending S&P 500 Index						
IPO	**No of neg.**	**% of neg.**	**Average**	**No of pos.**	**% of pos.**	**Average**
IPOS	87	21.70%	−0.419	314	78.30%	0.905
FPX	165	62.98%	−0.352	97	37.02%	1.259
FPXI	253	17.61%	−0.421	1184	82.39%	0.985
Mean	124	49.40%	−0.297	127	50.60%	0.934
	157	**37.92%**	**−0.372**	**431**	**62.08%**	**1.021**
Descending S&P 600 Small Cap Index descending						
	No of neg.	**% of neg.**	**Average**	**No of pos.**	**% of pos.**	**Average**
IPO	273	75.62%	−1.081	88	24.38%	0.386
IPOS	196	79.67%	−0.568	50	20.33%	0.903
FPX	985	78.24%	−1.089	274	21.76%	0.436
FPXI	177	74.68%	−0.680	60	25.32%	0.573
Mean	**408**	**77.05%**	**−0.855**	**118**	**22.95%**	**0.575**
Ascending S&P 600 Small Cap Index						
	No of neg.	**% of neg.**	**Average**	**No of pos.**	**% of pos.**	**Average**
IPO	74	18.23%	−0.381	332	81.77%	0.889
IPOS	171	61.96%	−0.355	105	38.04%	1.206
FPX	226	16.17%	−0.401	1172	83.83%	0.994
FPXI	132	50.00%	−0.327	132	50.00%	0.919
Mean	**151**	**36.59%**	**−0.366**	**435**	**63.41%**	**1.002**

Benchmark-adjusted returns						
	No of neg.	**% of neg.**	**Average**	**No of pos.**	**% of pos.**	**Average**
IPO	182	49.73%	−0.643	184	50.27%	0.517
IPOS	51	19.62%	−1.218	209	80.38%	0.794
FPX	555	45.49%	−0.448	665	54.51%	0.566
FPXI	78	31.20%	−0.628	172	68.80%	0.693
Mean	**217**	**36.51%**	**−0.734**	**308**	**63.49%**	**0.643**
Ascending S&P 500 Index						
	No of neg.	**% of neg.**	**Average**	**No of pos.**	**% of pos.**	**Average**
IPO	199	49.63%	−0.509	202	50.37%	0.515
IPOS	211	80.53%	−0.895	51	19.47%	1.461
FPX	681	47.39%	−0.566	756	52.61%	0.405
FPXI	170	67.73%	−0.789	81	32.27%	0.601
Mean	315	**61.32%**	**−0.690**	273	**38.68%**	**0.745**
Descending S&P 600 Small Cap Index descending						
	No of neg.	**% of neg.**	**Average**	**No of pos.**	**% of pos.**	**Average**
IPO	154	42.66%	−0.564	207	57.34%	0.547
IPOS	43	17.48%	−1.260	203	82.52%	0.944
FPX	390	30.98%	−0.477	869	69.02%	0.723
FPXI	52	21.94%	−0.681	185	78.06%	0.789
Mean	**160**	**28.26%**	**−0.745**	**366**	**71.74%**	**0.751**
Ascending S&P 600 Small Cap Index						
	No of neg.	**% of neg.**	**Average**	**No of pos.**	**% of pos.**	**Average**
IPO	220	54.19%	−0.575	186	45.81%	0.466
IPOS	217	78.62%	−1.054	59	21.38%	1.256
FPX	908	64.95%	−0.706	490	35.05%	0.458
FPXI	198	75.00%	−0.865	66	25.00%	0.661
Mean	**386**	**68.19%**	**−0.800**	**200**	**31.81%**	**0.711**
Abnormal returns						
Descending S&P 500 Index						
	No of neg.	**% of neg.**	**Average**	**No of pos.**	**% of pos.**	**Average**
IPO	177	48.36%	−0.638	189	51.64%	0.523
IPOS	73	28.08%	−1.227	187	71.92%	0.467
FPX	592	48.52%	−0.462	628	51.48%	0.557
FPXI	99	39.60%	−0.759	151	60.40%	0.509
Mean	235	**41.14%**	**−0.771**	289	**58.86%**	**0.514**
Ascending S&P 500 Index						
	No of neg.	**% of neg.**	**Average**	**No of pos.**	**% of pos.**	**Average**
IPO	199	49.63%	−0.509	202	50.37%	0.516
IPOS	191	72.90%	−0.529	71	27.10%	1.382
FPX	713	49.62%	−0.555	724	50.38%	0.405

Abnormal returns						
Ascending S&P 500 Index						
	No of neg.	**% of neg.**	**Average**	**No of pos.**	**% of pos.**	**Average**
FPXI	141	56.18%	−0.543	110	43.82%	0.721
Mean	**311**	**57.08%**	**−0.534**	**277**	**42.92%**	**0.756**
Descending S&P 600 Small Cap Index descending						
	No of neg.	**% of neg.**	**Average**	**No of pos.**	**% of pos.**	**Average**
IPO	175	48.48%	−0.619	186	51.52%	0.497
IPOS	73	29.67%	−1.211	173	70.33%	0.491
FPX	607	48.21%	−0.562	652	51.79%	0.566
FPXI	90	37.97%	−0.790	147	62.03%	0.509
Mean	**236**	**41.08%**	**−0.795**	**290**	**58.92%**	**0.516**
Ascending S&P 600 Small Cap Index						
	No of neg.	**% of neg.**	**Average**	**No of pos.**	**% of pos.**	**Average**
IPO	197	48.52%	−0.500	209	51.48%	0.508
IPOS	192	69.57%	−0.546	84	30.43%	1.243
FPX	725	51.86%	−0.560	673	48.14%	0.493
FPXI	152	57.58%	−0.551	112	42.42%	0.715
Mean	**317**	**56.88%**	**−0.539**	**270**	**43.12%**	**0.740**

This table presents a trend analysis of IPO ETF returns, which considers whether the overall stock market, successively represented by the S&P 500 Index and the S&P 600 Small Cap Index, moves upward or downward. The types of returns considered are the absolute, benchmark-adjusted returns and abnormal return of ETFs and displayed in the table are the number and percentage of days presenting negative and positive returns over the descending and the upward cycle of the stock market as well as the corresponding average returns of ETFs.

Table 5.
Market trend return analysis.

probability to present a negative abnormal return. Overall, the analysis of abnormal returns leads to conclusions similar to these reached through analyzing the benchmark-adjusted returns, namely IPO ETFs can be useful defending investment tools during bear markets, but their usefulness may be weakened during bull stock markets.

6. Conclusion

In this paper, we examine the performance of the four IPO ETFs traded on the US stock market, which invest in equity indices comprised of companies that have recently gone public. We assess the short- and long-term performance of these funds by estimating their absolute, benchmark-adjusted and abnormal returns. The benchmark-adjusted and abnormal returns are computed against the S&P 500 Index and the S&P 600 Small Cap Index.

In the short-run, we first compute the first-trading-day return of ETFs and then the average daily returns over the first 2, 3, 4, 5, 21, and 63 trading days. At the long-run level, we calculate cumulative absolute, benchmark-adjusted and abnormal returns over 6-, 12-, 18-, and 24-month investment horizons as well as over the whole trading history of each single ETF up to October 31, 2016. The same intervals are used to compute relevant buy-and-hold returns.

Apart from computing short- and long-run returns, we use a six-factor regression model to assess the relation of ETFs' performance with certain variables, which include the market portfolio, the Fama & French size, value, investment and profitability factors and the momentum factor of Carhart. Our study concludes with a market trend analysis, which assesses the behavior of IPO ETFs during the descending and upward phases of the overall stock market.

The results obtained are very comprehensive. At first, the analysis shows that the first-day return of ETFs is positive on average terms and, consequently, significant profits can be made on the first trading day of IPO ETFs. Going further, short-term analysis shows that average daily returns weaken after the first trading day and over a period ranging up to 63 trading days after the launch of each ETF on the stock exchange. These findings lead to the conclusion that day traders would be possibly attracted by IPO ETFs, but investors with a short-term investment horizon not exceeding a quarter should probably avoid IPO ETFs as short-term profits from such investments would be in question.

When it comes to long-term performance, positive cumulative absolute returns are computed for the majority of ETFs over the various periods examined. However, when cumulative benchmark-adjusted and abnormal returns are assessed, returns are positive only over the first 6 months of trading whereas returns become negative over the next time periods under study. When we consider the long-run buy-and-hold returns, our analysis reveals that ETFs deliver such substantial returns, either in their absolute or benchmark-adjusted form. In other words, from a buy-and-hold perspective, IPO ETFs can beat the market as it is represented by S&P 500 Index or the S&P 600 Small Cap Index. In summary, the analysis of long-run performance shows that investors looking for significant profits in the long run from entering the IPO business can resort to IPO ETFs to do so.

Regarding risk-adjusted performance, the regression analysis demonstrates that only one IPO ETF can deliver robust above market performance. The specific ETF was the first to enter the IPO ETF business, and it is about 8 years older than the other funds in the sample. This element provides a hint about a positive relation between age and long-run performance of ETFs. Moreover, regression results reveal that IPO ETFs are more conservative than the market. This assertion is verified by the systematic risk of ETFs which is, on average, significantly lower than unity. Furthermore, a positive effect of the size factor on ETF performance is revealed. On the contrary, a negative relation is revealed between ETF performance and the value factor of Fama & French. When it comes to momentum, results indicate that IPO ETFs are aligned with the stock market in the short-run but they deviate from it in the long term. Going further, the results concerning the Conservative Minus Aggressive factor verify a negative relation between investment and expected rate of return. Finally, as far as the Robust Minus Weak factor is concerned, the results reveal a negative relationship between the performance of ETFs and RMW, which combined with the CMA slopes indicates that the returns of IPO ETFs resemble the returns of those firms with low profitability which nevertheless invest a lot.

In the last step, the market trend return analysis shows that when the stock market descends, the absolute return of IPO ETFs declines too on about 76% of negative trading days. On the other hand, when the market moves upward, the prices of ETFs increase on 63% of the corresponding days. The opposite behavior is displayed by the benchmark-adjusted and abnormal return of ETFs. This means that when the market goes down, the ETF benchmark-adjusted and abnormal returns move to the opposite direction with a probability of 57% or more (depending on the type of return considered and the index used as the market portfolio). The main conclusion drawn from the market trend analysis is that IPO ETFs can be useful hedging investment tools during bear markets, but their hedging efficiency weakens during bull markets.

Author details

Gerasimos G. Rompotis
National and Kapodistrian University of Athens, Attica, Greece

*Address all correspondence to: geras3238@yahoo.gr

References

[1] Miller RE, Reilly FK. An examination of mispricing, returns, and uncertainty for initial public offerings. Financial Management. 1987;**16**(2):33-38

[2] Tinic S. Anatomy of initial public offerings of common stock. Journal of Finance. 1988;**43**(4):789-822

[3] Ibbotson RG, Sindelar JL, Ritter JR. Initial public offerings. Journal of Applied Corporate Finance. 1988;**1**: 37-45

[4] Carter RB, Manaster S. Initial public offerings and underwriter reputation. Journal of Finance. 1990;**45**(4): 1045-1067

[5] Ritter JR. The hot issue market of 1980. Journal of Business. 1984;**57**(2): 215-240

[6] Ritter JR. The costs of going public. Journal of Financial Economics. 1987;**19**: 269-281

[7] Ritter JR. The long-run performance of initial public offerings. Journal of Finance. 1991;**46**(1):2-27

[8] Loughran T, Ritter JR. Why don't issuers get upset about leaving money on the table in IPOs? Review of Financial Studies. 2002;**15**(2):413-444

[9] Loughran T, Ritter JR. Why has IPO underpricing changed over time? Financial Management. 2004;**33**(3):5-37

[10] Ritter JR. Equilibrium in the initial public offering market. Annual Review of Financial Economics. 2011;**3**:347-374

[11] Loughran T, Ritter JR, Rydqvist K. Initial public offerings: International insights. Pacific-Basin Finance Journal. 1994;**2**(2–3):165-199

[12] Ma S, Faff R. Market conditions and the optimal IPO allocation mechanism in China. Pacific-Basin Finance Journal. 2007;**15**(2):121-139

[13] Jia C, Xie Z, Zhang D. Analyst coverage in the premarket of IPOs. Working Chapter. 2014

[14] Lee PJ, Taylor SL, Walter TS. Australian IPO pricing in the short and long run. Journal of Banking & Finance. 1996;**20**(7):1189-1210

[15] Kryzanowski L, Lazrak S, Rakita I. The behavior of prices, trades and spreads for Canadian IPO's. Multinational Finance Journal. 2005;**9**(3–4):215-236

[16] Hamao Y, Packer F, Ritter JR. Institutional affiliation and the role of venture capital: Evidence from initial public offerings in Japan. Pacific-Basin Finance Journal. 2000; **8**(5):529-558

[17] Levis M. The long-run performance of initial public offerings: The UK experience 1980-1988. Financial Management. 1993;**22**:28-41

[18] Arosio R, Paleari S, Giudici G."The market performance of Italian IPOs in the long-run. Working Chapter, EFMA 2001 Lugano Meetings. 2001

[19] Chahine S. Block-holder ownership, family control and post-listing performance of French IPOs. Managerial Finance. 2007;**33**(6):388-400

[20] Loughran T, Ritter JR, Rydqvist K. Initial public offerings: International insights. Pacific-Basin Finance Journal. 1994;**2**(2-3). Available from: https://site.warrington.ufl.edu/ritter/files/2016/05/Int2016.pdf [Accessed: 11 December 2017]

[21] Ibbotson RG. Price performance of common stock new issues. Journal of Financial Economics. 1975;**2**:235-272

[22] Rajan R, Servaes H. Analyst following of initial public offerings. Journal of Finance. 1997;**52**(2):507-529

[23] Carter RB, Frederick HD, Singh AK. Underwriter reputation, initial returns, and the long-run performance of IPO stocks. Journal of Finance. 1998;**53**(1): 285-311

[24] Gompers PA, Lerner J. The really long-run performance of initial public offerings: The pre-Nasdaq evidence. Journal of Finance. 2003;**58**(4): 1355-1392

[25] How JCY, Ngo K, Verhoeven P. Dividend initiations and long-run IPO performance. Australian Journal of Management. 2011;**36**(2):267-286

[26] Moshirian F, Ng D, Wu E. Model specification and IPO performance: New insights from Asia. Research in International Business and Finance. 2010;**24**(1):62-74

[27] Kirkulak B. The initial and long-run returns of Japanese venture capital-backed and non-venture capital-backed IPOs. International Journal of Managerial Finance. 2008;**4**(2):112-135

[28] Kooli M, Suret JM. The aftermarket performance of initial public offerings in Canada. Journal of Multinational Financial Management. 2004;**14**(1): 47-66

[29] Espenlaub S, Gregory A, Tonks I. Testing the robustness of long-term under-performance of UK initial public offerings. Working Chapter. 1998

[30] Khurshed A, Mudambi R, Goergen M. On the long-run performance of IPOs. Working Chapter, University of Reading. 2000

[31] Gregory A, Guermat C, Al-Shawawreh F. UK IPOs: Long run returns, behavioural timing and pseudo timing. Journal of Business Finance and Accounting. 2010;**37**(5–6):612-647

[32] Ljungqvist AP. Pricing initial public offerings: Further evidence from Germany. European Economic Review. 1997;**41**:1309-1320

[33] Stehle R, Ehrhardt O, Przyborowsky R. Long-run stock performance of German initial public offerings and seasoned equity issues. European Financial Management Journal. 2000;**6**(2):173-196

[34] Bessler W, Kurth A. Agency problems and the performance of venture-backed IPOs in Germany: Exit strategies, lock-up periods, and bank ownership. European Journal of Finance. 2007;**13**(1):29-63

[35] Aussenegg W. Short and long-run performance of initial public offerings in the Austrian stock market. Working Chapter, Vienna University of Technology. 1997

[36] Alvarez S, Gonzalez V. Long-Run Performance of Initial Public Offerings (IPOs) in the Spanish Capital Market, Working Chapter, University of Oviedo, EFMA 2001 Lugano Meetings; 2001

[37] Boissin R, Sentis P. Long-run performance of IPOs and the role of financial analysts: Some French evidence. European Journal of Finance. 2012;**20**(2):1-25

[38] Neneh BN, Smit VA. Factors affecting the absolute and relative long-term performance of initial public offerings (IPOs) on the Johannesburg security exchange (JSE). Investment Management and Financial Innovations. 2014;**11**(4):244-253

[39] Sapusek A. Benchmark-sensitivity of IPO long-run performance: An empirical study for Germany.

Schmalenbach Business Review. 2000; **52**:374-405

[40] Karolyi GA, Martell R. Terrorism and the stock market. International Review of Applied Financial Issues and Economics. 2010;**2**(2):285-314

[41] Coakley J, Hadass L, Wood A. Hot IPOs can damage your long-run wealth! Applied Financial Economics. 2008; **18**(14):1111-1120

[42] Fama EF, French KR. Common risk factors in the returns on stocks and bonds. Journal of Financial Economics. 1993;**33**:3-56

[43] Carhart M. On persistence in mutual fund performance. Journal of Finance. 1997;**52**(1):57-82

[44] Fama EF, French KR. A five-factor asset pricing model. Journal of Financial Economics. 2015;**116**:1-22

[45] Merikas A, Gounopoulos D, Nounis C. Global shipping IPOs performance. Maritime Policy and Management. 2009;**36**(6):481-505

[46] Ahmad-Zaluki NA, Abidin S. IPO pricing in Malaysia: An analysis of REITs and non-REIts. International Journal of Economics and Management. 2011;**5**(1):319-332

[47] Younesi N, Ardekani A, Hashemijoo M. Performance of Malaysian IPOs and impact of return determinants. Journal of Business Studies Quarterly. 2012;**4**(2):140-158

Chapter 7

The Independence of Indexed Volatilities

Katlego Kola and Tumellano Sebehela

Abstract

Studies on indexed volatility spillovers are unique because indices encompass more information than other parameters used in illustrating volatility movements. Further, indices encompass most of the constituents listed on different stock exchanges around the globe. This chapter uses vector autoregression (VAR) for volatility spills and the Markov regime switching model to understand how different volatility regimes behave among bonds, commodities, equities and real estate indices of emerging markets. The results illustrate that volatility spillovers occur within (same) indices and across different indices. Moreover, those spillovers are within and across emerging countries. Interestingly, illiquid indices in certain situations move in between different volatility regimes more than liquid indices. Volatility strategies emanating from this study are equally applicable to both sell and buy sides in securities markets.

Keywords: BRICS, duration, Markov-regime switching, VAR(1), volatility spillovers

1. Introduction

Formation of organisation that represents countries with similar interests or likeminded goals can be traced many decades ago. Some of those organisations are continentally focused (i.e. African Union, former Organisation of African Unity in 1963 and European Union in 1958-its original roots) while other are global (i.e. United Nations in 1945). Recently, we have seen organisations that are Transatlantic-Brazil, Russia, India, China and South Africa (BRICS hereafter) countries. South Africa (SA) joined BRIC countries in 2009 through invitation by other member states while the four founding members originate from a term coined by Jim O'Neil (former Managing Partner of Goldman Sachs). While the origination of the BRIC term is influenced by the economic similarities, there are other interesting similarities about BRIC countries. The similarities of BRICS nation are (i) political structure-ruling parties stay in power for least 10 years without much challenge; although, we have recently seen the rising of opposition parties or citizens, (ii) country governance-ruling elites combine free market policies with socialism, and privatisation of government owned entities is extremely rare and (iii) economic policies-ruling parties champion economic direction and by extension economic of countries [1]. Some market commentators called that approach statism. However, statism is beyond the scope of this study. Those three traits have strong influence of the capital markets of those countries. The key question is what relationship exists between investments and associated risks. For this article, the special focus is on volatility spills.

That concept is commonly known as volatility transfer hypothesis (VTH). VTH is well documented across and within different traditional asset classes (i.e. stocks, bonds and money market instruments especially cash). Fundamentally, VTH argue that as one become familiar with a firm, the volatility of that firm decreases due to decrease in information asymmetry. However some scholars argue that VTH does not hold in every situation. On the practical side, specifically in among alternative asset classes, there are virtually no studies on VTH. This is the main gap that this article fills in. In analysis, the study draws data on bonds, commodities, equities and listed real estate from the BRICS countries. The analysis is essentially empirical. Both empirical and theoretical studies offer little, if any, insight on how volatility spillovers behave and their effects in the BRICS countries. The closest study that explores this theme is [2]. In [2], multivariate general autoregressive conditional heteroscedasticity (GARCH) and disaggregated value-at-Risk (VaR) are used to study traditional asset classes. This study goes beyond traditional asset classes and uses other models such as the regime-switching models. Similarly to [2], international diversification and risk management is central to volatility spillovers in BRICS countries.

A lot of policy documents show that jointly BRICS account for over billions of dollars investments including listed investments-in 2012 BRICS received over $1 billion in foreign aid. The population is highly consumptuous with a high percentage of population eligible to work for foreseeable future. In all those countries, ruling governments encourage their working force to save some of their earnings for later use in their life. Among the type of investments that potential future retiree can invest in include bonds, commodities, equities and listed real estate investments. Besides the type of investments that potential future retiree investments in, BRICS have their own special economic traits. South Africa offers one of the highly sophisticated capital markets in the world and China is the second biggest economy after the Unites States (U.S.). More, China has been moving at least 30 million people out of the poverty over the last 20 years. Given those massive investment opportunities in BRICS countries, how do investors maximise their returns and minimise their risks? One of the ways of minimising risks in the BRICS is by mitigating against volatility investment movements in the BRICS countries.

The consensus emerging from literature on asset co-movements is that asset markets are linked internationally, and volatility is transmitted from one market to another. Earlier studies of market linkages were habitually focused on developed countries however due to the financial liberalisation and trade openness of emerging economies, research has also focused on investigating cross-border links in emerging economies from developed countries. Emerging markets have increasingly played an important role in financial markets and were not spared from the impact of the global financial crisis. A better understanding of how emerging markets respond to exogenous shocks can assist investors and portfolio managers better understand if there are any diversification possibilities.

This article explores volatility spillovers in the BRICS countries based on alternative investment strategies. That is, alternative investment strategies involve investment in bonds, commodities, equities and real estate. For this study, seems real estate is listed because on one hand, the relationship between listed real estate and unlisted real estate is a mixed bag [3] and other the other hand, real estate is seen as a proxy for macroeconomic risks [4]. The macroeconomic risk proxy is also evident in other industries such as commodities. Moreover, diversification plays part in influencing commodity prices. Listed real estate is either real estate investment trusts (REITs) or real estate operating companies (REOCs). Further, those studies illustrate that those effects are trans-Atlantic. The reason why cash is not analysed in this article is because cash and money asset classes have been extensively researched. For example, over 60% of international trade is done on U.S. dollars and currency markets are the most liquid of all capital markets [5]. For this study, it is important to drive risk management strategies, especially when information is asymmetric.

The article similar to this study is one by Liow [6]. That study analysed spillovers of four major asset classes (public real estate, general equity, currency and bond) during 2007–2009 period. Given the longer period for this study, one foresees more interesting results than ones of Liow [6]. He used regime-switching, VAR and GARCH (1;1) models. This uses models used in [6] plus the regime-switching model. Liow [6] draws data from four continents; (i) Asia emerging countries, (ii) European emerging markets, (iii) Latin American emerging countries and (iv) South Africa. Other than being emerging countries, the BRICS are similar in the sense that ruling political elites stay in power for long periods (i.e. 15 years), more, those governments have come up with organisations that are most likely to compete with established institutions, i.e. the BRICS Bank is most likely to compete with the World Bank in future. Further, there is close political will among the BRICS which is not prevalent among all emerging countries. As volatility spills are driven by financial integration, liberalisation and crises contagion [6] among other factors, the former factors are likely to be key drivers for volatility spills among the BRICS countries. So far, it seems there are no major crises contagion reported in any of the BRICS countries.

To sum up, the results show that the indices (bonds, commodities, equities and real estate) illustrate that volatility spills are within and in between emerging countries. The volatility movements between countries are sporadic without any specific pattern(s)-most volatility spills are within countries. Those spills are evident in both out and in-sample data. Thus, lagged data of indices have evident volatility spillovers. Consistent with prior studies, the volatility spills move between different volatility regimes. Interestingly, liquid indices have less persistent regimes than illiquid indices. That would imply that illiquid indices are suitable for investments by intraday investors such as hedge funds while liquid indices are suitable for long-term investments-a rare finding. In [7], Markov-Switching-GARCH model is used, while this study uses general Markov regime switching model. The former model is univariate and discrete in nature while the latter is 'multivariate' and continuous in nature. Hedging was effectively reduced by 64% in [8] while in this study volatility risk is appropriately modelled.

The balance of this article is structured as follows: Section 2 is on literature review. Section 3 is on data and modelling, and Section 4 presents the analysis. Section 5 concludes the study.

2. Literature review

In criticising the prior studies this article divides literature review as per the four asset classes; (iii) bonds, (i) commodities, (ii) equities, and (iv) listed real estate. In this way, specific traits of each asset class are disentangled.

2.1 Bonds

In [9], it is explored volatility spills and return between equity and bond markets for Australia during the period of 1992–2006. They argue that volatility spills are important for diverse purposes; (i) asset allocation, (ii) portfolio management,

(iii) financial risk management, and (iv) capital market regulation. In this article, volatility spills are important largely for financial risk management. Among confirmed concepts on volatility spills (i) hedging demands increase with prices changes, (ii) positive news increases stock prices while prices fall when the discount rate rises. Normally, asymmetric price adjustment hypothesis (APAH) state that bad news affect bonds and stocks equally than good news. For modelling, they used joint process of conditional means, asymmetric Baba, Engle, Kraft and Kroner (BEKK) model, dynamic conditional correlation (DCC) model and bivariate GARCH model.

The data sample is on Australian equity and government bond markets, and the equity index was on 500 companies listed on Australian Stock Exchange. The preliminary results of [9] illustrate that equity volatility is lowest when returns of both markets are positive, and highest equity (bond) returns are negative (positive). More, when equity returns are negative, conditional correlation is stronger. As expected, distribution of returns are skewed and leptokurtic. Bond (equity) markets seem to react predominantly to negative (positive) news than positive (negative) ones. When the bond shock moves from negative angle to positive side, then equity variance surface tilts. Most volatility spills for equities are evident when returns are negative and visa verse for bonds. None of the used models were fully able to explain observed spills.

In [10], co-movements of volatilities in the international equity and bond markets were explored. They argue that genitive returns are more common and dependent than positive returns in international equity markets. In investigating volatility spills [10], the issue of fat tails was taken into account. The data presents the dependence between two leading markets in North-America (U.S. and Canada) and two major markets of the Euro zone (France and Germany). The U.S. equity index is based on the S&P500 index and Canadian equity index returns are based on DataStream index. The bond series are from 5-year government bond indices. The statistical tools used are exceedance correlation, extreme value theory (EVT) in order to capture fat tails and Gaussian bivariate GARCH or regime-switching models, specifically M-GARCH because of its ability to capture many variables. Copulas are used to increase the ability to capture asymmetric dependence.

The preliminary results of [10] show that there is a large, extreme dependence in international equity and bond markets while bond-equity dependence has a negative effect. The latter statement encourages international diversification and switching form equities into the domestic bonds. Historically, correlation between Canadian equity and bond markets has been relatively high. Further, results show that asymmetric regime of dependence and negative shocks are more likely to be transmitted to other markets than positive shocks. After the introduction of the Euro, France and Germany became more dependent. Broadly, high volatilities are associated with asymmetric dependence.

Ehrmann et al. [11] disentangled complexity of financial transmission process across different assets-domestically and internationally. They focus spillovers on two largest economies in the world-the U.S. and Euro area. The period covered is from 1998 to 2008 for two-daily returns over a 20-year period for seven asset prices: short-term interest rates, bond yields and equity market returns. For the U.S., data includes the 3-month Treasury bill rate for the short rate, the 10-year Treasury bond rate for the long rate and the S&P500 index for the stocks. For the Euro area, data is 3-month interbank rate-the FIBOR rate before 1999, the EURIBOR after 1999-for short rate, the German 10-year government bond for the long rate, and the S&P Euro index for the equity market and the U.S. dollar-euro since 1999. Every data is expressed as a percentage.

To model those spills [11], it was used a behavioural model that incorporated seven variables which had a 7 × 7 matrix. For reduced estimators, they used ordinary least squares (OLSs) model. Other methods used for Cholesky decomposition, alternative methodology for identification known as identification through heteroscedasticity (IH). They assume that structural shocks are uncorrelated and the matrix is stable for the entire. The latter principles are consistent with prior literature especially for ARCH and GARCH models. In presenting results [11], international transmission (i.e. direct effects and overall effects), response of the exchange rate and variance decomposition are shown. On international transmission, the direct effects show that spillovers are positive, both domestically and internationally. In those spills, the rise in foreign equity markets leads the spills. For overall effects, the key finding is that international transmissions are large for most assets but there are also international cross-market linkages. Moreover, the U.S. shocks led Euro shocks. Most of the co-movements were among the bond markets. Overall, the U.S. equity markets played a central role of influencing world stock markets. In relation to response of the exchange rate, the overall changes in relation to exchange rate reaction to bond yield changes are fairly small than direct effects. On the variance decomposition, during the 1989–2008 financial period, major spills were driven by the U.S. markets across every asset class in the study. The robustness tests support the earlier findings of the study. Thus, in global asset allocation one should mitigate against spills across most asset classes.

2.2 Commodities

In [12], volatility spills were investigated in commodity markets since 1700. They argue that some authors raised questions regarding the volatility of commodity prices been more than manufacturing ones, the secular trend since 1700 and relationship between globalisation and commodity volatilities. However, none of the scholars have addressed those questions using a long term series indeed.
For poor countries [12], it was argue that volatilities for those countries should be high because those countries specialise in agriculture and mineral production. The data used in [12] is for the world and various trends are outlined during specific periods. This is to consolidate reasons that drove commodity prices during those periods. They calculated log prices for their study, and used Dickey-Fuller and Phillips-Perron tests to validate their illustrate volatilities. Prebisch-Singer hypothesis was central to their analysis. Preliminary results of [12] show that volatilities among different commodities are different. In poor countries, volatilities tend to be higher because those countries are dependent on agriculture and mineral production. Sauerbeck-Statist shows no evidence of secular patterns from 1800 onwards. Further analysis illustrates that French and American Revolutionary Wars, the Napoleonic Wars and the War of 1812 contributed to increase in volatilities. In order to test the robustness of their results [12], GARCH (1;1) model and GARCH (1;1) was used and it was confirmed that results are robust. Seasonality also played a role in driving higher volatilities.

Antonakakis and Kizys [13] investigated dynamic spills between commodity and currency markets. In [13], it is argued that precious metals (gold, silver, platinum and palladium) have been seen as safe havens during final crisis. Further, they state that inclusion of precious metals in equity portfolios decreases systematic risk of investments; therefore, diversification accrues in those investments. They research is centred on these questions; (i) how time-varying spills differ among commodity and currency markets, and (ii) what is the relationship between returns and volatilities during financial transmission. In answering those questions, Antonakakis and Kizys [13] used the spillover index which is performed by using rolling-window forecast error variance decomposition (FEVD) by transmitters and receivers of shocks.

The weekly data in [13] is made up of the spot prices of the four precious metals, crude oil spot prices, euro (EUR/USD), Japanese yen (JPY/USD), British pound (GBP/USD) and the Swiss franc (CHF/USD) spot exchange rate, each versus U.S. dollar. They use weekly daily in order to synchronise data and error elimination [13]. The period of the data is from January the 6th, 1987 to July the 22nd, 2014, totalling 1438 observations. The usage of the four precious metals is well documented by numerous studies. The preliminary analysis of data illustrate that volatilities increased dramatically especially from 2000/2001 period for the precious metals and oil, while currencies volatility decreased from 2000/2001 onwards. Moreover, preliminary analysis shows that spot prices are positively skewed with exception of GBP/USD and CHF/USD. The absolute returns (volatility) for all parameters are positively skewed. And the Jarque-Berra tests confirm non-normality of distributions. Further analysis includes using vector autoregressive (VAR) model to illustrate return transmission across all the parameters. One of the advantages of VAR model is that it can cater for many variables.

The results of the VAR model illustrate volatility spills across all variables. Total spillovers index indicates 42.41% average contribution. Most transmission was from gold, followed by silver and then platinum. Crude oil had lowest transmissions. On the other hand, crude oil's demand is linked to four commodities as for production of those metals, crude oil is used. One of notable thing about [13] is that negative skewness has higher probabilities. Normally, the opposite should be true because positive skewness constituent more risk than a negative one. For all variables, the curves are positively skewed and leptokurtic. The latter statement would imply that prices spreads are significantly probably due to high volatilities. According [13], volatilities in commodity and currency markets are likely to occur during less volatile episodes. For robustness test, they used h-step-ahead forecast error variance decompositions and alternative rolling windows, and robustness tests confirmed that results main qualitatively similar.

Basak and Pavlova [14] modelled financialization for commodities markets. Prior studies have documented index and non-index commodities; however, the theory of financialization which is far-reaching implications had limited synthetisation [14]. The latter point is central to study of [14]. The main variables that were analysed in the study are (i) commodity supply shocks, (ii) commodity demand shocks, and (iii) (endogenous) changes in wealth shares of the two investor classes. The theoretical model that they built is a closed form. Fundamentally, in [14], it was argued that value assets pay off more in high-index states. In building the model, they assumed that the model follow Brownian motion (BM). The model included a parameter that signal arrival of news, supply news of uncorrelated commodities, model distinguish between index and non-index commodities, and the inventors were accounted for; (i) normal investors and (ii) institutional investors. Moreover, equilibrium effects of financialization of commodities were accounted for. Centrally to the last statement, instead of the model behaving like a trading model, it behaved like one for normal investor. Other equilibrium issues included (i) equilibrium commodity futures prices shaped on corollary, (ii) futures volatilities and correlations, and (iii) economy with demand shocks. Further, the illustrated commodity prices and inventories. For the commodity prices and inventories, they (i) incorporating storage where additional economic agents (i.e. consumers and firms) were added, (ii) equilibrium commodity prices and inventories. The second proposition is on how the discount factor is affected by institutional inventors. And finally, (iii) cross-commodity spillovers and the import of income shocks. The latter proposition is about how institutional demand increases for all assets are positively correlated with index, especially demand for commodity storage.

The results for [14] illustrated those volatilities in futures markets do spillover into other commodities. Further, there is a trade-off between investors due to relative performance fluctuates. The latter phenomenon is consistent with what is illustrated by VIX volatility index [14]. In addition, the model information is 'asymmetric and investors have the same beliefs'.

In [15], excess co-movements of commodity prices in developed (118 variables from Australia, Canada, France, Germany, Japan, the UK and the U.S.) and emerging markets (six variables from China, Brazil, Brazil, Taiwan, Mexico, etc.) were investigated. They argue that prior studies illustrate that financialization in the commodities markets lead to excess price volatility. One possible reason for that is that commodities especially of currency nature such as gold are characterised by spikes in prices. Central to their investigation is that (i) co-movements imply that 'demands and supplies are affected by unobserved forecast of the economic variable' and (ii) portfolio management strategies are affected by co-movements. The latter phenomenon resonates with this study. The variables that [15] are (i) the U.S. index of industrial production, (ii) consumer price index (CPI), (iii) effective $US exchange rate, (iv) three-month Treasury bill interest rate, (v) M1 monetary measure and (vi) S&P500 stock index.

One thing which is evident in [15] is that they are dealing with a large database which has numerous variables. And in order to probably account for those variables, you need a model that accounted for such variables. For the commodity prices, they used wheat, copper, silver, soybeans, raw sugar, cotton, crude oil and live cattle. Further, arbitrariness and computational difficulties should be minimised. One of the ways of how to avoid arbitrariness and computational difficulties is to use principal component analysis (PCA) and stepwise regression, although stepwise is time consuming when one uses many variables. In their analysis [15] focused on filtering commodity returns using large approximate factors models. And for that [15] used (i) static factor model and (ii) ARCH-LM for illustrating spillovers and (iii) SUR model to test whether residuals are unrelated.

The preliminary analysis of [15] the skewness of all commodities except of wheat is negatively skewed. Thus, wheat should have high volatilities than the rest of the commodities. And the Jarque-Berra test confirms non-normality for all commodities. The latter illustration is consistent with other studies on commodities. The correlation matrix shows that all commodities are correlated with one another except with live cattle. That is, live cattle in when compared with the seven commodities might offer diversification benefits. The results of returns show that crude oil and copper are costly correlated with variables of emerging markets. Monetary measures have more influence in emerging markets than developed countries. When they test for excess co-movement of commodity returns, results exemplify that commodity co-movements are common and influencing across all markets. Moreover, those co-movements are sampling dependent. In [15], it stated that given that the speculation is rife in commodity markets, some co-movements might be driven by speculation. The OLS model confirms the presence of endogeneity.

2.3 Equities

The Black Monday of October 1987, the U.S. born global financial crisis of 2008 and 2009, as well as the European debt crisis that occurred in late 2009 are known as the some of the few financial crisis in the past three decades that have resulted in the volatility of financial markets and further resulted in wide spread international crisis. These are known as co-movements of financial markets defined as volatility spillovers from one market to another. Volatility spillover studies have come to the vanguard as they are largely associated with risks that have implications on (i) optimal portfolio construction, (ii) financial stability and (iii) implementation of policies that may render harmful shock transmissions in financial markets. Recent studies that address the issue of volatility dynamics indicate that volatility spillover effects among countries or financial markets are time varying, most importantly during times of crisis. This has particularly significant consequences for investors and policy makers. Consequently, understanding the changing aspects of volatility spillovers is imperative.

In [16], both implied and realised volatility linkages were analysed through a rolling correlation analysis across global equity markets. This covers the U.S., European, German, Japanese, and Swiss markets during the sample period of 1999 to 2009. Implied volatility indices provide information regarding future uncertain expectations of stock price movements. Using the VAR method, the study indicates that both unconditional and conditional correlations for implied and realised volatility exhibit large fluctuations during that sample period. These results coincide with market fluctuations that occurred during the period of the global financial crises.

The consensus emerging from literature on asset co-movements is that asset markets are linked internationally, and volatility is transmitted from one market to another. Earlier studies of market linkages were habitually focused on developed countries however due to the financial liberalisation and trade openness of emerging economies, research has also focused on investigating cross-border links in emerging economies from developed countries. Emerging markets have increasingly played an important role in financial markets and were not spared from the impact of the global financial crisis. A better understanding of how emerging markets respond to exogenous shocks can assist investors and portfolio managers better understand if there are any diversification possibilities.

On another standpoint [2], volatility spillover effects were identified on a sectorial basis (industrial and financial sectors) from the U.S. as a developed country to BRICS nations as emerging markets using a VAR(1)-GARCH (1,1) framework. In the industrial sector, overall results indicate that the volatility transmission from the U.S. predominantly affects Brazil, Russia and India, while in the financial sector; it predominantly affects Brazil and Russia. In [17], the volatility impact is also indicated from developed markets by looking at regional spillovers across transitioning emerging markets and frontier equity markets, particularly in the Middle East and Africa together with the U.S. as the developed market. The study examines the stock markets of Saudi Arabia, UAE, South Africa and Israel from the period of 1994 to 2010 using a multi-timescale analysis using a wavelet-based time and frequency distributions compositions. The study finds that the Middle Eastern countries were more susceptible to the U.S. subprime crisis as compared to South Africa, however indication of short-term shocks that produced additional vulnerability in the South African equity market prior to the global financial crisis are noted, which could have potentially been due to investor sentiment.

Despite the increased studies of volatility spillover analyses from developed to emerging markets, there continues to be limited cross-market studies that are undertaken in equity markets of emerging nations. The possible integration of emerging markets continues to be of great concern as theory suggests that expected returns might be expected to reduce, following a greater integration of emerging markets in the world economy. Ref. [8] contributes to the empirical literature of volatility spillover dynamics between equity markets by examining the returns and volatility dynamics of Ghana, Kenya, Nigeria and South Africa for the period

2005–2010. The study employs a multivariate VAR-EGARCH framework and finds that Nigeria is the dominant in volatility transmission to Ghana, Kenya and South Africa and while it is not a receiver of volatility from these markets. The study however finds that the domestic volatility indices of these markets are the highest coefficients for all these markets, which implies that domestic shocks may impact these markets more than external shocks.

In [2], it was positioned that a more effective way of better understanding efficient asset pricing, volatility forecasting, efficient cross-market allocation and hedging decisions along with optimal international portfolio strategies is through understanding the stock market dynamics and volatility spillover effects of listed asset sectors individually in particular markets. Several literatures have focused on volatility spillovers in financial markets on a global, regional and country level. This section particularly focuses on volatility spillovers among equity stocks in financial markets. Cross-market volatility linkages in global developed equity markets attracted much attention in research. An earlier study of [18] studied the return volatility dynamics and transmission among the G-7 countries' equity markets using both the GARCH and VAR models. They find that while in these markets, domestic market shocks are the largest single source of domestic volatility variation for other markets, (apart from the U.K. and U.S.) shocks to foreign markets account for a significant portion of domestic market volatility. The study provides empirical evidence of volatility spillover effects in the equity markets of these industrialised countries. The results also indicate that volatility spillovers in these equity markets for this period had significant changes due to the global financial crises.

Studies such as [19] find that during tranquil times there are particular countries that are net transmitters of risk and others are net receivers of risk in global financial markets. The study particularly analyses the global financial shifts of volatility spillovers by employing the [20] forecast-error variance decomposition and incorporating a Markov switching framework which considers economic regime changes, into the generalised vector autoregressive (VAR) model. The study uses the following daily stock market volatility indices as proxies of market risk; the VIX (S&P 500 volatility, U.S.), VFTSE (FTSE 100 volatility, U.K). VCAC (CAC 40 volatility, France), VDAX (DAX 30 volatility, Germany). VAEX (AEX 25 volatility Netherlands), VSMI (SMI 20 volatility, Switzerland), VHSI (HIS 50 volatility, Hong Kong) and JNIV (Nikkei 225 volatility, Japan) for the period 2001 to 2017. The results of the study support the theory of shock transmissions and volatility spillovers by finding that all markets are more intense and are at the frequent risk of shock transmission and reception during turbulent times.

2.4 Listed real estate

The co-movement of real estate stocks and financial markets has been studied extensively. Previous literature has documented the theory that low correlation of an asset with other capital markets, international and domestic portfolios provides the opportunity for risk reduction and diversification in an investment [21]. In [22], the local, regional and global linkage of securitized real estate and stock markets and possible integration in nine developed markets from the three regions of North America (the U.S.), Europe (Germany, France, Netherlands and the U.K.) and Asia-Pacific (Japan, Hong Kong, Singapore and Australia) in the period 1990–2011 were investigated.

The study employs the spillover index of [20] that produces variance decompositions that are insensitive to variable ordering by allowing correlated shocks and historically observed distribution of the errors to account for the shocks. The spillover index is further based on a multivariate VAR that can capture market fluctuation of more than two countries concurrently rather than bivariate models. Liow [22] finds evidence of the following: (i) time-varying return co-movement and volatility spillovers in all markets and positive association with the global financial crisis (ii) a bi-directional and regime-dependant relationship of cross-volatility spillover effects, (iii) synchronisation between co-movements of volatility spillovers and correlation spillover cycles. Liow [23] studied time-varying co-movements of Asian real estate and the linkages of local, regional and global stock markets over the period of 1995 to 2009. Correlations of assets are interpreted to indicate co-movement and integration across financial markets. The integration of markets is also interpreted to indicate interdependence of markets which can lead to transmission crises.

Liow [23] demonstrates through an Asymmetric Dynamic Conditional Correlation (ADCC) model, also a specific class of multivariate GARCH models. Liow [23] finds time-varying conditional real estate-stock correlations at local, regional and global stock markets and some asymmetry and furthermore real estate-global stock correlation is impacted significantly by volatilities at local, regional and global levels. In this period, Liow [23] also finds that real estate and stock volatilities are more substantial in influencing co-variances more than correlations during and post the global financial crises. Hoesli and Reka [24] provided evidence on a national and international basis by investigating volatility spillovers between the U.S. and the U.K. real estate market, The U.S. and Australian real estate market as a national analysis and the U.S equity and real estate markets as an international analysis. The period of the study extends from 1990 to 2010 and the volatility spillovers are studied using the covariance matrix of the asymmetric t-BEKK (Baba-Engle-Kraft-Kroner) specification. On a national basis, the U.S is the net transmitter of volatility spillovers; this can be expected as the subprime crisis originated in the U.S. On an international basis, the three markets have more influence of volatility of the global market than the reverse, indicating quite the importance of these developed markets.

Liow and Ye [25] employed both univariate and multivariate switching regime beta models in the period of 2000–2015 to illustrate regime-dependant excess return distribution and volatility spillovers pre and post the global financial crises. The study examines the developed markets of the U.S., the U.K., France, Germany, Australia, Japan, Hong Kong and Singapore and their linkages with the world stock market and world real estate markets. The study uses switching regime models to allow for different economic conditions as well to capture the changes in the stochastic volatility process driving the real estate markets. The study reports a higher volatility parameter in response to the global financial crises compared to the 'normal' period. The real estate market linkages with the world market were affected differently by the global financial crises however they are amplified post-crises particularly for the European region, while the Asian real estate markets displayed reduced volatility spillovers with world markets in low volatility state post-crises.

Regime changes are associated with significant shifts in the fundamental relation between the risks and return trade-off and the probability that a switch can be initiated from one regime to another [26]. In [26], it was incorporated multiple regimes changes by modelling the return-volatility transmissions of real estate through the multivariate regime-dependent asymmetric dynamic covariance (MRDADC) model. They study the real estate markets of the U.S., the U.K, Japan, Hong Kong and Singapore for the period of 1990 to 2009. Firstly, the study finds that asymmetry, variance and covariance, associated with multiple regime changes, jointly influence return-volatility transmission in real estate markets and secondly the study finds that the five markets generally interact well with one another by finding significant mean-volatility linkages under different volatility regimes. Consequently, this has implications on diversification benefits that these markets can offer.

3. Data and modelling

3.1 Data

The weekly data is for the five BRICS countries (general equities, real estate, commodities and bonds) for the period 1 January 2007–31 December 2017 obtained from Bloomberg. The out-sample is from 2007 to 2017 and in-sample from 2012 to 2017. The in-sample is for parameters estimation and out-sample for evaluating forecasting performance. The use of weekly data ameliorates concerns over non-synchronicities and bid-ask effects in daily data [13]. The phenomenon of using returns to illustrate the descriptive nature of volatility spillovers is synonymous with [6, 27]. The returns are logarithm returns and they are consistent with VAR model. All returns are calculated based on the indices of those countries. The indices are as follows; (i) general equities, Brazil IBRX 50 for Brazil, Moex Russian index for Russia, Nifty 50 for India, SSE50 for China and JSE top 40 index for South Africa, (ii) listed real estate, IMOB for Brazil, for Russia the index is created based on PIKK Group, PJSC LSR Group, World Trade Centre 'ordinary shares' and World Trade Centre 'preferred shares' because Russia does not have a listed real estate index-the market capitalisations of those firms where aggregated over time, Nifty Realty for India, SHROP for China and all Property index (J803) for South Africa, (iii) commodities, BM&F BOVESPA for Brazil, MICEX Oil and Gas Index-from the Moscow exchange for Russia, Nifty Commodities for India, CCI for China and JCGMSAG (gold mining index) for South Africa and (iv) bonds, for Brazil-Brazil 8 7/8 04/15/24 bond, Russia-RFLB 08/29/18 bond, India-Nifty 10 yr. benchmark, China-GT USDCN 15yr bond and South Africa-SAGB 10 ½ 12/26 bond. Skintzi and Refenes [28] used indices to investigate regional and country shocks. This article is the first one that uses indices to illustrate shocks in the BRICS countries. According to [28], one of the advantages of modelling volatility shocks using indices is that

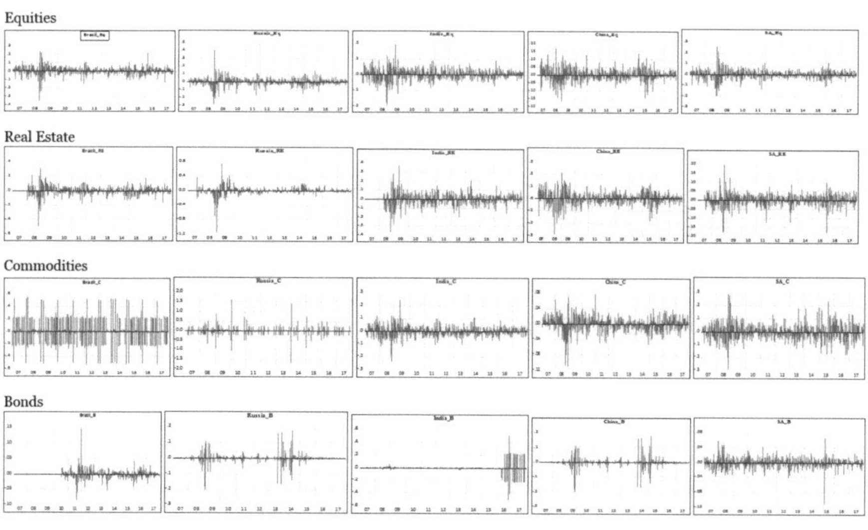

Figure 1.
BRICS log returns.

shocks are captured both as endogenous and exogenous variables. Just like [6, 27], this article presents diagnostic analysis based on graphs as part of volatilities transmission investigation.

For every index per a row, the first country is Brazil, followed by Russia, then India; thereafter, China and finally South Africa. A close inspection of **Figure 1** illustrate that the log returns of BRICS countries as shown by different graphs, BRICS returns were characterised by spikes during 2007–2017 period. The latter statement might be interpreted as the presence of changing volatility patterns and probably spillovers. Similar arguments were put forward by [6, 27] on return patterns. The years are on the x-axis and the log-returns on the y-axis. During 2008/2009, there was a global financial crisis that mainly affected western countries-western Europe and U.S. were the hardest hit by that subprime crisis. According to the Bank of International Settlements (BIS) Brazil only reacted to the global subprime crisis after Lehman Brothers collapsed. Due to that reaction, there was panic in Brazil lead to property market falling but IBOVESPA rose by 20%-in local currency; local capital issuance stood around $165 billion around 5.6% of Brazilian GDP. And bank credit increased to 36% from 32% during that period. Although, there still spikes after 2009, but they hoovered around same levels until 2017. For Russia, one sees similar pattern to Brazil. For both countries-Brazil and Russia, during subprime crisis, real estate reacts more than other indices. Does that imply that during subprime crisis volatilities are much higher in real estate?

Volatility modelling will provide answer(s) to that. Similar patterns are observable about Indian and Chinese indices. However, India and China have very strong capital markets and those countries are self-reliant on financing countries infrastructure. It seems that India and China tend to be insulated from external capital shocks [29]. South Africa is a unique member of the BRICS which joined through invitation. During year 2008, South African indices reacted to global capital markets movement; however, there was no subprime crisis effects felt in South Africa [30]. A study by PWC South Africa in 2016 illustrate that there was (i) a decline in new equity capital raised in South Africa, (ii) active and growing bond market in South Africa and (iii) number of corporate transactions decreased in South Africa. The decline in commodities index during 2014–2016 can be attributed to decline in commodities price and demand in commodities by South Africa trading partners. All those graphs illustrated diagnostic analysis on volatility spills. Now, the article takes the analysis further and it explores formative assessment of global transmission in the BRICS countries. The next section presents descriptive statistics of indices of the BRICS countries.

3.2 Data description and preliminary statistics

Table 1 provides the descriptive statistics of the returns of general equities, real estate, commodities and bonds.

Panel 1 indicates the equity information across all countries. Russia leads with the highest return at 28.41% while China has the lowest maximum return of 16.80%. Over the full period, Russian equities are also the most volatile with a standard deviation of 5.20% and the lowest volatile equities being that of China at 3.72%. The distribution of returns over time is negatively skewed with the exception of India and China. In addition, for all countries, the excess kurtosis exceeds 3, indicating that the return series is leptokurtic which is inconsistent with a normal distribution. The real estate data in panel 2 for the five countries indicate Russia with the highest return of 52.82% while the South Africa closed off with a lowest maximum return of 17.81% return. Russia is the most volatile with a weekly standard deviation of 7.65% while South Africa reports the lowest standard deviation of

Descriptions	Mean	Minimum	Maximum	SD	Kurtosis	Skewness	JB
Panel 1: general equity							
Brazil	0.0007	−0.3547	0.2385	0.051	7.0571	−0.6941	1235.05
Russia	0.0009	−0.4031	0.2841	0.052	9.1638	−0.0484	1987.64
India	−0.001	−0.1906	0.1956	0.037	3.2816	0.2699	264.06
China	−0.001	−0.1704	0.168	0.04	2.1323	0.0068	106.28
South Africa	−6E − 04	−0.2606	0.1984	0.043	5.1509	−0.0227	633.49
Panel 2: real estate							
Brazil	−0.002	−0.5044	0.3097	0.066	8.8189	−1.0306	1780.53
Russia	−0.001	−0.7145	0.5282	0.077	22.483	−1.3087	11613.2
India	0.003	−0.3752	0.3719	0.072	4.0292	0.2754	384.67
China	−0.002	−0.2161	0.2894	0.054	2.6673	0.3788	179.68
South Africa	−0.001	−0.1961	0.1781	0.037	4.2404	0.4225	428.42
Panel 3: commodities							
Brazil	0.0002	−0.529	0.5435	0.177	2.0477	0.0046	100.11
Russia	−8E − 04	−1.6035	1.6337	0.199	22.8521	−0.2209	12.385
India	0.0009	−0.2369	0.2432	0.042	3.8767	−0.0754	359.35
China	0.0005	−0.1096	0.0768	0.02	4.0293	−0.7607	442.87
South Africa	−0.002	−0.2866	0.286	0.065	2.0176	0.3055	106.1
Panel 4: bonds							
Brazil	0.0001	−0.0845	0.1474	0.016	21.5203	1.6562	7763.32
Russia	−2E − 04	−0.2019	0.1777	0.029	20.4736	−0.7622	9466
India	−3E − 04	−0.5151	0.5113	0.065	26.9833	−1.1651	17455.1
China	−3E − 04	−0.1126	0.0661	0.015	7.2105	−0.5118	1266.32
South Africa	−1E − 04	−0.2019	0.1777	0.029	20.4549	−0.7619	9431.2

Note: SD stands for standard deviation and JB for Jarque-Bera test for the return normality.

Table 1.
Descriptive statistics.

3.68%. All five countries exceed the kurtosis of 3 and with the exception of Brazil and Russia, the data is positively skewed.

For commodities indicated in panel 3, Russia reports the highest maximum of 163.37% in returns, while India reports the lowest at 7.68%. Russia commodity stocks are more volatile with a standard deviation of 19.87% and the Chinese stocks are the least volatile at the standard deviation of 2.02% All countries exceed the kurtosis of 3 and the data is negatively skewed with the exception of Brazil and South Africa. In the bonds market indicated in panel 4, India has the highest return at 51.13% while China has the lowest maximum return at 6.61%. India is also the most volatile with a standard deviation of 6.50% and China. The data is also leptokurtic and is negatively skewed with the exception of Brazil. JB values in all panels (i.e. 1–4) illustrate that the four indices are abnormal and that can be interpreted as the presence of shocks. In [6], the same view on JB values was stated. The skewness values show that some countries have negative skews while others have positive skews for different capital markets. That mixture of different skewness assist in hedging volatility while positive skewness assist in generating high alpha and/or arbitrage opportunities. The former phenomenon is ideal for risk managers while the latter phenomenon is suitable for intraday investors-traders.

3.3 Volatility spillover modelling

Volatility and volatility transmission can be illustrated using most econometric models including VAR model. The formula for VAR model is:

$$y_t = c + A_1 y_{t-1} + A_2 y_{t-2} + \dots + A_p y_{t-p} + e_t \quad (1)$$

Where the l-periods back observation y_{t-1} is called the l-th lag of l-th lag of y, c is a $k * 1$ vector of constants (intercepts), A_j is the time-invariant $k * k$ matrix and e_t is a $k * 1$ vector of error terms satisfying $E(e_t) = 0$, every error term has mean zero. $E(e_t e_t') = \Omega$, the contemporaneous covariance matrix of error terms is Ω (a $k * k$ positive-semidefinite matrix. $E(e_t e_{t-k}') = 0$, for any non-zero k, there is no correlation across time; in particular, no serial correlation in individual error terms.
In order to have a deeper insight in volatility spills, this article proposes using regime-switching model in order to capture different spills regimes. The common model used for regime-switching variables is Markov switching model. The simple Markov model of conditional mean presented when s_t denotes an unobservable state variable assuming the value one or zero. A simple switching model for the variable z_t involves two AR specifications:

$$z_t = \begin{cases} \alpha_0 + \beta z_t + \varepsilon_t, s_t = 0, \\ \alpha_0 + \alpha_1 + \beta z_t + \varepsilon_t, s_t = 1, \end{cases} \quad (2)$$

where $|\beta| < 1$ and ε_t are i.i.d. random variables with mean zero and variance σ_ε^2. This is a statitionay AR (1) process with the mean $\frac{\alpha_0}{1-\beta}$ when $s_t = 0$, and it switches to another stationary AR (1) process with mean $\frac{\alpha_0 + \alpha_1}{1-\beta}$ when $s_t = 1$. If $\alpha_1 \neq 0$ then the model admits two dynamic structures at different levels, depending on the value of the state variable s_t. In this case, z_t are governed by two regimes with distinct means, and s_t determines switching between two different regimes. The transition matrix for the Markov is:

$$\mathcal{P} = \begin{bmatrix} IP(s_t = 0|s_{t-1} = 0) IP(s_t = 1|s_{t-1} = 0) \\ IP(s_t = 0|s_{t-1} = 1) IP(s_t = 1|s_{t-1} = 1) \end{bmatrix} \quad (3)$$

and

$$= \begin{bmatrix} p_{00} \; p_{01} \\ p_{10} \; p_{11} \end{bmatrix}, \quad (4)$$

where p_{ij} $(i,j = 0, 1)$ denote the transition probabilities of $s_t = j$ given that $s_t = i$. The transition probabilities satisfy $p_{i0} + p_{i1} = 1$. The matrix governs the random behavior of the state variable, and it contains two parameters $(p_{00}$ and $p_{11})$.
One can extend model (5) such that a more general dynamic structure is captured. Then model (2) is extended into:

$$z_t = \alpha_0 + \alpha_1 s_t + \beta_1 z_{t-1} + \dots + \beta_k z_{t-k} + \varepsilon_t \quad (5)$$

where $s_t = 0, 1$ are still the Markovian state variables with the transition matrix (3a) and ε_t are i.i.d. random variables with zero and variance σ_ε^2. This is a model with a general $AR(k)$ dynamic structure and switching intercepts. For the d-dimensional time series $\{z_t\}$, Eq. (4) can be re-written as:

$$z_t = \alpha_0 + \alpha_1 s_t + B_1 z_{t-1} + \dots + B_k z_{t-k} + \varepsilon_t \tag{6}$$

while $s_t = 0, 1$ are still the Markovian state variables with the transition matrix (3a), $B_i(i = 1, \dots, k)$ are matrices of parameters, and ε_t are i.i.d. random vectors with zero and variance–covariance matrix $\sum_0$. Eq. (5) is a VAR model with switch intercepts. Although generalisation is easy but some parameters such as d variables might be difficult to estimate.

4. Analysis

In presenting the empirical results, the article starts with VAR calculations. Thereafter, Markov regime-switching results are presented in order to explore if one can infer interdependence of volatilities regimes. In order to verify which VAR is suitable, the first and second order tests (i.e. residual serial correlation) testing validity are used. Thereafter, a lag-length criterion is used. All those tests confirmed the appropriateness of VAR (1) model. Further, in order to interpret the results Cholesky decomposition is used. Generally, when using Cholesky decomposition the order of VAR parameters order matters. The BRICS countries are inputted in alphabetical order because that order is consisted with normal writing order. Although, VAR results might be different when one inputs them in a different format, one views normal order as an appropriate one. It can be inferred from [31] alphabetical order modelling leads to better estimates. In **Tables 2** and **3** all variables highlighted in grey are statistically significant for VAR values as they are at least 2 irrespective of being negative or positive. The F-statistic is basically Anova values and one reads the in the following manner. Assume the following inequality $F(2, 12) = 22.59, p < 0.05)$, the 2 is the degrees of freedom numerator, 12 is total observations of freedom denominator, 22.59 is the calculated Anova value and 0.05 is alpha (i.e. significance level). This article assumes that both the degrees of freedom numerator and total observations of freedom denominator are infinities in order to illustrate the best case scenario. In the latter situation, the critical value is 1.22. Thus, F-statistic values highlighted in grey fall within the non-rejection (i.e. acceptable) regions while values which are not highlighted fall within rejection regions. That is, latter values exemplify autocorrelation for those VAR(1) model.

The results panel 5 of **Table 2** illustrates that one-lag in Brazilian indexed volatility of bonds cause one-lag in Brazilian indexed volatility of bonds by 0.18 units. The letter statement is sensible given that what happens in one market should have similar effect in the short run-regimes show that regimes time is just over 2 weeks. Similarly, a one-lag in Brazilian indexed volatility of bond cause one-lag in South African indexed volatility of bonds-this probably that of similarities between the two countries, i.e. ruling political parties stay in power much longer; historically, Brazil and South Africa have good trade relations and further, the BRICS formation is strengthening that relationship even more. The one-lag in Indian volatility of bonds cause one-lag in Indian volatility of bonds. The phenomenon is similar with the one of Brazil lags; however, Indian one is negative while Brazil one is positive. One possible explanation for India negative lag is that in India the government is highly involved in driving economic growth than in Brazil.

Panel 5: bonds

	Brazil	China	India	Russia	South Africa
Brazil	0.1833 (4.4095)	−0.0202 (−0.2429)	0.2881 (1.5718)	−0.0201 (−0.24301)	0.0332 (0.7153)
China	0.0077 (0.0038)	1.7959 (−0.4477)	−0.8782 (−0.0993)	−1.4175 (−0.3533)	0.2652 (0.1185)
India	−0.0004 (−0.0440)	0.0050 (0.2812)	−0.4140 (−10.5584)	0.0049 (0.2801)	0.0114 (1.1494)
Russia	−0.0226 (−0.0113)	1.4237 (0.3549)	0.8546 (0.0966)	1.0447 (0.2605)	−0.2573 (−0.1150)
South Africa	0.1055 (2.7839)	−0.0280 (−0.3701)	0.0383 (0.2292)	−0.0280 (−0.3697)	−0.0003 (−1.9232)
F-statistic	5.2479	17.9005	23.0227	17.9331	1.1701
Akaike AIC	−5.8292	−4.4438	−2.8618	−4.4433	−5.6106
Schwarz SC	−5.7830	−4.3973	−2.8157	−4.3907	−5.5643

Panel 6: commodities

	Brazil	China	India	Russia	South Africa
Brazil	−0.4092 (−10.5168)	−0.0125 (−2.6652)	−0.0063 (−0.6138)	0.0339 (0.7887)	−0.0089 (−0.5621)
China	0.3609 (0.9718)	0.2844 (6.3448)	0.0436 (0.4442)	−0.5516 (−1.3461)	−0.2129 (−1.4044)
India	0.0028 (0.0162)	0.0159 (0.7539)	0.0670 (1.4443)	0.1208 (0.6232)	−0.0092 (−0.1288)
Russia	−0.0701 (−1.9894)	0.0059 (1.3848)	0.0048 (0.5099)	−0.2919 (−7.5058)	0.0033 (0.2270)
South Africa	−0.0943 (−0.8626)	−0.0078 (−0.5876)	0.0627 (2.1706)	0.1935 (1.6049)	−0.0114 (−0.2545)
F-statistic	22.7883	11.7035	2.3085	12.2434	0.7016
Akaike AIC	−0.8059	−5.0351	−3.4670	−0.6091	−2.5984
Schwarz SC	−0.7597	−4.9888	−3.4208	−0.5629	−2.5522

Panel 7: equities

	Brazil	China	India	Russia	South Africa
Brazil	−0.1469 (−2.0726)	−7.4597 (−1.3644)	1.2495 (0.2433)	2.5543 (0.3575)	7.1695 (1.2132)
China	0.0000 (−0.0920)	0.0178 (0.4235)	0.1028 (2.5982)	−0.0552 (−1.0039)	−0.0616 (−1.3525)
India	−0.0002 (−0.3129)	−0.0531 (−0.8988)	−0.0257 (−0.4625)	0.1499 (1.9421)	0.0724 (1.1336)
Russia	−0.0008 (−2.0001)	−0.0213 (−0.6589)	−0.0082 (−0.2684)	−0.0094 (−0.2233)	0.0520 (1.4883)
South Africa	−0.0004 (−0.4955)	0.0826 (1.2342)	0.1263 (2.0106)	0.0982 (1.1239)	−0.0959 (−1.3261)

Panel 7: equities					
	Brazil	**China**	**India**	**Russia**	**South Africa**
F-statistic	1.9912	2.5000	2.7793	2.7791	2.7064
Akaike AIC	−12.2983	−3.6080	−3.7334	−3.0728	−3.4525
Schwarz SC	−12.2520	−3.5618	−3.6871	−3.0266	−3.4062
Panel 8: real estate					
	Brazil	**China**	**India**	**Russia**	**South Africa**
Brazil	−0.0197 (−0.3642)	−0.1362 (−2.9988)	−0.0720 (−1.2489)	0.0276 (0.4412)	0.0031 (0.1009)
China	0.0236 (0.4708)	−0.0399 (−0.9456)	0.1344 (2.5099)	−0.0325 (−0.5584)	−0.0011 (−0.0391)
India	−0.0259 (−0.5738)	−0.0286 (−0.7487)	0.0162 (0.3345)	−0.1256 (−2.3889)	0.0097 (0.3717)
Russia	−0.0229 (−0.6359)	−0.0504 (−1.6582)	0.0466 (1.2075)	0.1679 (4.0062)	0.0332 (1.6033)
South Africa	0.0107 (0.1145)	−0.0780 (−0.9927)	0.1783 (1.7871)	0.0010 (0.0093)	−0.0233 (−0.0449)
F-statistic	0.2134	2.6753	3.8118	5.8949	0.6335
Akaike AIC	−2.6706	−3.0149	−2.5382	−2.3731	−3.7809
Schwarz SC	−2.6244	−2.9687	−2.4919	−2.3269	−3.7347

Note: in each cell, the first number is the coefficient and the number in brackets is the t-test. All variables highlighted in grey are statistically significant for VAR values as they are at least 2 irrespective of being negative or positive. The interpretation of results is based on Cholesky decomposition.

Table 2.
VAR (1): out-sample period (2007–2017).

All other indexed volatilities of bonds in other BRICS countries are statistically insignificant. However, those latter results should be read with caution as using Cholesky decomposition for curves for those countries to start at zero. Panel 6 of **Table 2** illustrates results for commodities indexed volatilities.

The statistically significant results are for Brazil and Brazil-this is for the same reasons as in panel 5, Brazil and China-Brazil is the producer of commodities while China is a consumer. This implies that the one-lag in producer of commodities indexed volatilities causes one-lag in consumer indexed volatilities but not visa verse. More, the coefficient is negative because the effects spillover to the consumer from the producer. The results for China lags can be explained by same reasons as the Brazil lags. Similarly, the one-lag in Indian index volatility cause a one-lag in South African indexed commodities volatility-the same as the Brazil and China one lags. The Russian lags are the same as China lags. Note that China lag with itself is positive while Russia lag with itself is negative. The positive lag for China lag with itself is probably due the economic influence that China has on the major world issues. The influence of Russian on major economic issues is limited. Thus, it might imply that South Africa needs to establish itself globally before the South African government can play a major on South African economic issues.

Panel 7 shows that spillovers which are statistically significant are for Brazil lags with itself-this pattern has been explained before, Brazil lag with Russian lag-in

Panel 9: bonds					
	Brazil	**China**	**India**	**Russia**	**South Africa**
Brazil	0.1876 (3.8632)	−0.0120 (−0.1567)	0.2688 (1.1956)	−0.0121 (−0.1578)	0.0278 (0.6435)
China	−0.0817 (−0.0304)	−2.0308 (0.4779)	−1.6449 (−0.1322)	−1.5335 (−0.3608)	−0.7866 (−0.3289)
India	0.0001 (0.0114)	0.0056 (0.3399)	−0.4205 (−8.7141)	0.0056 (0.3386)	0.0099 (1.0653)
Russia	0.0553 (0.0259)	1.6457 (0.3874)	1.6068 (0.1292)	1.1477 (0.2701)	0.7689 (0.3216)
South Africa	0.1664 (3.0025)	0.08445 (0.9643)	−0.1679 (−0.6544)	0.0837 (0.9552)	−0.1354 (−2.7462)
F-statistic	4.5645	14.0761	15.7002	14.1098	2.0675
Akaike AIC	−5.5172	−4.6011	−2.4522	−4.6006	5.7506
Schwarz SC	−5.4585	−4.5423	−2.3935	−4.5419	−5.6919
Panel 10: commodities					
	Brazil	**China**	**India**	**Russia**	**South Africa**
Brazil	−0.3855 (−7.4290)	−0.0166 (3.4736)	−0.0097 (−0.9339)	0.0746 (1.2989)	(−1.0249)
China	0.8517 (1.3579)	0.1761 (3.0423)	0.0542 (0.4329)	−1.2171 (−1.7521)	(−1.6324)
India	−0.3983 (−1.3512)	0.0242 (0.8910)	0.0728 (1.2363)	−0.1864 (−0.5711)	(1.2772)
Russia	−0.1453 (−3.0541)	0.0010 (0.2295)	0.0015 (0.1561)	−0.3677 (−6.9804)	(1.1867)
South Africa	0.0280 (0.1981)	0.0177 (1.3538)	0.0216 (0.7648)	0.1967 (1.2551)	(1.2906)
F-statistic	12.6282	5.3503	0.7579	11.8936	0.0651
Akaike AIC	−0.8229	−5.5888	−4.0445	−0.6187	−2.6074
Schwarz SC	−0.7506	−5.5165	−3.9722	−0.5464	−2.5350
Panel 11: equites					
	Brazil	**China**	**India**	**Russia**	**South Africa**
Brazil	0.0795 (1.0222)	−6.1630 (−0.9579)	−3.1423 (−0.6267)	−15.9395 (−2.1685)	−4.7373 (−0.8339)
China	0.0011 (1.6271)	0.0537 (0.9391)	0.0342 (0.7611)	−0.1100 (−1.6849)	−0.1395 (−2.7636)
India	0.0009 (0.8208)	−0.0566 (−0.6371)	0.1208 (1.7324)	−0.0125 (−0.1229)	−0.0386 (−0.4921)
Russia	−0.0002 (−0.2543)	−0.1442 (−2.3803)	0.0363 (0.7626)	−0.1418 (−2.0488)	0.0223 (0.4165)
South Africa	0.0009 (0.7747)	0.0287 (0.3102)	−0.0790 (−1.0876)	0.1526 (1.4447)	−0.0512 (−0.6272)
F-statistic	0.8648	1.5195	1.2508	3.1221	1.6589
Akaike AIC	−12.7912	−3.9589	−4.4415	−3.6926	−4.2078

Panel 11: equites					
Schwarz SC	−12.7188	−3.8867	−4.3692	−3.6203	−4.1355
Panel 12: real estate					
	Brazil	**China**	**India**	**Russia**	**South Africa**
Brazil	0.0041 (0.0635)	0.0284 (0.4825)	−0.0729 (−0.9954)	−0.1126 (−2.1609)	−0.0207 (−0.4699)
China	0.1213 (1.8983)	−0.0306 (−0.5308)	0.1037 (1.4455)	0.0393 (0.7707)	−0.0794 (−1.8378)
India	−0.0482 (−0.8873)	−0.0046 (−0.0943)	0.0426 (0.6990)	−0.0174 (−0.4013)	−0.0282 (−0.7678)
Russia	−0.0309 (−0.4209)	−0.0771 (−1.1644)	−0.0512 (−0.6213)	−0.0362 (−0.6179)	−0.0266 (−0.5363)
South Africa	−0.0128 (−0.1304)	0.0293 (0.3308)	0.1061 (0.9652)	−0.1355 (−1.7336)	−0.0415 (−0.6271)
F-statistic	1.0215	0.3552	0.0529	1.5103	0.8958
Akaike AIC	−3.2510	−3.4551	−3.0200	−3.7027	−4.0345
Schwarz SC	−3.1787	−3.3828	−2.9477	−3.6305	−3.9622

Note: in each cell, the first number is the coefficient and the number in brackets is the t-test. All variables highlighted in grey are statistically significant for VAR values as they are at least 2 irrespective of being negative or positive. The interpretation of results is based on Cholesky decomposition.

Table 3.
VAR(1;1): In-sample period (2012–2017).

both countries, commodities firms are the main constituents of equities indices. And the causal relationship is slightly negative. Thus, 1 unit lag in Brazilian indexed volatilities emanating from equities cause −0.0008 lag in Russian indexed volatility of the same index. The latter strategy is synonymous with hedging and speculation in equity markets. More, straddles work in a similar manner. Panel 8 shows the results of lags in real estate indices. The statistically significant lags are for Russia with itself-that pattern has been explained before, China and Brazil-Brazil is probably the most powerful economy in South American while China is the second biggest economy after the United States. China has been on major infrastructure projects including real estate and many academics and practitioners have questioned whether the bubble is in the horizon in China. The negative coefficient is probably due to 'overbuilding' in China. Indian lagged volatility cause a positive lag in China. The latter finding is probably due to ruling parties' influences in managing their economies. Interestingly, one-lag in Russian volatility causes one-lag in India. Normally, collapse of currencies and commodities markets precede other capital markets products. Overall, one can see that volatility spillovers in the BRICS countries based on four indices during 2007–2017 period, exemplify opportunities to diversification opportunities-when indexed volatilities move in different directions and risk management opportunities-when indexed volatilities move the same direction.

The influence of Brazil lag to South Africa lag during period of 2012–2017 is the same as during the 2007–2017 period as illustrated in panel 9. The period of 2012–2017 was largely a bull market while 2007–2017 had some bearish years, i.e. 2008/2009 period. This implies that indexed volatilities of bonds during out-sample

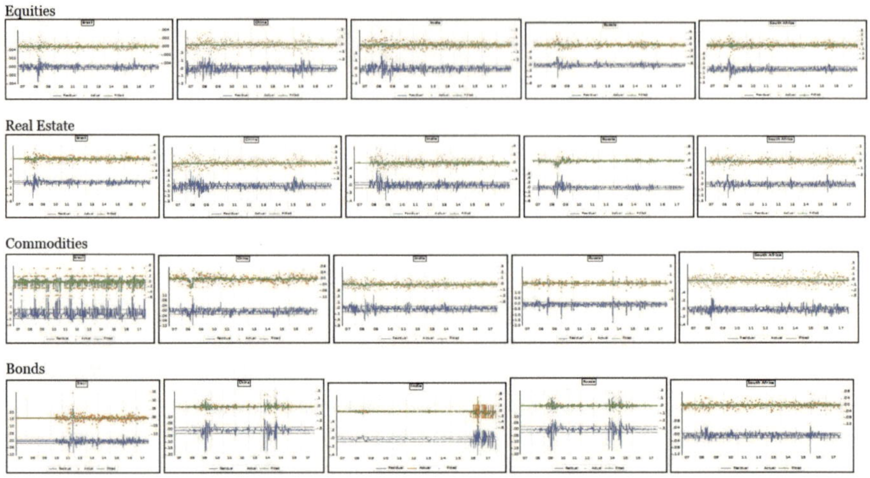

Figure 2.
Filtered regime probabilities-out sample: 2007–2017.

reflect similar patterns as in-sample period. The sample phenomenon can be advocated on the influence the one-lag of Indian volatility on the lag of India. The interesting result in panel 9 is the one-lag of South Africa with itself-during the in sample period the lag is influential. During 2012–2017, the South African long-and short-term yields were on an upward trajectory. This is probably why one-lag for South Africa in during the in-sample period had a casual effect. For commodities indices-panel 10, the rests are the same as in **Table 2** except the one-lag of Brazilian volatility on one-lag of Russia. During 2012–2017, commodities prices were stable. In panel 11, one-lag of China has influence on one-lag of Russia and one-lag of South Africa had one-lag on China-all the lags are negative. This is probably to declining consumption on commodity products by China. The rest of results are in panel 11 are the same as in panel 7. For panel 12, only one-lag of has a negative influence one-lag of Brazil. In short-run volatilities tend to be spiky than in the long run. That is, the volatility spillovers might be temporary.

For every index type in **Figure 2** in every row, the first country is Brazil followed by China and then India; thereafter Russia. The last country is always South Africa. For equities indices, all the five countries have main shocks in 2007–2008 period as illustrated by residuals. This is the period of the last subprime crisis. However, the actual date reveals a similar picture. The upward regimes in all countries were during 2007–2009 period. It can be inferred from [6, 27] that when indices move in the same direction, the volatilities should follow a similar pattern. But, those graphs do not tell one from and to which are the volatilities. The equities volatilities in Brazil and South Africa seem to hover around the same level during the entire out sample. In [30], it was illustrated the subprime effects of 2007–2009 in South Africa were minimal. From what was reported in media, Brazil never suffered much from the subprime effects of 2007–2009. Real estate indices show the similar patterns as equities indices except for China and India. Sometimes during subprime crises, equities movements preceded real estate movements. The real estate indices of China and India show similar and strong patterns. One of the reasons for that is the BRIC relation between those two countries precedes the establishment of the BRIC countries. More, they have large populations and their respective governments are at the heart of driving those economies.

For the commodities indices, Brazil and South Africa have the most and similar volatile indices patterns. One of the reasons of that is that Brazil and South Africa

Panel 13: equities										
	Brazil		**China**		**India**		**Russia**		**South Africa**	
CTP	1	2	1	2	1	2	1	2	1	2
1	0.5703	0.4297	0.5009	0.4991	0.4943	0.5057	0.5058	0.4942	0.5661	0.4339
2	0.4993	0.5107	0.5126	0.4874	0.5034	0.4967	0.5216	0.4784	0.6033	0.3967
CED	1	2	1	2	1	2	1	2	1	2
	2.3274	2.0436	2.0034	1.9507	1.9775	1.9864	2.0233	1.9171	2.3047	1.6577
Panel 14: real estate										
CTP	1	2	1	2	1	2	1	2	1	2
1	0.4983	0.5017	0.0000	1.0000	0.9827	0.0173	0.4689	0.5311	0.3442	0.6558
2	0.4893	0.5107	0.0244	0.9756	0.8896	0.1004	0.0210	0.9789	0.0074	0.9926
CED	1	2	1	2	1	2	1	2	1	2
	1.9932	2.0439	1.0000	40.9669	57.7020	1.1116	1.8827	47.5343	1.5248	134.6585
Panel 15: commodities										
CTP	1	2	1	2	1	2	1	2	1	2
1	0.5206	0.4795	0.9093	0.0907	0.4737	0.5263	0.4965	0.5035	0.0000	1.0000
2	0.5024	0.4976	0.0021	0.9979	0.4544	0.5456	0.4998	0.5002	0.0141	0.9859
CED	1	2	1	2	1	2	1	2	1	2
	2.0857	1.9903	11.0248	485.6439	1.8999	2.2007	1.9859	2.0007	1.0000	70.8325
Panel 16: bonds										
CTP	1	2	1	2	1	2	1	2	1	2
1	0.4959	0.5040	0.2862	0.7138	0.9919	0.0081	0.4817	0.5185	0.5067	0.4933
2	0.0018	0.9985	0.4598	0.5402	0.7747	0.2253	0.3799	0.6201	0.4853	0.5147
CED	1	2	1	2	1	2	1	2	1	2
	1.9841	556.1991	1.4009	2.1748	123.8068	1.2908	1.9285	2.6323	2.0270	2.0605

Note: CTP and CED stand for constant transition probabilities and expected duration, respectively.

Table 4.
Markov transition-out sample: 2007–2017.

are rich in mineral resources. On the other hand, China and India consume most of commodities products. Surprisingly, Russia had the most stable commodity index during 2007–2017 period. Unlike Brazil and South Africa, Russia is mainly rich in oil while the other two countries are rich in minerals. The bonds indices show similar patterns to real estate indices. Numerous studies illustrate that listed real estate exhibit traits of other capital markets, especially bonds. The patterns of bonds indices are dissimilar except for China and Russia. It can be inferred that bonds volatilities of those two countries follow in the same direction. The graphs show diagnostic patterns and in order to have more depth, this article illustrates Markov transitions as shown in **Table 4**. In most studies, transition probabilities and expected durations, are used to illustrate Markov transitions.

Panel 13 (14) illustrates Markov transitions for equities (real estate) while panel 15 (16) shows Markov transitions for commodities (bonds). For equities indices, for the four countries; Brazil, China, India and Russia, there is considerable transition dependence between the two regimes as the original regimes start from as low 0.50 and increase to as high as 0.57. The non-original regimes are as low as 0.50.

Although the original regime for South Africa 0.56 (relative high) but the non-original regime seems less dependent on the original regime. The expected durations of all countries are approximately 2 weeks. The quickly changing patterns in equities would be excepted given that equities markets are quite volatile that other capital markets. For real estate indices, China and South Africa show an interesting pattern-the original regimes are very low but the non-original regimes are highly dependent of the original regimes. That rare scenario is hardly observable in most countries in the world. That could be possibly due to the influence of governments which translate into financial markets in those countries. For Brazil, India and Russia, the two regimes seem to be dependent on each other. The excepted durations for real estate indices show interesting results-the expected durations are shorter their equities counter-parts mostly for first regimes. That is high unexpected. One possible explanation is that real estate indices in those countries are quite thin and represent a few constituencies. For commodities indices, the original regimes and non-original regimes are dependent. South Africa is the only country that illustrate a unique regime-non original regime is not some much dependent on original regime. All the regimes with exception of China and South Africa last for a few weeks. The reason why China and South Africa have longer accepted durations is because China consumes most commodities in the world while South Africa is a country rich in minerals. The regimes of bonds indices of all countries seem to be dependent. One possible explanation for that is that bonds are the oldest market in the capital markets. More, bonds are used mostly in those countries to finance private and public infrastructure. The expected durations of Brazil and China are entirely longer. Probably those two countries use their bond markets frequently for their capital markets offerings.

For every index type in **Figure 3** in every row, the first country is Brazil followed by China and then India; thereafter Russia. The last country is always South Africa. For equities indices, the later periods of China, Russia and South Africa show similar regimes patterns. Thus, there is a possibility that equities indexed volatilities of those move from and to with each other. For all the five countries, in year 2014, equities indexed volatilities show similar movements. Most of the 2014 year was characterised by bull markets most countries throughout the world. At that time, probably volatilities are spillover each other. The real estate indices for of all for

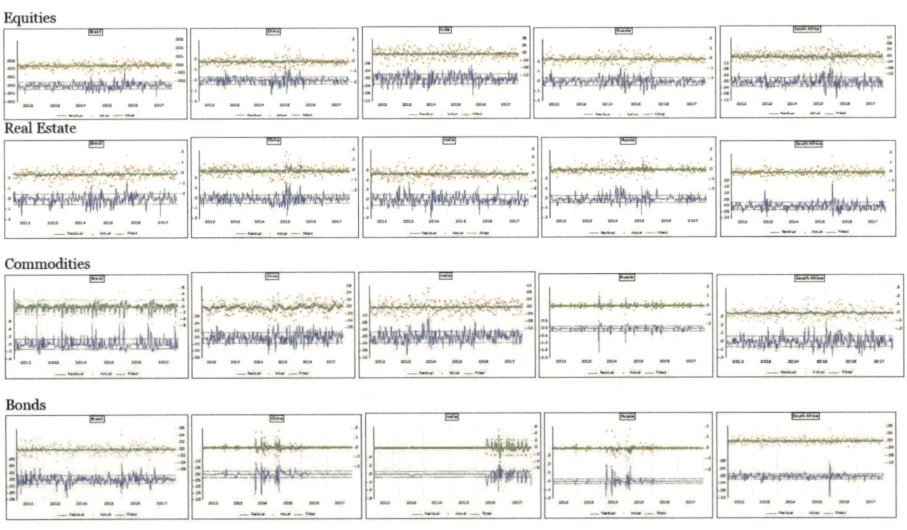

Figure 3.
Filtered regime probabilities-in sample: 2012–2017.

Panel 17: equities										
	Brazil		China		India		Russia		South Africa	
CTP	1	2	1	2	1	2	1	2	1	2
1	0.5147	0.4853	0.4494	0.5506	0.9731	0.0269	0.9756	0.0244	0.0000	1.0000
2	0.5159	0.4841	0.5897	0.4102	0.9977	0.0023	0.6888	0.3112	0.3045	0.6955
CED	1	2	1	2	1	2	1	2	1	2
	2.0605	1.9382	1.8161	1.6955	37.1527	1.0023	40.9446	1.4518	1.0000	3.2839
Panel 18: real estate										
CTP	1	2	1	2	1	2	1	2	1	2
1	0.0000	1.0000	0.9847	0.0153	0.0000	1.0000	0.1127	0.8873	0.9934	0.0066
2	0.0544	0.9456	0.5366	0.4634	0.0343	0.9657	0.0744	0.9256	1.0000	0.0000
CED	1	2	1	2	1	2	1	2	1	2
	1.0000	18.3795	65.2176	1.8635	1.0000	29.1281	1.1271	13.4442	153.0187	1.0000
Panel 19: commodities										
CTP	1	2	1	2	1	2	1	2	1	2
1	0.0000	1.0000	0.3956	0.6044	0.1097	0.8903	0.0189	0.9811	0.4853	0.5147
2	1.0000	0.0000	0.0466	0.9534	0.9999	0.0000	0.0000	0.9997	0.3379	0.6621
CED	1	2	1	2	1	2	1	2	1	2
	1.0000	1.0000	1.6545	21.4513	1.1232	1.0000	1.0193	3059.4310	1.9430	2.9595
Panel 20: bonds										
CTP	1	2	1	2	1	2	1	2	1	2
1	0.9738	0.0262	0.0000	0.9999	0.5174	0.4826	0.0000	1.0000	0.0000	1.0000
2	1.0000	0.0000	1.0000	0.0000	0.5776	0.4224	0.0197	0.9802	0.0033	0.9967

Panel 17: equities										
	Brazil		China		India		Russia		South Africa	
CED	1	2	1	2	1	2	1	2	1	2
	38.2366	1.0000	1.0000	1.0000	2.0720	1.7314	1.0000	50.6053	1.0000	303.1733

Note: CTP and CED stand for constant transition probabilities and expected duration, respectively.

Table 5.
Markov transition-in sample: 2012–2017.

countries with exception of Brazil exemplify the same pattern. One possible reason is that listed real estate mimics similar movements. So far, the diagnostic assessments illustrate that there is some relationship between indexed volatilities of equities (real estate). This might imply that volatilities of indices move together during bullish periods than bearish periods.

The indexed commodities volatilities of Brazil, China, India and South Africa exemplify similar movements. Brazil and South Africa are some of the main producers of minerals while China and India are some of the main consumers of mineral products. The bonds volatilities show different all countries show different movements. The indexed volatilities for in-sample period seem to be spiky than ones of out-sample period. It can be inferred from [32] that volatilities flatten out in the long-run because of diversification benefits which are more prevalent in the long-run. Broadly, the graphs of in-sample regimes are similar to ones of out-sample. Just like in the out-sample analysis for indexed volatilities, Markov transitions are calculated in order to deepen the insights on how indexed volatilities during in-sample period behave.

Panel 17 of **Table 5** illustrates that non-original regimes are dependent for indexed volatilities; however, the original regimes are not necessarily trend setters. One of the reasons that might explain that pattern is that during 2012–2017 period most equities market experience bull phase. The expected durations for all equities volatilities are fairly short with exception of the Russian market. Panel 18 illustrates the same pattern as panel 17 except in the case of South Africa. Surprisingly, excepted durations of real estate are far shorter than ones of equities. The patterns of regimes in panels 19 and 20 show similar patterns as in **Table 5**. The interesting part is that excepted durations for Russia-excepted durations of Russia are fairly long. Normally, currencies markets lead movements in stock markets, followed by equities, then bonds and final the real estate. Based on the latter principle, Russian commodities Markov transitions are longer because of long excepted duration of Russian bond index which was preceded by equities volatilities. Similar, real estate volatilities follow the same pattern. The Russian commodities volatilities are higher because Russian is major player in the commodities market in the world.

5. Conclusion

To sum up, this study illustrates that; firstly, there are spillovers that happen across, in-between and within bonds, commodities, equities and real estate indices. Secondly, sometimes the illiquid indices contribute more to volatility spillovers than liquid indices. Thirdly, expected durations of illiquid indices have shorter time spans than liquid indices. Fourth, in most cases, the volatility spillovers patterns during the out-sample period are similar to ones emanating during the in-sample period. Finally, periodical movement patterns vary across, in-between and within bonds, commodities, equities and real estate indices.

The implications from this study as follows. Firstly, similar governmental formations should be encouraged throughout the world provided that there economic benefits associated with those formations. Secondly, investing in different indices should be encouraged-diversification pays. Thirdly, there are risk management strategies that one can design based on volatility spillovers across, in-between and within bonds, commodities, equities and real estate indices. Fourth, the BRICS formation has indirectly influenced how capital markets (i.e. bonds, commodities, equities and real estate indices) behave. Finally, there are numerous investment strategies that investment managers can build based on volatility spills.

Acknowledgements

We are grateful to Carlos Campani for providing data on Brazilian commodities index. The remaining errors are our own.

Conflict of interest

The authors declare no conflict of interest.

Additional classification

JEL: C32, C33.

Author details

Katlego Kola* and Tumellano Sebehela*
School of Construction Economics and Management, WITS University, Johannesburg, South Africa

*Address all correspondence to: 461696@students.wits.ac.za and tumellano.sebehela@wits.ac.za

References

[1] Nayyar D. BRICS, developing countries and global governance. Third World Quarterly. 2016;**37**(4):575-591

[2] Syriopoulos T, Markam B, Boubaker A. Stock market volatility spillovers and portfolio hedging: BRICS and the financial crisis. International Review of Financial Analysis. 2015;**39**: 7-18

[3] Lee ML, Lee MT, Chiang KC. Real estate risk exposure of equity real estate investment trusts. Journal of Real Estate Finance and Economics. 2008;**36**(2): 165-181

[4] Naranjo A, Ling DC. Economic risk factors and commercial real estate returns. Journal of Real Estate Finance and Economics. 1997;**14**(3): 283-307

[5] Kumar M, Moorthy U, Perraudin W. Predicting emerging market currency crashes. Journal of Empirical Finance. 2003;**10**(4):427-454

[6] Liow KH. Conditional volatility spillover effects across emerging financial markets. Asia-Pacific Journal of Financial Studies. 2015;**44**:215-245

[7] Lee CL, Stevenson S, Lee ML. Futures trading, spot price volatility and market efficiency: Evidence from European real estate securities futures. Journal of Real Estate Finance and Economics. 2014;**48**(2):299-322

[8] Kuttu S. Return and volatility dynamics among four African equity markets: A multivariate VAR-EGARCH analysis. Global Finance Journal. 2014; **25**:56-69

[9] Dean WG, Faff RW, Loundon GF. Asymmetry in return and volatility spillover between equity and bonds markets in Australia. Pacific-Basin Finance Journal. 2010;**18**(3):272-289

[10] Garcia R, Tsafack G. Dependence structure and extreme comovements in international equity and bond markets. Journal of Banking & Finance. 2011; **35**(8):1954-1970

[11] Ehrmann M, Fratzsher M, Rigobon R. Stocks, bonds, money markets and exchange rates: Measuring international financial transmission. Journal of Applied Econometrics. 2011; **26**(6):948-974

[12] Jacks DS, O'Rourke KH, Williamson JG. Commodity price volatility and world market integration since 1700. Review of Economics & Statistics. 2011;**93**(3):800-813

[13] Antonakakis N, Kizys R. Dynamic spillovers between commodity and currency markets. International Review of Financial Analysis. 2015;**41**:303-319

[14] Basak S, Pavlova A. A model of financialization of commodities. Journal of Finance. 2016;**71**(4):1511-1556

[15] Le Pen Y, Sévi B. Futures trading and the excess co-movement of commodity prices. Review of Finance. 2017;**22**(1):381-418

[16] Ding L, Huang Y, Pu X. Volatility linkage across equity markets. Global Finance Journal. 2014;**25**:71-89

[17] Dewandaru G, Masih R, Masih M. Regional spillovers across transitioning emerging and frontier equity markets: A multi-time scale wavelet analysis. Economic Modelling. 2017;**65**:30-40

[18] Leachman LL, Francis B. Equity market return volatility: Dynamics and transmission among the G-7 countries. Global Finance Journal. 1996;**7**(1):27-52

[19] BenSaïda A, Litimi H, Abdallah O. Volatility spillover shifts in global financial markets. Economic Modelling.

2018;**73**:1-11. Available from: https://doi.org/10.1016/j.econmod.2018.04.011

[20] Diebold FX, Yilmaz K. Better to give than to receive: Predictive directional measurement of volatility spillovers. International Journal of Forecasting. 2012;**28**(1):57-66

[21] Liow KH, Chen Z, Jingran L. Multiple regimes and volatility transmission in securitized real estate markets. Journal of Real Estate Finance and Economics. 2011;**42**(3):295-328

[22] Liow KH, Schindler F. An assessment of the relationship between public real estate and stock markets at the local, regional and global levels. International Real Estate Review. 2014; **17**(2):157-202

[23] Liow KH. Co-movements and correlations across Asian securitized real estate and stock markets. Real Estate Economics. 2012;**40**(1):97-129

[24] Hoesli M, Reka K. Volatility spillovers, co-movements and contagion in securitised real estate markets. Journal of Real Estate Finance and Economics. 2013;**47**(1):1-35

[25] Liow KH, Ye Q. Switching regime beta analysis of global financial crisis: Evidence from international public real estate markets. Journal of Real Estate Research. 2017;**39**(1):127-164

[26] Liow KH, Zhu H, Ho D, Al K. Regime changes in international securitized property markets. Journal of Real Estate Portfolio Management. 2005;**11**(2):147-167

[27] Mensi W, Boubaker FZ, Al-Yahyaee KH, King SH. Dynamic volatility spillovers and connectedness between global, regional and GIPSI stock markets. Finance Research Letters. 2018;**25**:230-238

[28] Skintzi VD, Refenes AN. Volatility spillovers and dynamic correlation in European bond markets. Journal of International Financial Markets, Institutions & Money. 2006;**16**(1):23-40

[29] Bianconi M, Yoshino JA, De Sousa MOM. BRIC and the US financial Crisis: An Empirical Investigation of Stock and Bond Markets. Emerging Markets Review. 2013;**14**:76-109

[30] Sebehela T. The impact of the subprime mortgage financial crisis on housing finance in South Africa. Housing Finance International. 2009; **23**(4):44-46

[31] Van Griensven A, Meixner T, Grunwald S, Bishop T, Diluzio M, Srinivasan R. A global sensitivity analysis tool for the parameters of multi-variable catchment models. Journal of Hydrology. 2006;**324**(1–4): 10-23

[32] Borenstein S. The long-run efficiency of real-time electricity pricing. Energy Journal. 2005;**63**(3): 93-116

Chapter 8

The Impact of Exchange Rates on Stock Markets in Turkey: Evidence from Linear and Non-Linear ARDL Models

Mustafa Çakır

Abstract

In this chapter we investigate the asymmetric impact of exchange rates on three major stock market indices in Turkey using four different ARDL models between 2003M1 and 2018M12. This chapter also attempts to differentiate the short-run and the long-run relationship between exchange rates and stock market indices namely BIST All shares, BIST National 100 index, and BIST National 30 index. Our motivating question is whether the relationship between exchange rates and three major stock market indices are symmetric or asymmetric in Turkey? To answer this, we first use the linear bivariate and multivariate models assuming the effects are symmetric. We then use the non-linear bivariate and multivariate models to examine whether exchange rate have symmetric or asymmetric effects on selected stock stock market indices in Turkey. The findings show that exchange rates have asymmetric effects on all three major stock market indices both in the short and long run. When we look at the long-run, the currency appreciation has positive and significant impact on selected stock markets but currency depreciation does not have an effect. This finding is in line with the understanding that Turkish sectors heavily depends on the import of raw and intermediate goods. The results also show that the economic activity has positive and significant effects on all stock markets implying that it is the main determinant in the long-run. Moreover, interest rates and volatility index were negative and significant in all markets. Thus, it has important implications for policy makers to provide stable prices and diverse investors.

Keywords: asymmetric effects, exchanges rates, stock markets, ARDL models, Turkey

1. Introduction

Some of the major developments in Turkey's economy during the past decades has been the liberalization of capital markets and implementation of floating exchange rate regime. These developments with the rapid growth of Turkey's economy has attracted international investors and thus increased Turkey's integration into the global economy. Turkey, as emerging market, became attractive to foreign investors for portfolio diversification but shocks in exchange rate markets create volatility in the stock market. It can react positively or negatively to fluctuations in foreign exchange markets. Thus, exporters can benefit from the local currency depreciation due to higher export competitiveness, while importers will pay higher prices for imported goods, thus determining a company's cash flow and market value. Causality refers to exchange rates that vary from stock markets. On the other hand, if a country's exports depend mainly on foreign inputs, the resulting relationship between equity and exchange rates may be insignificant. Since Turkey is a net importer of goods and services, potentially, the depreciation of Turkish lira will cause the value of shares to fall.

There are two main theories suggesting a relation between exchange rates and stock prices. The first is the flow-oriented exchange rate models [1] that focus on the current account or trade balance and predicts that changes in exchange rates will affects the country's real economic variables and therefore stock prices by affecting international competition and trade balance. According to this approach, there is a positive relationship between the two and the causality from exchange rate to stock prices. Fluctuations in exchange rates makes the domestic companies more competitive in case of the depreciation of the national currency, thus increase their exports. Because, these fluctuations affect the costs and profits of many companies due to borrowing in foreign currencies to finance their operations. This affects the stock prices of firms [1].

Second approach is the stock-oriented approach which predicts that movements on stock prices affect exchange rates and thus a causality from stock prices to exchange rates via capital account [2]. As capital is part of the stock, it can influence the exchange rate through the demand of money. According to this, a rising stock prices will attract capital inflows to a country and this will lead to a decline in exchange rates by increasing demand for local currency [3].

It has become a generally accepted notion that these two variables are the way to go for emerging economies to enable economic growth and development. The role of exchange rate is much more important for small open economies in particular emerging markets. In this chapter we seek to shed some light on the analysis of the symmetric and asymmetric effects of exchanges rates on the stock prices in Turkey at industry level using a linear and nonlinear framework. This study is of great interest for a country that has import-oriented economy and completed its financial liberalization in the early 1990s. Because the empirical studies trying to prove the relationship between the exchange rates and the stock prices have mixed results regarding the two main views mentioned above.

Figure 1 shows the dynamics of Turkey's three major stock market indices. The 2008 crisis is seen as the most important point of decline in the trend. Since Borsa Istanbul is generally a foreign-invested market, the performance of the Turkish stock markets is negatively affected by foreign investors via the global financial crises. During this period, the risk premium was raised for Turkey. In parallel, CDS values increased. A similar effect occurred after 2018. The Turkish economy has shown that it is not fragile and has exceeded stress tests. Thus, after 2008, the index displayed a strong rise. The depreciation of the exchange rates at the end of the period led to a downward trend in three major stock market indices.

On the other hand, **Figure 2** shows the developments in the exchange rate market in Turkey. The exchange rates displayed a stable outlook in the first half of the period, but an upward trend in the second half of the period. Recently, the depreciation of the exchange rate accelerated. Thus, it seems to have a negative impact on stock market performance especially when the index gets cheaper in Turkish Lira terms, so the trend is expected to turn up.

Therefore to see whether the relationship between exchange rates and three major stock market indices is symmetric or asymmetric in Turkey, we employed four different methods: linear bivariate ARDL model is applied to investigate linear

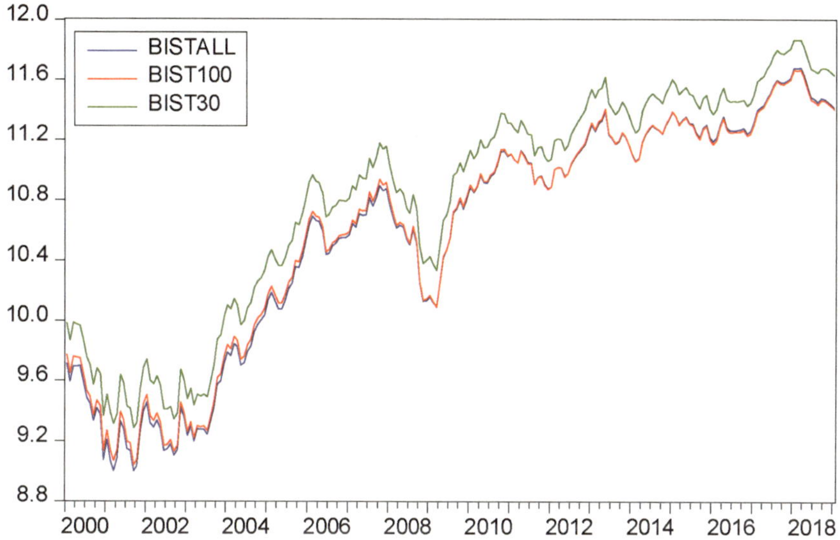

Figure 1.
Stock market dynamics in Turkey (logs in TRY).

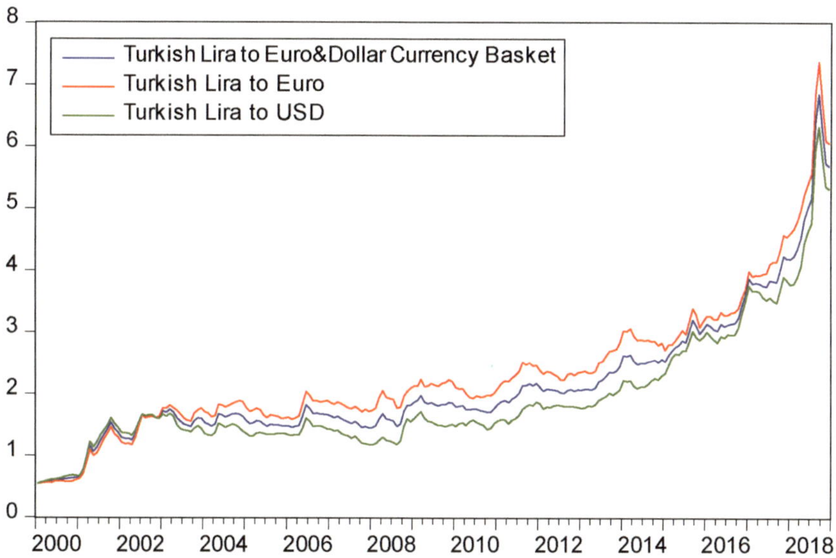

Figure 2.
Turkish lira to Euro&Dollar Currency Basket.

relationship between stock prices and the exchange rates; linear multivariate ARDL model employed to show that changes in some additional variables such as interest rates and industrial production have symmetric or asymmetric effects on stock prices; as exchange rates has different impact on different sectors of the economy, multivariate ARDL models employed to analyze the relationship between them. Moreover, the relationship should not be based on the linear but also on nonlinear dimension. Thus finally, nonlinear bivariate and multivariate ARDL models applied to analyze the non-linear relationship between stock prices and the exchange rates in Turkey.

This study is of great interest for a country that has import-oriented economy, has completed its financial liberalization in the early 1990s, and become an attractive destination for foreign investors. The rationale for assessing the role of symmetric and asymmetric effects of exchanges rate on stock prices in Turkey is based on the perception, as expressed by [1, 2], that the stock prices can react positively or negatively to fluctuations in exchange rates. Determining the factors that cause movements in stock prices is very important and is of great interest to policy makers and investors. The role of exchange rate on stock prices is much more important for small open economies in particular emerging markets. There is no sufficient research evidence showing the links between foreign exchange rate and Turkish stock market. We believe that this study will fill the gap in the literature in this area.

The rest of the chapter is organized as follows: Section 2 review the related literature; Section 3 describes data and methods applied; Section 4 presents empirical findings and discusses the implications of the analysis; and, finally, Section 5 concludes the paper and provides policy implications.

2. Literature review

The relationship between stock prices and exchange rates has been extensively studied by many researches. Some find positive association between the two [4, 5] others discover negative relations [6, 7] and even no relationship at all [8].

Studies on the relationship between exchange rate and stock prices in the literature can be summarized in different categories according to their empirical results. Firstly, there are some studies that find significant positive relationship between the two. For instance, the relationship between stock prices and exchange rates on financial, manufacturing, and services indices and fifteen sub-indices in Turkey investigated using Johansen cointegration test and the results show evidence that there is a long-run relationship among these indices and exchange rates. The results suggest that exchange rate exposure on financial and manufacturing industries have positive forex beta for the dollar exchange rate, but in terms of service industries there is negative forex beta [9]. A similar exercise undertook to investigate the effects of changes in foreign exchange on the stock returns on company level using panel data analysis. The results show evidence that changes in real exchange rate has positive and significant impact on stock returns in the manufacturing and trade sectors between the years 2006–2014 [10].

Secondly, there are some studies that find negative relationship between the two [6, 11]. For example, Akıncı and Küçükçayşı analyses the relationships between stock markets and exchange rates in 12 countries and finds that the exchange rate has negative effect on the stock market index [6]. Belen and Karamelikli investigates the causality between the exchange rates and stock returns in Turkey and finds no evidence supporting any causal relationship between the dollar exchange rate and the BIST-30 Index [11]. Tsai examine the relationship between stock price index and exchange rate in six Asian countries, namely Singapore, Thailand, Malaysia, the Philippines, South Korea, and Taiwan. Their results show that all countries in the study have negative the relationship between stock prices and exchange rates, which is in line with the portfolio balance effect [12]. Recently, the relationships between real exchange rate returns and real stock price returns in Malaysia, the Philippines, Singapore, Korea, Japan, the United Kingdom and Germany examined using dynamic conditional correlation (DCC) and multivariate generalized autoregressive conditional heteroskedasticity (MGARCH) models. The results show that there is a negative relationship between real exchange rate return and real stock price return in Malaysia, Singapore, Korea and the UK [13].

Thirdly, there are some studies that find two-way causality between the exchange rate and stock prices [14]. For instance, Zeren and Koç examines the relationship between exchange rates and stock market indices in Turkey, Japan and England. They use using the time varying causality test and find two-way causality between the exchange rate and stock prices for during the global crises period. However, some empirical studies find one-way causality between the exchange rate and stock prices [14]. Coskun et al. investigate the link between stock index and macroeconomic variables (USD exchange rate, exports and imports, industrial production index, and gold price using monthly data for Turkey. Using Granger causality, they find one-way causality from exchange rate to BIST, and using impulse response function their results suggest positive response of BIST to exchange rate shock [4]. Aydemir and Demirhan analyses the causality between exchange rates and stock prices for national 100, services, financials, industrials, and technology indices. The results suggest that there is positive bi-directional causal relationship from technology indices to exchange rate, but in terms of national 100, services, financials and industrials indices to exchange rate the paper does provide negative causality [15]. On the other hand, Kendirli and Çankaya (2016) analyze the causal relationship between the USD and Istanbul Stock Exchange National 30 Index from 2009:01 to 2014:12 monthly data and find no causal relationship between USD and BIST-30 index returns [8].

Fourthly, there are some studies that investigates short and long-run relationship between the two [16]. Recently, the relationship between the stock prices and exchange rates, specifically BIST 100 and 23 sectors indexes investigated using ARDL model. The results suggest that the long run relationship exist only between exchange rate and textile, wholesale and retail, and technology indices [17]. The short and long-term relations between exchange rate and financial sector index, industrial sector index, service sector index and technology sector index investigated in Turkey [18]. The results suggest that exchange rate has no long term relationship with stock prices and the sectors. However, in short term relationship, the results show that exchange rate has bidirectional causality with stock prices, technology and service sectors while a unidirectional causality with financial sector index. Akel and Gazel (2014) investigate the long-run and short-run equilibrium relationships between real effective industrial index in Turkey. Based on ARDL cointegration analysis, they find that there is a positive relationship between industrial index and Dollar Index and Euro/TL exchange rate, but there is no evidence on the relationship between real effective exchange rate and industrial index. Based on VECM model, they find that industrial index is positively related to the REER while it is negatively related to the Dollar Index and Euro/TL exchange rate [19].

3. Methodology

This study investigates symmetric and asymmetric effects of exchange rates on three major stock market indices in Turkey using four different models. Firstly, linear and nonlinear bivariate ARDL models are estimated where the exchange rates are the only determinant of stock prices. The linear models are used to capture the symmetric effects of exchange rate changes while the nonlinear models are applied to capture asymmetric effects of exchange rate changes on stock prices.

Following Pesaran et al. [20] and Shin et al. [21] we apply the following the bivariate model to account for cointegration between exchanges rate and stock prices in Turkey.

$$LnSP_t = \alpha + \beta LnEX_t + \varepsilon_t \tag{1}$$

where a is the drift component, SP_t is the stock price index, EX_t is the nominal effective exchange rate, and ε_t is an error term. In order to estimate the short-run effects, the error correction form, proposed by Pesaran et al. [20] of the Eq. (1) can be written as follows:

$$\Delta LnSP_t = \alpha + \sum_{k=1}^{n1} \beta_k \Delta LnSP_{t-k} + \sum_{k=0}^{n2} \delta_k \Delta LnEX_{t-k} + \gamma_1 \ln SP_{t-1} + \gamma_2 \ln EX_{t-1} + u_t \tag{2}$$

By now, we basically assume that exchange rate changes have symmetric effects on stock prices, but it might be possible that the effects could be asymmetric. In order to assess whether exchange rate changes have asymmetric effects on stock prices, we decompose the exchange rates into its positive and negative partial sums. For example, there might be differences between increases and decreases of the short-run interest rates. The partial sum of positive values is computed by replacing negative values with zeros as $POS_t^+ = Ln\mathrm{EX}_t^+ = \sum_{j=1}^{t} \Delta \mathrm{Ln}EX_j^+ = \sum_{j=1}^{t} max\left(\Delta\mathrm{LnEX}_j, 0\right)$, and the partial sum of negative values are computed by replacing positive values with zeros as $NEG_t^- = Ln\mathrm{EX}_t^- = \sum_{j=1}^{t} \Delta \mathrm{Ln}EX_j^- = \sum_{j=1}^{t} min\left(\Delta\mathrm{LnEX}_j, 0\right)$ where ΔEX_j^+ *is the* positive sum of changes in exchange rates, and ΔEX_j^- is the negative sum of changes in exchange rates.

The *LnEX* in Eq. (2) is replaced by new generated POS and NEG variables in the nonlinear ARDL models as follows:

$$LnSP_t = a + \beta POS_t + NEG_t + \varepsilon_t \tag{3}$$

Thus, the error correction form of the Eq. (3) takes the following form with POS and NEG variables.

$$\begin{aligned} \Delta LnSP_t = \alpha &+ \sum_{i=1}^{n1} \beta_i \Delta LnSP_{t-i} + \sum_{i=0}^{n2} \delta_{1,i} \Delta POS_{t-i} + \sum_{i=0}^{n3} \delta_{2,i} \Delta NEG_{t-i} + \lambda_1 LnSP_{t-1} \\ &+ \lambda_2 POS_{t-1} + \lambda_3 NEG_{t-1} + u_t \end{aligned} \tag{4}$$

Secondly, linear and nonlinear multivariate ARDL models are estimated where industrial production index (IP), volatility index (VIX) and interest rates (IR) are used as a determinants of stock prices in Turkey. In order to account the effect of these variables on stock prices we employ a linear multivariate model of Moore & Wang [22] and Bahmani-Oskooee & Saha [23] as follows:

$$ln\, SP_t = a + \beta LnEX_t + \gamma LnIPI_t + \delta LnIR_t + \theta LnVIX_t + \varepsilon_t \tag{5}$$

where IPI_t is an index of industrial production, IR_t is the short term (overnight) interest rates, VIX_t is a measure of stock market volatility index and ε_t is an error term. The coefficient sign of β could be positive or negative depending on the firm's international competitiveness and production costs due to depreciation in exchange rates. When firms gain international competitiveness, they export more and thus exchange rate affects stock prices positively. However, increased costs due to depreciation in exchange rate are expected to affect stock prices negatively. Since there is a common consensus that economic activities affect stock prices positively [23, 24], the industrial production index is used as a proxy for measuring economic activity. Thus, we can expect stock prices to increase through increasing industrial production. Thus, we can expect the coefficient sing of γ to be positive.

As the interest rates are significant determinants of stock prices [25, 26], we use the short term (overnight) interest rates as a broad measure of financing costs. However, the effects of on stock prices are ambiguous [27, 28]. And finally, considering the international effects and theoretical predictions [29, 30], the volatility index is included in the model.

From Eq. (5), the coefficients estimate we get are the only long run effects. In order to infer the short-run effects, the Eq. (5) need to be rewrite in an error correction modeling format proposed by Pesaran et al. [20]. Therefore, we follow Pesaran et al.'s [20] bound testing approach and consider the following error-correction forms of multivariate model respectively:

$$\begin{aligned}\Delta LnSP_t = \alpha &+ \sum_{k=1}^{n1} \beta_k \Delta LnSP_{t-k} + \sum_{k=0}^{n2} \delta_k \Delta LnEX_{t-k} + \sum_{k=0}^{n3} \theta_k \Delta LnIPI_{t-k} \\ &+ \sum_{k=0}^{n4} \varphi_i \Delta LnIR_{t-k} + \sum_{k=0}^{n5} \vartheta_k \Delta LnVIX_{t-k} + \lambda_1 LnSP_{t-1} + \lambda_2 LnEX_{t-1} \\ &+ \lambda_3 LnIPI_{t-1} + \lambda_4 LnIR_{t-1} + \lambda_5 LnVIX_{t-1} + u_t \end{aligned} \tag{6}$$

The Eq. (6) give short-run as well as long-run estimates in one step, where λ_1, λ_5 are the long run parameters, Δ are the first difference operator, n and q are the optimal lag lengths for each variable, and u_t is the usual White noise residuals. The estimates of coefficients attached to first-differenced variables gives the short-run effects while the estimates of $\lambda 2$–$\lambda 5$ normalized on $\lambda 1$ give the long-run effects. In order for the long-run estimates to be valid, the F test proposed by Pesaran et al. [20] is applied to joint significance of lagged level variables $\lambda_1 = \lambda_2 = \lambda_3 = \lambda_4$ in equation [6] as a sign of cointegration. The F test has obviously new critical values depending on whether variables in the model are I(0) or I [1], and whether the model contains an intercept and/or a trend.

Once the cointegration established, the long-run effects of exchange rates, industrial productions, interest rates and volatility index on stock prices are captured by the estimates of $\lambda_2 - \lambda_5$ normalized on λ_1 . The short-run effects are gathered by the estimates of the coefficients of the first differenced variables such as the short-run effects of industrial production index on stock prices are determined by θ_k. The lag length of the first differences in Eq. (6) is chosen according to the Schwarz Bayesian Criteria (SBC) where we consider a maximum lag length of six.

The nonlinear multivariate ARDL models are constructed to assess the asymmetric effects of exchange rate changes on stock prices as follows:

$$\begin{aligned}\Delta LnSP_t = \alpha &+ \sum_{k=1}^{n1} \beta_k \Delta LnSP_{t-i} + \sum_{k=0}^{n2} \delta_{1,k} \Delta POS_{t-i} + \sum_{k=0}^{n3} \delta_{2,k} \Delta NEG_{t-i} + \sum_{k=0}^{n4} \theta_k \Delta LnIPI_{t-i} \\ &+ \sum_{k=0}^{n5} \varphi_k \Delta LnIR_{t-i} + \sum_{k=0}^{n6} \vartheta_k \Delta LnVIX_{t-i} + \lambda_1 LnSP_{t-1} + \lambda_2 POS_{t-1} + \lambda_3 NEG_{t-1} \\ &+ \lambda_4 LnIPI_{t-1} + \lambda_5 LnIR_{t-1} + \lambda_6 LnVIX_{t-1} + u_t \end{aligned} \tag{7}$$

Where the exchange rate is replaced by new generated POS and NEG variables. Thus the nonlinearity comes from the two new variables where POS refers appreciation of home currency and NEG refers depreciation of the home currency.

4. Empirical findings

In this chapter both linear and nonlinear ARDL models are estimated for bivariate and multivariate models by using monthly data over the period of 2003 M1 to

2018 M12 for three major stock market indices in Turkey. The results of short and long-run estimates of both linear and nonlinear for the bivariate and multivariate models are reported in **Tables 1** and **2**. Each of the tables consist of three panels: Panel A reports the short run estimates, Panel B reports the long-run estimates and the diagnostic statistics are then reported in Panel C. To ensure one of the requirements of Pesaran et al.'s [20] method that the variables could be I(0) or I [1] but not I [2], we use the traditional Augmented Dickey-Fuller (ADF) tests on levels as well as the first differenced variables. The lag order of the ADF test statistics is determined by the Akaike Information Criterion (AIC) and the results show that there are no I [2] variables.

4.1 Results of the bivariate models

In the bivariate models, the exchange rates are considered as the determinant of stock markets. **Table 1** gives the result of the linear bivariate modes. Looking at the linear model from Panel A, the short run coefficients associated with exchange rates are significant for all stock markets. The results show that all stock market indices are effected negatively by exchange rates changes as expected in the economic theory. The panel B shows that there is a positive long-run relationship between exchange rates and all markets.

Panel C reports the diagnostics statistics. The results of F test are slightly above the upper bound critical value of 3.35 in all stock indices. The error-correction model denoted by ECM test which shows negative and significant coefficients for all markets. Moreover, the LM test is also applied and the results show insignificant for all markets suggesting that there is no autocorrelation in the optimum model. Ramsey's RESET statistics are also reported to judge misspecification. For instance, if the test statistics of RESET test is more than the critical value of 3.84, it indicates a misspecification problem in the model at some significance level. Given its critical

Variables	BIST All	BIST 100	BIST 30
Panel A: Short Run Estimates			
$\Delta lnSP_{t-1}$	−0.46(−7.01) ***	−0.45(6.94)* **	−0.45(−6.97) ***
$\Delta lnEX$	−1.21 (−5.20) ***	−1.25(5.37)* **	−1.28(−5.46) ***
$ln\, \Delta EX_{t-1}$	−0.62 (−2.52) *	−0.62(2.53)**	−0.6 (−2.4) *
Constant	0.46(2.93) **	0 .47(2.95)***	0.51(3.03) **
Panel B: Long Run Estimates			
lnEX	1.86 (3.45) ***	1.82(3.43)***	1.76(3.46) ***
Panel C: Diagnostic Statistics			
Adjusted R^2	0.327	0.33	0.33
F	4.35	4.47	4.72
ECM_{t-1}	−0.05 (−2.84) **	−0.04(2.87)***	−0.05(−2.95) **
LM	3.91 (0.14)	3.97(0.14)	3.68(0.16)
RESET	0.69 (0.56)	0.62(0.60)	0.55(0.65)
CS (CS^2) (5%)	Stable	Stable	Stable

*Notes: Numbers inside the parentheses are t-ratios. Superscript *** represents the significance at 1% level, ** at the 5% level and * at the 10% level. The Δ denotes the first difference of the variables.*

Table 1.
Results of the linear bivariate models.

Variables	BIST All	BIST 100	BIST 30
Panel A: Short Run Estimates			
$\Delta lnSP_{t-1}$	−0.45 (−6.76)***	−0.442(6.70)***	−0.44(−6.69)***
ΔPOS	−1.58(−5.13)***	−1.62(5.27)* **	−1.66(−5.33)**
ΔPOS_{t-1}	−0.92(−2.85)**	−0.92(2.84)* **	−0.88(−2.68)**
ΔNEG	0.02 (0.20)	0.0219(0.25)	0.02(0.23)
Constant	0.88** (3.05)**	0.88(3.09)***	0.94(3.18)**
Panel B: Long Run Estimates			
POS	0.81 (1.20)	0.81(1.20)	0.78(1.19)
NEG	0.22 (0.19)	0.266(0.23)	0.24 (0.21)
Panel C: Diagnostic Statistics			
Adjusted R^2	0.335	0.34	0.34
F	4.67*	4.76*	5,01**
ECM_{t-1}	−0.08(−2.68) **	−0.082(2.71)***	−0.09(−2.81) ***
LM	3.64 (0.16)	3.51(0.17)	3.31(0.19)
RESET	1.11 (0.35)	1.05(0.37)	0.99(0.40)
CS (CS^2) (5%)	Stable	Stable	Stable
Wald (short run)	37.99***	39.34***	38,28***
Wald (long run)	0.79	0.71	0.76

*Notes: Numbers inside the parentheses are t-ratios. Superscript *** represents the significance at 1% level, ** at the 5% level and * at the 10% level. The Δ denotes the first difference of the variables.*

Table 2.
Results of the non-linear bivariate models.

value, the RESET statistic is insignificant for all stock market indices, suggesting that the model is correctly specified in the sector. The CUSUM and CUSUM square tests are also reported to establish stability of the short run and the long run estimates. The test results show that the estimated parameters for all stock market indices are stable. As can be seen, estimates are stable at least by one of the tests. Based on the above results, we can conclude that the exchange rate has short-run effects on three major stock market indices (BIST All, BIST100 and BIST30) in Turkey.

However, we would also like to see whether the short-run effects change if non-linear adjustment process used. Then the answer will be based on the results of non-linear ARDL models reported in **Table 2**. The results show that the currency appreciation (ΔPOS) has significant negative short-run effects on all markets, while depreciation (ΔNEG) has no effect as it is insignificant. This results suggests that exchange rate changes in Turkey have asymmetric effect on stock indices in Turkey.

When we look at the long-run effects in Panel B, the currency appreciation has positive impact on all stock indices, but the effects are statistically insignificant. The currency depreciation also has no effect on any indices in Turkey. In order to see whether the long-run assessment is valid, we report F test and ECMt-1 test results. In order to further validate the short-run and long-run asymmetric effects, the equality of short-run and long-run coefficient estimates is also tested applying Wald test. As for the long-run asymmetry we test whether $\lambda 2 = \lambda 3$. According to the Wald test statistic, the asymmetry effects between exchange rates and stock prices are supported for all markets in the short-run.

4.2 Results of the multivariate models

Tables 3 reports the results of short and long-run estimates of linear multivariate models for BIST All Shares, BIST 100 and BIST 30 stock prices. Panel A captures the symmetric effects of exchange rates on stock prices as well as other macroeconomics explanatory variables. The results show that all markets namely, BIST All, BIST100 and BIST30, are negatively affected by exchange rate changes. These markets on the other hand have a positive and statistically significant relationship with industrial production index implying that economic activity in Turkey has a significantly positive impact on the stock markets in the short run.

However, all markets have affected negatively by an increase in interest rates which implies that high interest rates lead to decrease in the investment level in the country and hence decrease economic activity. Likewise, volatility index (VIX) have a negative relationship with all stock market indices which implies that an increase in uncertainty lead to decrease the profitability of firm and thus lead to decrease stock prices in the short run.

When we look at the long run coefficient presented in Panel B, the industrial production index carries significant and positive relationship with all markets while interest rates and volatility index carries negative and significant relationship with stock prices in Turkey. Focusing on the exchange rate on stock prices, we found that

Variables	BIST All	BIST 100	BIST 30
Panel A: Short Run Estimates			
$\Delta lnSP_{t-1}$	−0.23(3.98)***	−0.19(3.43)***	−0.20(.50)***
$\Delta lnEX$	−0.84(4.23)***	−1.00(5.07)***	−1.01(5.03)***
$\Delta lnEX_{t-1}$	−0.45(2.26)**		
$\Delta lnIR$	−0.60(3.88)***	−0.56(3.64)***	−0.57(3.56)***
$\Delta lnIPI$	1.36(4.10)***	1.41(8.24)***	1.36(7.84)***
$\Delta lnVIX$	−0.15(2.06)**	−0.14(3.82)***	−0.14(3.72)***
Constant	0.69(2.06)**	0.71(2.10)**	0.87(2.56)**
Panel B: Long Run Estimates			
$lnEX$	0.22(1.09)	0.13(0.65)	0.15(0.75)
$lnIR$	−2.98(4.61)***	−2.88(4.33)***	−2.95(4.35)***
$lnIPI$	1.75(4.06)***	1.74(3.93)***	1.60(3.50)***
$lnVIX$	−0.17(1.96)*	−0.21(2.25)**	−0.21(2.22)**
Panel C: Diagnostic Statistics			
Adjusted R^2	0.59	0.58	0.57
F	4.61**	429**	4.22**
ECM_{t-1}	−0.20(3.76)***	−0.19(3.63)***	−0.19(3.62)***
LM	2.29(0.31)	4.28(0.11)	2.69(0.26)
$RESET$	2.48(0.06)	2.43(0.07)*	1.54(0.20)
CS (CS^2) (5%)	Unstable	Stable	Stable

*Notes: Numbers inside the parentheses are t-ratios. Superscript *** represents the significance at 1% level, ** at the 5% level and * at the 10% level. The Δ denotes the first difference of the variables.*

Table 3.
Results of the linear multivariate models.

in the long run the exchange rate changes affect stock prices positively. Thus the short run relationship between stock prices and exchange rate is not sustained in the long run. When cointegration established among variables then the long run relationship will be relevant. And thus we carry diagnostic statistics reported under Panel C. The F statistic is slightly above the upper bound critical value of 3.35 in all stock prices. The F statistic is statistically significant for all markets which establishes cointegration among variables. We also carry ECM test which is another indication of cointegration and the lagged error term (ECM_{t-1}) results show significant and negative coefficient. The results of ECM test results supports cointegration among variables. Panel C also reports Langrange Maltiplier (LM) test in order to check for autocorrelation among residuals. The LM test results are insignificant implying that there is no autocorrelation in the residuals. The Ramsey's Regression Specification Error Test (RESET) is also applied to check whether or not the model is misspecified. The results of RESET test statistics are insignificant for all models implies that the models are correctly specified except BIST100. Lastly, we applied the

Variables	BIST All	BIST 100	BIST 30
Panel A: Short Run Estimates			
$\Delta lnSP_{t-1}$	−0.22(3.83)***	−0.19(3.39)***	−0.20(3.45)***
ΔPOS	−1.07(4.11)***	−1.21(4.61)***	−1.23(4.57)***
ΔPOS_{t-1}	−0.58(2.04)**		
ΔNEG	−0.06(0.45)	−0.19(1.41)	−0.16(1.24)
$\Delta lnIR$	−0.45(2.29)**	−0.33(1.73)*	−0.35(1.74)*
$\Delta lnIPI$	1.38(7.98)***	1.37(7.83)***	1.32(7.39)***
$\Delta lnVIX$	−0.16(4.27)***	−0.17(4.37)***	−0.17(4.25)***
Constant	0.86(1.64)*	1.21(2.38)**	1.35(2.57)**
Panel B: Long Run Estimates			
POS	−0.017(0.06)	−0.26(1.06)	−0.22(0.85)
NEG	−0.029(0.46)	−0.84(1.46)	−0.77(1.27)
$lnIR$	−2.00(2.43)**	−1.48(1.89)*	−1.60(1.94)**
$lnIPI$	1.65(3.07)***	1.31(2.33)**	1.19(2.00)**
$lnVIX$	−0.19(1.62)*	−0.31(2.58)**	−0.30(2.42)**
Panel C: Diagnostic Statistics			
Adjusted R^2	0.59	0.58	0.57
F	4.18**	4.17**	4.08**
ECM_{t-1}	−0.22(4.16)***	−0.22(4.11)***	−0.21(4.05)***
LM	2.51(0.28)	4.56(0.11)	2.97(0.22)
$RESET$	1.4(0.22)	1.48(0.21)	0.77(0.50)
CS (CS^2) (5%)	Stable	Stable	Stable
Wald (short-run)	13.35***	10.06***	10.44***
Wald (long-run)	0.49	2.50	2.06

*Notes: Numbers inside the parentheses are t-ratios. Superscript *** represents the significance at 1% level, ** at the 5% level and * at the 10% level. The Δ denotes the first difference of the variables.*

Table 4.
The results of the non-linear multivariate models.

cumulative sum of recursive residuals (CUSUM denoted CS) and the cumulative sum of recursive residuals of square (CUSUMQ denoted CS^2) tests. According to both CS and CS^2 test results, the models are stable except BIST All Shares.

We also test the asymmetric effects of exchange rate changes on stock prices using the nonlinear multivariate models (see **Table 4**). Thus we decompose the exchange rates changes into its positive (*POS*) and negative (*NEG*) partial sums to test whether stock prices have asymmetric relationship with exchange rates changes. The results show that the currency appreciation (ΔPOS) has a negative and significant coefficient but the currency depreciation (ΔNEG) do not have significant coefficient. This implies that there is asymmetric relationship between the exchange rate and stock prices in the short-run. This asymmetric relationship is not continue in the long-run as in Panel B, *POS* and *NEG* variables have insignificant coefficients. When we look at the effects of other variables we see that the industrial production index has positive and significant effect both in the short and long run.

5. Conclusion

The aim of this chapter is multiresolution analysis with the application of advanced economic techniques using four different ARDL models to shed some light on the analysis of the symmetric and asymmetric impact of exchange rates on three major stock market indices in Turkey using monthly data from 2003M1 to 2018M12. This chapter also attempts to differentiate the short-run and long-run relationship between exchange rates and market indices. The motivating question is whether the relationship between the two is symmetric or asymmetric in Turkey? To answer the question, we employed four different methods: linear bivariate ARDL model is applied to investigate linear relationship between stock markets and the exchange rates; linear multivariate ARDL model employed to show that changes in some additional variables such as interest rates and industrial production have symmetric or asymmetric effects on stock markets; as exchange rate has different impact on different sectors of the economy, multivariate ARDL models employed to analyze the relationship between them. Moreover, the relationship should not be based on the linear but also on non-linear dimension. Thus finally, non-linear bivariate and multivariate ARDL models applied to analyze the non-linear relationship between stock market indices and the exchange rates in Turkey.

This study is of great interest for a country that has import-oriented economy, has completed its financial liberalization in the early 1990s, and become an attractive destination for foreign investors. The rationale for assessing the role of symmetric and asymmetric effects of exchanges rate on stock markets in Turkey is based on the perception, as expressed by (Dornbusch and Fischer 1980 and Frankel 1992), that the stock markets can react positively or negatively to fluctuations in exchange rates. Determining the factors that cause movements in stock markets is very important and is of great interest to policy makers and investors. The role of exchange rates on stock markets is much more important for small open economies in particular emerging markets. There is no sufficient research evidence showing the links between foreign exchange rate and Turkish stock market. We believe that this study will fill the gap in the literature in this area.

The findings show that exchange rates have asymmetric effects on all three major stock market indices both in the short and long-run. When we look at the long-run, the currency appreciation has positive and significant effect on stock market indices but currency depreciation does not have an effect. This finding is in line with the understanding that Turkish sectors heavily depends on the import of raw and intermediate goods. The results also show that the economic activity has positive and significant effects on three major stock market indices implying that it is the main determinant in the long-run. Moreover, interest rates and volatility index were negative and significant in all markets. Thus, it has important implications for policy makers to provide stable prices and diverse investors.

Acknowledgements

https://orcid.org/0000-0003-4565-9581.

Author details

Mustafa Çakır
Department of Economics, Istanbul Sabahattin Zaim University, Istanbul, Turkey

*Address all correspondence to: mustafa.cakir@izu.edu.tr

References

[1] Dornbusch BR, Fischer S. Exchange Rates and the Current Account. Am Econ Rev. 1980;70(5):960–71.

[2] Frankel JA. Monetary and portfolio-balance models of exchange rate determination. Int Econ Policies their Theor Found. 1992;793–832.

[3] Ahmed AD, Huo R. Linkages among energy price, exchange rates and stock markets: Evidence from emerging African economies. Applied Economics. 2020;52(18):1921–35.

[4] Coşkun M, Kiracı K, Muhammed U. Seçilmiş Makroekonomik Değişkenlerle Hisse Senedi Fiyatları Arasındaki İlişki: Türkiye Üzerine Ampirik Bir İnceleme. Finans Polit Ekon Yorumlar. 2016;53 (616).

[5] Abdalla ISA, Murinde V. Exchange rate and stock price interactions in emerging financial markets: Evidence on India, Korea, Pakistan and the Philippines. Appl Financ Econ. 1997;7 (1):25–35.

[6] Akıncı GY, Küçükçaylı F. Hisse Senedi Piyasası ve Döviz Kuru Mekanizmaları Üzerine Bir Panel Veri Analizi. Muhasebe ve Finans Derg. 2016;(71):127–49.

[7] Yang Z, Tu AH, Zeng Y. Dynamic linkages between Asian stock prices and exchange rates: new evidence from causality in quantiles. Appl Econ. 2014; 46(11):1184–201.

[8] Kendirli S, Çankaya M. Dolar Kuru'nun Borsa Istanbul-30 Endeksi Üzerindeki Etkisi ve Aralarindaki Nedensellik İlişkisinin Incelenmesi. Celal Bayar Üniversitesi Sos Bilim Derg. 2016;14(2):307–24.

[9] Doğukanlı H, Özmen M, Yücel E. İMKB'de Sektörel Açıdan Döviz Kuru Duyarlılığının incelenmesi. Çukurova Üniversitesi Sos Bilim Enstitüsü Derg. 2010;19:63–86.

[10] Boyacıoğlu MA, Çürük D. Effect of Foreign Exchange Rate Changes to the Stock Returns: An Application on the İstanbul Stock Exchange 100 Index. Muhasebe ve Finans Derg. 2016;(70): 143–56.

[11] Belen M, Karamelikli H. Türkiye'de Hisse Senedi Getirileri ile Döviz Kuru Arasındaki İlişkinin İncelenmesi: ARDL Yaklaşımı. İstanbul Üniversitesi İşletme Fakültesi Derg. 2016;45(1):34–42.

[12] Tsai IC. The relationship between stock price index and exchange rate in Asian markets: A quantile regression approach. J Int Financ Mark Institutions Money. 2012;22(3):609–21.

[13] Wong HT. Real exchange rate returns and real stock price returns. Int Rev Econ Financ. 2017;49(February): 340–52.

[14] Zeren F, Koç M. Time varying causality between stock market and exchange rate: Evidence from Turkey, Japan and England. Econ Res Istraz. 2016;29(1):696–705.

[15] Aydemir O, Demirhan E. The relationship between stock prices and exchange rates: Evidence from turkey. Int Res J Financ Econ. 2009;23(2): 207–15.

[16] Rjoub H. Stock prices and exchange rates dynamics: Evidence from emerging markets. African J Bus Manag. 2012;6(13).

[17] Eyüpoğlu DS, Eyüpoğlu DK. Borsa İstanbul Sektör Endeksleri İle Döviz Kurları Arasındaki İlişkilerin İncelenmesi: ARDL Modeli. Ömer Halisdemir Üniversitesi İktisadi ve İdari Bilim Fakültesi Derg. 2018;11(1):8–28.

[18] Keskin Benli Y. Empirical Analysis of the Realationship Between Exchange Rate and Istanbul Stock Exchange 100 and Sector Indexes. Int Ref J Humanit Acad Sci. 2015;4(12):55–55.

[19] Akel V, Gazel S. Döviz Kurlari ile BIST Sanayi Endeksi Arasındaki Eşbütünleşme İlişkisi: Bir ARDL Sınır Testi Yaklaşımı. Erciyes Üniversitesi İktisadi ve İdari Bilim Fakültesi Derg. 2014;0(44):23.

[20] Pesaran MH, Shin Y, Smith RJ. Bounds testing approaches to the analysis of level relationships. J Appl Econom. 2001;16(3):289–326.

[21] Shin Y, Yu B, Greenwood-Nimmo M. Modelling Asymmetric Cointegration and Dynamic Multipliers in a Nonlinear ARDL Framework. In: Festschrift in Honor of Peter Schmidt. New York, NY: Springer New York; 2014. p. 281–314.

[22] Moore T, Wang P. Dynamic linkage between real exchange rates and stock prices: Evidence from developed and emerging Asian markets. Int Rev Econ Financ. 2014;29:1–11.

[23] Bahmani-Oskooee M, Saha S. Do exchange rate changes have symmetric or asymmetric effects on stock prices? Glob Financ J. 2016;31:57–72.

[24] Bahmani-Oskooee M, Saha S, Halicioglu F, Bahmani S, Alagidede P, Panagiotidis T, et al. Spillover Effects between Exchange Rates and Stock Prices: Evidence from BRICS around the Recent Global Financial Crisis. Appl Financ Econ. 2017;15(1):459–71.

[25] Erdem C, Arslan CK, Erdem MS. Effects of macroeconomic variables on Istanbul stock exchange indexes. Appl Financ Econ. 2005;15(14):987–94.

[26] Ferrer R, Bolós VJ, Benítez R. Interest rate changes and stock returns: A European multi-country study with wavelets. Int Rev Econ Financ. 2016;44: 1–12.

[27] Moya-Martínez P, Ferrer-Lapeña R, Escribano-Sotos F. Interest rate changes and stock returns in Spain: A wavelet analysis. BRQ Bus Res Q. 2015 Apr 1;18 (2):95–110

[28] Kasman S. The relationship between exchange rates and stock prices: A causality analysis. Dokuz Eylül Üniversitesi Sos Bilim Enstitüsü Dergisi. 2003;5(2):70–9.

[29] Delisle RJ, Doran JS, Peterson DR. Asymmetric pricing of implied systematic volatility in the cross-section of expected returns. J Futur Mark. 2011 Jan;31(1):34–54.

[30] Pesaran MH, Shin Y, Smith RJ. Bounds testing approaches to the analysis of level relationships. J Appl Econom. 2001;16(3):289–326.

Chapter 9

Volatility Effects of the Global Oil Price on Stock Price in Nigeria: Evidence from Linear and Non-Linear GARCH

David Oluseun Olayungbo

Abstract

This present study examines the volatility effects of the oil price on the stock price returns in Nigeria from the period of 2000M(12) to 2020M(4) on a monthly data using both standard GARCH and non-linear GARCH models. The motivation for the present study is the recent fall in the global oil price of Brent Crude to US$15.25 per barrel due to the outbreak of the Corona Virus (COVID-19). Consequentially, the Nigerian stock market (NSE) responded with a fall of 4172 point or by a fall of 15.53%. After establishing the presence of heteroscedasticity through the ARCH test and volatility clustering through the returns, the outcome of the study contributes to knowledge by providing financial information and signals to investors about the best GARCH model response to proactively and successfully use to model global oil price shocks so as to reduce financial risk in Nigeria's stock market.

Keywords: oil price volatility, stock market returns, linear and non-linear GARCH models, Nigeria

1. Introduction

Oil price changes have been known to have direct impact on stock market returns depending whether the affected country is an oil-exporting or importing country [1–4]. The effects are usually different across countries. For oil-importing countries, the increase in oil price usually leads to fall in stock market returns, while the increase may not necessarily reduce the stock market returns in oil exporting countries. The experience in Nigeria has also been a significant one, not only as an oil exporting county but also as an oil-dependent one. Nigeria depends on oil exports such that it represents 90% of foreign exchange earnings and greatly determines the execution of the country's yearly budget [5]. The transmission of oil price volatility to the stock market returns stems from two channels. The first channel may be limited to investment in oil companies and this can occur when there is fall in equity investment of oil companies in oil-exporting countries due to fall in the global oil price. The second channel is broader and affects all sectors of the economy. It can come from foreign portfolio investors moving their financial assets from an oil dependent economy due to fall in the global oil price. This is usually due to the investors' perception that they may suffer huge financial loss if their investments are not quickly moved. Therefore, the stock market is so sensitive and important that it serves as long term funds for investment, businesses, financial institutions, private and the public. It is such that investors are much more concerned about the volatility of their returns in terms of gain and losses.

Apart from the theoretical and the empirical support, the stock market returns have been further verified to respond to the global oil price during the period of study in Nigeria (**Figure 1**). Therefore, since oil price volatility has been the major source of uncertainty in stock market returns especially in an oil-dependent economy like the sample country, it is then imperative to study their relationships. The unpredictability in the movement of oil price and its correlation with stock price returns have made it imperative for financial investors, practitioners, risk managers and policy makers to be interested in appropriate volatility model that best predicts minimum variance of the stock returns. Some previous studies in Nigeria have examined volatility using GARCH models. Salisu [6] examined comparative performance of both Brent oil and Western Texas Intermediate (WTI) oil across subsamples in Nigeria using GARCH models and found that bad news in the oil market increased oil price than good news. Najjar [7] applied ARCH, GARCH and EGARCH to Amman stock exchange in Jordan to study the return volatility of the market and found GARCH model to explain the extent of volatility clustering and leptokurtosis in the stock market. Uyaebo et al. [8] used non-linear GARCH models on the all share index of six selected stock market of Nigeria, Kenya, Germany, South Africa, China and United States for the period of February 2000 to February 2013. The study found volatility to be faster and persist in Nigeria and Kenya only. The study by [9] also investigated volatility of banks' equity returns on weekly basis for six commercial banks using GARCH models from January 2010 to June 2016. The study found EGARCH and CGARCH as the best volatility model in Nigeria. This present paper is different from the previous papers and contributed to the literature in two ways. First, we used different error distributions in the estimation of the standard GARCH and the non-linear GARCH models which previous studies have failed to take into consideration. Second, this study extends into the period of the COVID-19, the first quarter of the year 2020, which is another period of global shocks to both the oil market and the stock market.

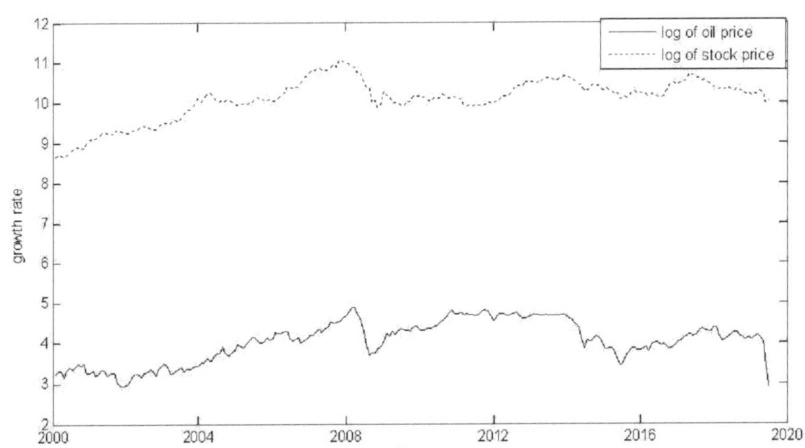

Figure 1.
The movement of change in oil price and stock price over the study period.

2. Literature review

The literature review on the relationship between stock price and oil price volatility in this study is done along the type of generalized autoregressive conditional heteroscedasticity GARCH type adopted. Hammoudeh and Aleisa [10] studied the causal relationship between oil price and stock price and found causality emanating from the variables for Saudi Arabia. Also, Bashar [11] examined the effects of oil price on stock market of five GCC countries such as Bahrain, Kuwait, Oman, Saudi Arabia and Abu Dhabi with daily data from the period of 25th May, 2001 to 24th May, 2005. The study found a bidirectional respond between Saudi stock market and the oil price shocks in vector autoregression (VAR) analysis.

In another paper for GCC, [12] investigated the volatility and channel of shocks among US equity market, global oil market and the equity market of Saudi Arabia, Kuwait and Bahrain. Of all the three equity markets, only Saudi Arabia equity market had significant volatility spillover to the oil market with the multivariate (GARCH) with BEKK. Arouri et al. [13] applied a generalized VAR-GARCH approach to examine the volatility channel between oil and stock market of Europe and the US. After analyzing the optimal weights and hedge ratio for oil-stock portfolio, the study found different volatility spillover for the selected European and the US stock market with VAR-GARCH being the best asset-hedging model. Khalfao et al. [14] investigated the relationship between West Texas Intermediate (WTI) crude oil market and the stock market of G-7 countries using wavelet-based MGARCH method. The mean and the variance of the study showed significant volatility spillover between the G-7 stock market returns and the oil market. Bouri [15] also applied ARMAX-GARCH to model and predict stock market returns of investors of oil-exporting countries like Lebanon and Jordan. The selected MENA countries are Morocco and Tunisia. The study found volatility spillover from the oil market to only Jordan stock market. In another paper, [16] examined directional connectedness between oil market and equity by applying implied volatility indices for 11 stock markets for the period of 2008–2015. A one-way transmission was found from oil market to equity market. Khamis et al. [17] used causality and multivariate regression method with daily data from the year 2012 to 2015 to examine the response of Saudi Arabia stock market to oil price fluctuation at the sectoral level. The finding is that Saudi Arabia stock market showed different to oil market. In recent paper, [18] examined the connection between oil price and stock market for net oil-exporting and net oil-importing countries such as Russia, Canada, United States and Japan using cointegration analysis. The study found significant and positive connection only between Russian stock market and oil price for the study period of 2007–2016.

3. Source of data and variable definition

The data used for this study were monthly data from the period of January 2000 to April 2020. The data were sourced from the Statistical Bulletin [19] published by Central bank of Nigeria (CBN) and the United State (US) Energy Information Administration [20]. Specifically, the Brent oil price was sourced from the US Energy Information Administration while the equity All Share Price Index (ASPI) was sourced from CBN and augmented with the monthly online data of Nigerian Stock Exchange [21]. The reason for the choice of equity stock price over bond is due to its high risk, high volatility and its sensitivity to market events and financial news which normally affect its returns. Bonds, on the other hand, offer lower returns with fixed interest and less sensitive to financial news and risk. Also, the choice of Brent spot oil price as against West Texas Intermediate (WTI) oil price is because the Nigeria's oil export is usually measured and priced in Brent oil market while the WTI is a bench mark for North American market. The stock price is measured as the monthly equity investment of ASPI in Naira on Nigerian Stock exchange while the Brent oil price is the monthly global oil price in US dollar per barrel (pbl) in the international oil market. The returns of both stock price and oil price were generated through the log of difference ($d\log X$) of the series which can be mathematically written as: $d\log X = \log X - \log X(-1)$.

3.1 Descriptive statistics

The statistical distributions of the 252 monthly observations of stock price and oil price with their returns used in this study are presented in **Table 1**. The average monthly observation of the oil price returns is −0.0013%, which implies that there were losses and low returns on oil revenue during the period of study. The high difference between the maximum oil price of $US132.72 and the minimum value of $US18.38 confirms the high volatile nature of the oil price. For the stock price returns, the minimum value is negative with a value of −0.3659. This implies that the stock price returns is less volatile than the oil price returns with minimum value of −0.55%. Although, there is also a large difference between the maximum value of the stock price with N65652.38 in billion and the minimum values of N5892.8 billion. The variability is just lower compared to that of the oil price. The standard deviation, skewness and kurtosis greater than zero imply that distribution is not normally distributed except for both returns that are close to zero and being normal. The positive skewness of 0.39% and 0.55% for oil price and stock price imply that their distributions are skewed to the right. On the other hand, the negative skewness of −1.75% and −0.47% for oil price returns and stock price returns imply that their distributions are skewed to the left. Furthermore, the kurtosis of oil price with value of 2.09% and the stock price with value 3.51 imply normal distribution because the values are less than 3. However for the returns, the kurtosis value of 9.08 and 7.71% for both oil price returns and stock price returns denote leptokurtic characteristic. Lastly, the null hypothesis for Jarque-Bera is that the data is normally distributed, however, with the probability value of 0.00 less than 0.05% in **Table 1**, then the null hypothesis is rejected and the alternative hypothesis that the data are

Statistics	Oil price	Oil price returns	Stock price	Stock price returns
Mean	64.35	−0.0013	27315.4	0.0056
Median	61.96	0.0164	26011.64	0.0024
Maximum	132.72	0.1979	65652.38	0.3235
Minimum	18.38	−0.5548	5892.8	−0.3659
Std-dev	29.91	0.1035	11756.38	0.0708
Skewness	0.39	−1.7543	0.55	−0.4734
Kurtosis	2.09	9.0837	3.51	7.71
Jarque-Bera	14.69	499.37	14.74	233.47
Prob.	0.00	0.00	0.00	0.00
Observation	252	252	252	252

Table 1.
Descriptive analysis.

Augmented Dickey Fuller test			Phillips-Perron test		
Variables	**Levels**	**Status**	**Variables**	**Levels**	**Status**
Oil price returns	−10.0663	I(0)	Oil price returns	−10.015	I(0)
Stock price returns	−13.5579	I(0)	Stock price returns	−13.5579	I(0)
The critical values are −3.4573, −2.8733 and −2.5731 for 1, 5, and 10%, respectively.					

Table 2.
Results of the unit root tests.

F-Statistics	7.9138	Prob. F(1,241)	0.00
Obs*R-squared	7.7257	Prob. Chi-Square(1)	0.00
Scale explained SS	5854	Prob. Chi-Square(1)	0.00

Table 3.
Breusch-pagan-Godfrey test.

not normally distributed is accepted. It is evident that the statistical properties of the variables used in this study can be described as fat tailed, leptokurtic and deviated from normal distribution which is typical of financial time series, risks and returns.

3.2 Preliminary test

The first exercise after the descriptive analysis is to verify the stationary properties of the variables used in the analysis and then test for the ARCH effect on the variables. Once the variables are stationary and ARCH effect is present, then we can proceed to estimate the GARCH models. The Augmented Dickey Fuller [22] and the Philips-Perron [23] tests were conducted and the results shown in **Table 2**. The unit root results show that both oil price returns and stock price returns are stationary at levels. The stationarity of the returns of the variable of interest is one of the conditions for carrying out the GARCH process.

The final preliminary test is to test for ARCH effects using Breusch-Pagan-Godfrey method of Engle [24] to verify the presence of heteroscedasticity and proceed to the GARCH process. The heteroscedasticity test presented in **Table 3** shows the presence of heteroscedasticity, which means that the variance is not constant over time (see also Appendix 5 for additional evidence of heteroscedasticity with the fat tail of the histogram distribution). The null hypothesis is that there is no presence of heteroscedasticity in the returns series. And since the probability value is less than 0.05%, then the null hypothesis is rejected and the alternative hypothesis of presence of ARCH effects or heteroscedasticity is accepted.

4. The linear and non-linear GARCH models

The presence of the ARCH effects in our variables as presented in **Table 3** endorses the use of the GARCH models. There are many types of GARCH models. We have the symmetric (linear) GARCH, which is the normal GARCH and asymmetric (nonlinear) GARCH such as exponential GARCH (EGARCH) and the Threshold GARCH (TGARCH) or Glosten, Jagannathan and Runkle GARCH (GJR-GARCH).

We started with the ARCH model formulated in two parts, the mean equation and the variance equation proposed by Engle [24] and written as:

$$Y_t = \alpha + \beta' X_t + \mu_t \tag{1}$$

Eq.(1) is the mean equation, where Y_t is a column vector of response variables, α is the constant term, β' is a row vector of unknown parameters, X_t is a column vector of explanatory variables and μ_t is a column vector of random error terms with $\mu_t = z_t\sqrt{h_t}$. Where $z_t \approx (0, h_t)$ and h_t is a scaling factor. The variance equation of the ARCH model on the other hand in general term is stated as:

$$h_t = \gamma_0 + \sum_{i=1}^{q} \gamma_i u_{t-i}^2 \tag{2}$$

The limitation of the ARCH model is that it is more of a moving average (MA) model where the variance is only responding to the errors. The autoregressive (AR) parts of the model are not captured, hence the use of more superior model like the GARCH model propounded by Bollerslev [25]. The mean equation still remains the same while the variance equation in general term is written a bit differently from the ARCH model as:

$$h_t = \gamma_0 + \sum_{i=1}^{p} \lambda_i h_{t-i} + \sum_{i=1}^{q} \gamma_i u_{t-i}^2 \tag{3}$$

The GARCH model equally has its own deficiency; it cannot accounts for the impacts of news and events that can have asymmetric effects on financial assets. For instance, investors would react differently to the occurrence of good or bad news to financial assets or the market. Whenever bad news happen in the financial market, the volatility is usually higher and larger than a state of tranquility. To address such asymmetric effects, non-linear or asymmetric GARCH models such as TGARCH and EGARCH are propounded. The TGARCH model propounded by Zokoian [26] can be stated in its general form as:

$$h_t = \gamma_0 + \sum_{i=1}^{p} \lambda_i h_{t-i} + \sum_{i=1}^{q} (\phi_i + \eta_i D_{t-i}) u_{t-i}^2 \tag{4}$$

Where $D_{t-i} = 1$ is bad news for $u_t < 0$ and 0 otherwise, β_i measures good news, η_i denotes the asymmetry or leverage term, $\eta_i > 0$ implies asymmetry, while $\eta_i = 0$means symmetry. If η_i is found to be significant and positive, then negative shocks have larger impacts on the conditional variance, h_t than the positive shocks. Another asymmetric GARCH model is EGARCH propounded by Nelson [27] described in logarithm form as:

$$\log(h_t) = \gamma_0 + \sum_{i=1}^{p} \beta_i \left| \frac{u_{t-i}}{\sqrt{h_{t-i}}} \right| + \sum_{i=1}^{q} \gamma_i \frac{u_{t-i}}{\sqrt{h_{t-i}}} + \sum_{i=1}^{m} \alpha_i \log(h_{t-i}) \tag{5}$$

where good news is denoted by positive value of u_{t-i} with total effect as $(1 + \gamma_i)|u_{t-i}|$ and bad news given by u_{t-i} being negative with total effect as $(1 - \gamma_i)|u_{t-i}|$. If $\gamma_i < 0$ then bad news is assumed to have higher effects on volatility than good news. There is symmetry if $\gamma_i = 0$ and there is asymmetry if $\gamma_i \neq 0$. In short, γ_0 is the constant term, β_i measure the ARCH effect, γ_1 measures the leverage effect and lastly, α_i account for the GARCH effect.

DOI: http://dx.doi.org/10.5772/intechopen.93497

5. Empirical analysis and result discussions

Having described both the symmetric and asymmetric GARCH, we expressed the variables of interest from the mean equation as:

$$RSP_t = \alpha + \beta ROP_t + u_t \qquad (6)$$

Eq. (6) expresses stock price return as a function of oil price return. Where RSP_t is the return of the stock price over time, α is the constant term, ROP_t is the returns of the oil price, β is the marginal effect of the oil price on the stock price while u_t is the error term. The variance equation with the parsimonious GARCH (1,1) model is stated as:

$$h_t = \gamma_0 + \lambda_1 h_{t-1} + \gamma_1 u_{t-1}^2 \qquad (7)$$

Where $\lambda_1 + \gamma_1 < 1$ implies stationarity and $\lambda_1 + \gamma_1 > 1$ signifies non-stationarity of the ARCH and GARCH. The justification for the choice of GARCH (1,1) apart from being parsimonious is that the variance model depends on the most recent past variance. The use of any higher lags would result to loss of degree of freedom, information and over parameterization of the GARCH model [28]. The GARCH (1,1) model is estimated with different error distributions so as to identify the model with minimum variance using the Schwarz criterion (SC) and the log likelihood. The GARCH model with the minimum variance represents the model with minimum asset risk. The result of the of the GARCH (1,1) model with different error distributions is presented in **Table 4** (See the Appendix 1 for the log likelihood of the distributions). It can be observed from the **Table 4** that all the GARCH (1,1) result with the different errors are stationary given that their parameter values of $\lambda_1 + \gamma_1 < 1$. In addition, the previous period of volatility of all the error distributions have significant effects on the current conditional volatility. For the GARCH (1,1) with normal distribution error, the sum of the coefficients of the ARCH and GARCH [the sum of the residual square and Garch(−1)] are positive and statistically significant at 0.05% with a value of 0.9037. The value is less than 1, which satisfies the stability condition of the GARCH process. That of the[1] student-t error distribution is 0.8473 and 0.8731 for the generalized error distribution model. The result suggests that the persistence of volatility effects of oil price on stock price is large for Nigeria (the volatility clustering in **Figure 2** equally suggests the persistence of volatility movement of the two series). The large volatility for Nigeria is supported by previous study done by Uyaebo et al. [8] done for six selected countries with Nigeria inclusive. For the GARCH (1,1), the error distribution for the student-t error distribution is 0.85%, 0.87% for generalized error distribution, and there is highest value of 0.90% for normal distribution. The mean equation, on the other hand, implies that 1% change in oil price affects the stock price by 0.13% for the GARCH (1,1) using normal distribution and the generalized error distribution while it is a bit higher at 0.14% for student-t error distribution. However, in terms of the model with goodness of fit and with minimum variance, the GARCH (1,1) model with student-t error distribution behaves optimally with minimum SC value of −2.56 and with the highest log likelihood value of 327.18. The implication of the optimality of the student-t error distribution implies that stock price returns in Nigeria is unpredictable and volatile because of the effect of the global oil price. We therefore conclude here that GARCH (1,1) process with student-t error distribution

[1] More exposition on student-t distribution can be found in Fisher (1925).

Dependent variable: stock price				
Normal Dist.				
Mean equation				
Variables	Coefficient	Std. error	z-Statistics	Prob.
dlogoilprice	0.1257	0.0265	4.7473	0.00***
Constant	0.0117	0.0046	2.5352	0.01***
Variance equation				
Variables	Coefficient	Std. error	z-Statistics	Prob.
Constant	0.0005	0.0003	1.8414	0.07*
residual square	0.1562	0.0699	2.2362	0.03**
Garch(−1)	0.7475	0.101	6.7968	0.00***
Log likelihood	321.37			
Schwarz criterion	−2.53			
Student t dist.				
Mean equation				
Variables	Coefficient	Std. error	z-Statistics	Prob.
dlogoilprice	0.1384	0.0324	4.2693	0.00***
Constant	0.0079	0.004	2.013	0.04**
Variance equation				
Variables	Coefficient	Std. error	z-Statistics	Prob.
Constant	0.0007	0.0006	1.2456	0.21
Residual square	0.0995	0.0769	1.2943	0.19
Garch(−1)	0.7478	0.174	4.2983	0.00***
Log likelihood	327.18			
Schwarz criterion	−2.56			
Generalized error				
Mean equation				
Variables	Coefficient	Std. error	z-Statistics	Prob.
dlogoilprice	0.1286	0.0315	4.0756	0.00***
Constant	0.0084	0.0039	2.1526	0.03**
Variance equation				
Variables	Coefficient	Std. error	z-Statistics	Prob.
Constant	0.0006	0.0005	1.3042	0.19
Residual square	0.1230	0.0889	1.3836	0.17
Garch(−1)	0.7501	0.1619	4.6326	0.00***
Log likelihood	326.01			
Schwarz criterion	−2.54			

****, **, * represent significance level at 1, 2, and 10%, respectively.*

Table 4.
GARCH (1,1) results of stock prices and oil prices volatility.

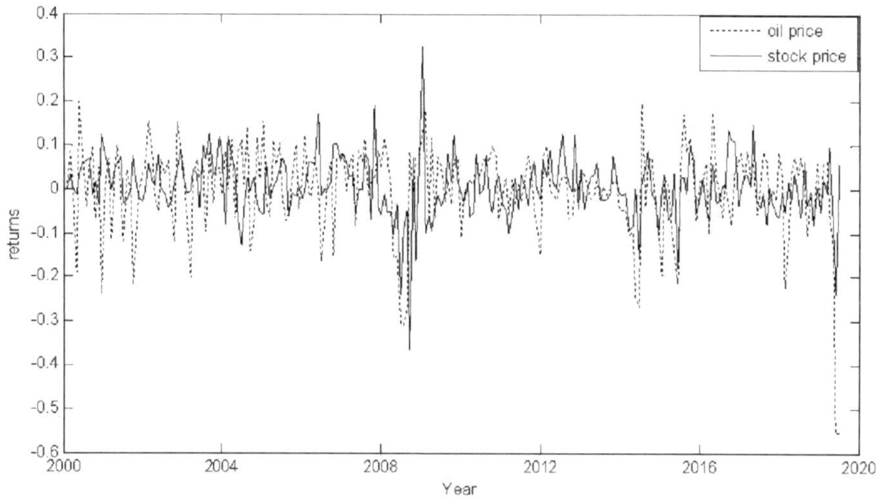

Figure 2.
Graph of the monthly returns of oil price and stock price over the period of study.

is the best selection model for financial investors when taking decisions on the volatility effects of oil price on stock price in Nigeria.

Due to the limitation of the standard ARCH and GARCH model of not capable of capturing news, events and incidents that result in asymmetric impacts on financial assets in financial markets, the use of TGARCH and EGARCH that are more superior in accounting for good and bad news (the asymmetric and non-linear effects) became popular. The GARCH model usually treats the innovation in absolute term with the squared residual. However, with the TGARCH and EGARCH, the residual is decomposed into negative effects ($u_{t-i} < 0$) and the positive effects ($u_{t-i} > 0$). The parsimonious TGARCH (1,1) model can be written as: $h_t = \gamma_0 + \lambda_1 h_{t-1} + \gamma_1 u_{t-1}^2 + \alpha_1 u_{t-1}^2 D_{t-1}$ and the result presented in **Table 5** with the error distributions. The marginal effects of oil price on stock price is almost similar with the GARCH (1,1) result with almost 0.13 at 1% significance level for all the error distributions. Also, the GARCH effect is significant at 1% for all the error distributions, suggesting significant effects of past conditional volatility on the current volatility. This implies volatility effects of oil price on stock price in Nigeria. For TGARCH (1,1) model of the normal distribution, we found the positive effect (good news) to be insignificant with coefficient value of 0.02% while that of the negative effect (bad news) is significant at 5% with coefficient value of 0.26% (sum of 0.0176 and 0.2454). The difference between the positive effect and negative effect is 0.2454, which is the leverage effect. The result shows presence of leverage effect and negative effect of oil price has more significant impact on stock prices than positive effect. In the same vein, the positive and negative effects of the TGARCH (1,1) model using the student-t error distribution are 0.0373 and 0.1341, respectively, though the negative effect is not significant like the TGARCH (1,1) normal distribution. The negative effect also has larger effect of 0.13% than the positive effect with 0.04%. This finding supports previous study in Nigeria by Salisu [6] that also found bad news to have large effect than good news in oil market. The TGARCH (1,1) for the generalized error distribution also show asymmetric effect though the negative effect is also not significant. The negative effect has coefficient value of 0.1940 while the positive effect is 0.0276. In overall, similar to the GARCH (1,1) model, the student-t error distribution is also found to have the minimum variance with SC value of −2.54 and the maximum log likelihood value of 327.98. We, therefore, conclude

Dependent variable: stock price				
Normal Dist.				
Mean equation				
Variables	Coefficient	Std. error	z-Statistics	Prob.
dlogoilprice	0.1271	0.0293	4.3383	0.00***
Constant	0.0106	0.0045	2.3545	0.02**
Variance equation				
Variables	Coefficient	Std. error	z-Statistics	Prob.
Constant	0.0008	0.0004	1.9647	0.05*
Residual square	0.0176	0.0726	0.2424	0.81
resid square(resid(−1) > 0	0.2454	0.123	1.9957	0.04**
Garch(−1)	0.6862	0.1319	5.2028	0.00***
Log likelihood	324.67			
Schwarz criterion	−2.53			
Student t dist.				
Mean equation				
Variables	Coefficient	Std. error	z-Statistics	Prob.
dlogoilprice	0.1393	0.0338	4.1172	0.00***
Constant	0.0080	0.0040	2.0086	0.04**
Variance equation				
Variables	Coefficient	Std. error	z-Statistics	Prob.
Constant	0.0008	0.0006	1.3834	0.17
Residual square	0.0373	0.0886	0.4214	0.67
Resid square(resid(−1) > 0	0.1341	0.1327	1.0100	0.31
Garch(−1)	0.7111	0.1838	3.8685	0.00***
Log likelihood	327.98			
Schwarz criterion	−2.54			
Generalized Error dist.				
Mean equation				
Variables	Coefficient	Std. error	z-Statistics	Prob.
dlogoilprice	0.1305	0.03335	3.8936	0.00***
Constant	0.0082	0.0040	2.0685	0.04**
Variance equation				
Variables	Coefficient	Std. error	z-Statistics	Prob.
Constant	0.0008	0.0005	1.4810	0.13
Residual square	0.0276	0.0902	0.3060	0.75
Resid square(resid(−1) > 0	0.1940	0.1496	1.2969	0.19
Garch(−1)	0.6974	0.1766	3.9499	0.00***
Log likelihood	327.62			
Schwarz criterion	−2.53			

****, **, * represent significance level at 1, 2, and 10%, respectively.*

Table 5.
TGARCH (1,1) results of stock prices and oil prices volatility.

that news, information and events on oil prices are very significant to stock price volatility in Nigeria.

In order to have a robust estimation and result, the EGARCH, another asymmetric or non-linear model, is considered to compare its result with the TGARCH model. The parsimonious EGARCH (1,1) is also specified as: $\log(h_t) = \gamma_0 + \beta_1 \left| \frac{u_{t-1}}{\sqrt{h_{t-1}}} \right| + \gamma_1 \frac{u_{t-1}}{\sqrt{h_{t-1}}} + \alpha_1 \log(h_{t-1})$. The result of the EGARCH (1,1) model is presented in **Table 6**. Looking at the mean equation of the EGARCH (1,1) result with the normal distribution, we found oil price to have 0.17% significant effect on stock price in Nigeria at 1% significance level. The ARCH and the leverage term are not significant while the GARCH terms are significant at 10%. For the ARCH term,

Dependent variable: stock price				
Normal dist.				
Mean equation				
Variables	Coefficient	Std. error	z-Statistics	Prob.
dlogoilprice	0.1700	0.0285	5.9670	0.00***
Constant	0.0053	0.0050	1.0484	0.29
Variance equation				
Variables	Coefficient	Std. error	z-Statistics	Prob.
Constant	−7.8302	1.4262	−5.4903	0.00***
Residual square	0.0112	0.1446	0.0773	0.94
Leverage term	0.1330	0.0850	1.5640	0.12
Garch(−1)	−0.4560	0.2709	−1.6831	0.09*
Log likelihood	307.63			
Schwarz criterion	−2.44			
Student t dist.				
Mean equation				
Variables	Coefficient	Std. error	z-Statistics	Prob.
dlogoilprice	0.1375	0.0342	4.0190	0.00***
Constant	0.0091	0.004	2.2437	0.02**
Variance equation				
Variables	Coefficient	Std. error	z-Statistics	Prob.
Constant	−1.0114	0.6257	−1.6165	0.11
Residual square	0.2042	0.1322	1.5447	0.12
Leverage term	−0.0567	0.0783	−0.7248	0.47
Garch(1)	0.8421	0.1064	7.9128	0.00***
Log likelihood	327.20			
Schwarz criterion	−2.53			
Generalized error dist.				
Mean equation				
Variables	Coefficient	Std. error	z-Statistics	Prob.
dlogoilprice	0.1257	0.0334	3.7506	0.00***
Constant	0.0090	0.0040	2.2599	0.04**

Dependent variable: stock price				
Variance equation				
Variables	Coefficient	Std. error	z-Statistics	Prob.
Constant	−0.9643	0.5425	−1.7777	0.08*
Residual square	0.2227	0.1404	1.5859	0.11
Leverage term	−0.0838	0.0805	−1.0418	0.30
Garch(−1)	0.8537	0.0914	9.3394	0.00***
Log likelihood	326.65			
Schwarz criterion	−2.53			

****, **, * represent significance level at 1, 2, and 10%, respectively.*

Table 6.
EGARCH (1,1) results of stock prices and oil prices volatility.

the result shows a positive relationship between the shock of the oil price and the volatility of stock price returns. Also, the leverage effect is positive meaning that good news prevails over bad news in the oil market on stock price volatility. Negative effect is found between the past volatility and the future. The past volatility negatively predicts the future volatility at 10% significance level. We further examine the EGARCH (1,1) result with the student-t distribution and we found the marginal effect of oil price on stock price returns to be 0.14%, lower than the 0.17% of the EGARCH (1,1) model with normal distribution. Similar to the result of the normal distribution, the ARCH and the leverage term are also not significant only the GARCH term is significant at 1%. The ARCH term shows a positive relationship between the oil price shocks and the stock price volatility returns. 1% increase in oil price shock, stock price fluctuates by 0.20%. The leverage effects on the other hand are negative. This implies that 1% increase in the negative shocks in the oil price; it reduces the stock price returns by 0.06%. The GARCH term is significant at 1% level suggesting that the previous volatility predicts significantly the future volatility in the effect of oil price volatility on stock price returns. A 1% increase in past volatility leads to 0.84% increase in future volatility significantly at 1% level. Lastly, we examine the EGARCH (1,1) result using the generalized error distribution and we found the marginal effect of oil price volatility on stock price returns to be 0.13% at 1% significance level. The result of the ARCH, leverage and GARCH term of the generalized error term is similar to that of the student-t distribution. The ARCH term shows that 1% increase in the oil price shock insignificantly increases the stock price returns by 0.22%. The leverage effect also shows prevalence of bad news with 1% increase in bad news in the oil market reducing stock price returns by 0.08%. The GARCH term is significant with 0.85% future volatility increase resulting from 1% increase in past volatility in relation to the effect of oil price on the stock price in Nigeria. Of all the distributions, the EGARCH (1,1) of the student-t distribution is found to be the best model with minimum variance looking at the SC and likelihood. The EGARCH (1,1) with student-t distribution has SC with minimum value of −2.53 and likelihood maximum value of 327.20. We therefore conclude that both the standard GARCH and non-linear GARCH process driven by the student-t distribution is the best selection model for investors for valuing the volatility effect of oil price on stock price in Nigeria. Finally, considering the diagnostic tests of our model, the serial correlation for all the error distributions used are presented at the

Appendix 4 showing rejection of the null hypothesis of presence of serial correlation with p-values greater than 0.05.

6. Conclusion and policy implications

In this study we examined the volatility effects of oil price behavior on stock price in Nigeria from the first month of year 2000 to the fourth month of year 2020 using both standard and asymmetric GARCH. Before performing the GARCH, TGARCH and EGARCH, we carried out some preliminary tests such as the ARCH tests for heteroscedasticity, unit root test for stationary test and all the tests show evidence of volatility clustering which necessitate the use of GARCH process on the variables. The standard GARCH was first done and the model with student-t distribution showed goodness of fit. We proceeded to use the non-linear GARCH models such as the TGARCH and EGARCH to account for news, events and information that can filter into the oil market and thereby create asymmetric behavior in the financial market. The non-linear GARCH models also confirm the student-t distribution as the best model for traders in the financial market in Nigeria. In this study, we found oil price volatility to be a significant predictor of stock price returns. Secondly, our study showed that the volatility movement is high and persist over the study period. Also, we found leverage effects in stock price response to oil price. Bad news tends to increase volatility than good news. One of the implications of the findings of this study is that oil price volatility should be considered in the prediction of stock price returns by investors and financial analyst in Nigeria. In addition, the finding implies that most of the investors in the financial market are risk averse; this is because they are more sensitive in their asset decisions to bad news than to good news. This study concludes that bad news have much effects on investors than good news in the movement of oil price effect to stock price returns.

A. Appendix

A.1 The probability density function of normal distribution is written as:

$$f(x|\mu,\sigma) = \frac{1}{\sigma\sqrt{2\pi}} e^{\frac{-(x-\mu)^2}{2\sigma^2}} \quad (8)$$

and its log likelihood function in GARCH term is:

$$-\frac{n}{2}\ln(2\pi) - \frac{n}{2}\ln(h) - \frac{1}{2h}\sum_{j=1}^{n}(x_j-\mu)^2. \quad (9)$$

A.2 The probability density function of thc student-t distribution is:

$$f(y,\nu) = \frac{\Gamma\frac{\nu+1}{2}}{\sqrt{\pi(\nu-2)}\Gamma\frac{\nu}{2}\left(1+\frac{\nu^2}{\nu-2}\right)^{\frac{\nu+1}{2}}} \quad (10)$$

Its log likelihood function in GARCH term is:

$$\log\left[\Gamma\left(\frac{\nu+1}{2}\right)\right] - \log\left[\Gamma\left(\frac{\nu}{2}\right)\right] - \frac{1}{2}\log(\pi(\nu-2)) - \frac{1}{2}\sum_{j=1}^{n}\left[\log(h_t) + (\nu+1)\log\left(1+\frac{\varepsilon_t^2}{h_t(\nu-2)}\right)\right] \quad (11)$$

A.3 The probability density function of the generalized error distribution is:

$$f(x|\mu, \sigma, \kappa) = \frac{e^{-\frac{1}{2}|x-\mu|^{\frac{1}{n}}}}{2^{\kappa+1}\sigma\Gamma(\kappa+1)} \tag{12}$$

Its log likelihood function in GARCH term is:

$$-\frac{1}{2}|x-\mu|^{\frac{1}{n}} - (\kappa+1)\log(2) - \log(h) - \log(\Gamma) - \log(\kappa+1) \tag{13}$$

A.4 Diagnostic test of student's t for serial correlation

Date: 05/12/20 Time: 00:06						
Sample: 2000:01 2020:12						
Included observations: 243						
Autocorrelation	Partial Correlation		AC	PAC	Q-Stat	Prob*
.|. |	.|. |	1	−0.028	−0.028	0.1887	0.664
.|. |	.|. |	2	−0.025	−0.025	0.3376	0.845
.|* |	.|* |	3	0.107	0.106	3.1875	0.364
.|. |	.|. |	4	0.040	0.045	3.5767	0.466
.|. |	.|. |	5	0.024	0.031	3.7163	0.591
.|. |	.|. |	6	−0.002	−0.010	3.7169	0.715
.|. |	.|. |	7	0.039	0.032	4.1050	0.768
.|. |	.|. |	8	0.014	0.009	4.1571	0.843
.|. |	.|. |	9	−0.054	−0.054	4.9051	0.842
.|. |	.|. |	10	−0.024	−0.036	5.0550	0.887
.|* |	.|* |	11	0.101	0.093	7.6682	0.743
.|. |	.|. |	12	0.023	0.038	7.8105	0.800
.|. |	.|. |	13	−0.051	−0.036	8.4859	0.811
.|. |	.|. |	14	−0.039	−0.059	8.8732	0.839
.|. |	.|. |	15	−0.035	−0.054	9.1869	0.868
.|. |	.|. |	16	−0.062	−0.063	10.192	0.856
.|. |	.|. |	17	0.004	0.014	10.195	0.895
.|. |	.|. |	18	0.004	0.010	10.199	0.925
.|. |	.|. |	19	−0.039	−0.025	10.601	0.937
.|. |	.|. |	20	−0.038	−0.023	10.977	0.947
.|. |	.|. |	21	−0.023	−0.014	11.121	0.960
.|. |	.|. |	22	−0.040	−0.048	11.545	0.966
.|. |	.|. |	23	−0.050	−0.057	12.227	0.967
.|* |	.|* |	24	0.136	0.146	17.252	0.838
.|. |	.|. |	25	−0.052	−0.028	17.992	0.843
.|. |	.|* |	26	0.059	0.092	18.936	0.839
*|. |	*|. |	27	−0.069	−0.083	20.253	0.820

Autocorrelation	Partial Correlation		AC	PAC	Q-Stat	Prob*
.|. |	.|. |	28	-0.028	-0.038	20.471	0.847
.|* |	.|* |	29	0.157	0.126	27.294	0.556
.|. |	.|. |	30	−0.024	−0.004	27.457	0.599
.|. |	.|. |	31	0.046	0.058	28.054	0.618
.|. |	.|. |	32	−0.013	−0.045	28.101	0.664
.|. |	.|. |	33	0.013	0.022	28.145	0.708
.|. |	.|. |	34	0.054	0.053	28.981	0.712
*|. |	*|. |	35	−0.069	−0.106	30.354	0.692
.|. |	.|. |	36	−0.003	−0.036	30.357	0.734

* no serial correlation since p-values >0.05%.

Diagnostic test of Normal distribution for serial correlation

Date: 05/12/20 Time: 00:08						
Sample: 2000:01 2020:12						
Included observations: 243						
Autocorrelation	**Partial Correlation**		**AC**	**PAC**	**Q-Stat**	**Prob***
.|. |	.|. |	1	−0.014	−0.014	0.0483	0.826
.|. |	.|. |	2	−0.041	−0.041	0.4578	0.795
.|. |	.|. |	3	0.069	0.068	1.6444	0.649
.|. |	.|. |	4	0.005	0.005	1.6495	0.800
.|. |	.|. |	5	0.031	0.036	1.8822	0.865
.|. |	.|. |	6	0.017	0.014	1.9549	0.924
.|. |	.|. |	7	0.035	0.037	2.2564	0.944
.|. |	.|. |	8	0.008	0.006	2.2729	0.971
.|. |	.|. |	9	−0.052	−0.052	2.9643	0.966
.|. |	.|. |	10	−0.034	−0.041	3.2544	0.975
.|. |	.|. |	11	0.066	0.059	4.3691	0.958
.|. |	.|. |	12	0.033	0.037	4.6579	0.968
*|. |	.|. |	13	−0.068	−0.059	5.8644	0.951
.|. |	.|. |	14	−0.053	−0.060	6.5925	0.949
.|. |	.|. |	15	−0.048	−0.057	7.1937	0.952
*|. |	*|. |	16	−0.074	−0.072	8.6166	0.928
.|. |	.|. |	17	0.021	0.022	8.7326	0.948
.|. |	.|. |	18	0.012	0.013	8.7734	0.965
.|. |	.|. |	19	−0.038	−0.027	9.1536	0.971
.|. |	.|. |	20	−0.043	−0.032	9.6408	0.974
.|. |	.|. |	21	−0.024	−0.011	9.7969	0.981
.|. |	.|. |	22	−0.036	−0.039	10.139	0.985

Autocorrelation	Partial Correlation		AC	PAC	Q-Stat	Prob*
.|. |	*|. |	23	−0.060	−0.070	11.101	0.982
.|* |	.|* |	24	0.152	0.155	17.408	0.831
.|. |	.|. |	25	−0.047	−0.039	18.003	0.842
.|* |	.|* |	26	0.076	0.110	19.586	0.811
*|. |	*|. |	27	−0.085	−0.102	21.580	0.758
.|. |	.|. |	28	−0.037	−0.030	21.949	0.784
.|* |	.|* |	29	0.173	0.133	30.315	0.398
.|. |	.|. |	30	−0.013	−0.008	30.366	0.447
.|. |	.|* |	31	0.060	0.074	31.367	0.448
.|. |	.|. |	32	−0.012	−0.047	31.407	0.496
.|. |	.|. |	33	0.017	0.039	31.486	0.543
.|* |	.|. |	34	0.075	0.072	33.071	0.513
*|. |	*|. |	35	−0.084	−0.121	35.098	0.464
.|. |	.|. |	36	0.015	−0.014	35.160	0.508

* no serial correlation since p-values >0.05%

Diagnostic test of Generalised error distribution for serial correlation

Date: 05/12/20 Time: 00:10

Sample: 2000:01 2020:12

Included observations: 243

Autocorrelation	Partial Correlation		AC	PAC	Q-Stat	Prob*
.|. |	.|. |	1	−0.022	−0.022	0.1171	0.732
.|. |	.|. |	2	−0.034	−0.035	0.4108	0.814
.|* |	.|* |	3	0.084	0.083	2.1762	0.537
.|. |	.|. |	4	0.018	0.021	2.2581	0.688
.|. |	.|. |	5	0.025	0.031	2.4107	0.790
.|. |	.|. |	6	0.007	0.003	2.4232	0.877
.|. |	.|. |	7	0.034	0.033	2.7153	0.910
.|. |	.|. |	8	0.015	0.012	2.7737	0.948
.|. |	.|. |	9	−0.057	−0.056	3.5908	0.936
.|. |	.|. |	10	−0.028	−0.037	3.7903	0.956
.|* |	.|* |	11	0.084	0.076	5.6165	0.898
.|. |	.|. |	12	0.025	0.034	5.7782	0.927
.|. |	.|. |	13	−0.060	−0.049	6.7146	0.916
.|. |	.|. |	14	−0.047	−0.060	7.2915	0.923
.|. |	.|. |	15	−0.042	−0.055	7.7527	0.933
*|. |	*|. |	16	−0.067	−0.066	8.9174	0.917
.|. |	.|. |	17	0.011	0.016	8.9485	0.942
.|. |	.|. |	18	0.012	0.014	8.9844	0.960

Autocorrelation	Partial Correlation		AC	PAC	Q-Stat	Prob*
.|. |	.|. |	19	−0.041	−0.030	9.4252	0.966
.|. |	.|. |	20	−0.039	−0.027	9.8406	0.971
.|. |	.|. |	21	−0.024	−0.015	10.000	0.979
.|. |	.|. |	22	−0.040	−0.046	10.438	0.982
.|. |	.|. |	23	−0.056	−0.065	11.286	0.980
.|* |	.|* |	24	0.148	0.155	17.255	0.838
.|. |	.|. |	25	−0.051	−0.036	17.956	0.844
.|. |	.|* |	26	0.068	0.102	19.242	0.826
*|. |	*|. |	27	−0.076	−0.091	20.830	0.794
.|. |	.|. |	28	−0.030	−0.031	21.072	0.822
.|* |	.|* |	29	0.163	0.127	28.470	0.493
.|. |	.|. |	30	−0.019	−0.006	28.572	0.540
.|. |	.|. |	31	0.051	0.064	29.312	0.553
.|. |	.|. |	32	−0.010	−0.046	29.343	0.602
.|. |	.|. |	33	0.016	0.035	29.417	0.646
.|. |	.|. |	34	0.067	0.065	30.701	0.630
*|. |	*|. |	35	−0.077	−0.113	32.379	0.595
.|. |	.|. |	36	0.009	−0.021	32.402	0.640

*no serial correlation since p-values >0.05%

A.5 The presence of fat tail confirm heteroscedasticity of the GARCH process

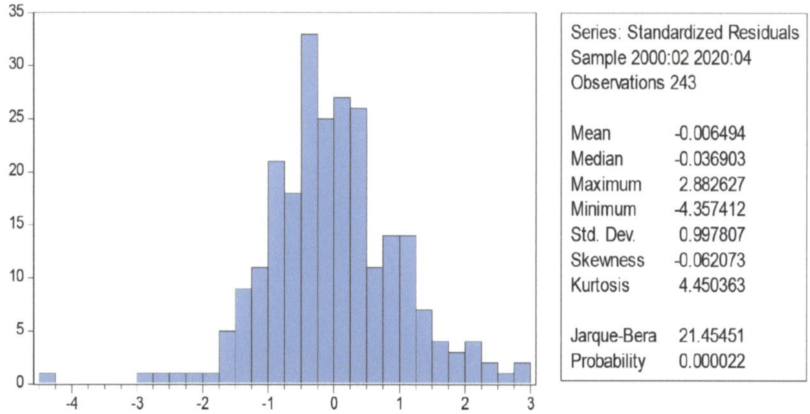

Conflict of interest

The author declares no conflict of interest.

Author details

David Oluseun Olayungbo
Obafemi Awolowo University, Ile-Ife, Nigeria

*Address all correspondence to: doolayungbo@oauife.edu.ng

References

[1] Jones CM, Kaul G. Oil and the stock markets. Journal of Finance. 1996;**51**(2): 463-491

[2] Huang RD, Masulis RW, Stoll HR. Energy shocks and financial markets. Journal of Futures Markets. 1996;**16**:1-27

[3] Sadorsky P. Oil Price shocks and stock market activity. Energy Economics. 1999;**2**:449-469. DOI: 10.1016/S0140-9883(99)00020-1

[4] Basher SA, Sadorsky P. Oil Price risk and emerging stock markets. Global Finance Journal. 2006;**17**:224-251

[5] Olayungbo DO. Asymmetric effects of oil revenue shocks on government spending composition and productive sectors: New evidence from Nigeria. OPEC Energy Review. Wiley; 2019; **43**:1-18

[6] Salisu AA. Modelling oil price volatility before, during and after the global financial crisis. OPEC Energy Review. 2014;**38**:469-495

[7] Najjar AL, D. Modelling and estimation of volatility using ARCH/ GARCH models in Jordan's stock market. Asian Journal of Finance and Accounting. 2016;**8**(1):152-167

[8] Uyaebo SO, Atoi VN, Usman F. Nigeria stock market volatility in comparison with some countries: Application of asymmetric GARCH models. CBN Journal of Applied Statistics. 2015;**6**(2):133-160

[9] Asemota OJ, Ekejiuba UC. An application of asymmetric GARCH models on volatility of banks equity in Nigeria's stock market. CBN Journal of Applied Statistics. 2017;**8**(1):73-99. ISSN: 2476-8472, the Central Bank of Nigeria, Abuja

[10] Hammoudeh S, Aleisa E. Dynamic relationship among GCC stock markets and NYMEX oil futures. Contemporary Economic Policy. 2004;**22**:250-269

[11] Bashar AZ. Wild oil-prices, but brave stock markets. The case of GCC stock markets. Operational Research International Journal, Springer. 2006;**6**: 145-162. DOI: 10.1007/BF02941229

[12] Malik F, Hammoudeh S. Shock and volatility transmission in the oil, US and gulf equity markets. International Review of Economics and Finance. 2007;**16**(3):357-368

[13] MEH A, Jouini J, Nguyen DK. Volatility spillover between oil prices and stock sector returns: Implications for portfolio management. Journal of International Money and Finance. 2011; **31**(7):1387-1405. DOI: 10.1016/j.jimonfin.2011.07.008

[14] Khalfao R, Boutahar M, Boubaker H. Analyzing volatility spillover and hedging between oil and stock markets: Evidence from wavelet analysis. Energy Economics. 2015;**49**: 540-549. DOI: 10.1016/j.eneco.2015.03.023

[15] Bouri E. Oil volatility shocks and the stock markets of oil-importing MENA economies: A tale from financial crisis. Energy Economics. 2015;**51**:590-598. DOI: 10.1016/j.eneco.2015.09.002

[16] Maghyereh AI, Awartani B, Bouri E. The directional volatility connectedness between crude oil and equity market: New evidence from implied volatility indexes. Energy Economics. 2016;**57**: 78-93. DOI: 10.1016/j.eneco.2016.04.010

[17] Khamis R, Anasweh M, Hamdan A. Oil prices and stock market returns in oil-exporting countries: Evidence from Saudi Arabia. International Journal of Energy Economics and Policy. 2018; **8**(3):301-306

[18] Kurtar H, Kapusuzoglu A, Ceylan NB. Oil prices and stock markets: An empirical analysis from Russia, Canada, USA and Japan. Journal of Business Research-TURK. 2019;**11**(1): 558-574. DOI: 10.20491/isarder.2019.619

[19] Central Bank of Nigeria, Statistical Bulletin. 2020. Abuja, Nigeria. Available from: www.cbn.gov.ng [Accessed: 07 May 2020]

[20] United State Energy Information Administration. Available from: www.eia.gov [Accessed: 07 May 2020]

[21] Nigerian Stock Exchange (NSE, 2020). Lagos, Nigeria. Available from: www.nse.com.ng [Accessed: 07 May 2020]

[22] Dickey DA, Fuller WA. Distribution of the estimators for autoregressive time series with a unit root. Journal of the American Statistical Association. 1979; **74**:427-431

[23] Phillips PCB, Perron P. Testing for a unit in time series regression. Biometrica. 1988;**75**:335-346. DOI: 10.1093/biomet/7.52.335

[24] Engle R. Autoregressive conditional heteroscedasticity with estimates of the variance of United Kingdom inflation. Econometrica: Journal of the Econometric Society. 1982;**50**:987-1007

[25] Bollerslev T. Generalized autoregressive conditional heteroscedasticity. Journal of Econometrics. 1986;**31**:307-327

[26] Zakoian JM. Threshold Heteroscedastic models. Journal of Economic Dynamics and Control. 1994; **18**(931):955

[27] Nelson D. Conditional heteroscedasticity in asset returns: A new approach. Econometrica: Journal of the Econometric Society. 1991;**59**: 347-370

[28] Asteriou D, Hall SG. Applied Econometrics, A Modern Approach using Eviews and Microfit. New York, N.Y: Palgrave Macmillan; 2006. p. 10010

Chapter 10

An Econometric Investigation of Market Volatility and Efficiency: A Study of Small Cap's Stock Indices

Muhammad Jawad and Munazza Naz

Abstract

By utilization the context of econometric models, this chapter investigates three significant research parameters and tries to find out the positive outcome for further studies. The first question, is the volatility of Small Cap foreseeable?. The second question, does the volatility of Small Cap exhibition the same pragmatic regularities stated in the literature about the behavior of further stock prices?, The third and Final question, can Small Cap clear the test of market efficiency?. The results of these research questions will provide the answers of following objectives: First, economic representatives investing in Small Cap Stock markets. Second, the business professors/professionals/educationist is more concerned in Small Cap for their teaching and research. Third, the policy makers who are observing the stock market volatilities because of its significances and impulsive behavior to invest for more incentives among other consequences.

Keywords: ARCH type models, market volatility, market efficiency, small Cap's stock

1. Introduction

There are two constants in company change and danger which demonstrate unpredictability of money-related resources. Budgetary resources instability is presently unsurprising because of the historic work of Engle [1] which brought forth ARCH models equipped for foreseeing the until now flighty heteroskedastic residuals from the mean equation [2]. Subsequently, a basic inquiry rises: Is exact investigation of budgetary resource instability important; If things being what they are, which substances will see it as significant?

The investigation of budgetary resources instability is essential to scholastics, policymakers, and money related market members for a few reasons. To begin with, the forecast of money related resources instability is basic to financial specialists since it encourages them make sane portfolio hazard broadening, chance decrease, and the board choices. Instability is fundamentally critical to financial operators since it speaks to a proportion of hazard presentation in their ventures. Second, an unpredictable financial exchange is a temperamental securities exchange. Also, an unsteady securities exchange is a genuine worry of policymakers on the grounds that the shakiness of the financial exchange impacts the U.S. economy contrarily [3]. An ongoing declaration expresses that when markets are seen as exceptionally

IntechOpen

unstable the apparent instability "may go about as a likely hindrance to contributing" ([4], p. 445). Pindyck [5] suggests that the drop in product expense in the United States in the 1970s can be explained by rises in chance rates coupled with increasing market volatility.

Third, the negative effect of securities exchange instability has pulled in the consideration of numerous researchers. For instance, Garner [6] found that the securities exchange crash in 1987 got a decrease customer spending in the U.S. Likewise, Maskus [7] found that outside trade advertises unpredictability impacts exchange. Fourth, from a hypothetical point of view, unpredictability involves a middle stage in the evaluating of subordinate protections. The core strands of the Black Scholes equation indicate, for example, that the value of an America's calling option is an uncertain aspect. Pragmatically then, options markets can be viewed as an exchange of unpredictability between financial operators.

Finally, stock returns estimation may be assumed to be volatility unpredictability, and this is a major US sector where econometric models of volatility unpredictability are varied. In this regard, a few researchers (e.g., [8]) accept that experimental exploration in displaying instability may in reality bring about the decrease of certainty spans in volatility time-fluctuating certainty time frames bring arrangement back. In the event that this result is legitimate, the study of figure precision will improve. All in all, the former audit obviously shows that securities exchange unpredictability is a beneficial subject of useful and scholarly interests.

Thus, more speculations are rising about the significance of monetary resources instability, and this time from industry specialists. Specifically, venture and money industry examiners hypothesize that financial specialists see little capitalization stock records to be less unstable than enormous capitalization stock lists.' For instance, The Invest Mentor (June 16, 1997) talks about this wonder and infers that it is an uncertain fantasy. Among all little capitalization stock lists, Small Cap (SC) 600 is especially well known, as per industry onlookers. This little top stock list is claimed and overseen by the Standard and Poor's Corporation who accepts that SC 600 is a significant individual from the universe of little tops. Since SC 600 is a subset of the whole populace of little top lists, the individuals who put resources into SC 600 are consequently hostages to the equivalent uncertain fantasy expressed previously. Subsequently, we contend that the instability of SC 600 entices for exact investigation.

In the first place, it is conceivable that the nonappearance of exact examination about the conduct of SC 600 may have added to this uncertain legend in financial specialists' observations. Consequently, there is a requirement for observational examination to advise speculators about the basic factual conduct of SC 600. Second, it is essential to inspect whether the factual portrayals of SC 600 as far as its unpredictability are unique in relation to watched regularities of stock costs by and large. We additionally accept that such observational examination will be an essential preface to resulting investigation into the perceptual legend of speculators. As far as we could possibly know, no examination has done this. We presume that this examination void is a hole in the current information on unpredictability elements and expectation. To this end, at any rate three exploration addresses come into view: (1) Are the volatilities of SC 600 unsurprising? (2) Do the volatilities of SC 600 show the equivalent exact regularities in the conduct of other stock costs? (3) Can SC 600 breeze through the severe structure assessment of market productivity?

The current money-based econometric writing divides these statistical regularities into two increasing, based classifications: I asymmetric or power and (ii) fat-tail distribution or leptocurtosis. Whilst we do not speak politely, excellent reports and talks are made available in writing [9–11]. First of all, the allocation of production prices is exceptionally high. Negative returns (advanced news) are tracked by higher market valuation changes than positive returns of a comparable scale (uplifting). This wonder, which is now widely called effect effects, is recorded by the landmark focus by Black [12]. More or less the principle of control attests that the responsibility to profit of the shareholding-influenced business proportion will decline in general as stock costs drops. As a result, the expanded interest-based duty would extend the income unpredictability of asset investors. A similar miracle was recorded by Black [12], Christie [13] and Schwert [14]. Dark reveals, however, that financial leverage alone is not enough to explain the magnitude of the asymmetry he has found experimentally. In that spirit, several scholars have argued that the impact (asymmetry) of dangerous prices may be caused by a critique of unpredictability of supply values, leading of shifts in volatility ([15]; World [16, 17]).

The second accuracy of the experiment established leptocurtosis or fat dispersion of product costs. In other words, the distribution of stock interest is more common than Gauss. Mandelbrot [18] and Fama [19] are the basic investigations about it; all provide fat descriptions of allocations of stock interest. This mystery leaves the US government nervous ([3], p. 54.); it makes it difficult [20] for researchers and econometrists to check it ([9], p. 335). Although leptokurtosis cannot be minimized as stock return procedures are standardized, it remains a challenge for the experts to figure out how to minimize kurtosis to the degree of modern conveyor systems.

At long last, when all is said in done, money related resource returns may show zero autocorrelation despite the fact that their squared qualities regularly demonstrate sequential reliance, consequently recommending the nearness of nonlinear conditions in the slacked estimations of the profits—alleged volatility clustering. Volatility clustering (or fleeting varieties) is a noteworthy factor in the disappointment of the experimental appropriations of the arrival arrangement to follow the Gaussian circulation [21]. Comparably, the experimental conveyance of budgetary resource returns displays non-Gaussian appropriation attributes, for example, leptokurtosis just as negative and positive skewness. Despite the fact that these experimental regularities are accounted for in considers concentrating on enormous stock lists, for example, the S&P 500 [14, 22], the degree the equivalent exact regularities are pervasive in SC 600 list is not known.

The research chapter tries to response on the following hypotheses stated in the null.

Null Hypothesis 1: The volatility of SC 600 is not foreseeable.

Null Hypothesis 2: SC 600 does not define the same empirical symmetries detected in the performance of other stock prices.

Null Hypothesis 3: SC 600 does not pass the severe form test of market efficiency.

2. Data and empirical analysis

We accumulate information on day by day shutting costs of the Small Cap (SC) 600 stock value list from January 1990 to August 2019. (The example size is directed by information accessibility, and information are liberally provided by Standard and Poor's Corporation). We follow different researchers (e.g., [23, 24]) to change the arrival arrangement into their log-contrasts registered as log(P) — log (PJ-l)), t = 1, 2, 3, ..., T, yielding exchanging days.

This technique manages two points of interest. To begin with, it disposes of the conceivable reliance of changes in the stock value record on the value level of the list. Second, the adjustment in the log of the stock value record yields a persistently intensified arrangement.

Series	Results and observations
Sample	1/01/1990 to 8/19/2019
Observations	7422
Mean	0.000397
Median	0.000841
Maximum	0.134563
Minimum	−0.088775
Standard deviation	0.012459
Skewness	0.424301
Kurtosis	13.41909
Jarque-Bera	9057.557
Probability	0.000000

Table 1.
Descriptive statistics.

The mean of the arrangement is incredibly little, near zero (0.0004), and the unqualified standard deviation a proportion of variety is very little (0.01). This finding recommends the nonattendance of non-simultaneous (dainty) exchanging during the example time frame. Precluding non-simultaneous exchanging, the watched little variety might be because of some type of market vanity.

The arrangement is adversely slanted (−0.26) with abundance kurtosis more than double the kurtosis for a Gaussian dispersion. In total, the arrangement is profoundly non-ordinary (asymmetric) as affirmed by the Jarque-Bera2 test for ordinariness. At the end of the day, the invalid of ordinariness is firmly dismissed, as the proof in **Table 1** recommends. At long last, the first experimental outcomes prove various examinations on stock value conduct.

In this way, hypothesis 2 is dismissed. Equally, as our theories are expressed in the invalid, a dismissal of the invalid implies that SC 600 shows indistinguishable watched regularities from other stock costs and stock cost records. At last, despite the fact that this primer experimental proof gives defense for ARCH demonstrating for our informational collection, we in any case give extra support to ARCH displaying following the proposals by Engle and Ng [25].

3. ARCH modeling

Both the observational writing on ARCH demonstrating systems [10] and ongoing surveys of ARCH models [9, 22] offer help showing that ARCH displaying is fitting for the current chapter. For instance, Bera and Higgins [9] announce that "leptokurtosis in the unqualified dissemination is an attribute of contingent heteroskedasticity information." This affirmation by Bera and Higgins focuses to the proof appeared in **Table 1** above. Second, stock record returns are famously known for positive autocorrelation at high frequencies [19, 26, 27] which incorporates every day frequencies for the current chapter. The information for the current chapter fulfills this condition. Third, one of the experimental regularities talked about above stock return circulations is autocorrelation in the crude arrangement and their squares. Autocorrelation in the squares of the crude arrangement is characteristic of instability bunching (fleeting variety) in the heteroskedastic second snapshot of the arrival arrangement. It is regular practice to accept these highlights as proof on the side of the way that an ARCH model will fit the informational collection of intrigue.

To address the former concerns identified with autocorrelation, we test for autocorrelation in the crude returns and their squares. We dismiss the invalid of no autocorrelation in both the crude returns and their squares utilizing Ljung-Box (L-B) Q-insights. We figure Ljung-Box Q-insights for 36 slacks (we report 10 slacks) for both crude returns and their squares to test for straight and nonlinear conditions, separately. We dismissed the invalid of no straight conditions in the profits and no nonlinear conditions in their squares. The outcomes are appeared in **Table 2** beneath. All the slacks are noteworthy, and the squares are obviously bigger. Once more, straight conditions might be because of some type of market defects, as non-simultaneous exchanging is managed due to the unqualified standard deviation examined previously. Moreover, nonlinear conditions are generally ascribed to the nearness of autoregressive restrictive heteroskedasticity (i.e., ARCH) proposing that ARCH kind displaying is essential [28]. At long last, the bunching present in the squared returns proposes that an ARCH kind definition will rough the structure of the heteroskedastic second, and that is actually what ARCH models are intended to achieve [29].

At last, a few researchers recommend that a factual test should initially affirm the nearness of an ARCH impact in the arrangement as opposed to force an ARCH sort model on the information [25, 30]. We will call this methodology ex-risk test for ARCH impact. To this end, we utilize a system proposed by Breusch and Pagan [30] and talked about in Wooldridge [31]. In particular,

$$RS_t = C + RS_{t.t} + U_t \tag{1}$$

where RS denominates the raw returns, C denominates the constant, RQ is a one-day lag of the raw returns and U is the error of the OLS framework. The results are in panel A in **Table 3**.

Next, our purpose is to collect U, and fit the following regression:

$$\hat{u}_t^2 = c + RS_{t\text{-}1} + \hat{e}_t \tag{2}$$

where û denominates the square of the residual from equation and is regressed on a constant and one lag of raw returns. The results are in panel B in **Table 3**. Finally, we fit

$$\hat{u}_t = c\text{-}\hat{u}_t + \hat{e} \tag{3}$$

where û, one period lag of (û}_,) and C are as defined âi equation above. We report the results in panel C in **Table 3**.

Drawing experiences from Wooldridge (2fD3) to define the conclusion of Breusch and Pagan (B-P) tests in **Table 3**, the outcomes are striking in key regards.

	1	2	3	4	5	6	7	8	9	10
Lag1	0.086	−0.047	0.027	0.024	0.011	0.030	0.012	0.036	−0.004	−0.045
	(14.9)	(19.3)	(20.7)	(21.9)	(22.1)	(23.8)	(24J)	(26.7)	(26.8)	(30.8)
Lag2	0.112	0.082	0.098	0.094	0.057	0.075	0.057	0.070	0.011	0.056
	(29.5)	(42.8)	(61.9)	(79.4)	(85.8)	(97J)	(104)	(I13)	(140)	(146)

All values are significant at P = 0.000.

Table 2.
Sample autocorrelation.

Panel A: model (1)			
Variable	**Coefficient**	**T-statistics**	**P-value**
C	0.00029 (0.0002)	29	0.21
RS_{t-1}	0.089 (0.022)	3.9	**0.0001**
Panel B: model (2)			
Variable	**Coefficient**	**T-statistics**	**P-value**
C	0.0001 (1.19E−5)	13.1	0.0000
RS_{t-1}	−0.005 (0.001)	−4.7	0.0000
Panel C: model (3)			
Variable	**Coefficient**	**T-statistics**	**P-value**
C	0.00009 (1.31E−05)	9.9	**0.0000**
$\hat{u}_t$	0.15 (0.0198)	7.0	0.0000
Panel D: model (4)			
Variable	**Coefficient**	**T-statistics**	**P-value**
$\hat{u}_t$	0.0051 (0.019)	0.19	0.79

Table 3.
ARCH analysis.

To start with, the t-measurement (− 4.7) on the slacked return in board B recommends solid proof of heteroskedasticity in the profit's arrangement. Second, the negative coefficient (−0.005) can be deciphered as follows. The instability of SC 600 is higher when the past return is low, and the other way around (cf. [31], p. 415). Accordingly, this finding confirms a piece of the revealed regularities about the unpredictability of stock value returns examined in past areas of the current chapter (cf. [31], p. 415). Third, this finding supports bountiful examinations in the account writing showing that the normal estimation of stock returns is not an element of past return esteems however a component of the change of past returns. Equally, in settling on their speculation choices, normal financial specialists would assess the difference of profits in their venture choices and not the normal (mean) estimation of the profits. The fluctuation of profits is definitely more a basic factor in venture choices than are the normal (mean) returns.

Despite the fact that these results are intriguing in their own right, our principle design is the ex-bet test for an ARCH impact. To this end, we tum to board C in **Table 3**. The t-measurement (t = 6.6) on the one-time frame slack of the mistake shows an ARCH impact (cf. [31], p. 417). At long last, after Wooldridge [31] we utilize the previous system to test the market effectiveness of the SC 600 stock list by relapsing $\hat{u}$, on $\hat{u}_{t-1}$ as expressed in condition (3) above. The outcomes are accounted for in board D in **Table 3**. The effective market theory (EMH) translation of this outcome originates from the finding that the OLS residuals squared are autocorrelated, highlighting heteroskedasticity of the subsequent second. In any case, the OLS residuals (not squared) are not autocorrelated. These outcomes recommend that a speculation technique dependent on notable data in the profit's arrangement is useless. At the end of the day, this is the exacting type of the EMH test [19] as in data seized in past stock costs is pointless in foreseeing current and future costs revenue driven abuses.

At last, a subsequent method to test for an ARCH impact is to fit an ARCH sort model on the information of intrigue and test whether there is any staying ARCH impact in the model assessed. We will consider this methodology the ex-post-test for the nearness of ARCH impact. This is the most widely recognized methodology in the surviving money related econometric writing where the Lagrange multiplier (LM) test measurement has become the workhorse (e.g., [10]). These outcomes are accounted for under the ARCH models introduced underneath.

Despite the fact that we have indicated proof defending ARCH models for the current chapter, we cannot continue without sifting the autocorrelation announced in **Table 2**. Autocorrelation renders fixed arrangement non-fixed, as exhibited by Bera and Higgins [9]. Commonly, a moving normal of request one [i.e., MA (1)] has been discovered sufficient to cleanse autocorrelations of this greatness (cf. [32]). Henceforth, MA (1) is fit the raw returns in the system of the model (4). That is,

$$R_t = S_t + \delta X_{t\text{-}1} \tag{4}$$

Next, let é be a gauge of the deviations of the raw returns back from a MA (1) of anticipated (mean) return. This amount is a contribution to the ARCH models talked about beneath.

Since ARCH models are a group of models, we test and locate that a summed-up ARCH (i.e., GARCH) is the best miserly model portraying the information producing procedure of SC 600 for the accompanying reasons. Initial, a GARCH model is an unbounded request ARCH model [33]. Second, a GARCH model is an ARMA model [29] having a place with model (4) above. At last, our examination 3 recommended ARMA (0,1)- GARCH (1,1) model as a lower request of the higher-request type appeared in conditions (5) to (7) underneath, (cf. [33]). That is:

$$r_t = \mu + \sum_{i=1}^{p} a_i r_{t\text{-}1} + \sum_{i=1}^{q} b_i \varepsilon_{t\text{-}1} + \varepsilon_t \tag{5}$$

$$\varepsilon_t = z^{th}{}_t \approx N(0,1) \tag{6}$$

$$h_t^2 = \omega + \sum_{i=1}^{p} \alpha_i \varepsilon_{t-1}^2 + \sum_{i=1}^{q} \beta_i h_{t-1}^2 \tag{7}$$

It regularly is expected that the mean procedure in condition (5) is direct and the unsettling influences are developments following the Gaussian circulation. Elective plans of the contingent fluctuation work.

There is Eq. (5). Sub-set constraints on the general structure's parameters define special cases and allow for limited heterogeneity and stationarity in such alternate formulations (see [33]). In model (7), q is the number of lagging conditions and p is the number of lagging sample variances (the squared random return component) [1, 33]. The characteristic of the symmetrical GARCH model is that it involves and parsimoniously integrates heteroscedasticity in the volatility calculation. Nevertheless, the model is well established because the infinite self-reign organized coefficients are all non-negative, and the roots lie behind the moving average polynomial of quadrangular inventions. The restricting of the value parameter, 'p = z′o + z'b < 1, should: (1) calculate the magnitude of continuous shock fluctuations, (2) ensure the consistency and stationary covariance of the error mechanism, and (3) ensure that finite unconditional variations are essential. Halfway-life4 is 1/2 L = [-In(2)/In(T)] persistence of the shake. Eventually, in Eq. (8), we approximate a lower GARCH model number as defined in **Table 4**.

The mean of the index return is the linear function of the time-divergent variance (h) under the ARMA (0,1)-GARCH (1.1) model. If the errors (e,) are serially associated and obey a method of MA (1), the variances (ht or volatility) are cantered in the time-t-1 data set f2. In fact, f1 makes past (volatility) conditional

Equation of mean				Equation of variance					
x	t	θ	t.	a_o	t	α	t	β	t
0.0009	4.9	0.19	5.9	1.7E−6	3.1	0.19	7.1	0.862	40
[0.000]		[0.026]		[6.9E−07]		[0.025]		[0.021]	
(0.000)		(0.023)		(3.24E−07)		(0.012)		(0.011)	

Table 4.
ARCH (0,1) and GARCH (1,1).

variances and squared error terms crucial. Thanks to the positive result in **Table 4** and the restriction •F = Z, + T, {ii < 1 is fulfilled, the model has a stationarity of second order [33]. The role of both x and d supports the predicted ARCH and GARCH impact.

The following statement is that "i" = Z;'; + Z, $, < l = 0.996, suggests strong durability uncertainty. The mean-revision is also found to almost fulfill the requirement of unity. Such findings contribute to the methodological regularities that confuse financial cyans ([9], p. 342).

It is evidence that Hypothesis 2 is not appropriate. Finally, the half lifespan is 1/2 L = [-In(2)/In('P)] = 69 days, while the uncertainty is only half large. We are turning now to the alerts mentioned so far on the basic GARCH model.

The source of GARCH norm caveats is the calculation, for the first time, of the variation in finance as predicted square deviations from a standard position. A linear combination of a constant, past conditional variance, lagged, squared errors — and that is a symmetrical GARCH model — is thus a statistical logical way of approaching the direction of time variance to present conditional variance [33]. [33] The quadrature of past mistakes to prevent negative differences imposes a symmetrical structure which implies a significant effect on the variability of current shocks from the past. Among others, the leverage effect cannot be captured by a symmetric GARCH model. Furthermore, in the sense that the squaring is a symmetrical layout from GARCH is essentially a quadratic specification. The symmetric GARCH model is thus not effective if the shock effect on current returns approaches a quadratic magnitude. In addition, the degree to which the retour-generating process of a given data set displays such alerts represents the limitations and assumptions based on GARCH's symmetrical models. In other words, asymmetric models from GARCH are required.

Engle and Ng [34] show, according to this criterion, that the TGARCH model Glosten, Jagannathan and Runkle [35] is the best parsimonious GARCH model that is available. We thus show the Glosten, Jagannathan and Runkle concept for the first time. We shall then use it for the purposes of this article.

The appeal of asymmetric GARCH models is based on the capture volatility asymmetries. It is possible to describe the pattern Glosten, Jagannathan and Runkle as follows. Consider expanding the above model (10) with the inclusion of a D indicator component, so that the first error lag is negative with a Dt-l < 0 and null, if the mean function is not positive.

This yields the regime switching model with zero as the threshold in

$$h_t^2 = \omega + \sum_{i=1}^{p} \alpha_i \varepsilon_{t-1}^2 + \sum_{i=1}^{q} \beta_i h_{t-j}^2 + \gamma \varepsilon_t^2 d_{t-1} \quad (8)$$

TGARCH has curious properties: it makes the effect on subsequent variance of positive (negative) shocks (c2) when y > 0 (< 0). Note that IX alone catches good news (increasing interest for the asset) during bad news during bad news.

	Coefficient	Std. error		T-ratio
Panel A: mean equation				
X	0.0006	[0.0002]	(0.0006)	2.9
Θ	0.174	0.0275	(0.0220)	6.3
Panel B: variance equation				
ω	2.11E−6	[7.21E−7]	(2.81E−7)	3.1
α	0.057	[0.030]	(0.0130)	1.93
y	0.189	[0.044]	(0.0208)	4.3
β	0.845	[0.010]	(0.0104)	80.88

Table 5.
TGARCH test.

(Activity price decrease) shall be captured at n + y. If >0 happens, the leverage effect would be measured by the sum n + y for poor messages (reduced asset price). If y 0, the results of the news are asymmetric. If the (e} series implements an ARMA cycle, the vector (e^2,e^2) of shock may use an ARMA cycle as GARCH model. **Table 5** offers comprehensive findings.

There are remarkable findings in **Table 5** from the Glosten, Jagannathan and Runkle TGARCH. Next, the ARCH word (ti) is significant but not so unified that volatility shocks are not destructive. Furthermore, the nonlinear dummy coefficient is strong and positive. It means that: (a) the leverage effect persists and (b) the influence of news is asymmetrical, or similarly optimistic inno- vs. the negative effect of the news on uncertainty. Finally, with a powerful effect, the term GARCH (b) is significant. Critical to resolve a breach of the assumption of normality, again, two types of standard errors have been reported: (a) frequent and inefficient standard errors, which are not compliant with Gaussian distribution assumes, and (b) stable standard and covariance error by Bollerslev-Wooldridge, which is consistent and efficient when the assumption of normality is broken. You may inquire whether these versions are listed correctly. We apply a diagnostic device battery to determine product requirements.

4. A battery of diagnostic tests for model specifications

The residuals must be white noise unless the configuration is correctly defined (i.e. the stanch ionic remains must be zero mean and have unit variance). Remember in the above **Table l** that, on the raw series rates and squares, we dismissed the zero hypothesis with no self-correction. This autocorrelation will only exist if and only if the templates are properly defined in the typical waste materials and their square regions. We directly use Ljung-Box Q statistics to reach the adequacy of the model by analyzing the standardized (normalized) residuals (e,/h|′ 2) and standardized square residuals (s,/h ‘2). Directly let E and h be estimates of the error and conditional variance.

Kurtosis coefficients are around fifty per cent larger for the two models listed in **Table 6** than for the Gaussian distribution, although the figures showed that the model is acceptable. Second, the model misspecification concerns arise in the framework of above **Table 6** if the coefficient sample autocorrelation and partial autocorrelation (PACs), calculated as 2/(T), is more than double the value of their asymptotic standard error (ASEs) “2 = 0.044, **Table 6** does not have an AC or PAC

	Standard GARCH				TGARCH			
		AC	PAC	Q		AC	PAC	Q
(s,/h,′ 2)	L-B (10)	−0.011	−0.011	3.5	L-B (10)	−0.009	−0.010	3.9 s
(s,/h,″)′	L-B (10)	−0.028	−0.028	4.3	L-B (10)	−0.029	−0.030	5.0
Skewness	−0.369					−0.280		
Kurtosis	5.804	13.96••	6.048	14.00**				

*"••" and "**" shows the significance at p = 0.000*

Table 6.
Standard GARCH and TGARCH models.

value close to that value. This proposal is fulfilled, as shown in **Table 6**, because the kurtosis is more than twice that for the non-standardized residual. Fourth, in a proprietary unpublished paper reported by Keam and Pagan, we are using the Pagan and Sabau [36] specification test. In particular, Kearn and Pagan are proposing to square residue out of the mean equation and regress to perform their tests with a constant and conditional variation (h2) in the following ways: (24) Alles and Murray ([37], p. 140) included this test in "a diagnostic test":

$$s—c + bh + e \tag{9}$$

In fact, model (9) investigates how many variances can be clarified by situation variances in the unknown actual volatility (proxied by e). As the regressed as well as the regressor are at least theoretically the same in the ARCH model's framework, the equation slope (9) should ideally be equal to unity, with zero intercept. Then you can determine the fit of the model using R2. **Table 7** reports the results.

The findings of the Keam-Pagan (K-P) check in **Table 7** prove that the evidence supports the theoretical assumptions. First, the intercepts (called C) vary little to zero. Secondly, there are extremely positive and high slope coefficients. Third, with standard errors insignificantly different from zero, both coefficients are statistically significant in less than five percent. Fourthly, it is important to remember that the TGARCH is greater in R^2 than the regular GARCH, and the model's explanatory forces are R2-based. It should not come as a surprise that TGARCH should be able to collect asymmetries from the data better than the standard GARCH does. This is an indirect proof of the overall asymptotic superior success of Glosten et al. in the recording results gap for both models (1993) as Engle and Ng [34] models of capture of asymmetries in volatility. In the same way, the results discrepancies give subtle proof that the traditional GARCH model struggles to chart the data's asymmetries.

Finally, Diebold [38] suggests, among other things, that, if the GARCH model is defined correctly, no ARCH effects in mean and variance equations respectively in the uniform residual rates and squares will remain. This test is a Lagrange multiplier test asymptotically equivalent to T * R2, where T is the sample number, and R2 the known determination coefficient. This test is also a K-degree free chi-square test.

	Standard GARCH		t-ratio	TGARCH		t-ratio
C	7.1E−5	(1.6E−5)	4.4	3.1E−05	(1.3E−5)	1.79
b-coefficient	0.519	(0.049)	9.9	0.699	(0.08)	12.8
R^2	0.513			0.842		

Table 7.
Keam-Pagan (K-P) test.

For the standard GARCH model the results are (computed as T• R2) 0.109 (p = 0.74) and (T• R2) 0.043 (p = 0.834) for the TGARCH model. These trivial p- values thus suggest a dismissal of the null hypothesis that the results maintain ARCH impact. In summary, our diagnostic test battery overall indicates that models are stated correctly.

5. Conclusions

This chapter addresses the value of high stock market fluctuations and three predictions: economists, investors, and policy makers. The fact that uncertainty is an important phenomenon to these institutions is illustrated by quotes from current literature in financial economy. While much analytical attention has been paid to the volatility of large cap inventory indices, there is been little concern for the volatility of the small cap indices. At least three methodological problems to be explored using small caps (SC) 600 for analysis purposes are described in this article.

The primary focus of the chapter is on these testable theories. Hypothesis 1 is a validation of the statement that SC 600 variance cannot be expected. This theory has been refuted on the basis of evidence that low cap volatility of 600 can be forecasted in the same way as other stock prices are expected by regular GARCH and TGARCH models. Hypothesis 2 is a hypothesis to the extent that SC 600 is not similarly empirically compatible with other stock values. The findings demonstrate, in terms of observable methodological regularities that govern the empiric distribution of stock prices in general, that the SC 600 exhibits the same statistical characteristics.

In conclusion, hypothesis 3 tests the argument that SC 600 cannot pass a rigorous market efficiency test for the form. This hypothesis is dismissed, which indicates that SC 600 has passed the Effective Hypothesis Test (EMH). Our findings may be seen as the start of further research on the behavior, particularly with respect to the EMH measure, of other small equity indices. Our findings especially encourage further research into a closer empirical study of the unresolved myth in investor perceptions.

Author details

Muhammad Jawad[1*] and Munazza Naz[2]

1 PhD, Post Doctorate, Assistant Professor, Department of Commerce, Fatima Jinnah Women University, Pakistan

2 PhD, Post Doctorate, Assistant Professor, Department of Mathematical Sciences, Fatima Jinnah Women University, Pakistan

*Address all correspondence to: muhammad_jawad85@yahoo.com

References

[1] Engle, R. (1982). Autoregressive Conditional Heteroscedasticity with Estimates of the Variance of U.K. Inflation. Econometrica, 50, 987-1008.

[2] Engle, R., and V. Ng, "An Introduction to the Use of ARCH/ GARCH models in Applied Econometrics." University of California, San Diego (1991).

[3] Greenspan, Alan (1997). Maintaining Financial Stability in a Global Economy. *Symposium Proceedings*, The Federal Reserve Bank of Kansas City.

[4] Poshakwale, S., and V. Murinde (2001). Modeling the Volatility in East European Emerging Markets: Evidence on Hungary and Poland. Applied Financial Economics, 11, 445-456.

[5] Pindyck, R. (1984). Risk, Inflation, and the Stock Market. *American Economic Review*, 76, 335-351.

[6] Garner, C.A. (1990). Has the Stock Market Crash Reduced Consumer Spending?. *Financial Market Volatility and the Economy*, Federal Reserve Bank of Kansas City.

[7] Maskus, K.E. (1990). Exchange Rate Risk and U.S. Trade: A Sectoral Analysis. *Financial Market Volatility and the Economy*, Federal Reserve Bank of Kansas City.

[8] Yu, Jun (2002). Forecasting Volatility in the New Zealand Stock Market. Applied Financial Economics, 12, 193-202.

[9] Bera, A., and M. Higgins (1993). ARCH Models: Properties, Estimation and Testing. Journal of Economic Surveys, 7(4), 305-362.

[10] Bollerslev, T., R. Engle, and D. Nelson (1994). ARCH Models," in R. Engle and D. McFadden (eds.), Handbook of Econometrics, Vol. 4 (North Holland, Amsterdam, 1994).

[11] Pagan, A. (1996). The Econometrics of Financial Markets. Journal of Empirical Finance, 3, 15-102.

[12] Black, F. (1976). Studies in stock volatility changes, in Proceedings of the 197d Meetings of the Business and Economics Statistics Section, I 77-181.

[13] Christie, A. (1982). The Stochastic Behavior of Common Stock Variances: Value, Leverage and Interest Rate Effects. Journal of Financial Economics, 10, 407-432.

[14] Schwert, G.W. (1989). Why Does Stock Market Volatility Change over Time?. Journal of Finance, 54, 1115-1151

[15] Campbell, J.Y., and L. Hentschel (1992). No News is Good News: an Asymmetric Model of Changing Volatility in Stock Returns. Journal of Financial Economics, 31, 281-318.

[16] French, K., G. Schwert, and R. Stambaugh (1987). Expected Stock Returns and Volatility. Journal of Financial Economics, 19, 3-29.

[17] Wu, G. (2001). The Determinants of Asymmetric Volatility. Review of Financial Studies, 14, 837-859.

[18] Mandelbrot, B. (1963). The Variation of Certain Speculative Prices. Journal of Business, 36, 394-419

[19] Fama, E. (1965). The Behavior of Stock Market Prices. Journal of Business, 38, 34-105.

[20] McAleer, Michael, and Les Oxley (2002). The Econometrics of Financial Series. Journal of Economic Surveys, 16 (3), 237-243.

[21] Fomari, F. and A. Mele (1996). Modeling the Changing Asymmetry of

Conditional Variances. Economics Letters, 50, 197-203.

[22] Bollerslev, T., R.F. Engle, and J.M. Wooldridge (1998). A Capital Asset Pricing Model with Time Varying Variance. Journal of Political Economy, 96, l16-131.

[23] Engle, R.F., and J. Patton (2001). What Good is a Volatility Model?. NYU Stern School of Business.

[24] R.F. Engle, "New Frontiers for ARCH Models," J. of Applied Econometrics, Vol. 17, pp 425-46, 2002

[25] Engle, R., and V. Ng (1991). Measuring and Testing the Impact of News on Volatility. University of California, San Diego.

[26] Cutler, D.M., J.M. Poterb, and L.H. Summer (1991). Speculative Dynamics. Review of Economic Studies, 58, 529-546.

[27] Lo, A.W., and A.C. MacKinlay (1988). Stock Market Prices do not Follow Random Walk: Evidence from a Simple Specification Test. levies' of Financial Studies, 1, 41-66.

[28] Nelson, D.B. (1991). Conditional Heteroscedasticity in Asset Returns: A New Approach. Econometrica, 59, 347-370.

[29] Engle, R. (2002). Introduction: in ARCH Selected Reading. Advanced Texts in Econometrics (Oxford University Press).

[30] Breusch, T.S., and A.R. Pagan (1979). A Simple Test for Heteroskedasticity and Random Coefficient Variations. Econometrica, 50, 987-1007.

[31] Wooldridge, Jeffery M. (2003). Introductory Econometrics. A Modern Approach (Mason, Ohio: South-Western Publishing).

[32] Alles, Lakshman, and Louis Murray (2001). An Examination of Returns and Volatility Patterns on the Irish Equity Market. Applied Financial Economics, 11(2),137-146.

[33] Bollerslev, T. (1986). Generalized Autoregressive Conditional Heteroscedasticity. Journal of Econometrics, 31, 307-327.

[34] Engle, R., and V. Ng (1993). Measuring and Testing the Impact of News on Volatility. Journal of Finance, 48, 1749-1778.

[35] Glosten, L., R. Jagannathan, and D. Runkle (1993). Relationship between the Expected Value and Volatility of the Nominal Excess Returns on Stocks. Journal of Finance, 48, 1779-1802.

[36] Pagan and Sabau (1987)

[37] Alles, Lakshman, and Louis Murray, "An Examination of Returns and Volatility Patterns on the Irish Equity Market," Applied Financial Economics, 1 1, no. 2 (2001)

[38] Diebold, F. (1986). Temporal Aggregation of ARCH Processes and the Distribution of Asset Returns. Special Studies Paper 200, Fedeml Reserve Board, Division of Research and Statistics, Washington, D.C.

Chapter 11

More Credits, Less Cash: A Panel Cointegration Approach

Sureyya Dal

Abstract

In this study, the long-run relation among credit expansion and liquidity risk was analyzed by using data of 20 banks in Turkish banking sector for the period 2014.Q1–2017.Q4. In the analysis, dynamic panel cointegration methodology which depends on cross-sectional dependence and homogeneity was adopted in order to determine whether there is a long-run relation between variables. As a result of the cointegration analysis, a long-run relation was found between liquidity risk and credit expansion. Also, the result indicates that credit expansion positively affects liquidity risk. This result suggests that the banks may constrain their credit growth in the long term in order to decrease liquidity risk.

Keywords: panel data models, financial econometrics, banks, financial risk, risk management, cointegration analysis

1. Introduction

Liquidity risk, which is an important measure of the bank's success in the long run, is the ability to pay liabilities and swap debts when needed. Banks should keep optimal liquid assets to meet their loan activities, investments, and depositors' demands on time and adequately. In this respect, banks try to balance this situation. As a result, the bank is exposed to liquidity risk. Thanks to the liquidity risk management, it is ensured that banks continue their effectiveness against new risks that may arise due to changes in the operating environment or increases in the current risk level [1]. On the other hand, credit is the debt given to real persons and corporations within the framework of contracts. It is one of the important financial instruments that cause economic growth by gaining investors' savings to the economy and increasing private consumption expenditures [2].

Total amount of credits given by the Turkish banking sector have been increasing rapidly in the last decade. This situation was shown in **Figure 1**. However, there is a risk that the bank loan client is not able to meet the obligations of the agreement. In this case, it is expected that there will be a decrease in the income and capital of banks and an increase in expenses and losses [3].

Banks should have liquid funds in their hands in order to meet their credit activities on time and adequately. If they do not hold this fund, the liquidity risk will increase. Increasing liquidity risk will increase financial vulnerability and economic instability. Therefore, in this study, the long-term relationship between credit expansion and liquidity risk is investigated with a panel cointegration

IntechOpen

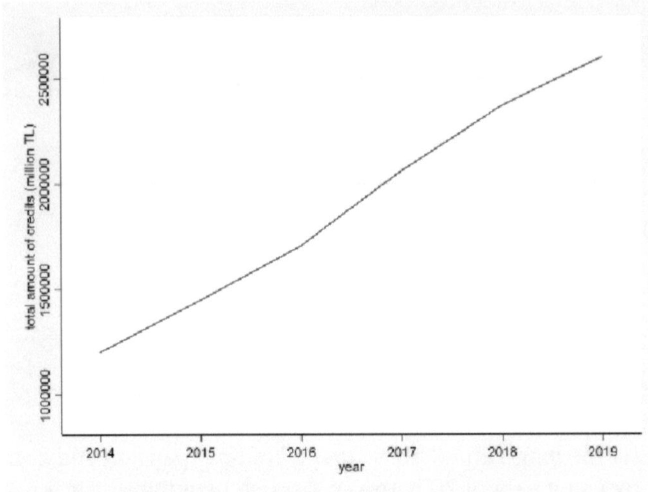

Figure 1.
Total amount of credits in the Turkish banking sector (million TL).

analysis. The rest of this study is organized as follows. In the second section, literature on credit expansion is given. The third section introduces the data set and variables used in this study. The fourth section examines the results of the econometric method used, and the last section concludes.

2. Literature on credit expansion

Credits can have positive and negative effects on the economy. For this purpose, studies conducted on credit expansion in Turkey were examined. Orhangazi explored the relation between capital inflows and credit expansion by using logit model. According to the findings, net private capital flows effect positively credit expansion by controlling other determinants [4]. Kara et al. made a cross-country comparison of credit growth by calculating a ratio of net credit use with respect to national income. They suggested a stable ratio of net credit relative to GDP that decreases slowly credit growth in the long-term period [5]. Kılıç examined relation between consumer credits and current account deficit. Time series methodology was adopted in order to find long-run dynamics. The study's results indicate one way Granger causality between consumer credits and current account deficit [6]. Karahan and Uslu analyzed relationship between credits extended by deposit banks to the private sector and current accounts deficit by using ARDL approach within time series framework. They found long-term relationship between variables [7]. Güneş and Yıldırım analyzed long-run relationship between credit expansion and current account deficit by using Johansen cointegration test. The results indicate existence of cointegration relation between vehicle and corporate loans and current account deficit [8]. Kılıç and Torun studied causality relation between consumer credits and inflation by using Granger causality test. The findings of the study gave evidence on two-way Granger causality relation between individual credit cards and inflation [9]. Köroğlu analyzed relation between credit expansion and current account deficit by using Granger causality test. He found one-way causality relation that credit expansion causes current account deficit [10]. Varlık investigated the effect of net and gross capital inflows and their components on credit boom by using logit model. The findings addressed that net and gross foreign direct investment inflows are negatively correlated with credit boom [11].

There is an extensive literature in Turkey examining the impact of credit expansion on macroeconomic factors. However, there is no study investigating the effect of credit expansion on liquidity risk by directly considering banks. The aim of this study is to fill this gap in the literature by using the panel data approach.

3. Data

This study examines long-run relation among liquidity risk and credit expansion. For this purpose, quarterly panel data was used in order to conduct analysis. Selected variables of 20 Turkish banks from 2014.Q1 to 2017.Q4 were obtained from the database of The Banks Association of Turkey in order to calculate liquidity risk and credit expansion from banks' balance sheet. The banks used in the study can be analyzed in three different groups. These are state-owned deposit banks, private-owned deposit banks, and foreign banks. Halkbank, Ziraat Bank, and Vakıf Bank were taken as state-owned deposit banks. Akbank, Fibabank, Şekerbank, Turkish Bank, Turkish Economy Bank, İş Bank, and Yapı Kredi Bank were used as private-owned deposit banks. Alternatif Bank, Arab Turkish Bank, Burgan Bank, Denizbank, ICBC Turkey Bank, ING Bank, QNB Finansbank, and Garanti BBVA Bank were taken as foreign banks. These banks constitute the units of the panel data set.

In this study, the ratio of the difference of loans and receivables from deposits to total assets was used as a measure of liquidity risk (LR) [12].

$$LR = \frac{Loans\ and\ Receivables - Deposits}{Total\ Assets} \tag{1}$$

The increase in credits, which causes an increase in production, income, exports, and profits of the financial sector, is expressed as credit expansion. Credit expansion (CE) which is the other variable of interest was created using equation below [13].

$$CE = \frac{Loans\ and\ Receivables}{Total\ Assets} \tag{2}$$

4. Methodology

The main purpose of this study is to explore long-run relationship among liquidity risk and credit expansion in the Turkish banking sector. This study adopts dynamic panel econometric methodology. It consists of four steps. First, the cross-sectional dependence of the units (banks) is investigated with the Pesaran CDLM test developed by Pesaran [14]. Second, Delta tests are applied to analyze whether the parameters change according to the units. Third, CIPS panel unit root test developed by Pesaran [15] is used to determine order of the integration of the variables. Finally, panel cointegration test developed by Westerlund [16] is conducted in order to explore the existence of the long-run relationship among the variables. In this section, theoretical background of methodology is explained.

4.1 Investigation of cross-sectional dependence

One of the important concepts that affects the choice of method to be used in dynamic panel data analysis is inter-units correlation. The inter-units correlation, in other words, cross-sectional dependence is the simultaneous correlation of series that may occur due to excluded, observed common factors, spatial spillover effects, and all common effects observed or not observed [17].

Model for panel data analysis can be written as in Eq. (3) [18]:

$$LR_{it} = \mu_i + \beta_i CE_{it} + \varepsilon_{it} \tag{3}$$

where $i = 1 \dots N$ denotes cross section dimension, which is banks here, $t = 1 \dots T$, is time series dimension which is the quarterly period. LR_{it} shows the liquidity risk, CE_{it} is a variable of credit expansion. μ_i represents the intercept of the model. The slope coefficients are β_i which vary across the cross section units. ε_{it} is the error term which may be cross-sectionally dependent.

The null hypothesis $(E(\varepsilon_{it}\varepsilon_{jt}) = 0\, for\ all\ \mathrm{i} \neq j)$ used to investigate whether there is a correlation between units in the error term of this model.

Rejecting the null hypothesis shows existence of the cross-sectional dependence. Pesaran [14] proposed a simple cross-sectional dependence test that can be applied to heterogeneous panel series with both stationary and unit roots [14]. The test statistic, *CD*, is the average of the pairwise correlation coefficients of the ordinary least squares residuals obtained from the individual regression coefficients. The test statistic is calculated as Eq. (4) [19]:

$$CD = \sqrt{\frac{2T}{N(N-1)}} \left(\sum_{i=1}^{N-1} \sum_{j=i+1}^{N} \hat{\rho}_{ij} \right) \tag{4}$$

where $\hat{\rho}_{ij}$ represents pairwise correlation coefficient and can be formulated by $\hat{\rho}_{ij} = \hat{\rho}_{ji} = \sum_{t=1}^{T} \hat{\varepsilon}_{it}\hat{\varepsilon}_{jt} / \left(\sum_{t=1}^{T} \hat{\varepsilon}_{it}^2\right)^{1/2} \left(\sum_{t=1}^{T} \hat{\varepsilon}_{jt}^2\right)^{1/2}$. $\hat{\varepsilon}_{it}$ shows the ordinary least square (OLS) estimate of ε_{it} which is based on T number of observation in each unit. Pesaran CD test works well even when there are few years and many units $(N > T)$ [20].

4.2 Investigation of homogeneity

Homogeneity means that constant and slope parameters do not change according to the units. Delta test which is an extension of Swamy S test is used to test homogeneity of parameters in this study. The purpose of the Swamy S test is to explore whether there is a difference between OLS estimator and weighted average matrices of within estimator. OLS estimator does not take into account panel structure of units. Conversely, within estimator considers panel-specific estimates with weighted average of parameters.

The null hypothesis of Swamy S test is H_0: $\beta_i = \beta \quad i = 1 \dots N$ which represents homogeneity of parameters estimated by two different estimation methods, OLS and within estimator [21].

Test statistic of Swamy [21] can be written as Eq. (5):

$$\hat{S} = \chi^2_{k(N-1)} = \sum_{i=1}^{N} \left(\hat{\beta}_i^{OLS} - \beta^{WWE}\right) V_i^{-1} \left(\hat{\beta}_i^{OLS} - \beta^{WWE}\right) \tag{5}$$

$$\beta^{WWE} = \left(\sum_{i=1}^{N} \hat{V}_i^{-1}\right)^{-1} \sum_{i=1}^{N} \hat{V}_i^{-1} \hat{\beta}_i^{OLS} \tag{6}$$

$\hat{\beta}_i^{OLS}$ indicates estimation of coefficients from ordinary least squares. β^{WWE} is the estimation of weighted (by $\hat{V}_i^{-1}$) average of parameters from within estimator. $\hat{V}_i$ is the weight which is difference between variances of OLS and within estimator. The test statistic is χ^2 distributed with $kx(N-1)$ degrees of freedom.

Pesaran and Yamagata [22] developed Swamy test by two different test statistics [22]. These two statistics differ according to the size of sample. They are delta ($\tilde{\Delta}$) for large samples and delta adjusted ($\tilde{\Delta}_{adj}$) for small samples. These tests explore whether slope coefficients are homogenous or not. Delta for large samples and delta adjusted for small samples are calculated as follows [23]:

$$\text{Large samples}: \tilde{\Delta} = \sqrt{N}\left(\frac{N^{-1}\hat{S}-k}{2k}\right) \sim \chi_k^2 \tag{7}$$

$$\text{Small samples}: \tilde{\Delta}_{adj} = \sqrt{N}\left(\frac{N^{-1}\hat{S}-k}{SE(T,k)}\right) \sim N(0,1) \tag{8}$$

in which $\hat{S}$ is Swamy test statistic, k is number of regressors, and SE denotes standard errors.

4.3 Investigation of unit roots

The first factor to be considered in panel unit root tests is whether the units forming the panel are correlated to each other. According to the existence of correlation between units, panel unit root tests are divided into two as first- and second-generation tests. Levin et al., Harris and Tzavalis, Breitung and Hadri are first-generation unit root tests that do not take into account cross-sectional dependence [24–27]. In these tests, all units are assumed to have a common autoregressive parameter. However, an autoregressive parameter changing according to the units is a more realistic approach. The second-generation unit root tests have been developed for this purpose. They deal with cross-sectional dependence in three different ways. First, first-generation unit root tests were transformed by reducing the correlation between the units by taking the difference from the cross-sectional averages, but unable to eliminate some types of correlation. As a result, these versions of tests are not used much in the literature [28]. Second, there are panel unit root tests such as the multivariate augmented Dickey-Fuller (MADF) panel unit root test and seemingly unrelated augmented Dickey-Fuller (SURADF) panel unit root test based on system estimation [29–32]. Third, there are panel unit root tests that eliminate cross-sectional dependence by modeling it via common factor [15, 33–40].

In this study, since the cross-sectional dependence was determined among the banks forming the panel, the stationarity of the series was tested by using the second-generation panel unit root tests. Cross-sectionally augmented Im, Pesaran, and Shin (CIPS) unit root test developed by Pesaran [15] was used to in order to determine stationarity of the series. CIPS unit root test is an extension of Im, Pesaran, and Shin (2003) unit root test. This method adds cross-sectional averages of the lagged series and first differences of series as factors to DF or ADF regression to eliminate correlation between units [15]. Dynamic heterogenous panel data model without autocorrelation is as Eq. (9).

$$LR_{it} = (1-\phi_i)\mu_i + \phi_i LR_{it-1} + \varepsilon_{it} \qquad i = 1\dots N, t = 1\dots T \tag{9}$$

ε_{it} with a single factor structure is shown in Eq. (10).

$$\varepsilon_{it} = \varphi_i f_t + \epsilon_{it} \tag{10}$$

where f_t is unobserved common factors, ϵ_{it} is individual specific error term. If we rearrange Eq. (9)., it is displayed in Eq. (11).

$$\Delta LR_{it} = \alpha_i + \beta_i LR_{it-1} + \varphi_i f_t + \epsilon_{it} \tag{11}$$

in which $\alpha_i = (1 - \phi_i)\mu_i$; $\beta_i = -(1 - \phi_i)$ and $\Delta LR_{it} = LR_{it} - LR_{it-1}$. Pesaran [15] used the cross-sectional average of LR_{it} $(\overline{LR}_t)$ and average of lagged values $(\overline{LR}_{t-1}, \overline{LR}_{t-2}, \ldots)$ as instrumental variable for common factor (f_t). Cross-sectionally augmented ADF (CADF) regression with intercept is defined as follow same as Equation 54 in Pesaran [15].

$$\Delta LR_{it} = \alpha_i + \beta_i LR_{it-1} + \omega_i \overline{LR}_{t-1} + \sum_{j=0}^{p} \psi_{ij} \Delta \overline{LR}_{t-j} + \sum_{j=1}^{p} n_{ij} \Delta LR_{it-j} + \epsilon_{it} \tag{12}$$

The unit root hypothesis of interest is: $H_0 : \beta_i = 0 \, for \; all \; i$; whereas alternatives are: $H_1 : \beta_i < 0 \; i = 1, 2 \ldots N_1, \beta_i = 0, i = N_1 + 1, N_1 + 2 \ldots N$. In order to test this hypothesis of interest, CIPS statistic is calculated as average of CADF.

$$CIPS = \frac{1}{N} \sum_{i=1}^{N} CADF_i = \frac{1}{N} \sum_{i=1}^{N} t_i \tag{13}$$

where t_i denotes the OLS t-ratio of β_i in the Eq. (12). Critical values were given by Pesaran [15].

4.4 Investigation of long-run relationship

Cointegration is the long-run equilibrium relationship between the variables despite permanent shocks affecting the system. Panel cointegration tests were developed to investigate long-run relationship in the panel data. They can be divided into two according to the existence of cross-sectional dependence. First-generation panel cointegration tests (Kao (1999); Pedroni (1999, 2004); McCoskey and Kao (1998); [16]) do not take into account correlation between units, while second-generation tests [16] with bootstrapping critical values (Gengenbach, Urbain and Westerlund (2016)) do. In this study, Westerlund [16] cointegration test was used to investigate long-run relationship between variables.

Westerlund [16] is an error-correction based panel cointegration test. In the test, the presence of long-run relationship is explored by deciding whether each unit has its own error correction [16]. So rejecting hypothesis of interest shows that there is not error correction and it means absence of the long-run relationship between variables. Error correction model is shown in Eq. (14) [41]:

$$\Delta LR_{it} = \delta_i' d_t + \alpha_i \left(LR_{it-1} - \beta_i' CE_{it-1} \right) + \sum_{j=1}^{m_i} \vartheta_{ij} \Delta LR_{it-j} + \sum_{j=-q_i}^{m_i} \gamma_{ij} \Delta CE_{it-j} + \varepsilon_{it} \tag{14}$$

Eq. (14) can be rewritten as below:

$$\Delta LR_{it} = \delta_i' d_t + \alpha_i LR_{it-1} + \lambda_i' CE_{it-1} + \sum_{j=1}^{m_i} \vartheta_{ij} \Delta LR_{it-j} + \sum_{j=-q_i}^{m_i} \gamma_{ij} \Delta CE_{it-j} + \varepsilon_{it} \tag{15}$$

where d_t represents deterministic components vector (intercept and trend), $\lambda_i'=-\alpha_i\beta_i'$ is the long-term parameter, ϑ_{ij} and γ_{ij} are short-term parameters. Westerlund [16] test is based on four statistics. Two of them are group mean statistics (G_α, G_T). Autoregressive parameter in group mean statistics varies from unit to unit. Group mean statistics can be formulated as in Eq. (16).

$$G_\alpha = \frac{1}{N}\sum_{i=1}^{N}\frac{T\hat{\alpha}_i}{\hat{\alpha}_i(1)}, \qquad G_T = \frac{1}{N}\sum_{i=1}^{N}\frac{\hat{\alpha}_i}{SE(\hat{\alpha}_i)} \tag{16}$$

in which SE denotes the standard error of $\hat{\alpha}_i$. Other two statistics of Westerlund [16] are panel statistics (P_α, P_T). They are calculated by using whole information on panel. Panel statistics are shown in the following equations:

$$P_\alpha = T\hat{\alpha}, \qquad P_T = \frac{\hat{\alpha}}{SE(\hat{\alpha})} \tag{17}$$

The rejection of the hypothesis of interest $(H_0 : \beta_i = 0 \, for\ all\ i)$ in both groups of tests signifies the existence of a cointegration relationship. If the variables are long-term cointegrated, the cointegration model can be estimated in different ways depending on whether the long-term covariance is homogeneous or not. Since the long-term covariance is homogeneous in this study, the panel dynamic least squares (PDOLS) estimator by Kao and Chiang [42] is used to estimate long-term relation. Kao and Chiang PDOLS estimator can be obtained by estimating regression model below [42]:

$$LR_{it} = \alpha_i + CE_{it}\beta + \sum_{j=-q}^{q} c_{ij}\Delta CE_{it+j} + v_{it} \tag{18}$$

where β is long-term parameter. According to Kao and Chiang's Monte Carlo simulation results, the PDOLS estimator and t statistics are successful in all cases of homogeneous and heterogeneous panels.

5. Empirical results

The aim of this study is to examine the long-term relationship between liquidity risk and credit expansion for the period from 2014.Q1 to 2017.Q4 using data from 20 banks in the Turkish banking sector. Since biased results can be obtained due to correlation between units forming panel data, the presence of cross-sectional dependence should be tested first. In this context, the presence of cross-sectional dependence of residuals obtained from error correction model and cross-sectional dependence of the liquidity risk and credit expansion variables were tested by Pesaran [14] CD test. The test results are given in **Table 1**.

According to the results represented in **Table 1**, the null hypothesis of cross-sectional dependence test states no correlation between units. There is enough

	LR		CE		Model	
	Statistic	**p-Value**	**Statistic**	**p-Value**	**Statistic**	**p-Value**
CD [14]	3.88	0.000	3.84	0.000	0.54	0.589

Table 1.
Test results of cross-sectional dependence.

evidence to reject the null hypothesis at 1% significance level for variables. It means that second-generation unit root tests are more appropriate in order to decide whether variables are stationary or not. However, test result for the residuals obtained from error correction model fails to reject the null hypothesis at any significance level. This result provides support for presence of cross-sectional independence in the error correction model. In this case, first-generation panel cointegration tests should be used. Westerlund [16] was chosen to explore long-run dynamics. However, Homogeneity tests should be realized before applying Westerlund [16]. If panel is homogenous then Westerlund's [16] results are valid. For this purpose, Pesaran and Yamagata [22] homogeneity test was applied to error correction model. Test results are given in **Table 2**.

There is not enough evidence to reject the null hypothesis of homogeneity tests at any significance level with respect to results presented in **Table 2**. The results indicate strong evidence for homogeneity of slope coefficients. Therefore, Westerlund [16] is suitable to explore cointegration relation if variables are nonstationary. Pesaran [15] CIPS unit root test was used in order to examine stationarity of variables. **Table 3** reports results of the CIPS unit root test for level and first difference of variables.

The test results in **Table 3** fail to reject the null hypothesis of CIPS unit root test in level of all variables. This result gives evidence of non-stationarity of variables. It means that a shock in the economy has permanent effect on liquidity risk and credit expansion. However, the results provide support for stationarity of variables after differencing them. Liquidity risk and credit expansion are integrated of order 1 (I (1)). Due to integration level of variables, panel cointegration relation can be analyzed. Selection of appropriate panel cointegration method depends on cross-sectional dependence and homogeneity of residuals. Westerlund [16] cointegration test was chosen due to homogeneity and cross-sectional independence of residuals. Westerlund's [16] null hypothesis indicates that there is not long-term relation between variables. Four statistics were calculated in Westerlund [16]. Test results were given in **Table 4**.

	Statistic	p-Value
$\tilde{\Delta}$	−0.417	0.676
$\tilde{\Delta}_{adj}$	−0.590	0.555

Table 2.
Test results of homogeneity tests.

Variables	Deterministic term	Pesaran CIPS statistic [15]
LR	Intercept only	−2.198
ΔLR	Intercept only	-4.421^{***}
CE	Intercept only	−1.780
ΔCE	Intercept only	-3.991^{***}

Note: Deterministic term was chosen by exploring graphs by panel.
****Indicates that the results can reject the null hypothesis at 1% significance level. The relevant 1% critical value for the cross-sectionally augmented Dickey-Fuller (CADF) statistic suggested by Pesaran is −2.1 [15].*
Δ represents first differences of variables.

Table 3.
Test results of CIPS unit root test.

Test statistic	Test value	z-Value	p-Value
G_T	−2.943	−5.785	0.000
G_α	−14.235	−5.804	0.000
P_T	−10.502	−3.857	0.000
P_α	−7.343	−2.912	0.002

Table 4.
Test results of Westerlund [16] cointegration test.

LR	Coefficient	z-Value
CE	1.31 (0.133)	9.82***
Wald $\chi^2(1)$	96.50***	

Note: Standard error is given in brackets.
****Indicates significant at 1% level.*

Table 5.
Estimation results of long-run relation model.

Westerlund [16] cointegration test results show rejection of the null hypothesis for all statistics. It points out that there is a long-term relationship between liquidity risk and credit expansion. Since the variables are cointegrated, long-run relationship can be estimated. Eq. (18) was estimated by the PDOLS estimation method developed by Kao and Chiang [42] in order to investigate the effect of credit expansion on liquidity risk in the long run. The estimation results were given in **Table 5**.

The Wald statistics in **Table 5** is significant at 1% level. It means that model is generally significant. The estimated parameter is the long-term parameter and it is statistically significant at 1% level. Therefore, the credit expansion affects the liquidity risk in the long run. This means that 1% increase in credit expansion increases liquidity risk by 1.31%.

6. Conclusion

Banks convert short-term assets received from depositors to long-term debt for borrowers. Therefore, banks try to maximize their expected profits by considering the risks that may arise from their activities. The concept of risk here is the state of uncertainty, which is uncertain but effective on institutional goals. Liquidity risk is one of the important risks faced by banks. Therefore, many studies on liquidity risk have been conducted in the literature. However, while assets and liabilities are two important components that constitute a bank's balance sheet, a panel study investigating long-run relation between credit expansion and liquidity risk has not been conducted in Turkey. This study aims to fill this gap in the literature. Panel cointegration approach was adopted in order to explore long-run dynamics. First, two important factors in panel methodology which are cross-sectional dependence and homogeneity were investigated properly. Pesaran [14] CD test was applied to the variables and error correction model in order to decide whether there is a cross-sectional dependence between units. The null hypothesis of Pesaran [14] CD test which states that there is a dependence between units was rejected for the variables, while it was not rejected for the model. It indicates that there is no cross-sectional dependence in the residuals of error correction model. Similarly, Delta test for large and small samples were conducted in order to determine homogeneity. The null hypothesis of homogeneity was not rejected. It indicates homogeneity of constant and slope coefficients. This result shapes dynamic panel methodology structure of the study. While there is an evidence on cross-sectional dependence in the variables, cross-sectionally augmented Im-Pesaran-Shin panel unit root test was used to determine integration level of variables. One of the strengths of this test is that it takes the cross-sectional averages of the lagged levels and first differences of the individual series instead of taking difference from the estimated common factors. According to the test results, variables were found to be nonstationary. Since the first order difference of both variables was stationary, existence of the long-run relation between two variables were explored by using Westerlund's [16] paper. Four test statistics were calculated in order to decide whether there is a cointegration relation or not. The null hypothesis which shows long-run relation between variables was rejected according to the test statistics. It allows us to estimate long-run effects. Long-run relation model was estimated by using PDOLS estimator. Model was found statistically significant at 1% level. Also, coefficient of explanatory variable which is credit expansion is found statistically significant at 1% level. Sign of the coefficient is positive. It indicates positive correlation between variables. According to this correlation relation, a growth in credit expansion leads an increase in liquidity risk which affects the costs and returns of banks. This result shows importance of credit expansion on risk management. Because, uncontrolled credit expansion leads to the financial fragility of banks. This study's findings suggest that the banks may limit their credit growth strategy in order to control liqudity risk [43].

Author details

Sureyya Dal
Department of Econometrics, Trakya University, Edirne, Turkey

*Address all correspondence to: sureyyadal@trakya.edu.tr

References

[1] Akkaya M, Azimli T. Türk Bankacılık Sektöründe Likidite Riski Yönetimi. Finans Politik & Ekonomik Yorumlar. 2018;**55**(638):35-48

[2] Göçer İ, Mercan M, Bölükbaş M. Bankacılık Sektörü Kredilerinin İstihdam ve Ekonomik Büyüme Üzerindeki Etkileri:Türkiye Ekonomisi için Çoklu Yapısal Kırılmalı Eş Bütünleşme Analizi. Hacettepe Üniversitesi İktisadi ve İdari Bilimler Fakültesi Dergisi. 2015;**33**(2):65-84

[3] Altıntaş A. Kredi Kayıplarının Makroekonomik Değişkenlere Dayalı Olarak Tahmini ve Stres Testleri: Türk Bankacılık Sektörü İçin Ekonometrik Bir Yaklaşım. İstanbul: Türkiye Bankalar Birliği; 2012. p. 179

[4] Orhangazi Ö. Capital flows and credit expansions in Turkey. Review of Radical Political Economics. 2014;**46**(4):509-516

[5] Kara H, Küçük H, Tiryaki ST, Yüksel C. In search of a reasonable credit growth rate for Turkey. Central Bank Review. 2014;**14**(1):1-14

[6] Kılıç C. Tüketici Kredileri ve Cari Açık Arasındaki İlişki: Türkiye Örneği. Atatürk Üniversitesi İktisadi ve İdari Bilimler Dergisi. 2015;**29**(2):407-420

[7] Karahan P, Uslu NÇ. Kredi Hacmi ile Cari Açık Arasındaki İliski: Türkiye için Dinamik Bir Analiz. EconWorld Working Papers 16007. Eskişehir: WERI—World Economic Research Institute; 2016. DOI: 10.22440/EconWorld.WP.2016.007

[8] Güneş S, Yıldırım C. Kredi Genişlemesi İle Cari Açık Arasındaki İlişki:Türkiye Örneği. Aydın İktisat Fakültesi Dergisi. 2017;**2**(1):43-60

[9] Kılıç F, Torun M. Bireysel Kredilerin Enflasyon Üzerindeki Etkisi: Türkiye Örneği. Yönetim Ve Ekonomi Araştırmaları Dergisi. 2018;**16**(1):18-40

[10] Köroğlu E. Kredi Genişlemesinin Cari Açığa Etkisi: Türkiye Örneği. Bulletin of Economic Theory and Analysis. 2018;**3**(3):175-193

[11] Varlık C. Türkiye Ekonomisinde Sermaye Girişlerinin Bileşenlerinin Aşırı Kredi Genişlemeleri Üzerindeki Etkileri. Uluslararası Yönetim İktisat ve İşletme Dergisi. 2020;**16**(2):219-238

[12] Işık Ö, Belke M. Likidite Riskinin Belirleyicileri: Borsa İstanbul'a Kote Mevduat Bankalarından Kanıtlar. Ekonomi, Politika & Finans Araştırmaları Dergisi. 2017;**2**(2):113-126

[13] Işıl G, Özkan N. İslami Bankalarda Likidite Riski Yönetimi: Türkiye'de Katılım Bankacılığı Üzerine Ampirik Bir Uygulama. Uluslararası İslam Ekonomisi ve Finansı Araştırmaları Dergisi. 2015;**1**(2):23-35

[14] Pesaran MH. General Diagnostic Tests for Cross Section Dependence in Panels. CESifoWorking Paper 1229; IZA Discussion Paper No. 1240. Bonn: IZA-Institute of Labor Economics; 2004

[15] Pesaran MH. A simple panel unit root test in the presence of cross-section dependence. Journal of Applied Econometrics. 2007;**22**:265-312

[16] Westerlund J. Testing for error correction in panel data. Oxford Bulletin of Economics and Statistics. 2007;**69**(6):709-747

[17] Matyas L, Sevestre P. The Econometrics of Panel Data. 3rd ed. Berlin: Springer; 2008. p. 949

[18] Sarafidis V, Yamagata T, Robertson D. A test of cross section dependence for a linear dynamic panel model with

regressors. Journal of Econometrics. 2009;**148**(2):149-161

[19] De Soyos RE, Sarafidis V. Testing for cross-sectional dependence in panel-data models. The Stata Journal. 2006;**6** (4):482-496

[20] Hepaktan CE, Çınar S. OECD Ülkeleri Vergi Sistemi Esnekliğinin Panel Eşbütünleşme Testleri ile Analizi. Sosyal Bilimler Dergisi. 2011;**4**(2): 133-153

[21] Swamy PAVB. Statistical Inference in Random Coefficient Regression Models. New York: Springer-Verlag; 1971. p. 203

[22] Pesaran MH, Yamagata T. Testing slope homogeneity in large panels. Journal of Econometrics. 2008;**142**: 50-93

[23] Göçer İ. Ekonomik Büyümenin Belirleyicisi Olarak İhracat: Gelişmekte Olan Asya Ülkeleri İçin Yatay Kesit Bağımlılığı Altında Çoklu Yapısal Kırılmalı Panel Eşbütünleşme Analizi. Bankacılar Dergisi. 2013;**86**:27-42

[24] Levin A, Lin CF, Chu CSJ. Unit root tests in panel data: Asymptotic and finite-sample properties. Journal of Econometrics. 2002;**108**:1-24

[25] Harris RDF, Tzavalis E. Inference for unit roots in dynamic panels where the time dimension is fixed. Journal of Econometrics. 1999;**91**:201-226

[26] Breitung J. The local power of some unit root tests for panel data. In: Baltagi BH, Fomby TB, Carter Hill R, editors. Nonstationary Panels, Panel Cointegration and Dynamic Panels. Vol. 15. Bingley: Emerald Group Publishing Limited; 2001. pp. 161-178

[27] Hadri K. Testing for stationarity in heteregenous panel data. Econometrics Journal. 2000;**3**:148-161

[28] Tatoğlu FY. İleri Panel Zaman Serileri Analizi. 2nd ed. İstanbul: Beta; 2018. p. 67

[29] Sarno L, Taylor MP. Real exchange rates under the current float: Unequivocal evidence of mean reversion. Economic Letters. 1998;**60**: 131-137

[30] Breuer J, McNown R, Wallace M. series specific unit root tests with panel data. Oxford Bulletin of Economics and Statistics. 2002;**64**(5):527-546

[31] Chang Y. Nonlinear IV unit root tests in panels with cross-sectional dependency. Journal of Econometrics. 2002;**110**(2):261-292

[32] Chang Y. Bootstrap unit root tests in panels with cross-sectional dependency. Journal of Econometrics. 2004;**120**(2): 263-293

[33] Phillips PCB, Sul D. Dynamic panel estimation and homogeneity testing under cross section dependence. Econometrics Journal. 2003;**6**:217-259

[34] Moon HR, Perron B. Testing for a unit root in panels with dynamic factors. Journal of Econometrics. 2004;**122**: 81-126

[35] Bai J, Ng S. A panic attack on unit roots and cointegration. Econometrica. 2004;**72**(4):1127-1177

[36] Bai J, Ng S. Panel unit root tests with cross-section dependence: A further investigation. Econometric Theory. 2010;**26**:1088-1114

[37] Breitung J, Das S. Panel unit root tests under cross-sectional dependence. Statistica Neerlandica. 2005;**59**:414-433

[38] Hadri K, Kurozumi E. A simple panel stationarity test in the presence of serial correlation and a common factor. Economics Letters. 2012;**115**(1):31-34

[39] Pesaran MH, Smith VL, Yamagata T. Panel unit root tests in the presence of a multifactor error structure. Journal of Econometrics. 2013;**175**(2):94-115

[40] Reese S, Westerlund J. Panicca: Panic on cross-section averages. Journal of Applied Econometrics. 2016;**31**:961-981

[41] Klein M. Inequality and household debt: A panel cointegration analysis. Empirica. 2015;**42**:391-412

[42] Kao C, Chiang MH. On the estimation and inference of a cointegrated regression in panel data. In: Baltagi BH, Fomby TB, Carter Hill R, editors. Nonstationary Panels, Panel Cointegration and Dynamic Panels. Vol. 15. Bingley: Emerald Group Publishing Limited; 2001. pp. 179-222

[43] Alves AJ Jr, Dymski GA, Paula LF. Banking strategy and credit expansion: A post-Keynesian approach. Cambridge Journal of Economics. 2008;**32**(3):395-420. DOI: 10.1093/cje/bem035

Chapter 12

Governance and Growth in the Western Balkans: A SVAR Approach

Gordana Djurovic and Martin M. Bojaj

Abstract

The quality of economic governance is one of the prerequisites for sustainable and faster economic development of the Western Balkan countries, having in mind their historical background, dissolution of the ex-Yugoslavia, specific economic circumstances during the transition recession of the 1990s, slow economic recovery at the beginning of the twenty-first century, strong impact of the global financial and economic crisis, and long and complexed path towards the European Union (EU). The main research problem in this paper is examining the dynamic relationships among government effectiveness, inflation, and GDP across Albania, Bosnia and Hercegovina, Kosovo, Montenegro, North Macedonia, and Serbia. We employ the Worldwide Governance Indicators of the World Bank, namely, the Governance Effectiveness Indicator, as one of the six broad dimensions of governance. Using a structural VAR approach, we examine the time-varying effects of economic governance shocks on inflation and economic growth dynamics for each of the Western Balkan (WB) countries in the period of January 2006 to December 2018. Our findings allow the WB policymakers to understand the impact of institutional strength involved in identifying the onset of sustainable development dynamics and the EU integration process in WB better and develop more effective government regulations that can be employed nationally.

Keywords: Western Balkans, economic governance, governance effectiveness, indicator, GDP, inflation

1. Introduction

What causes a fundamental lack of development in Western Balkan (WB) countries? The effectiveness of political and economic institutions is a vital determinant of long-run growth. Institutions constitute one of the underlying explanations for differences in growth across countries [1]. The structure of a societal organization is the central force behind differences in Albania, Bosnia and Hercegovina, Kosovo, Montenegro, North Macedonia, and Serbia [2]. The WB 6 shares a similar economic history. However, each of these countries has its differences. Today, the six Western Balkan countries are facing numerous economic and financial challenges and weak institutions, while future development dynamic is significantly dependent on the quality of economic governance.

Political institutions, which represent the governance structure, exercise public authority. Examining differences of the Western Balkan governance structures assists us to feature the efficiency of each country's public administration. On average, most of the WB 6 fare poorly on public services, implementation of policies, enforcement of property rights, and corruption. The relationship among these dimensions of economic governance and growth has been studied in recent literature [3–5]. Each of the WB 6 has tendencies to converge towards the European Union (EU), and each is expected to join the EU. Early in the 1990s, these countries started the transition mechanism. Countries with efficient institutions, well-advanced property rights, and sound public policies have stronger will to employ more efficiently physical and human capital and achieve a higher growth rate. Since each of the WB 6 has set its national development strategies, it is valuable to examine how the government efficiency indicator impacts this set of economic growth dynamics. Besides, we are interested in observing the behavior of inflation, as the new Member States eventually have to fulfill the Maastricht price criteria.

Based on the requirements of the Maastricht criteria for entering the EU, the inflation rate must be stabilized as a prerequisite to joining. The WB 6 has to bring its national legislation in line with EU law and meet price stability to ensure economic convergence. Convergence criteria explicitly report: "A price-performance that is sustainable and average inflation not more than 1.5% above the rate of the three best performing Member States [6]". The Union carefully monitors the progress in the alignment with and implementation of the *acquis* throughout the process of negotiating. For instance, in the case of Montenegro, one of the benchmarks for the chapter Economic and Monetary policy is the Country has adopted the required constitutional change. It has to ensure that the primary objective of price stability is defined in compliance with Articles 127 (1) and 282 (2) of the Treaty on the Functioning of the European Union—Article 143 of the Constitution [7].

Even though economic governance has been analyzed to a moderate extent within the EU, we find there is still sufficient space for enhancement using the WB 6 as an example. The novelty of this paper is that it uses a structural vector autoregressive approach for the economies of Albania, Bosnia and Hercegovina, Kosovo, Montenegro, North Macedonia, and Serbia to analyze the impact of economic efficiency to growth. This paper suggests examining time series data from January 2006 to December 2018 for WB 6. It evaluates and compares the empirical performances of forecasts of inflation, GDP, and economic governance effectiveness.

The annual economic reform program exercise led by the European Commission with all Western Balkan countries is a crucial tool for supporting the modernization of their economies and achieving closer economic coordination with the EU. The Commission will strengthen this exercise, bring it even closer in line with the current European semester for the EU Member States, and provide more advanced technical assistance.

In the context of the EU framework to support economic governance, all candidate countries and potential candidates are invited to submit a three-annual Economic Reform Programme (ERP) which comprises of the following components: macroeconomic framework, fiscal framework, and structural reforms. The ERPs contain medium-term macroeconomic projections and budgetary plans for the next 3 years, as well as a list of priority structural reform measures aiming at boosting competitiveness and inclusive growth. The ERP process has helped to focus on governments' attention to addressing urgent structural reform needs and to improve coordination. However, the tangible results of such reform efforts on people's lives still need to materialize. Awareness of the policy guidance by the relevant stakeholders and commitment to their implementation needs to be strengthened by the WB 6.

The objective is to reveal the dynamic relationship between economic governance, growth, and inflation for each of the WB 6 in the specified period and forecast the economic growth and inflation dynamics using an SVAR approach. Specifically, we aim at exploring how economic governance shocks impact GDP growth and vice versa. To achieve that objective, we estimate recursively structural VAR identified models for each of the Western Balkan countries. On purpose, we included the years of the global crisis to observe, analyze, and explore changes in this vital relationship between the exogenous shocks of the economic integration of the WB 6 and growth. We have to keep in mind that foreign direct investments could not penetrate the WB 6 markets as they did in the EU members because of economic disintegration. The data for governance quality are collected from the World Bank database [8, 9]. We must identify purely exogenous (policy or another type) shock to be able to trace out its dynamic effects: identify the structural VAR. Impulse responses trace the effects of structural shocks on the endogenous variables. Besides, we use forecast error variance decomposition to observe the proportion of the movements of a variable due to shocks to itself and to shocks to other variables.

Ceteris paribus, we hypothesize that shocks to government effectiveness positively affect economic growth and can be employed by the WB 6 governments as an anti-inflationary mechanism in the process of accessing the European Union. In short, this paper will show the impact of institutional strength on the development dynamics and dynamics of the EU integration process.

2. Literature review

Government effectiveness fosters growth and prosperity. The relationship between growth and government effectiveness in advanced countries has been a topic of many empirical and theoretical studies [10–19].

Papers that examine WB 6 economies are limited. To this end, various conceptual and empirical models are employed. The convergence of the WB 6 towards the EU-15 members has been examined by Siljak and Nagy, and they find the WB 6 converges faster, ranging from 1.3% to 3.6% [20]. Economic integrations, openness, and foreign direct investments impact growth based on recent literature in the EU [21]. EU membership prospect is the best trigger for foreign inflows [22]. Economic integration of CEE countries, between 1993 and 2001 and 1995–2007, revealed faster convergence towards the EU [23, 24]. The convergence patterns change across the WB 6 in different periods [25].

It looks like there is no integrated agreement in the empirical literature on the significance and the line or course on which it is moving. On the other hand, the economic catch-up integration of the WB 6 towards the EU still shows no convergence [26, 27]. Colak analyzed 33 EU (CEE 10, SEE 8, and EU 15) countries and found that economic governance has converged for each group of countries [28]. Badinger does not find a strong relationship between economic freedom and long-term growth [29]. The relationship between EU integrations and economic growth showed to be of positive and strong significance [30].

As far as the global economic crisis of 2008, different countries have had different sensitivities [31–33]. Matkowski et al. examines the convergence of EU-11 towards the EU-15 during the period 1993–2015 and reveals that a greater extent of convergence was before the financial crisis [34]. The convergence before the crisis was at a higher rate in the EU [35–37]. Western Balkans have continually underperformed compared to the average of the EU.

The WB 6 are heterogeneous, lacking similar convergence. Based on Zuk and Savelin (2018) the most successful central, eastern, and southeastern Europe

(CESEE) economic governances, in terms of the pace of convergence, share standard features such as, among other things, a sharp improvement in institutional efficiency and human capital, more outward-oriented economic policies, favorable demographic-economic developments, and the quick reallocation of labor from agriculture into other sectors [38]. Forward-looking, speeding-up, and sustaining convergence in the WB 6 requires in-depth efforts to improve institutional quality and innovation, reinvigorate foreign investment, and address the adverse impact of population aging seriously.

Stabilizing policies and implementation of reforms are the vital drivers of WB 6 growth, in the meantime declining the impact of initial conditions of the 1990s. Since the government efficiency indicator reflects perceptions of the quality of public services, the quality of the civil service and the degree of its independence from political pressures, the quality of policy formulation and implementation, and the credibility of the government's commitment to such policies, we give special attention to this indicator in explaining the growth differences among the WB 6 (through GDP) and macroeconomic stability (through inflation).

3. Methodology

Even though government efficiency has been studied to some extent, we reveal a significantly wider knowledge gap. First, conceptual specification, based on which empirical examinations of government efficiency is analyzed, is not prevailing combining theory and empirical analysis. Secondly, we identify six structural VAR models. To our knowledge, it has not been applied to WB 6 data. VARs turn out to be one of the key empirical tools in modern macroeconomics, and they allow one to model macroeconomic data informatively [39].

The range of the data is from January 2006 to December 2018. In order to control for time trends in our analysis, we include dummy variables. The expression referring to an SVAR model is used as follows:

$$Y_t = a_0 + \beta X_t + u_t \tag{1}$$

Here, we present parameter estimates and the main characteristics of the models. The identified recursive SVAR model is as follows:

$$y_t = a_t + \beta_1 GovEff_t + \beta_2 \pi_t + u_t \tag{2}$$

where y_t is the gross domestic product for each of the WB 6, $GovEff_t$ is the government efficiency indicator, and π_t represents inflation (a proxy for macroeconomic stability). This specification contains independently identically distributed stochastic disturbance term u_t $\{IID(0;\sigma_u^2)\}$. The above model will allow us to observe how economic governance shocks and macroeconomic stability impact GDP growth and vice versa. Of particular interest for this paper is to examine the role of economic integrations and macroeconomic stabilization in determining the growth of GDP in Albania, Bosnia and Hercegovina, Kosovo, Montenegro, North Macedonia, and Serbia. Thus, government efficiency and inflation are considered as important explanatory factors. For North Macedonia Model, we added purposely the corruption indicator variable, in order to observe the potential shocks to growth. As we will see, the indicator to this specific case shows no impact.

How well the models describe the dynamic behavior of economic variables? We will proceed with our VAR models for structural inference and policy analysis. One of the main objectives of our VAR model is forecasting, and it has common characteristics as a univariate AR model. Zivot and Wang emphasize that forecasting future values of a matrix Y_t, when the parameters Π of the Var(p) process are assumed to be known and there are no deterministic terms of exogenous variables, the best linear predictor, in terms of minimum mean squared error (MSE) of Y_{t+1} or one-step forecast, is [40]:

$$Y_{(T+1|T)} = c + \Pi_1 Y_T + \ldots + \Pi_p Y_{T-p+1} \tag{3}$$

and forecasts for longer horizons h (h-step forecasts) may be obtained using the chain rule of forecasting as:

$$Y_{(T+h|T)} = c + \Pi_1 Y_{(T+h-1|T)} + \ldots + \Pi_p Y_{(T+h-p|T)} \tag{4}$$

and h-step forecast error may be expressed as:

$$Y_{T+h} - Y_{(T+h|T)} = \sum_{s=0}^{h-1} \Psi_s \varepsilon_{T+h-s} \tag{5}$$

where the matrices Ψ_s are determined by recursive substitution:

$$\Psi_s = \sum_{j=1}^{p-1} \Psi_{s-j} \Pi_j \tag{6}$$

with $\Psi_0 = I_n$ and $\Pi_j = 0$ for $j > p$.

As already emphasized in the literature review, the logic behind employing these variables is clear: in an economically free societal environment, people and companies are free to work, manufacture, utilize their disposable income, and make investments in any way they please, with that liberty both ensured and protected by the state and unconstrained by the state [41]. Besides, low and stabilized inflation significantly indicates faster and mounting economic growth.

4. Empirical results

All variables are stationary based on unit root tests of ADF, PP, and KPSS stationary test. Visual inspection and statistical correlograms portray and confirm stationarity. Test results of *t*-statistics and *p* values reject the null hypothesis of a unit root.

We proceed with empirical construction and testing for potential structural breaks, which are crucial to identify for forecasting purposes as well as confidence bounds. Stability diagnostics, under recursive estimates, show that all coefficients have a lot of instability, indicating structural breaks. Chow breakpoint test confirms the above indication, having *F*-statistics and *p* values smaller than 5%, meaning to reject the null hypothesis of no breakpoints at 5% significance level. The Quandt-Andrews test indicates for rejecting the null hypothesis of no break. It reveals breaks for all cases Albania, Bosnia and Hercegovina, Kosovo, Montenegro, North Macedonia, and Serbia. Testing for multiple breaks in intercept and coefficients using Bai-Perron to sequentially test the hypothesis of L + 1 vs. L sequentially determined breaks. The Bai-Perron test recommends that there are breaks. We can conclude that all four tests indicate that there is a switch of parameters at 5% significance level, and we are dealing with multiple breaks in parameters. We will add the following dichotomous variables (**Table 1**):

Dummies	AL	B&H	KS	MNE	NM	SRB
1	d_2007	d_2007	d_2008	d_2008	d_2008	d_2008
2	d_2013	d_2008	d_2010	d_2010	d_2010	d_2010
3		d_2009	d_2011	d_2012	d_2012	d_2012
4		d_2011	d_2013		d_2013	d_2013
5		d_2013				d_2016

Source: Authors' calculation.

Table 1.
Dichotomous variables.

AL	B&H	KS	MNE	NM	SRB
0.979149	0.981038	0.975064	0.918688	0.987044	0.948791
0.917381	0.981038	0.975064	0.918688	0.987044	0.948791
0.814555	0.963392	0.927706	0.868723	0.979839	0.868408
0.814555	0.963392	0.927706	0.868723	0.979839	0.868408
0.383119	0.962341	0.725579	0.846442	0.943445	0.654013

VAR satisfies the stability condition. Source: Authors' calculation.
No root lies outside the unit circle in **Table 2.*

Table 2.
Root of characteristic polynomial.

Including 12 lags in the lag exclusion test or lag length criteria about deciding the maximum number of lags to be used in our VARs, we get an estimated fitting lag length denoted by an asterisk. We select 2, 11, 3, 2, 10, and 2 lags, respectively, as the appropriate lag length for our VAR models.

All inverse roots of the characteristic polynomial are <1, as seen in **Table 2**, confirming the stationarity of the VARs.

We have reached significant results, and based on the stationarity assessed so far, we can infer that impulse response standard errors are valid (**Table 3**). The largest inverse root of the AR characteristic polynomial is 0.987044. The correlograms of short-term error correlations of the estimated VARs suggest no autocorrelation. The entire lines lie within the 2 standard error bounds, showing at first lags another backup to the suggestion of missing autocorrelation in non-noticeable continual wave sinusoidal. Based on 95% significance level, the null hypothesis, which states there is no autocorrelation of residuals in our estimated VARs, cannot be rejected. It has p values of 44.15, 33.37, 86.14, 91.67, 76.31, and 96.69%, respectively, for lag orders up to 2, 11, 3, 2, 10, and 2 lags. Therefore, there is no indication, based on the LM tests, that there is the autocorrelation of errors.

4.1 Forecasting models

To generate a forecast, we can use known values or forecasted values. Using the known values for forecasting is static forecasting. In case we proceed using the predicted values from regression, then it is dynamic forecasting. There are two types of simulation processes. One is a deterministic simulation, where we get only one value for the solution, which does not respond to innovations. It calculates under the current set of assumptions or known facts without any shocks

Lags	AL	B&H	KS	MNE	NM	SRB
	Prob	Prob	Prob	Prob	Prob	Prob
1	**0.2790**	**0.2574**	**0.3468**	**0.9348**	**0.1017**	**0.6712**
2	**0.4415**	**0.1356**	**0.6129**	**0.9167**	**0.0639**	**0.9669**
3	0.0103	**0.7364**	**0.8614**	0.7818	**0.0545**	0.4213
4	0.1171	**0.1947**	0.8915	0.1140	**0.2147**	0.1376
5	0.4000	**0.2323**	0.9923	0.0169	**0.2487**	0.3582
6	0.9380	**0.1057**	0.0000	0.9868	**0.6963**	0.0611
7	0.6340	**0.4410**	0.5016	0.0019	**0.9956**	0.4222
8	0.8501	**0.1188**	0.0757	0.6773	**0.3241**	0.3912
9	0.3897	**0.4393**	0.2606	0.9880	**0.2077**	0.4678
10	0.9490	**0.5177**	0.3401	0.7466	**0.7631**	0.9671
11	0.8103	**0.3337**	0.9346	0.3383	0.5245	0.2678
12	0.0000	0.0000	0.0000	0.0000	0.0001	0.0000

Source: Authors' calculation.
Bold values represent lag values.

Table 3.
VAR residual serial correlation LM tests.

introduced, which is called the baseline. Deterministic simulation ignores the fact that relationships do not hold exactly, because of random disturbances and estimated coefficients, which are not known or predetermined values. We should account for these sources of uncertainty by using stochastic simulations. **Figure 1** performs gdp_gap and inflation stochastic simulations for static solution model simulators for period 2017m01 till 2017m12.

Forecasting performance of the static solution performs very well, both in terms of the fit and small standard error bounds, coming as a result of de facto one period ahead forecast.

It uses actual instead of forecasted lagged values over the forecast period. The blue lines portray the actual data for both gdp_gap and inflation, while the green lines represent the forecasting performance of the stochastic-static model. As seen in **Figure 1**, both predictions are very close to the real data and within the confidence bands, except in the 5th month for the North Macedonia GDP. The red lines show the upper and lower bounds of the stochastic-static solution model simulator. The comovement is noticeable for both variables. Including bootstrapped errors and coefficient uncertainty, we get forecast measures (**Table 4**).

Analyzing **Table 4**, the first thing we notice is low RMSE for all WB 6 countries. The RMSEs for gdp_gap and inflation are 0.1979 and 0.3768, respectively. Theil's coefficient U1, which measures the forecast accuracy, is acceptable for all variables of the VAR models.

4.2 Impulse responses

The impulse response function will tell us the change in endogenous variables for each structural shock at t, t + 1, and so on. Our goal is to trace out the effects of internal shocks to the WB 6 economies. First, we employ Sims' (1980) orthogonalized impulse response functions [42]. We will trace out the responses of the dependent variables in the SVAR models to shocks.

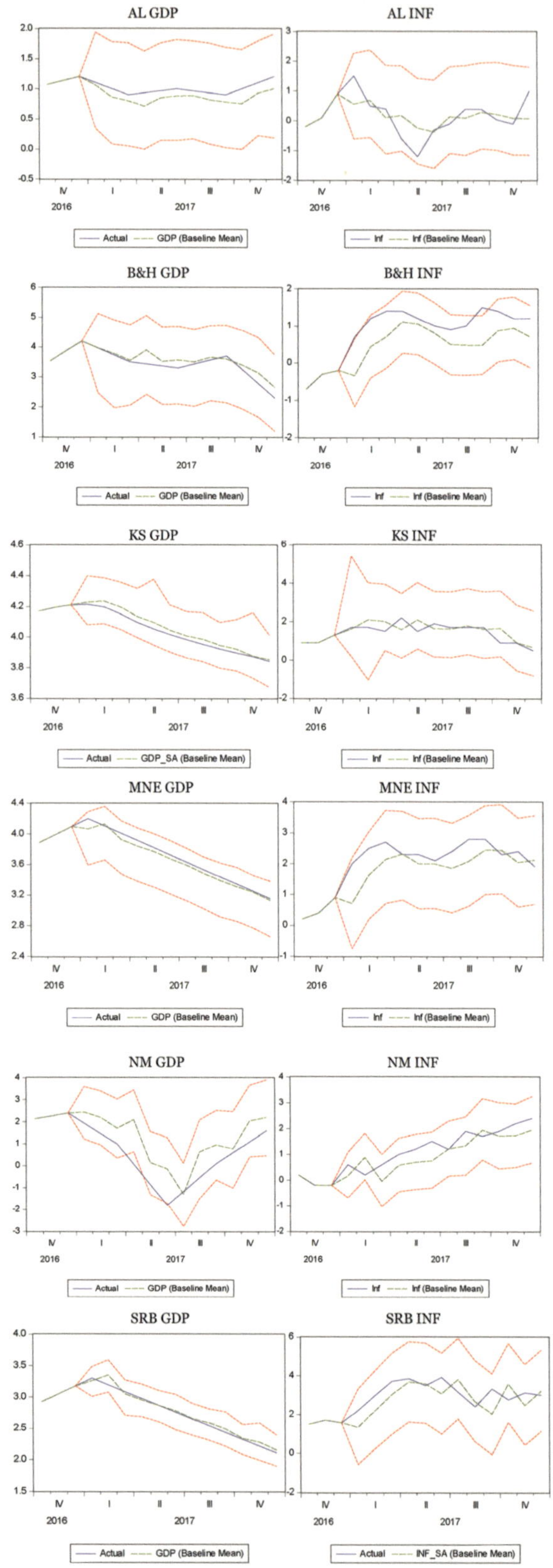

Figure 1.
GDP_GAP and inflation stochastic-static solution model simulator. Source: Authors' calculation.

	AL	B&H	KS	MNE	NM	SRB
RMSE	0.609466	0.471552	0.569857	0.623307	0.891088	1.618317
MAE	0.562789	0.365514	0.481942	0.558959	0.72649	1.353392
MAPE	192.5031	10.31633	10.45501	20.31178	1.223044	307.8459
Theil	0.404218	0.067415	0.066878	0.090758	0.007274	0.258264

Source: Authors' calculation.

Table 4.
GDP forecast measures.

The response of gdp_gap, in **Figure 2**, to the economic freedom shock, keeps increasing until the 19th month, up to 0.252388. As the economy is hit by the economic freedom shock, productivity increases for the first 6 months and then stops for a while till expectations of the market get to equilibrium and get positive perspective. Domestic investments increase until the 19th month. Closely, we must keep our eyes at how expectations of productivity and the labor market are formed.

We observe from **Figure 2** the response of GDP and inflation to the government efficiency shock. The response of AL GDP to GOVEFF shocks slightly decreases in the first quarter and afterwards continues with the same impulse. Moreover, the response of AL INF to GOVEFF shocks increases in the first two quarters and after that has no impact. Why? Moving to Bosnia and Hercegovina, we notice that the response of GDP to government efficiency shocks is positive. The GDP increases in the first 6 months then drops down until the end of the fourth quarter, while inflation increases from 0.15 to 0.23 from the first to the second month, respectively. Interestingly, inflation drops to 0.06 in the fifth month. In the second year, the shocks persist in lowering inflation (deflation) to −0.34. In the case of Kosovo, government efficiency shocks decrease GDP in the first two quarters to −0.19 and then keep mounting slowly till the 19th month, reaching 0. The response of inflation to the shock is that it increases just slightly until the 2nd month, following with a decrease until the 12th month, reaching deflation −0.47.

We have to take into consideration the role of expectations in explaining the impact of government efficiency shocks on GDP and inflation. As the economic government efficiency shock hits the economy, the productivity decreases for the first 10 months and then stops for a while till expectations of the market get to equilibrium and get a positive perspective. Domestic investments increase until the 19th month. Firmly, we must keep our eyes at how expectations of productivity and the labor market are formed. We observe from this case that the response of inflation to the shock immediately starts to decline after the second month, especially in the first year. Afterwards, it starts slowly to increase. Moreover, only after 23 months, it reaches the closest point to zero: 0.02. How can we interpret the above results? Having the good news that the region is moving ahead, towards the EU integrations, having positive expectations, and seeing everyday reforms within the economic activities in the real market, it is to be expected from a reasonable society to have a better perspective. This implies a correction of price expectations P^e in relation to the current price level P.

In the case of Montenegro, the GDP drops down in the first three quarters, reaching −0.28. Additionally, from the third quarter to the end of the 2nd year, the GDP keeps mounting. Inflation responds to the shock of government efficiency with an increase from 0 to 0.2 for the first 11 months. Why? How can we interpret the response of inflation to government efficiency shock? The enhancement of government efficiency changes the quality of the Montenegrin economy.

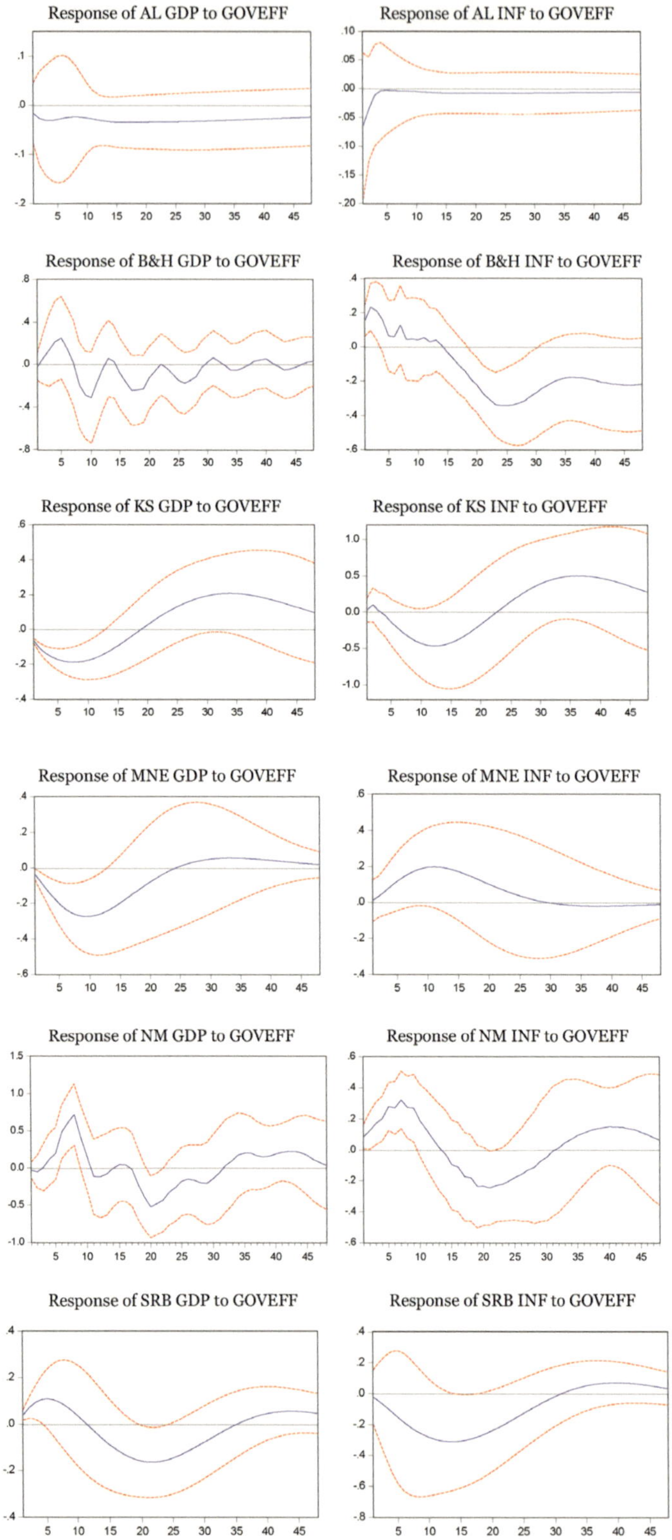

Figure 2.
Impulse responses to economic freedom and EGDI shocks. Source: Authors' calculation.

In the case of North Macedonia, the response of GDP to GOVEFF is positive from the very start, increasing the GDP to 0.72 until the 7th month. Afterwards, it falls to −0.12 after the 11th month. The inflation response is positive, reaching 0.32 until the 7th month, then drops down. This might be a piece of vital information for the macroprudential policymakers of North Macedonia.

The response of Serbia GDP to the government efficiency shock is positive. It starts mounting until the second quarter to 0.11 and then keeps decreasing until the 22nd month, reaching −0.17. Again, the mechanism of expectations is crucial in explaining the responses of GDP and inflation in the case of Serbia. This process, in this case, shifts the wage-setting relation, *WS*, to the right less than the PS, increasing employment and GDP. Workers' expectations are not higher than what firms expect, as a result of an increase in government efficiency. Thus, the wage-setting relation (*WS)* will shift less than the price-setting relationship (*PS*). This will decrease unemployment. As we can notice from Figure, inflation automatically starts to fall. The adjustment mechanism, in the case of Serbia, is very well set up between the workers and firms.

5. Conclusions

Given the strategic priority the government of Albania, Bosnia and Hercegovina, Kosovo, Montenegro, North Macedonia, and Serbia have to join the European Union, we felt compelled to identify an approach and methodology that the Governments of the WB 6 can use in developing anti-inflation macroeconomic stability and overall development strategy. Given the high increase in the interest of fulfilling the Maastricht convergence criteria before the accession and the lack of any uniform methodology, we believe that the findings presented in our paper will appeal to macroprudential policymakers. Although previous research papers have identified a few methods that could be used in forecasting growth, such as internal and external variables, the methodologies developed from those findings have been restricted and difficult to administer on a national level of the WB 6. Thus, our findings will allow the macroprudential policymakers to understand the factors involved in identifying the onset of macroeconomic efficiency dynamics and macroeconomic expectations in Western Balkan countries better and develop more effective policy measures that can be used nationally. In so doing, we hope that our research paper advances the toolset needed to combat the growth concerns of many macroprudential policymakers in the Western Balkan countries, especially the Central Banks.

This paper reveals a significantly wider knowledge gap: both theoretical and empirical. We identified recursively six SVAR models. Each model aggregates two critical macroeconomic variables to forecast GDP in the Western Balkans. We find that among the performance of the individual-predictor forecasts, all country models perform with high precision, based on the root mean square error and stochastic-static solution model simulator. This essential evidence shows that government efficiency and inflation are critical in promoting sustainable growth. The main implications of this study suggest that the government efficiency indicator is crucial in governing macroeconomic stability and sustainable growth in Western Balkans.

The impulse response findings reveal that the responses of GDP and inflation to a shock on economic governance are significant, except in the case of Albania, where the response of GDP and inflation are almost flat. Future papers are recommended to decompose the government efficiency to public services, civil services, independence from political pressures, policy formulations, and government commitment as individual independent variables. Meanwhile, the role of expectations are different for each of the Western Balkan countries, implying that each government has to take an in-depth analysis of different aspects of government efficiencies.

Future work should introduce new methods, e.g., Bayesian VAR (BVAR) and factor-augmented VAR (FAVAR); since central banks and the private sector have qualitative measures not reflected in the VAR, the time series which represent the economic concepts are arbitrary to some degree, and impulse responses are available only for the studied variables, constituting only a subset of the factors that policymakers are interested, especially in the Western Balkans. Thus, more massive data sets would be vital to identify the mechanism accurately. Finally, alternative estimation methods, identification schemes, and trying to interpret the estimated factors explicitly would be worthwhile and useful for macroprudential policymakers to forecast more precisely economic activities of the Western Balkans 6 especially in the dawn of entering the European Union.

Conflict of interest

The authors declare no conflict of interest.

Author details

Gordana Djurovic* and Martin M. Bojaj
Faculty of Economics, University of Montenegro, Montenegro

*Address all correspondence to: gordana@t-com.me

References

[1] Acemoglu D, Johnson S, Robinson J. The colonial origins of comparative development: An empirical investigation. The American Economic Review. 2001;**91**(5):1369-1401

[2] Rodrik D, Subramanian A, Trebbi F. Institutions rule: The primacy of institutions over geography and integration in economic development. Journal of Economic Growth. 2004; **9**(2):131-165

[3] Hellman J, Geraint J, Kaufmann D. Seize the State, Seize the Day: State Capture, Corruption and Influence in Transition. Policy Research Working Paper 2444. Washington: World Bank; 2001

[4] Kaufmann D, Kraay A. Growth without governance. Economia. 2002; **3**(1):169-229

[5] Kurtz M, Schrank A. Growth and governance: Models, measures, and mechanisms. The Journal of Politics. 2007;**69**(2):538-554

[6] European Commission. Convergence Report. Institutional Paper 078. European Economy. 2018. ISSN: 2443-8014

[7] European Union. Consolidated version of the Treaty on the functioning of the European Union. Official Journal of the European Union. 2012: C 326/47

[8] Worldwide Governance Indicators. Aggregate Governance Indicators 1996–2018 [Internet]. 2020. Available from: http://info.worldbank.org/governance/wgi/#home [Accessed: 12 January 2020]

[9] Kaufmann D, Kraay A, Mastruzzi M. The Worldwide Governance Indicators: A Summary of Methodology, Data and Analytical Issues. World Bank Policy Research Working Paper: No. 5430; 2010

[10] Kaufmann D. 10 myths about governance and corruption. Finance and Development. 2005;**42**(3):41-43

[11] De Amorim GM, Da Silva ME. A. Governance and Growth: A Panel Var Approach. Anais do XLIV Encontro Nacional de Economia. In: Proceedings of the 44th Brazilian Economics Meeting. Vol. 84. 2018; ANPEC

[12] Evans P, Rauch JE. Bureaucracy and growth: A cross-National Analysis of the effects of "Weberian" state structures on economic growth. American Sociological Review. 1999;**64**(5):748-765

[13] Ritzen J, Easterly W, Woolcock M. On "Good" Politicians and "Bad" Policies: Social Cohesion, Institutions, and Growth. World Bank Policy Research Working Paper: No. 2448; 2000

[14] Hopkin J. States, markets and corruption: A review of some recent literature. Review of International Political Economy. 2002;**9**(3):574-590

[15] Rodrik D. Why we learn nothing from regressing economic growth on policies. Seoul Journal of Economics. 2012;**25**(2)

[16] Sala-i-Martin X, Doppelhofer G, Miller R. Determinants of long-term growth: A Bayesian averaging of classical estimates approach. American Economic Review. 2004;**94**(4):813-835

[17] Temple J. The new growth evidence. Journal of Economic Literature. 1999; **37**(1):112-156

[18] Wacziarg R. Review of easterly's the elusive quest for growth. Journal of Economic Literature. 2002;**40**(3): 907-918

[19] Yanikkaya H. Trade openness and economic growth: A crosscountry

empirical investigation. Journal of Development Economics. 2003;**72**(1): 57-89

[20] Dz S, Nagy SG. Economic convergence between the Western Balkans and the New EU Member States (EU-13). Romanian Journal of European Affairs. 2019;**19**(1):50-64

[21] Friedrch C, Schnabel I, Zettelmeyer J. Financial Integration and Growth – Is Emerging Europe Different? European Bank for Reconstruction and Development. Working Paper 123; 2010

[22] Bower U, Turrini A. EU accession: A road to fast-track convergence? Economic and Financial Affairs Economic Paper: 393; 2009

[23] Matkowski Z, Próchniak M. Economic convergence in the EU accession countries. Composite Indicators of Business Activity for Macroeconomic Analysis. The RIED Papers and Proceedings, Vol. 74. SGH, Warsaw; 2004. pp. 405-425

[24] Jelnikar E, Murmayer U. Convergence in Europe. Empirical Analysis on Two Groups of Countries of the European Union. In: International Conference on Human and Economic Resources; 2004. pp. 246-260

[25] El Ouardighi J, Somun-Kapetanovic R. Do Balkan countries have a European future? An analysis of real economic convergence, 1989-2005. South East European Journal of Economics and Business. 2007;**2**(2):23-30

[26] Botric V. Output convergence between Western Balkans and EU-15. Research in Economics and Business: Central and Eastern Europe. 2013;**5**(1): 46-62

[27] Tsanana E, Katrakilidis C, Pantelidis P. Balkan area and EU-15: An empirical investigation of income convergence. In: Balkan and Eastern European Countries in the Midst of the Global Economic Crisis. Physica-Heidelberg; 2013. pp. 23-33

[28] Colak O. Convergence revisited: Case of EU and Eastern Europe. Regional Science Inquiry. 2015;**7**(1): 69-81

[29] Badinger H. Growth effects of economic integration. Review of World Economics. 2005;**141**(1):50-78

[30] Henrekson M, Torstensson J, Torstensson R. Growth effects of European integration. European Economic Review. 1997;**41**(8):1537-1557

[31] Berglof E, Korniyenko Y, Plekhanov A, Zettelmeyer J. Understanding the Crisis in Emerging Europe. European Bank for Reconstruction and Development: Working Paper 109; 2010

[32] Darvas Z. Beyond the Crisis: Prospects for Emerging Europe. Bruegel. Working Paper 2010-06; 2010

[33] Atoyan R. Beyond the Crisis: Revisiting Emerging Europe's Growth Model. Financial Theory and Practice. 2010;**34**(4):329-356

[34] Matkowski Z, Prochniak M, Rapacki R. Real Income Convergence between Central Eastern and Western Europe: Past, Present, and Prospects. EconStor Conference Papers 146992, ZBW - Leibniz Information Centre for Economics; 2016

[35] Strielkowski W, Höschle F. Evidence for economic convergence in the EU: The analysis of past EU enlargements. Technological and Economic Development of Economy. 2016;**22**(4):617-630

[36] Grela M, Majchrowska A, Michatek T, Muck J, Stazka-Gawrysiak A, Tchorek G, et al. Is Central and

Eastern Europe Converging towards the EU-15? Warsaw: Narodowy Bank Polski, Education & Publishing Department; 2017

[37] Micallef B. The Process of Economic Convergence in Malta and in the European Union. Central Bank of Malta Policy Note. Valletta: Central Bank of Malta; 2017

[38] Zuk P, Savelin L. Occasional Paper Series. Real Convergence in Central, Eastern, and South-eastern Europe. European Central Bank: 212; 2018

[39] Del Negro M, Schorfheide F. Chapter 7: Bayesian Macroeconometrics. In: Handbook of Bayesian Econometrics. Oxford: Oxford University Press; 2011. pp. 293-387

[40] The Heritage Foundation. Economic Freedom [Internet]. 2020. Available from: https://www.heritage.org [Accessed: 13 January 2020]

[41] Zivot E, Wang J. Vector autoregressive models for multivariate time series. In: Modelling Financial Time Series with S-PLUS. Berlin, Heidelberg: Springer Science; 2006. pp. 385-429

[42] Sims Ch A. Macroeconomics and reality. Econometrica. 1980;**48**(1):1-48

Chapter 13

Effects of Some Monetary Variables on Fixed Investment in Selected Sub-Saharan African Countries

Ombeswa Ralarala and Thobeka Ncanywa

Abstract

Monetary variables are not only important for the attainment of stable inflation but also for exercising influences in various ways on the behavior of the real economy, including the level of investment activity. Investment is very crucial in improving a country's productivity and growth and increasing its competitiveness in the long run. The study aims to investigate how monetary variables such as lending rates, exchange rate, and money supply affect investment actions in some selected Sub-Saharan African countries in the period 1980–2018. Using the panel autoregressive distributive lag method in the long run, a negative and significant relationship between lending rates and investment was discovered. Also, investment is positively related to both money supply and exchange rate in the long run. It is recommended that when central banks take contractionary measures, they must always consider the resulting change in investment as it is an essential part of aggregate demand. In a sluggish economy, interest rates should not be raised to the point where investment is discouraged and assets are suppressed.

Keywords: lending rates, exchange rate, money supply, investment, sub-Saharan Africa, panel autoregressive distributive lag

1. Introduction

The linkage between the monetary sector and the real sector plays a huge role in addressing the ills of economies such as achieving the price stability goal of the country's monetary policy, boosting economic growth, and reducing unemployment among the others [1]. Understanding the link between these sectors is important for the general economies, policymakers, and even households. For example, the use of both monetary and fiscal policy affects interest rates and has been seen after the global financial crisis that developed economies reduced interest rates until short-term rates were almost zero as a way to ease monetary policy. This led to household borrowing more than they could afford and suddenly, most households were indebted [2]. Thus, the demand side of many of the world's largest economies was affected to the point that the International Monetary Fund (IMF) and the World Bank downgraded their economic growth forecasts twice during 2008, mid-year [3]. Monetary variables are not only important for price stability only but also for influencing in various ways in the real economy, especially improving the level of investment activity [1].

Investment is very crucial in improving a country's productivity, growth and increasing its competitiveness in the long-run. To find the benefits of linking the monetary and real sector, it is imperative to investigate how monetary variables such as the lending rates, exchange rate and money supply can affect investment actions (a real sector variable). The investigation is conducted in a panel set-up of some selected Sub-Saharan African (SSA) countries such as Kenya, Mozambique, Nigeria, South Africa and Tanzania. The countries and study period are selected on the data availability basis. In Sub-Saharan Africa, there is limited literature addressing the linkage between the two sectors, as most studies stick to the relationship between variables of the same sector [4–6].

In the economic literature, one of the measures of investment activities is the gross fixed capital formation (GFCF) representing a total increase in fixed capital and is crucial to the economy because it builds an important part in gross domestic product. GFCF has always been identified as an important factor and an enhancer of economic growth in Sub-Saharan African countries [7–9]. It has three main components namely GFCF general government sector, GFCF private sector and GFCF public sector [10]. The GFCF government sector comprises of investment by the state; GFCF private sector includes investment by private enterprises; while GFCF public sector involves investment by public enterprises [11]. Ali [10] argues that because private investment is less associated with corruption, it has a more favorable effect on economic growth in comparison to public investment. Therefore, the investment needs to be handled carefully in that there are monetary policy instruments that assist in boosting investment, especially private investment. That is one of the reasons that a country's monetary policy should be designed in a manner that attracts investors. For example, in South Africa, business confidence and investment are mutually reinforcing, implying that for investment to take place business owners as investors must have the confidence to invest looking at policies adopted by the country and at the performance of the economy [12].

Business confidence is one of the factors that can contribute in boosting the economy in the sense that, owners have confidence and are certain about their growth and thus hire more staff, leading to increased employment and investment. However, it is distressing when Ndikumana [13] mentions that more than 30 of SSA countries experienced a decline in investment activities since the beginning of the 1980s. This has brought some concerns as an investment is a major enhancer of economic growth. For example, the Nigeria Bureau Statistics [14] report a yearly decline Nigeria's GCFC at the beginning of 2014. In the middle of 2015, Nigeria experienced negative growth in real terms which was for the first time since 2013 [13]. Changes in GCFC are regarded as a sign of economic incompetence. Thus, identifying how and to what extent monetary variables affect GCFC is of critical importance. This is because monetary variables are not only important for the attainment of stable inflation but also for exercising influences in various ways on the behavior of the real economy, including the level of investment activity.

The three monetary variables (exchange rates, money supply, and lending rates) selected for this study are crucial to explaining the link in the monetary-real sector nexus. The exchange rate is defined as a price relation of a country's currency to another country [14]. Its importance lies in the fact that they affect the relative prices of both the domestic and foreign countries. It is known that an appreciation in a country's currency leads to its goods abroad more expensive, and foreign goods in that country become cheaper, ceteris paribus [9]. Sub-Saharan African economies have at some point experienced appreciation in their currencies due to factors such as decreased trade barriers, decreased productivity and a rise in their price levels.

The following are the trends of the currencies in selected countries against the United States dollar; the Nigerian Naira has been reported to have reached an all-time high of 380 in March of 2020 [13]. The drop on oil prices in Nigeria put pressure on the monetary authorities to devalue the Naira to protect foreign exchange reserves. The Kenyan Shilling reached an all-time high of 106.80 in October of 2011, which might be due to the 2011 terrorist attacks in Kenya [15]. The Mozambique Metical reached an all-time high of 81.50 in October of 2016. The International Monetary Fund (IMF) discover that Mozambique has hidden some loans in three state-owned companies and this resulted in the IMF stopping its support [15]. Due to the declaration of a lockdown in South Africa as a way of preventing Corona Virus disease 2019 (COVID-19), the South African Rand reached an all-time high of 19.35 in April of 2020 [16].

One of the ways used by central banks to control the money supply is through the required reserves the banks ought to keep. For example, in South Africa, the South African Reserve Bank requires commercial banks to keep 2% of their total liabilities; the Bank of Ghana requires 10%; the Central bank of Kenya requires 5.25% and the Bank of Tanzania 7% [15, 16]. Reserve ratios in SSA have been accelerating since the mid-1990s and are quite high. In many SSA countries, the cash reserve requirements are accompanied by a liquid asset requirement (LAR) to finance the costs of deficits in banks. It should be noted that when central banks undertake policy decisions, expected inflation plays a huge role than the current rate of inflation. Inflation forecasting can be considered a comparative advantage of a central bank as it maintains information about the state of the economy over the public [17].

It had been argued that higher lending rates distort a country's level of investment, reduce the rate of economic growth and are an obstacle to smooth transmission of monetary policy impulse [18, 19]. Altman et al. [20] support this argument by adding that in response to a country's high lending rates, foreign investors reduce their investments. This is because consumer and business confidence in taking out risky investments is discouraged. Therefore, maintaining lower levels of lending rates will improve a country's investment levels. Comparing lending rates with an investment of 2008 in the selected countries, it can be seen in **Figure 1** that Mozambique is the only country that had lending rates exceeding gross fixed capital formation in 2008. Kenya, Nigeria and South Africa all have gross fixed capital formation levels higher than lending rates. In SSA, generally, this can be due to the stock of bank credit to the private sector that remains very low [21]. Several studies suggest that among others, monetary policy actions and macroeconomic uncertainty constrain bank lending rates [21–23].

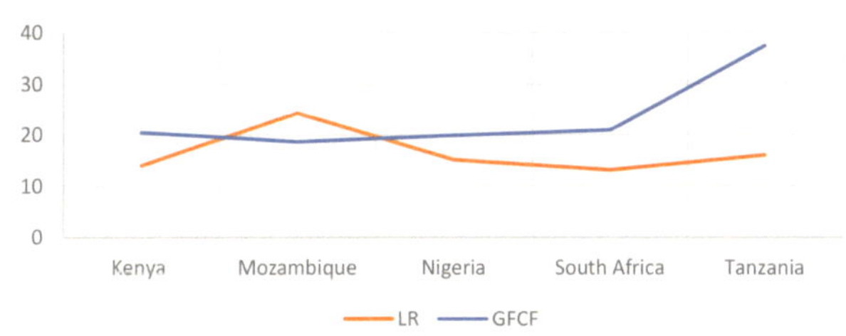

Figure 1.
Gross fixed capital formation (GFCF)-lending rate nexus, 2008.

2. Literature review

2.1 Theoretical literature

The effects of monetary policy variables on investment are based on the Keynesian theory of investment. The theory was developed by Keynes [24] who state that investment decisions are determined by a conducive environment for the investor and a long run survival behavior of an investor. For this to happen the investor need to consider the accumulation of capital which is influenced by lending rates [25–27]. The longer the investor survive in business, the more the economy can grow [26].

Keynes theory of investment further compares the marginal efficiency of capital (MEC) with interest rates [26, 28, 29]. If the MEC exceeds the rates, the investment will be increased. But because the production process demands the use of more and more capital, the MEC will suddenly fall. Once the MEC equals to the level of interest rate, there will not be any additional investments on income-earning assets. Additionally, Duesenberry [28] developed the financial theory of investment which assumes that there is a relationship between the cost of capital and interest rates.

The Keynesian theory of investment can be extended to include the effects of all the selected monetary variables on investment. For instance, according to Nucci and Pozzolo [30], investment is a function of the cost of capital and exchange rate. Also in Amiti and Weinstein [31] investment can be determined by money supply through bank supplies.

2.2 Empirical literature

It is vital to investigate the influence of monetary variables on investment activities as an investment is an important economic resource needed for economic growth. Literature suggests that monetary variables such as exchange rate do affect investment levels of a country in several setups. For instance, Osemene and Arotiba [32] advocate for a stable exchange rate environment to have positive effects of volatile exchange rate on foreign portfolio investment. Therefore, it can be argued that monetary authorities should formulate policies that result in a stable exchange rate as a way of boosting investors' confidence. These findings are enforced in Teddy [33] that a high volatile (highly unstable) exchange rate in Zambia harmed private capital inflows.

There are several conditions found in the literature on how the exchange rate can affect investment. These conditions vary depending on the developing state of the country. In Harchaoui, Harchaoui et al. [34], the exchange rate can influence investment through three channels: domestic and foreign demand, prices of variable inputs and the investment price. When a domestic currency depreciates, sales of goods and services yield higher revenues and profits. At the same time, the variable cost and imported capital increase to counterbalance the positive effects of higher revenues [34, 35]. This is because revenue from both domestic and foreign sales is increased. Nucci and Pozzolo [30] supported this argument when they investigated the exchange rate- investment nexus for some selected Italian manufacturing firms. The authors discovered that exchange rate depreciation impacts investment positively through revenue channel and negatively through the cost channel, and added that businesses need monopoly power to achieve this relationship.

The most important factors deliberated in the literature about what can cause positive effects of exchange rate on investment are stable exchange rate, monopoly power, the openness of trade, amount of imported inputs and developing level of a country [32, 34, 36, 37]. For instance, Atella et al. [36] emphasized that for a country's investment level to benefit from the exchange rate, the exchange rate has to be stable. Therefore it can be argued stable exchange rate can benefit any economic system through investment and profits due to its ability to strength firm market power. Servén [37] found a negative relationship between real exchange rate and investment in a highly open and less developed country scenario. This enlightens reasons why African countries depreciation of exchange rate would reduce investments as they use a lot of imported inputs with high variable input price. This explains why a country can benefit from its investment under stable exchange rates with high market power.

Money supply shocks can have differentiated effects on the real economy in several ways including investment. For example, Amiti and Weistein [31] found that money supply in bank loan can significantly determine investment activities, though there was a negative relationship. To identify the causal effect of money on the real economy, Brzezinski et al. [38] noted that reducing money supply can decrease real output. The study made use of local projections and autoregressive models to discover that clean identification requires that the money shock is not correlated with other shocks either contemporaneously, or across time. Karras and Stokes [39] also found a positive relationship in the money supply investment nexus and argued that investment is governed by asymmetries in money supply shocks which are similar to the ones that affect output.

Many studies established a positive relationship between money supply shocks and investment activities [31, 40, 41]. It is noted that the use of the money supply channel more financial markets and works well to positively influence investments where there are developed financial institutions [40]. Chen et al. [42] indicated that an increase in the money supply would increase money demand. This implies that the money supply can be one of the predictors of investment activities [42]. However, Gertler and Grinos [43] have the opposite that reducing money supply can enhance investment.

The relationship between lending rates (interest rates) and investment is widely understood in the macroeconomic sphere because the interest rate is one of the prospective determinants of investment [44–48]. It has been established in the literature that high-interest rates stimulate savings but harm investment especially of small businesses [44, 49–51]. The reasons for these harmful effects are because high-interest rates increase capital cost, and thus discourage investment [44]. Another view from Malawi and Bader [44] is that in less developed financial institutions private investment is inhibited by savings. Those are the instances where there is a positive relationship between the interest rate and investment.

Li and Khurshid [45] used the vector error correction model to investigate the effects of interest rate on investment in a Chinese province named Jiangsu. The study observed that in Jiangsu, interest rate and investment are positively related only in the short-run and negatively related in the long-run. It should be noted that some scholars believe that interest rates and investment have a one-way relationship. Onwumere et al. [46] revealed that, for Nigeria, the interest rate had a negative significant impact on investment for the period 1976 to 1999. In support of these findings, Muhammad et al. [47] also found that investment has an inverse association with the real interest rate in Pakistan for the period 1964 to 2012. Hyder and Ahmed [48] investigated the reasons for the fall of private investment in Pakistan. Their study concluded that a rise in the real interest rate causes a reduction in private investment.

3. Methodology

To analyze the effects of monetary variables on investment in the selected Sub-Saharan African countries (Kenya, Mozambique, Nigeria, South Africa and

Tanzania), the study used panel annual data collected from the World Bank. The study period 1980–2019 and countries are selected due to obtainability of data, the chosen variables are based on the Keynesian theory of investment and some reviewed empirical literature [25, 30, 31]. The selected three monetary variables are money supply, lending rates, and exchange rate and investment is measured by gross fixed capital formation as stipulated in the following equation:

$$GFCF_{it} = \alpha + \beta_1 MS_{it} + \beta_2 LR_{it} + \beta_3 ER_{it} + \mu_{it} \quad (1)$$

where GFCF measures gross fixed capital formation (investment); MS measures money supply; LR measures lending rates and ER measures exchange rates; α measures the constant of the model; β_{1-3} measures the estimates of monetary policy variables, and μ the error term to make the model more accurate and cater for any input variable omissions.

This study employs a panel analysis that is more time-series than cross-sectional. The first step is to check for stationarity of variables as it is the common characteristics in time series dominated analysis [52, 53]. To test for stationarity, three tests were used to ensure the inexistence of unit root in the study data namely Levin-Lin-Chu (LLC) test, the Im-Pesaran-Shin (IPS) test and the Fisher-ADF. The LLC test allows for heterogeneity in the intercept terms, the IPS and the Fischer are less restrictive as they allow coefficients to be heterogeneous [54, 55]. The Fischer outperforms the IPS when it comes to the size-adjusted power [56]. Therefore, all the tests are used to reinforce each other and allow us to make robust decisions about which panel type to use for the analysis. If there are different orders of integration, an autoregressive panel is eligible [52, 57].

Panel cointegration is useful to determine if there are long term effects between investment and the monetary variables. Additionally, panel cointegration can address issues of heterogeneity in the panel by looking at the parameters, how many cointegrating relationships across countries and if there is cointegration in different countries [57, 58]. For the cointegration exercise, the Pedroni, Kao and Johansen-Fisher tests are employed [52, 57]. The Pedroni consider four-panel statistics and three group panel statistics to test the presence of cointegration [59]. The advantage for the within-dimension-based four panels is to identify a first-order autoregressive process which is assumed to be the same in all countries in the series, and the three group panels are between-dimension-based and allow for parameters to vary across countries [59]. The Kao test reinforces the Pedroni as it uses the same approach but differs by specifying country-specific intercepts and homogeneous estimates on the first stage regressors. The Fischer combines individual cross-sections and gives results of the full panel [57, 60].

After the realization that there is cointegration (long-run relationship) and variables are integrated at different orders, a panel autoregressive distributed lag (ARDL) model is employed. The ARDL regression is necessary to find the nature of coefficients, whether the negative or positive relationship and significant or not. If variables show different orders of integration in the unit root analysis and cointegration exist, then the ARDL is the best estimator to find short-run, long-run and error correction estimates in a single model [59, 60]. In this model, the error correction term can be determined by integration of short-run adjustments with long-run equilibrium maintaining the long-run information. The advantage of having a large panel ARDL starting from 1980 to 2019 is to address the bias problem caused by correlating error terms with the mean-differenced regressors. The cointegrating form of the ARDL model called the pooled mean group estimator permits estimates to differ across sections [53].

4. Results and discussions

Brooks [61] emphasizes that variables should be free from a unit root to avoid spurious regression, therefore this study needed to difference the variables to attain stationary variables. **Table 1** provides panel stationarity tests as estimated using three stationarity test, LLC; IPS; and Fisher ADF.

Variable	Test	Test equation	Level p-value	1st order p-value
GFCF	LLC	I&I	0.0011	—
		II&T	0.0350	—
		None	0.0155	—
	IPS	I&I	0.0116	—
		II&T	0.0491	—
	Fisher-ADF	I&I	0.0124	—
		II&T	0.0304	—
		None	0.0342	—
MS	LLC	I&I	0.0138	—
		II&T	0.0000	—
		None	0.7522	0.0000
	IPS	I&I	0.0000	—
		II&T	0.0000	—
	Fisher-ADF	I&I	0.0000	—
		II&T	0.0000	—
		None	0.0000	—
ER	LLC	I&I	0.9968	0.0000
		II&T	0.1617	0.0000
		None	0.9999	0.0000
	IPS	I&I	1.0000	0.0000
		II&T	0.3255	0.0000
	Fisher-ADF	I&I	0.9999	0.0000
		II&T	0.3980	0.0000
		None	1.0000	0.0000
LR	LLC	I&I	0.4142	0.0000
		II&T	0.0376	—
		None	0.3539	0.0000
	IPS	I&I	0.3366	0.0000
		II&T	0.0967	0.0000
	Fisher-ADF	I&I	0.2363	0.0000
		II&T	0.0567	0.0000
		None	0.8643	0.0000

I&I: individual and intercept; II&T: individual, intercept, and trend.

Table 1.
Summary of panel unit root test results.

In **Table 1** gross fixed capital formation (GFCF) and money supply (MS) are generally shown to be integrated at levels I(0), while exchange rates (ER) and lending rates (LR) are integrated of order one I(1). Therefore, the variables used in the study are a mixture of I(0) and I(1) and none of them is I(2) which paves a way to run the panel ARDL [52, 60]. It is stated in Nkoro and Uko [60] that variables that show different orders of integration can be estimated best with ARDL. Moreover, cointegration results indicate the existence of a long-run relationship but do not give estimates, hence in addition to the cointegration analysis, there is a need for a robust estimation technique like ARDL.

Tables 2–4 provide results of panel cointegration tests as estimated for the model specified in Eq. 1 under the Pedroni, Kao and Fisher-ADF tests for cointegration, respectively.

The Pedroni test results presented in **Table 2** confirm cointegration in three out of seven statistics. One out of four within dimensions accept the alternative hypothesis of cointegration at 10% significance levels (Panel v-Statistics) whereas two out of three between dimensions accept the alternative hypothesis of cointegration at 1% significance level (Group PP- statistics and Group ADF statistics). The Kao panel cointegration tests results, as shown in **Table 3** also confirm cointegration by rejecting a null hypothesis of no cointegration at 1% level of significance. **Table 4** illustrates a strong cointegration between the variables in the Fisher-ADF test. This is displayed by both the trace and the max Eigenvalues which both detect at least two cointegrated relationships between investment and the selected independent variables. All three cointegration tests reveal that a long-run relationship exists between the variables for the selected panel. This implies that investment has a long-run relationship with the selected monetary variables in the chosen panel of five Sub-Saharan countries. **Table 5** provides estimates of the model specified in Eq. 1, where investments are regressed against monetary variables such as lending rates, money supply and exchange rate.

Panel	**T-statistics**	**P-value**
v-Statistic	1.316356*	0.0940
rho-Statistic	0.863098	0.8060
PP-Statistic	−0.312544	0.3773
ADF Statistic	−0.132706	0.4472
Group	**T-statistics**	**P-value**
rho-Statistic	0.350217	0.6369
PP-Statistic	-2.365533***	0.0090
ADF-Statistic	-2.938605***	0.0006

* *and* *** *indicate that the p-values are significant at 10 and 1% level of significance, respectively.*

Table 2.
Summary of Pedroni cointegration test results.

Variable	**T-statistics**	**P-value**
ADF	-2.77887***	0.0027
Residual variance	26.11567	
HAC variance	21.89175	

*** *indicates that the p-values are significant at 1% level of significance.*

Table 3.
Summary of Kao panel cointegration test results.

Table 5 shows the summary of panel ARDL long-run and short-run results. As depicted in **Table 5**, lending rates, money supply and exchange rates all have a strong long-run relationship significant at 1% level with investment. Lending rates, as economic theory suggests, have been found to have a negative relationship with investment in this study [25, 44, 51]. The results are found to be in line with those of Malawi and Bader [44] and Ashraf et al. [50] where an increase in the real interest rate by 1% reduces the investment. It has been found that interest rate plays an important role in investment decision making.

It turns out that the money supply is positively related to investment for our selected panel (**Table 5**). According to the results, when the money supply is increased, a relative increase in investment follows. Many scholars established that money supply has a positive long-run relationship with investment [38, 42, 62]. On the contrary, it has been discovered that there may exist a negative relationship between money supply and investment [31, 40, 43]. Li and Yang [40] further add that money supply is a weak instrument to be used to influence real estate investment in an inflation targeting environment.

The exchange rate also shows a significant and positive long-run relationship with investment in **Table 5**. It has been argued in the literature review section that a country's investment level can benefit from the exchange rate, provided exchange rate is stable [25, 30, 34, 36]. The argument is based on the fact that a depreciating exchange rate is associated with a stable environment and strong market power [36].

Hypothesized no. of CE(s)	Fisher stat. (from trace test)	P-value	Fisher stat. (from max-Eigen test)	P-value
None	75.81***	0.0000	47.55***	0.0000
At most 1	15.57**	0.0490	15.96**	0.0429
At most 2	7.841	0.4492	6.332	0.6101
At most 3	9.222	0.3239	9.222	0.3239

*** and *** indicate that the p-values are significant at 5% and 1% level of significance, respectively.*

Table 4.
Summary of Johansen-Fisher panel cointegration test results.

Variables	Coefficient	Std. Error	t-Statistic	P-value
Long run estimates				
Lending rates	-3.523144	0.677454	-5.200565***	0.0000
Money supply	18.87173	2.946935	6.403849***	0.0000
Exchange rates	0.012514	0.001282	9.763669***	0.0000
Short-run estimates				
Error correction term	-0.834634	0.371897	-2.244262**	0.0274
D(Investment)	0.133988	0.370028	0.362103	0.7182
D(Lending rates)	10.51841	3.009819	3.494700***	0.0008
D(Money supply)	14.16886	24.00636	0.590213	0.5566
D(Exchange rates)	0.019939	0.111209	0.179291	0.8581

***, and *** indicate that the p-values are significant at 5% and 1% level of significance, respectively.*

Table 5.
Summary of long-run and short-run panel ARDL estimates.

Market power effects tend to offset the volatility nature of exchange rate, hence it can positively affect investments.

The panel ARDL results in **Table 5** confirm that lending rates are positively related to investment in the short run at a 1% level of significance. Money supply and exchange rate, on the other hand, showed no significant short-run relationship with investment (**Table** 5). Most importantly, the error correction term met the requirement of being negative and is very high at 83% and significant at 5% level. This implies that investment will be very fast to go back to equilibrium following a change in the selected monetary variables. These results are valid and reliable as mentioned in Nkoro and Uko [60] that panel ADRL has Gaussian error terms implying normal distribution, no autocorrelation and no heteroscedasticity in error terms.

5. Conclusions and recommendations

The study investigated the effects of lending rates, money supply, and exchange rate on investment activities in selected Sub-Saharan African countries for the period of 1980–2018 using panel ARDL. To test for stationarity, Levin-Lin-Chu (LLC), the Im-Pesaran-Shin (IPS), and the Fisher-ADF tests were used, and variables were found to be integrated differently with a mixture of I(0) and I(1). Pedroni, Kao, and Johansen-Fisher tests for cointegration proved that all three monetary variables were cointegrated with investment and therefore have a long-run relationship.

The ARDL long-run results revealed a negative and significant relationship between lending rates and investment. Additionally, investment is positively related to both money supply and exchange rate in the long run. It can be concluded that the Sub-Saharan African region need to maintain low lending rates, increase the money supply, and keep a stable exchange rate to influence investments, which will ultimately affect the growth of the economy.

The study recommends that when central banks take contractionary measures, they should consider the resulting change in investment as it a crucial part of economic growth. For example, when an economy is sluggish, interest rates must not be raised to the point where investment is discouraged and assets are suppressed. The study concludes the role played by monetary variables on investment activities that there is a strong link between the monetary sector and the real sector.

Conflict of interest

We, as authors, declare that there is no conflict of interest concerning this study.

Author details

Ombeswa Ralarala and Thobeka Ncanywa*
Department of Economics, University of Limpopo, Sovenga, South Africa

*Address all correspondence to: thobeka.ncanywa@ul.ac.za

References

[1] Mishkin FS. Exchange Rate Pass-through and Monetary Policy. National Massachusetts, Cambridge, MA: Bureau of Economic Research; 9 May 2008

[2] Cardak BA, Martin VL. Once in a lifetime? The effects of the global financial crisis on household willingness to take financial risk. The Economic Record. 2019;**95**(311):442-461

[3] Walter S. Globalization and the demand-side of politics: How globalization shapes labour market risk perceptions and policy preferences. Political Science Research and Methods. 2017;**5**(1):55-80

[4] Kagochi J. Inflation and financial sector development in sub-Saharan African countries. Journal of Economic Studies. 2019;**46**(4):798-811

[5] Ibrahim M, Alagidede P. Financial sector development, economic volatility and shocks in sub-Saharan Africa. Physica A: Statistical Mechanics and its Applications. 2017;**484**:66-81

[6] Hartmann D, Guevara MR, Jara-Figueroa C, Aristarán M, Hidalgo CA. Linkingeconomiccomplexity,institutions, and income inequality. World Development. 2017;**93**:75-93

[7] Uneze E. The relation between capital formation and economic growth: Evidence from sub-Saharan African countries. Journal of Economic Policy Reform. 2013;**16**(3):272-286

[8] Ncanywa T, Makhenyane L. Can investment activities in the form of capital formation influence economic growth in South Africa? In: SAAPAM Limpopo Chapter 5th Annual Conference Proceedings; October 2016; Mokopane. 2016. pp. 270-279

[9] Ajose K, Oyedokun GE. Capital formation and economic growth in Nigeria. Accounting and Taxation Review. 2018;**2**(2):131-142

[10] Ali G. Gross fixed capital formation & economic growth of Pakistan. Journal of Research in Humanities, Arts and Literature Applied. 2015;**1**(2):21-30

[11] Ugochukwu US, Chinyere UP. The impact of capital formation on the growth of the Nigerian economy. Research Journal of Finance and Accounting. 2013;**4**(9):36-42

[12] Deloitte R. Closing the Infrastructure Gap: The Role of Public-Private Partnerships. London: Deloitte Development LLP; 2006

[13] Ndikumana L. Capital Flows, Capital Account Regimes, and Foreign Exchange rate regimes in Africa. Political Economy Research Institute. University of Massachusetts Amherst; 2003

[14] Nigerian Bureau of Statistics. Macro-Economic Data in Nigeria. Nigeria: NBS; 2013

[15] International Monetary Fund [IMF] [Internet]. 2020. Available from: http://www.imf.org [Accessed: 09 April 2020]

[16] South African Reserve Bank [SARB] [Internet]. 2020. Available from: http://www.resbank.co.za [Accessed: 14 February 2020]

[17] Narayan PK, Narayan S, Prasad AD. Modelling the Relationship between Budget Deficits, Money Supply and Inflation in Fiji. Pacific Economic Bulletin. Griffith University. 2019

[18] Mansour M, Sghaier A, Bannour B, Jabeur S. The interactions between the lending rates, deposit rates and money market rates. Iranian Economic Review. 2019;**23**(1):163-189

[19] Montiel PJ. Policies and Economic Growth: Theory, Evidence and Country-Specific Experience from Sub-Saharan Africa. Financial Nairobi, KE: African Economic Research Consortium; 1995

[20] Altman EI, Gande A, Saunders A. Bank debt versus bond debt: Evidence from secondary market prices. Journal of Money, Credit and Banking. 2010;**42**(4):755-767

[21] Amidu M. What influences banks' lending in sub-Saharan Africa? Journal of Emerging Market Finance. 2014;**13**(1):1-42

[22] Dymski GA. "New Markets" or old constraints? Financing community development in the post-"War on Poverty" era. In: National Economic Association Conference; 2 January 2005; Philadelphia

[23] VanHoose DD. Bank capital regulation, economic stability, and monetary policy: What does the academic literature tell us? Atlantic Economic Journal. 2008;**36**(1):1-4

[24] Keynes JM. The General Theory of Interest, Employment and Money. London: MacMillan; 1936

[25] Chick V. Keynes's theory of investment and necessary compromise. In: Dow SC, Hillard J, editors. Keynes, Uncertainty and the Global Economy: Beyond Keynes. Vol. 2. 2002. pp. 55-67

[26] Gordon MJ. The neoclassical and a post-Keynesian theory of investment. Journal of Post Keynesian Economics. 1992;**14**(4):425-443

[27] Crotty JR. Neoclassical and Keynesian approaches to the theory of investment. Journal of Post Keynesian Economics. 1992;**14**(4):483-496

[28] Duesenberry JS. Business Cycles and Economic Growth. San Francisco: University of Michigan Press; 1958

[29] Modigliani F, Miller MH. The cost of capital, corporation finance and the theory of investment. The American Economic Review. 1958;**48**(3):261-297

[30] Nucci F, Pozzolo AF. Investment and the exchange rate: An analysis with firm-level panel data. European Economic Review. 2001;**45**(2):259-283

[31] Amiti M, Weinstein DE. How Much Do Bank Shocks Affect Investment? Evidence from Matched Bank-Firm loan data. Journal of Political Economy. 1 Apr 2018;**126**(2):525-587

[32] Omorokunwa OG, Ikponmwosa N. Exchange rate volatility and foreign private investment in Nigeria. Asian Journal of Business Management. 15 Oct 2014;**6**(4):146-154

[33] Teddy KF. The effect of exchange rate volatility on private inflows in Zambia [Master's dissertation]. Lusaka: Department of Economics University of Zambia; 2015

[34] Harchaoui TM, Tarkhani F, Yuen T. The Effects of the Exchange Rate on Investment: Evidence from Canadian Manufacturing Industries. Ottawa, ON: Bank of Canada; 2005

[35] Campa JM, Goldberg LS. Investment, pass-through, and exchange rates: A cross-country comparison. International Economic Review. 1999;**40**(2):287-314

[36] Atella V, Atzeni GE, Belvisi PL. Investment and exchange rate uncertainty. Journal of Policy Modeling. 2003;**25**(8):811-824

[37] Servén L. Real-exchange-rate uncertainty and private investment in LDCs. The Review of Economics and Statistics. 2003;**85**(1):212-218

[38] Brzezinski A, Chen Y, Palma NP, Ward F. The Vagaries of the Sea: Evidence on the Real Effects of Money

from Maritime Disasters in the Spanish Empire. London: Centre for Economic Policy Research; 2019

[39] Karras G, Stokes HH. Why are the effects of money-supply shocks asymmetric? Evidence from prices, consumption, and investment. Journal of Macroeconomics. 1999;**21**(4):713-727

[40] Li YJ, Yang Y. The effect of interest rate and money supply impose on real estate investment in China: An empirical analysis. Journal of Xi'an Institute of Finance and Economics. 2005;**18**(5):47-51

[41] Moore BJ. How credit drives the money supply: The significance of institutional developments. Journal of Economic Issues. 1986;**20**(2):443-452

[42] Chen MC, Chang CO, Yang CY, Hsieh BM. Investment demand and housing prices in an emerging economy. Journal of Real Estate Research. 2012 Jan 1;**34**(3):345-373

[43] Gertler M, Grinols E. Monetary randomness and investment. Journal of Monetary Economics. 1982;**10**(2):239-258

[44] Malawi AI, Bader M. The impact of interest rate on investment in Jordan: A cointegration analysis. Journal of King Abdulaziz University: Economics and Administration. 2010;**105**(3055):1-26

[45] Li S, Khurshid A. The effect of interest rate on investment; Empirical evidence of Jiangsu Province, China. Journal of International Studies. 2015;**8**(1):81-90

[46] Onwumere JU, Okore OA, Ibe IG. The impact of interest rate liberalization on savings and investment: Evidence from Nigeria. Research Journal of Finance and Accounting. 2012;**3**(10):130-136

[47] Muhammad SD, Lakhan GR, Zafar S, Noman M. Rate of interest and its impact on investment to the extent of Pakistan. Pakistan Journal of Commerce and Social Sciences (PJCSS). 2013;**7**(1):91-99

[48] Hyder K, Ahmed QM. Why Private Investment in Pakistan Has Collapsed and how it can be restored. Pakistan: Lahore Journal of Economics. 2003;**9**(1):107-128

[49] Badar M, Javid AY. Impact of macroeconomic forces on nonperforming loans: An empirical study of commercial banks in Pakistan. Transactions on Business and Economics. 2013;**10**(1):40-48

[50] Ashraf BN, Arshad S, Hu Y. Capital regulation and bank risk-taking behaviour: Evidence from Pakistan. International Journal of Financial Studies. 2016;**4**(3):16

[51] Moudud-Ul-Huq S, Ashraf BN, Gupta AD, Zheng C. Does bank diversification heterogeneously affect performance and risk-taking in ASEAN emerging economies? Research in International Business and Finance. 2018;**46**:342-362

[52] Ncanywa T, Mabusela K. Can financial development influence economic growth: The sub-Saharan analysis? Journal of Economic and Financial Sciences. 2019;**12**(1):1-3

[53] Pesaran MH. On the interpretation of panel unit root tests. Economics Letters. 2012;**116**(3):545-546

[54] Levin A, Lin CF, Chu CS. Unit root tests in panel data: Asymptotic and finite-sample properties. Journal of Econometrics. 2002;**108**(1):1-24

[55] Im KS, Pesaran MH, Shin Y. Testing for unit roots in heterogeneous panels. Journal of Econometrics. 2003;**115**(1):53-74

[56] Nell C, Zimmermann S. Panel unit root tests term paper [PhD course: Panel data]. Lecturer: Prof. Dr Robert Kunst.

Department of Economics at University of Vienna; 2011

[57] Maddala GS, Wu S. A comparative study of unit root tests with panel data and a new simple test. Oxford Bulletin of Economics and Statistics. 1999;**61**(S1):631-652

[58] Verbeek M. Pseudo-panels and repeated cross-sections. In: The Econometrics of Panel Data. Berlin, Heidelberg: Springer; 2008. pp. 369-383

[59] Ramirez MD. Are foreign and public capital productive in the Mexican case? A panel unit root and panel cointegration analysis. Eastern Economic Journal. 2010;**36**(1):70-87

[60] Nkoro E, Uko AK. Autoregressive distributed lag (ARDL) cointegration technique: Application and interpretation. Journal of Statistical and Econometric Methods. 2016;**5**(4):63-91

[61] Brooks C. Introductory Econometrics for Finance. 2a Upplagan. Cambridge: Cambridge University Press; 2008. ISBN-13. 2008:978-0

[62] Saarenheimo T. Credit Crunch Caused Investment Slump? An Empirical Analysis Using Finish Data. Finland: Bank of Findland Discussion Papers; 1995

Chapter 14

Will Malawi's Inflation Continue Declining?

Hopestone Kayiska Chavula

Abstract

The main objective of this chapter is to examine and determine the main factors that have driven inflation rate in Malawi since 2001, with a special focus on the period 2013–2019, during which inflation rate has continuously declined reaching 9% in 2019, from 36% in 2013. The chapter also tries to assess whether this decline will continue as per the performance of the underlying economic fundamentals both in the short- and the long-run. The study employs the autoregressive distributed lag (ARDL) model framework to examine the drivers of inflation both in the short- and the long-run using quarterly data, over the period of 2001–2019. The results reveal that reduction in headline inflation has mainly been driven by money supply growth, fiscal deficits, and output growth in the short-run, while only output has driven inflation decline in the long-run. The results also show that after floating exchange rate in 2012, inflation decline has mainly been driven by output growth despite inflationary pressures from the exchange rate and import prices. Model forecasts show that inflation may increase up to 19.4% by December 2020, if money supply growth, fiscal deficits, and exchange rate movements are not taken care of.

Keywords: monetary policy, ARDL, unit root, co-integration, forecasts

1. Introduction

Malawi is a small country located in the Southern part of Africa, with a surface area of 118,484 square kilometres, total length of 853 km and a maximum width of 257 km. It is a former British colony that gained independence in 1964. Its economy is mainly dependent on agriculture which employs about 65% of the workforce in the country, and contributing about 36% to the economy's gross domestic product (GDP). More than 90% of the country's export revenues come from the agriculture sector. The sector is one of the main contributors to the country's building of inflationary pressures as it occupies the largest proportion of the country's inflation basket designed by the country's National Statistical Office (NSO).

High inflation and fluctuation in prices is not preferred as it leads to uncertainty and cost push shocks which affect the stability and performance of economies [1]. This being the case, maintaining relatively low inflation and price stability has been one of the core objectives targeted by the monetary authorities in designing and implementing monetary policy in Malawi. Before 2012, Malawi operated a de facto pegged exchange rate regime with periodic devaluations. The national currency was pegged to the US dollar and kept an overvalued exchange rate. However, in 2012 Malawi implemented a floating exchange rate regime where prices and exchange

IntechOpen

rates move based on economic fundamentals [1]. During the same period, the country adopted an automatic fuel pricing mechanism, which together with the newly implemented floating exchange rate regime was aimed at addressing the country's balance of payments problems.

As has been the case with most developing countries in Africa, the main objective of the monetary policy in Malawi has been to achieve low and stable prices that preserve the value of the Kwacha (the local currency), and encourages investment needed to achieve sustainable economic growth and create employment as stipulated in the Reserve Bank of Malawi Act of 1989 [2]. This is because price stability enhances investors' confidence as it reduces uncertainty in an economy and, thereby creating a favorable environment for growth and employment creation. Furthermore, low inflation contributes to the protection of the purchasing power of all households, particularly the poor who have no means of defending themselves against continually rising prices. However, the implementation of such a broad mandate could be practically challenging, since some of the policy objectives could be in conflict with each other [3]. Nonetheless, monetary policy pursued by most developing countries has managed to bring down inflation over the past two decades, with significant growth being experienced in most countries in the past decade or so [4].

In Malawi, monetary policy implementation continues to be underpinned by inflation dynamics especially by the dominance of the agricultural sector activities and the country's reliance on donor funding which contributed about 40% of the country's budget before the "Cash-gate scandal"[1] which led to withdrawal of donor funding in 2013. With the economy's dependence on agriculture, inflation in Malawi normally improves with improved food availability and tobacco sales, mostly from April to September every year. It then accelerates with food scarcities and excessive demand for foreign exchange from October to March [5]. However, it is claimed that the country's monetary policy does not seek to address these dynamics but rather to achieve a balance between output growth and monetary aggregates as well as smoothening of exchange rate movements. With the belief that these inflation dynamics will improve over time as production structures respond to macroeconomic stability in the context of a market-determined exchange rate [2]).

Figure 1 shows that interest rates reached as high as 52% in 2000, mainly driven by increased deficit financing as the IMF stopped aid disbursements due to corruption concerns in December 2000, and many individual donors followed suit, resulting in an almost 80% drop in Malawi's development budget. The continued deficit financing led to an increase in liquidity in the economy, exerting pressure on both interest rates and domestic prices. Since then both interest rates and inflation declined significantly due to improved fiscal management and increased real growth, with interest rates, inflation, money supply and GDP growth averaging 24.3%, 10.9%, 1.9% and 6.3% respectively over the period 2005–2009.

However, since 2005, Malawi enjoyed price stability as inflation declined from 16% to 7.2% in March 2011. Overall, inflation remained moderate and in single digits since 2007, mainly due to a relentless adherence to a tight monetary policy, heavily buttressed by fiscal discipline and stable exchange rate up-to January 2012 when it jumped to 10.3% (**Figure 1**). However, inflation remained persistently high since 2012, mainly due to the country's switch from a fixed to a floating exchange rate regime, which led to a sharp depreciation of the exchange rate which was further exacerbated by the withdrawal of external budget support following the

[1] "Cashgate" is a financial scandal involving looting, theft and corruption that happened at Capital Hill the seat of Government of Malawi.

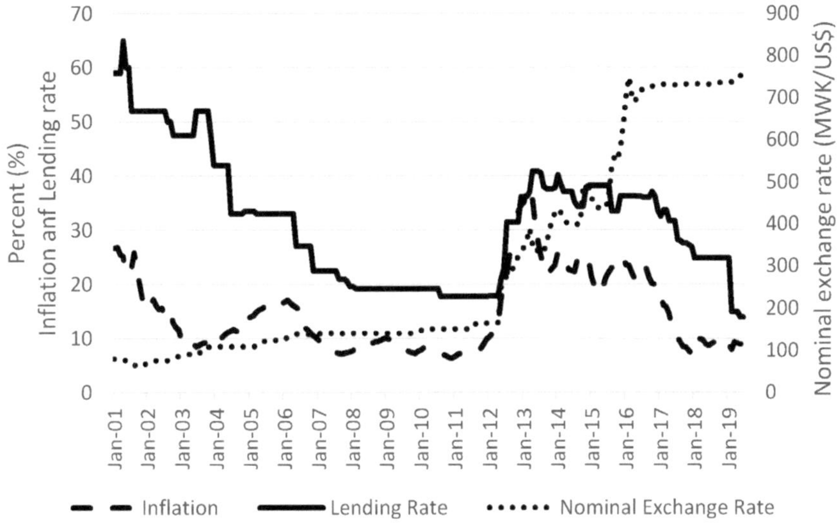

Figure 1.
Inflation, exchange rate and interest rate dynamics, January 2001–June 2019. Source: [6].

large scale theft of public funds coined the "cash-gate scandal". These developments exerted inflationary pressures in the economy, with inflation hovering to as high as 37.9% by February 2013, mainly driven by food prices, especially maize prices following poor agricultural performance and depreciation of the exchange rate [2]. Furthermore, financing of the fiscal deficits in the aftermath of the scandal was done through printing of money and the issuing of government securities to the private sector. In addition, the economy suffered from the effects of a combination of droughts and floods resulting in a reduction in agricultural production leading to a sharp increase in food inflation [1].

During this period, in May 2012, the exchange rate depreciated by 49% against the major currencies leading to a significant increase in inflation rate. As a consequence, interest rates increased to contain the inflationary pressures induced by the depreciation of the local currency, and also to contain inflationary expectations pressure accumulated over the preceding period. Furthermore, apart from the inflationary expectations arising from the continued uncertainty in the exchange rate policy, increasing food prices, especially maize prices, exacerbated the situation [2]. Inflation rates, interest rates and nominal exchange rates reached their highest levels over the period May 2012 to May 2013. Rising as high as 38%, 41% and 355 Kwacha per US/$ respectively, the highest levels after a long time. **Figure 1** shows that after this period both inflation and interest rates begun to decline, while the exchange rate continued to depreciate.

Continued exchange rate depreciation and relatively tight monetary policy have further resulted into inflationary pressures, exacerbated by the substantial increase in government domestic borrowing due to donor suspension of direct budget support to the Malawi Government due to the Cashgate scandal [2]. This raised domestic financing requirements by government, hence creating more liquidity in the economy. This also heightened pessimistic inflation expectations by the public and precipitated exchange rate depreciation. These developments led to an increase in money supply growth and inflation [2]. It should also be noted that despite the continued decline in the global oil prices during the period, its impact has not fully been translated into the Malawian economy because the automatic pricing mechanism on energy prices adopted since 2012 has not consistently been reflecting this decline [2]. Food prices especially maize during the harvesting seasons were also not significantly declining to have an impact on inflation during the period January 2013 to February 2016. However, inflation in Malawi has continued to decline since early 2013, declining by 29 percentage points from 36% in February 2013 down to 9% in June 2019 (**Figure 1**). This is despite the theoretical economic fundamentals behaving to the contrary as fiscal balances widened from −1.9% of GDP in 2011 to −7.2% in 2018; and the country switched from a de facto pegged exchange rate regime to a floating exchange rate regime, leading a 33% devaluation of the local currency in 2012. Authorities' adoption of the automatic fuel pricing mechanism during the period meant that fuel prices should reflect the recent increases in global fuel prices. However, on the contrary, money supply grew at an average of 1.6% between February 2013 and September 2019, while policy rate declined from 25% in 2013 to 13.5% in 2019, theoretically easing the inflationary pressures in the economy.

Since Wu [1], there has been no study (to the author's knowledge) that has looked at inflation dynamics in Malawi over the period 2000–2019 as carried out in this study. However, the most recent study by Wu [1] focused mainly on the period up to 2015, investigating mainly the effects of the exchange rate regime change in 2012 and the switch to an automatic fuel pricing mechanism. This study, however, focuses on a relatively much longer period investigating the factors behind inflation movements in Malawi noting that a number of policy and structural changes have taken place over the period 2000–2019, which might not have been fully captured by Wu [1]. Authorities claim that most of these policy and structural changes have contributed to the recent continuous decline in headline inflation in the country. The main objective of this chapter is therefore to examine the factors that have led to inflation movements in the Malawian economy with a special focus on the recent continuous decline, and assessing whether it is a reflection of the performance of the country's economic fundamentals and whether it is something that will persist in the short to medium term.

The rest of the chapter is organized as follows. The next presents a brief literature review of some previous studies in the area. Section 3 presents the methodology employed in the chapter, while Section 4 presents the results of the analysis and Section 5 concludes the chapter.

2. Literature review

A number of studies have looked at the effectiveness of monetary policy in Malawi or the effect of selected monetary policy variables on the economy, but very few (if any) have focuses on inflation in the past few years. For example, Wu [1] looked at the causal relationship between food and non-food inflation in Malawi before examining the exchange rate pass-through process to headline inflation and how it has evolved during the pre- and post-exchange rate regime change in 2012. The paper further investigates the possible drivers of headline inflation in Malawi over the period 2001–2015 [1]. However, the period 2012–2015 could not have offered longer enough time horizon for the exchange rate policy regime change implemented in 2012 to have had a significant impact on inflation. This study, with a much longer time span, covering the period 2012–2019, is expected to provide more insights on the impact of both structural and policy changes on inflation in the country. Ngalawa and Viegi [7] uses the structural vector autoregressive model to investigate the transmission mechanism through which monetary policy affects domestic prices and output growth in Malawi. The results of the study reveal that the bank rate remained a more effective measure of monetary policy than reserve money over the period of the study. The results also support the narrative that price stability remains the main objective of monetary policy in Malawi, despite revealing that monetary authorities also put emphasis on increasing economic growth and employment in the country. The results show also that the responses of exchange rate changes to monetary policy are stronger than those of consumer prices, suggesting that monetary factors may not be the dominant determinants of inflation in Malawi.

As is the case with Ngalawa and Viege [7], Mangani [8] examines the effectiveness of monetary policy in Malawi, but using bank rate and reserve money as measures of monetary policy stance, while using lending rate and broad money as intermediate targets. The results show that changes in the bank rate have an instantaneous impact on the lending rate and also the results reveal that the lending rate had an impact on changes in money supply. However, it was further observed that these effects were hardly transmitted to prices, indicating the ineffectiveness of the Keynesian interest rate view of the monetary policy transmission mechanism [8]. The results showed also that changes in exchange rate and money supply had a significant impact on prices, which is contrary to the classical view of the policy transmission mechanism, while the exchange rate itself was in turn affected by changes in money supply. Hence, it could be argued that the changes in consumer prices are more attributable to the exchange rate channel of the monetary policy transmission mechanism. However, further analysis shows that monetary policy played no role in the effects of the exchange rate movements on domestic prices over the period under study.

Jombo et al. [9] employs the augmented Phillips curve and vector autoregressive approaches to estimate the exchange rate pass-through to domestic inflation in Malawi over the period 1990–2013. The results show that exchange rate movements had a modest impact on domestic prices. However, it is argued that the dynamic exchange rate pass-through elasticity of 0.2 signifies that exchange rate still stood as a potential important source of inflation over the period of the study, hence the need for monetary authorities to pay attention to its movements. Mwabutwa et al. [10] uses the time varying parameter (TVP) VAR model with stochastic volatility that allows for the capturing of the variation of macroeconomic structure and changes in the transmission mechanism overtime, to examine the impact of bank rate, exchange rate and private credit shocks on output and price level. The model is used to simulate the impulse responses of output and price levels to financial and monetary policy shocks. The results reveal that by demarcating the analysis to focus on the period before and after financial reforms carried out between 1988 and 1994. The results indicate that changes in the transmission mechanism became clearer only after 2000, with monetary policy transmission performing in tandem with economic theory predictions without price surprises in the period after reforms especially after 2000, while it performed with price surprises in the period before the financial reforms carried out between 1988 and 1994. However, the results found a weak transmission mechanism through the credit channel especially through loans supply, calling for more financial strategies to improve the credit market system.

As per the results of other studies mentioned earlier, the findings from both Mangani [11] and Ngalawa [12] show that an increase in money supply leads to a decrease in price levels, which contradicts with the conventional monetary policy theory of inflation in Malawi, where an increase in money supply leads to an increase in price levels. In fact, in most of the periods an increase in money supply is associated with periods of falling inflation most of the times. In addition, and in line with the findings of Jombo et al. [9], these studies also reveal that while lending rate instantaneously responds to bank rate adjustments and though the lending rate somewhat influences money supply, the effects are hardly transmitted to prices. So they also observe that the Keynesian interest rate view of the monetary policy transmission mechanism does not apply to Malawi. Interest rates are found to affect inflation through the cost of production effect rather than through money supply effects. Also as is the case with Mangani [8] and Jombo et al. [9], these studies show that exchange rates have a much stronger effect on price levels in Malawi, reflecting the country's high level of openness and import dependence, making it highly vulnerable to foreign reserve situation due to the country's reliance on a narrow range of sources, most notably foreign aid and tobacco exports [13]. Matchaya [14] looks at the possible sources of inflation in Malawi and finds out that changes in money supply, exchange rates, past values of inflation, recessions and booms were the main determinants of inflation. These results are further supported by the findings from Simwaka et al. [15] where the results indicate that monetary and supply side factors drove inflation in Malawi over the period January 1995–March 2011. The study finds that money supply growth, exchange rate adjustments and decreases in output growth had a significant positive impact on inflation over the period. This result is also supported by Lungu et al. [16] which found that output gap has a negative impact on inflation over the period to some extent signifying the dominance of food prices in the consumer price index in Malawi.

3. Methodology

3.1 Model specification and estimation techniques

The main purpose of this chapter is to examine the drivers of inflation the Malawian economy, with a special focus on its recent continuous decline since 2013, and also to assess whether this decline is a reflection of the economic fundamentals performance and whether this decline will persist in the short- to medium-term.

It makes use of the Phillips curve (aggregate supply) or a price-setting model that evaluates the effect of past and expected inflation, fiscal deficits, import prices, output gap (measured as output relative to its potential output[2]) and exchange rate to capture the external effects of an open economy. Furthermore, the proposed model encompasses both the monetarists' and the structuralists' approach in determining factors that affect inflation, for instance the conventional output gap term is included to capture the rigidity of the labor market [17]. An increase in output will lead to a rise in labor demand as firms will need to hire more workers to further expand production. This increase in labor demand will lead to an increase in inflation as real wages and marginal costs rise. However, if labor supply is highly elastic, then the rise in real wages will be small, marginal cost will not rise significantly, and inflation will not move a lot in response to changes in output gap [18]. The model also takes into consideration full and immediate pass-through of imported prices (and hence exchange rate changes) into consumption prices. The exchange rate reflects the price effects of exchange rate changes on imported goods in the consumption basket which is common in small open economies like that of Malawi.

With reference to the effects of changes in money supply, literature reveals that one of the basic tenets of the quantity theory of money is that a change in the growth rate of money induces an equal change in the rate of price inflation [19]. Since nominal interest rates are based on real return and the expected rate of inflation, it suggests that the level of nominal interest rates should be positively correlated with average rates of inflation in the long-run. Furthermore, nominal

---

[2] Potential output was estimated using the Hodrick-Prescott (HP) filter.

interest rates and money growth rates are also expected to be positively correlated because of the positive correlation between average inflation rates and average money supply growth rates [18].

Fiscal deficits are one of the main factors that have been exerting inflationary pressures in most African countries. Especially when a country implements a regime of fiscal dominance or active fiscal policy, and passive monetary policy where monetary policy adjusts to deliver the level of seignorage required to balance the government's intertemporal budget [18]. In this case, the monetary authority is forced to generate enough seigniorage to satisfy the intertemporal budget balance condition. This will have an effect on prices and inflation since the changes in seignorage affect the current and future money supply.

An increase in the bank rate by the monetary authorities induces a rise in short term rates such as interbank rate and treasury bill rates which have an impact on other long-term lending rates. As a result of the rise in lending rates, both households and firms reduce their consumption and investment expenditures respectively, as real cost of borrowing increases. Households will mostly reduce their expenditures on consumption of luxury or durables goods due to the increased costs of borrowing. This leads to a decline in aggregate demand and consequently easing the inflationary pressures in the economy (see [20–22] among others for more details). Furthermore, when domestic interest rates increase relative to foreign interest rates, assuming uncovered interest rate parity, domestic currency depreciates in order to maintain equilibrium in the foreign exchange market of the domestic economy. This expected future depreciation induces an initial appreciation of the domestic currency making domestically produced goods more expensive than foreign-produced goods. Hence leading to a decline in net exports and aggregate demand as well as inflationary pressures. Also, the rise in domestic interest rates above foreign interest rates could also attract capital inflows, leading to an appreciation of the local currency. Thus, the precise impact of changes in exchange rate may be uncertain.

The general form of the model to be estimated can be represented as:

$$inf_t = f((m2_t), (i_t), (fd_t), (e_t), (m_t)(y_t)) + \varepsilon_t \tag{1}$$

where inf_t is the inflation rate, i_t is the interest rate, fd_t is the fiscal deficit, y_t is the output gap, e_t is the nominal exchange rate, and ε_t is the error term. It is important to note that there could theoretically be interrelationships between the chosen explanatory variables in the model hence having an impact on inflation through different channels. For instance, based on the conventional real interest rate channel, interest rates could affect the output gap (y_t) and hence having an impact on inflation. The exchange rate would have a direct impact on domestic prices through its impact on the cost of imported goods and through wages, but also indirectly through its impact on output and net exports, hence affecting the inflation rate.[3] In this regard, this calls for caution in taking care of instances of autocorrelation and heteroscedasticity in the model.

Since the objective of the chapter is to examine the drivers of inflation both in the short- and the long-run, the ARDL framework is deemed appropriate for this analysis because of the advantages it has over other methodologies. Contrary to the traditional error correction methodology, where it is imperative to carry out and establish the stationarity of the variables to be used in the short- and long-run analysis to establish their order of integration, the ARDL methodology, while

---

[3] See [23] for more details.

utilizing the Bounds Test, does not require this pre-testing of the order of integration. It uses the F- and t-statistics to test the significance of the lagged variables in a univariate error correction system without establishing the order of integration of the data generation process underlying the series. However, it is important to establish the order of integration beforehand to ensure the absence of I(2) series since their presence would violate the properties of an ARDL model which requires variables to be only I(0), I(1) or they should be mutually integrated. The ARDL methodology also has an advantage over other methodologies in that the its parameters can be estimated consistently without invoking exogeneity and residual serial correlation, especially if the order of the ARDL is appropriately augmented by the suitable specification of the lag structure of the variables [25].

This being the case the objective of the chapter could therefore be investigated by using the ARDL model and Error Correction Model (ECM) frameworks. In this regard Eq. (1) can mathematically be specified as an ARDL model with p lags of *inf* and q lags of $\boldsymbol{X}$ (where $\boldsymbol{X}$ is a $kx1$ vector of independent variables, which include in this case money supply growth, lending rate, nominal exchange rate, import prices, fiscal deficits and output gap), ARDL (p, q) as:

$$inf_t = \sum_{i=1}^{p} \theta_i (inf_{t-i}) + \sum_{i=0}^{q} \boldsymbol{\alpha}_i' \boldsymbol{X}_{t-i} + \varepsilon_t \tag{2}$$

where t is the time period, θ_i are $kx1$ coefficient vectors; α_i are scalars and ε_t is a disturbance term with a zero mean and constant variance. Eq. (2) can be re-parameterized and expressed in error correction model form as:

$$inf_t = \varnothing inf_{t-1} + \gamma' \boldsymbol{X}_t \sum_{i=1}^{p} \theta_i (\Delta inf_{t-i}) + \sum_{i=0}^{q} \boldsymbol{\alpha}_i' \Delta \boldsymbol{X}_{t-i} + \varepsilon_t, \tag{3}$$

where $\varnothing$ is the speed of adjustment and Δ is the difference operator.

3.2 Data

The paper uses quarterly time series data for analysis for the period January 2001-June 2019. The data for all the variables is obtained from Malawi's Central Bank, the Reserve Bank of Malawi, except import price index which is obtained for the Economist Intelligence Unit database [24]. Real GDP were in annual frequency and had to be interpolated to transform them into quarterly data frequency.

4. Model estimation and results

The estimation of the model starts with the examination of the time series properties of the data, using the Augmented Dickey-Fuller test to test for stationarity of the variables. The results of the unit root tests indicate that all the variables, except output gap and money supply growth are integrated of order 1 (I(1)) at below 5% significance level (**Table 1**). This means that in this model some variables have integration of zero order, I(0), and others have integration of the first order, I(1). This result satisfies the requirement for the application of the ARDL methodology which is further supported by the results of the Bounds test (**Table 2**). The result of the Bounds test for co-integration proposed by Pesaran et al. [25] within the ARDL framework, shows that the null hypothesis of no

Augmented Dickey-Fuller test results				
Variable	**Test statistics**			
	Levels (I(0))		**First difference (I(1))**	
	t statistics	**P-value**	**t-statistics**	**P-value**
Inflation	2.5932	0.0991	5.1882	0.0000
log(M2)	growth)	3.1711	0.0261	
Lending rate	2.3613	0.1563	6.554	0.0000
Log(Import price)	0.8814	0.7884	3.5046	0.0107
Fiscal deficit	2.467	0.1277	12.2825	0.0000
Nominal exchange rate	1.1499	0.9976	6.9521	0.0000
Output_gap	6.1783	0.0000		

Note: Values in parentheses are P-values.

Table 1.
The results of the augmented Dickey-Fuller unit root test.

F-bounds test		**Null hypothesis: no levels relationship**		
Test statistic	**Value**	**Signif.**	**I(0)**	**I(1)**
F-statistic	8.956687	10%	1.99	2.94
K	6	5%	2.27	3.28
		2.5%	2.55	3.61
		1%	2.88	3.99

Notes: k=no. of explanatory variables.

Table 2.
Bounds test results for co-integration relationship.

equilibrium level relationship is rejected at below 1% error level by the F-test statistic (**Table 2**).

The Bounds test results in **Table 2** show that F-statistic has the computed value of 8.96 which exceeds the upper bound value of, I(1) which is 3.99 at 1% level of significance, implying that inflation rate and its determinants in the model are co-integrated and approach the long-run equilibrium, calling for the application of the ARDL approach [25]. The implication of this is that the parameters of the model can be estimated consistently without invoking exogeneity and residual serial correlation. The parameter stability test based on the plot of the cumulative sum of recursive residuals squares (CUSUM test) and the plot of the cumulative sum of squares of recursive residuals show that the estimated parameters of the ARDL specification are stable at least over the study period (**Figures 1A(a)** and **(b)** in the Appendix).

4.1 Estimation results

The short-run analysis results in **Table 3** reveal that all the variables, except import prices, have a significant impact on inflation in the short-run. Money supply growth and fiscal deficits are found to have a significant negative impact on inflation, contrary to what the theoretical literature stipulates. However, this could be due to the tight monetary policy being exercised by monetary authorities in Malawi,

Variable	Coefficient	Std. error	P-value
Δinf_{t-1}	0.522715	0.090417	0.0000
$\Delta m2_t$	−0.121076	0.050711	0.0211
$\Delta m2_{t-1}$	−0.378424	0.065234	0.0000
$\Delta m2_{t-2}$	−0.267229	0.056639	0.0000
$\Delta m2_{t-3}$	−0.220042	0.050737	0.0001
Δi_{t-2}	0.118637	0.065816	0.0780
Δfd_t	5.31E−05	1.33E−05	0.0002
Δfd_{t-1}	−6.01E−05	2.06E−05	0.0054
Δfd_{t-2}	−4.56E−05	1.51E−05	0.0041
Δe_{t-2}	0.024740	0.006614	0.0005
Δe_{t-1}	0.016306	0.008573	0.0634
Δe_{t-2}	0.015709	0.007222	0.0348
Δe_{t-3}	0.025733	0.006304	0.0002
Δy_t	0.000295	0.000371	0.4308
Δy_{t-1}	−0.000582	0.000179	0.0021
ect_{t-1}	−0.775206	0.085318	0.0000
R-squared: 0.744337			
Breusch-Godfrey serial correlation LM Test: F-statistic 0.226575 (0.7982)			
Durbin-Watson stat:		2.132180	2.132180
Heteroskedasticity test: ARCH: F-statistic		1.4387 (0.2345)	

Table 3.
Short-run ARDL error correction regression results.

signified by the decline in average monthly growth of money supply from 2.3% over 2001–2011 to 1.6% over the period 2012–2019, and the fiscal consolidation efforts exacerbated by the withdrawal of donor funding. In line with the findings of Mangani [8] and Chavula [5], the results from this study indicate that the quantity theory of money to some extent does not seem to hold in Malawi, as the rising money supply seem to lead to a decline in consumer prices. Further analysis of the relationship between money supply growth and inflation rate shown that since 2000 the growth in money supply has persistently been lower than growth in overall inflation, averaging 3.8% and 15.5%, respectively over the period 2015Q1–2019Q2 to some extent contributing to the forces dragging down inflation over the period. While fiscal deficits have had very minimal but significant impact on inflation over the period, with a positive impact in the first quarter before turning to having a negative impact in the second quarter. With the fiscal consolidation efforts being put in place, the time lag in affecting inflation could be suggesting that the funds have been directed towards some productive sectors which could have had a negative impact on inflation over the period. However, lending rates and exchange rates seem to be the main factors exerting positive inflationary pressures in the Malawian economy in the short run, while output initially exerts a negative impact before having a positive impact on inflation after a certain period conforming to economic theory.

Table 4 presents results of the long-run coefficients computed from the dynamic model shown above. The findings reveal that money supply growth, lending rate and

Variable	Coefficient	Std. error	P-value
$\Delta m2_t$	0.473708	0.170419	0.0079
Δi_t	0.319709	0.127466	0.0157
$\Delta fd_t)$	0.000172	0.000104	0.1038
Δe_t	−0.013703	0.019788	0.4921
Δm_t	0.374323	2.060464	0.8566
Δy_t	−0.000771	0.000241	0.0025
c	−2.438828	1.025090	0.0216
Breusch-Godfrey serial correlation LM test: 0.226575 (0.7982)			
Heteroskedasticity test: ARCH: 1.439651 (0.2345)			

Note: Values in parentheses are P-values.

Table 4.
Long run ARDL estimation results.

fiscal deficit appear to have a positive and statistically significant impact on inflation in the long-run. Money supply growth and lending rate are found to have a positive and statistically significant impact at below 1% level of significance, whereas fiscal deficits are found to be significant at 10% level. To some extent signifying the negative effects of increased fiscal deficits due to the weakening of the country's fiscal consolidation efforts in the long run and also the impact of county's spending on its early 2019 elections. Output gap is found to have a negative and significant impact on inflation at below 1% level of significance, which conforms to the existing theoretical literature.

The chapter further examines whether there has been any change with regards to what has been driving inflation before and after the exchange rate regime change in 2012. The study again uses the same ARDL model framework based on Eq. (2) applied over the two separate periods, 2001–2011 and 2012–2019. The short-run results covering the period 2001–2011 (the period before the regime change), show that money growth, lending rate, fiscal deficit, output and import price had an instantaneous positive impact on inflation over the first few months, before rebounding and absorbing the shock soon after, especially through increases in output and money growth. On the other hand, fiscal deficits and import prices had an instantaneous negative impact on inflation before exerting inflationary pressures soon after the first quarter. While nominal exchange rate had a significant negative impact on inflation, to some extent reflecting the impact of price controls as they weakened its impact in the short-run over the period.

The long-run estimation results show that between 2001 and 2011 money supply growth exerted significant inflationary pressures in the Malawian economy, while import prices had had a negative and significant impact on inflation as monetary authorities operated a de facto pegged exchange rate regime over the period (see **Table A1** in the Appendix).[4] This result to some extent could be attributed to the capital management and price controls operated before 2012 by monetary authorities (see [1] for more details). However, the exchange rate is found to have a positive but insignificant impact on inflation, while output gap has a negative but insignificant impact on inflation in the long-run.

After floating the exchange rate and implementing the oil price automatic adjustment mechanism covering the period 2012–2019, the short-run estimation

[4] Though not reported, kindly not that the model estimation methodology followed all the necessary analytical and evaluation tests assessing its suitability for analysis.

results show that inflation was mainly affected by changes in the nominal exchange rate, with a 1% depreciation leading to a 0.01 percentage increase in inflation rate. However, increases in output are found to have outweighed inflationary pressures as output led to a significant decline in inflation over the period, with a 1% increase in output leading to a 0.004% decline in inflation rate with a 3-month time lag.

The long-run results in **Table A2** show that inflation rate was found to have mainly been influenced by import prices over the period, reflecting the removal of price controls and floatation of the exchange rate. Analysis results show that between 2012 and 2019, a 1% increase in import prices led to a 0.2% increase in inflation. While over the short-run, results show that inflation was mainly affected by changes in the nominal exchange rate, with a 1% depreciation leading to a 0.01% increase in inflation rate. However, increases in output are found to have outweighed inflationary pressures as output led to a significant decline in inflation over the period.

Lastly, the analysis carried out earlier was used to provide the basis in providing the answer to the main question asked in the title of this paper, "Will Malawi's inflation rate continue to decline? To answer this question, we use the model estimated for the results in **Table 3** to produce forecasts based on the fundamentals that have been driving inflation in Malawi over the period 2001–2019. The model is firstly evaluated for its suitability for forecasting and its predictability power using the Theil Inequality Coefficient. The results of the evaluation (in **Figure A2(a)**) show that the model's predictive power is good since the value of the Theil Inequality Coefficient is close to zero. We also employed the CUSUM and CUSUM square tests to validate the stability of the model, and the results show that the plot of the CUSUM statistics stay within the 5% significance level, meaning that the estimates from the model are stable over the period under consideration, and could produce reliable forecasts. The model performance is also further evaluated by comparing the actual and the fitted values from the model. **Figure A2(b)** shows that the simulated values track the actual values well, thereby justifying the model's suitability for forecasting.

The results from the forecasting process (**Figure 2**) reveal that inflation rate might not continue declining as has been the case over the past few years if the status quo stays as it is currently. Inflation rate may increase up to 19.4% by the end of 2020 mainly driven by exchange rate variability, import prices and money supply as they are projected to rise significantly in the short- to medium term. Monetary authorities should therefore continue to put in place measures that will continue controlling money supply growth, import prices and maintain exchange rate stability as these seem to be the main drivers of inflation in the short- to medium-term.

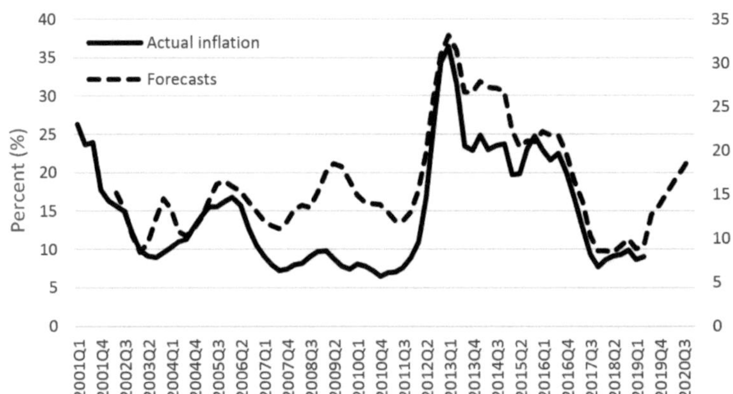

Figure 2.
Inflation forecasts, 2001Q1–2020Q4.

5. Conclusions

In this paper we have tried to examine the main factors behind the country's inflation dynamics since 2001, putting emphasis on the factors behind its continuous decline since early 2013. We have also tried to assess if at all this decline will persist as per the performance of the underlying economic fundamentals both in the short- and long-run amidst the existing opposing forces.

The results of the study show that based on the full sample (2001–2019), money supply, fiscal deficits and output growth had a significant negative impact on inflation in the short-run, while exchange rate movements and interest rates exerted inflationary pressures in the economy over the period. However, results reveal that only output had a significant negative impact on inflation in the long-run over the same period, while money supply, interest rates and fiscal deficits exerted significant inflationary pressures in the economy.

Inflation dynamics in the period before the change in exchange rate regime are found to have been influenced mainly by money supply, interest rates, exchange rate movements and import prices in the short-run while in the long-run inflation was mainly influenced by changes in import prices. The results based on the sub-sample (2012–2019), capturing the period after the exchange rate regime change, the decline in inflation is found to have been mainly influenced by output growth in the short-run while exchange rate movements exerted inflationary pressures in the economy over the period. However, in the long-run, import prices continued to have significant positive effects on inflation.

The results from the forecasting process reveal that inflation rate might not continue declining as has been the case over the past few years if the status quo stays as it is currently. The forecasts show that inflation rate may increase up to 19.4% by the end of 2020. Monetary authorities should therefore continue to put in place measures that will control money supply growth, import prices and maintain exchange rate stability as these seem to be the main drivers of inflation in the short- to medium-term in the country.

The results seem to suggest that, while price stability remains the principal objective of monetary authorities in the country [7], they should not only place more emphasis on the objective of stabilization and achieving low inflation, but also focus on supporting strong, sustained and shared growth, as output seems to play a significant role in bringing down inflation in the country. As they continue to put money supply, fiscal deficits and exchange rates in check, they should ensure that the strategies being implemented and the associated transmission mechanisms aim at increasing the country's output growth. In line with the findings of Simwaka et al. [15], these results may be suggesting that the movement and relationship between inflation and money growth could be further suggesting that while monetary and fiscal policy tightening remain central to lowering inflation, structural measures to boost productivity and growth in the economy remain necessary in ensuring a more sustainable disinflation growth path.

Noting very well that cutting of interest rates that the country has undertaken recently could not bear fruits if the economy does not produce enough goods and services to meet the existing demand, lack of supply would lead to a rise in inflation, which force monetary authorities to raise interest rates again.

In line with the findings of Mangani [8] and Chavula [5], an increase in money supply seems to lead to a decline in inflation and the increase in interest rates seem to lead to a decline in prices. These results to some extent indicate that the quantity theory of money does not seem to hold in Malawi. To some extent suggesting the need for the continued use of reserve money and money supply to control inflation.

Acknowledgements

I would like to thank Dr Kisiyawo Simwaka, Ms Marietta Kaval0, and Mr Wyton Jombo, all from the Reserve Bank of Malawi for making the data available in coming up with this chapter.

Conflict of interest

The authors declare no conflict of interest.

Notes/Thanks/Other declarations

The views expressed in this paper do not in any way represent the views of the United Nations Economic Commission for Africa (ECA). All the remaining errors and omissions are my responsibility.

A. Appendix

See **Figures A1** and **A2** and **Tables A1** and **A2**.

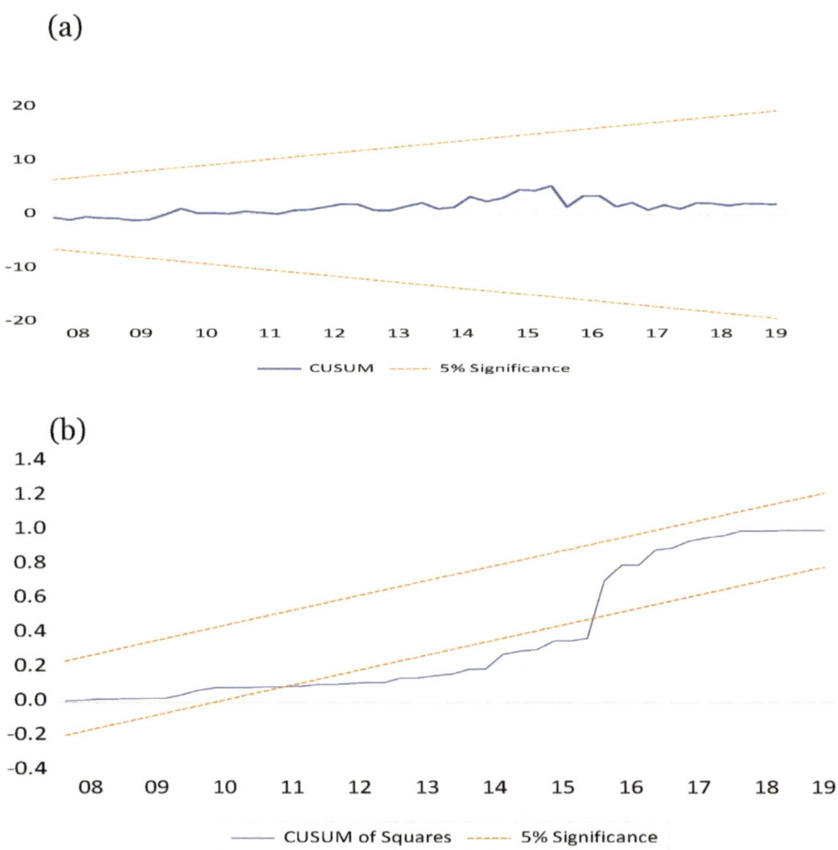

Figure A1.
Stability tests: (a) CUSUM test results for model stability and (b) CUSUM square test results for model stability.

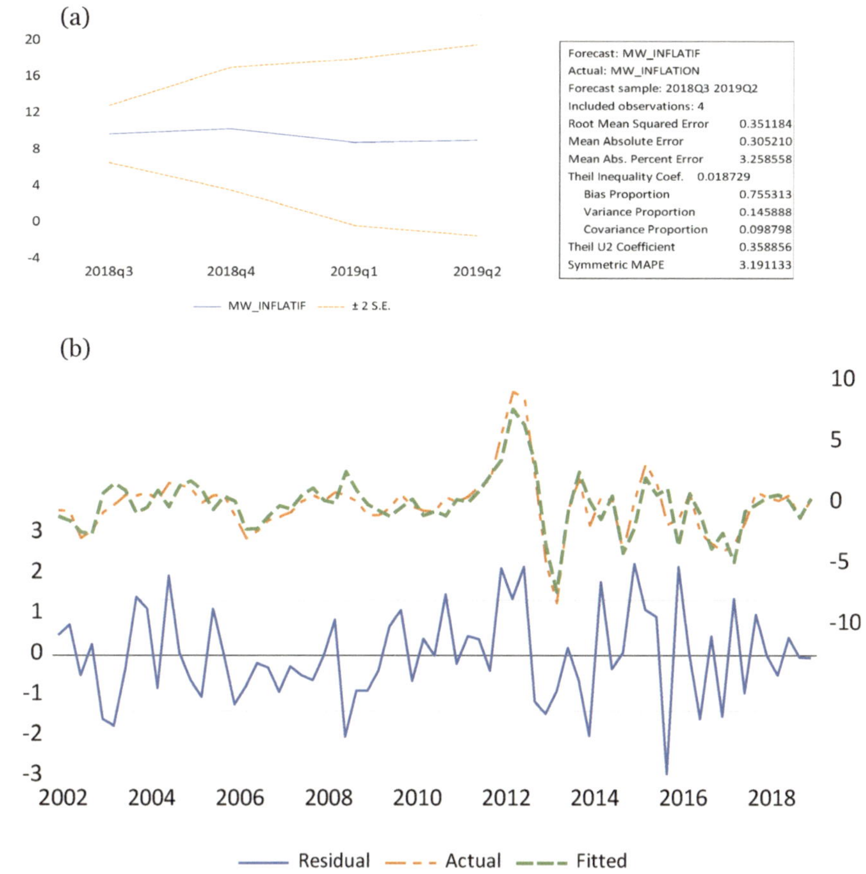

Figure A2.
Model forecasting performance tests. (a) The Theil Inequality Coefficient test and (b) comparing the actual and fitted or estimated values from the model.

	ARDL short-run results				ARDL Long-run results		
Variable	**Coefficient**	**Std. error**	**P-value**		**Coefficient**	**Std. error**	**P-value**
$\Delta\, inf_{t-1}$	0.093212	0.043127	0.0589	$m2_t$	1.454819	0.440133	0.0092
$\Delta\, inf_{t-2}$	−0.350365	0.034636	0.0000	i_t	−0.071854	0.049039	0.1769
$\Delta m2_t$	0.212724	0.015561	0.0000	fd_t	−0.000180	0.000102	0.1125
$\Delta m2_{t-1}$	−0.251965	0.015112	0.0000	Δe_t	0.523396	0.327125	0.1441
Δi_t	0.145083	0.023975	0.0002	Δm_t	−0.429097	0.095834	0.0015
Δi_{t-1}	−0.059094	0.027057	0.0568	y_t	−0.000370	0.000350	0.3188
Δi_{t-2}	0.047333	0.027611	0.1206	C	−7.675094	2.359756	0.0100
Δi_{t-3}	−0.036347	0.025592	0.1892				
Δfd_t	−6.85E−05	8.90E−06	0.0000				
Δfd_{t-1}	6.75E−05	8.92E−06	0.0000				
Δe_t	−0.021708	0.018230	0.2642				
Δe_{t-1}	−0.184993	0.017992	0.0000				
Δe_{t-2}	−0.195165	0.018680	0.0000				

	ARDL short-run results			ARDL Long-run results		
Variable	Coefficient	Std. error	P-value	Coefficient	Std. error	P-value
Δe_{t-3}	−0.031946	0.015896	0.0754			
Δm_t	−0.050171	0.004835	0.0000			
Δm_t	0.070395	0.004778	0.0000			
Δm_t	0.051798	0.004011	0.0000			
Δm_t	0.051419	0.004266	0.0000			
Δy_t	−5.67E−05	7.73E−05	0.4820			
Δy_{t-1}	1.07E−05	5.22E−05	0.8416			
Δy_{t-2}	0.000108	4.19E−05	0.0302			
Δy_{t-2}	−0.000286	3.21E−05	0.0000			
ect_{t-1}	−0.322544	0.018502	0.0000			
R-squared: 0.978508						
Breusch-Godfrey Serial Correlation LM Test: F-statistic 0.3274 (0.7313)						
Heteroskedasticity test: Breusch-Pagan-Godfrey: F-statistic 1.9140 (0.1538)						

Note: Values in parentheses are P-values.

Table A1.
ARDL results for the period 2001–2011.

	ARDL short-run results			ARDL long-run results			
Variable	Coefficient	Std. Error	P-value	Variable	Coefficient	Std. error	P-value
Δinf_{t-1}	0.526685	0.112450	0.0003	$m2_t$	−0.019378	0.142288	0.8935
Δe_t	0.012223	0.006129	0.0646	Δi_t	−0.074744	0.278291	0.7919
Δy_t	−0.001064	0.000987	0.2977	Δfd_t	4.91E−05	2.98E−05	0.1205
Δy_{t-1}	−0.003913	0.000962	0.0010	Δe_t	−0.015466	0.023154	0.5143
ect_{t-1}	−0.782070	0.105332	0.0000	m_t	0.205028	0.087456	0.0332
				y_t	−0.000472	0.000913	0.6122
				c	−9.288554	4.007864	0.0350
R-squared: 0.794218							
Breusch-Godfrey serial correlation LM test: F-statistic 2.4729 (0.1230)							
Heteroskedasticity test: Breusch-Pagan-Godfrey: F-statistic 1.0836 (0.4326)							

Note: Values in parentheses are P-values.

Table A2.
ARDL results for the period 2012–2019.

DOI: http://dx.doi.org/10.5772/intechopen.91764

Author details

Hopestone Kayiska Chavula
Macroeconomics and Governance Division, Economic Commission for Africa, Addis Ababa, Ethiopia

*Address all correspondence to: chavulah@yahoo.com; chavula@un.org

References

[1] Wu F, Dong. Understanding inflation in Malawi: A quantitative investigation. In: IMF Working Paper, WP/17/48. Washington, DC: African Department, IMF; 2017

[2] Reserve Bank of Malawi (RBM). Monetary Policy Statement #2 March 2015. Lilongwe, Malawi: RBM. p. 2015

[3] Kwalingana S. The monetary policy reaction function for Malawi [MA (economics) thesis]. Zomba: University of Malawi; 2007

[4] United Nations Economic Report on Africa. Fiscal Policy for Financing Sustainable Development. Addis Ababa: UNECA; 2019

[5] Chavula HK. Monetary policy effects and output growth in Malawi: Using a small macroeconometric model. Open Journal of Modelling and Simulation. 2016;**4**:169-191

[6] Reserve Bank of Malawi. Financial and economic review. RBM. 2019;**53**(3)

[7] Ngalawa V. Dynamic effects of monetary policy shocks in Malawi. South African Journal of Economics. 2011;**79**(3):224-250

[8] Mangani R. The effects of monetary policy on prices in Malawi. In: AERC Research Paper 252. Nairobi, Kenya: African Economic Research Consortium (AERC); 2011

[9] Wytone J, Simwaka K, Chiumia A. Exchange rate pass-through in Malawi: Evidence from augmented Phillips curve and vector autoregressive approaches. Standard Global Journal of Business Management. 2014;**1**(2):34-40

[10] Mwabutwa C, Bittencourt M, Viegi N. Evolution of monetary policy transmission mechanism in Malawi: A TVP-VAR approach. In: Working Paper Series. South Africa: Department of Economics, University of Pretoria; 2013

[11] Mangani R. Market reaction to monetary policy pronouncements in Malawi. In: Working Paper. Zomba: Chancellor College, University of Malawi; 2009

[12] Ngalawa H. Dynamic effects of monetary policy shocks in Malawi. In: The 14th Annual Conference of the African Econometrics Society, Abuja, 8–10 July. 2009

[13] Deraniyagala S, Kaluwa B. Macroeconomic policy for employment creation: The case of Malawi. In: Employment Working Paper No. 93. Geneva: Employment Sector, Employment Policy Department, ILO; 2011

[14] Matchaya G. The nature of inflation in Malawi up to the early 2000s. Journal of Economics and International Finance. 2011;**3**(5):289-304

[15] Simwaka K, Ligoya P, Kabango G, Mtendere C. Mone supply and inflation in Malawi: An econometric investigation. The International Journal of Applied Economics and Finance. 2012;**6**(3):74-88

[16] Lungu M, Jombo W, Chiumya A. Determining the output gap and its link with price dynamics in Malawi. Journal of Research in Economics and International Finance. 2012;**1**(4):124-135

[17] Akinboade A, Oludele S, Franz K, Elizabeth NW. The determinants of inflation in South Africa: An econometric analysis. In: African Economic Research Consortium (AERC) Research Paper No. 143, Nairobi. 2004

[18] Walsh E, Carl. Monetary Theory and Policy. 4th ed. Cambridge, Massachusetts: The MIT Press; 2017

[19] Lucas RE. Two illustrations of the quantity theory of money. American Economic Review. 1980;**70**(5): 1005-1014

[20] Were M, Nyamong E, Kamau AW, Sichei MM, Wambua J. Assessing the effectiveness of monetary policy in Kenya: Evidence from a macroeconomic model. Economic Modelling. 2014;**2014** (**17**):193-201

[21] Ireland PN. The monetary transmission mechanism. In: Working Paper 06-1. Boston: Federal Reserve Bank of Boston; 2005

[22] Mishkin FS. Symposium on the monetary transmission mechanism. Journal of Economic Perspectives. 1995; **9**:3-10

[23] Batini N, Haldane AC. Forward-looking rules for monetary policy. In: Working Paper No. 9. Bank of England; 1999. Available from: https://www.bankofengland.co.uk/-/media/boe/files/working-paper/1999/forward-looking-rules-for-monetary-policy.pdf?la=en&hash=0CF3AD6AADB76ACA59FD60FF8F5CFEC37A085F43

[24] EIU (Economist Intelligence Unit). EIU database. 2020. Available from: www.eiu.com

[25] Pesaran MH, Shin Y, Smith R. Bounds testing approaches to the analysis of level relationships. Journal of Applied Econometrics. 2001;**16**:289-326

Chapter 15

Efficiency of the City Councils Using Cross-Sectional Model: Challenges in Times of Change and Political Tension

Claudio Elórtegui-Gómez, Hanns de la Fuente-Mella, Mauricio Alvarado and Matías Guajardo

Abstract

The efficiency of city councils is a matter of concern in public discussion in Chile, due to the growing political relevance that citizens demand of them for social and economic management, in the face of the effects of the pandemic and recent social unrest. Despite the marked historical centralization of power in the capital city, the efficiency of the Chilean municipalities will be key to improving the quality of life of the communities, especially in times of political tension, greater social needs and discredit toward national institutions, not well the local ones. A cross-sectional econometric regression model was developed to explain the determinants of the efficiency of the municipalities and identify the variables that have the greatest impact on said efficiency. City councils that are regional capitals with more than 50,000 inhabitants were selected for this study.

Keywords: econometric model, city council, efficiency, life quality, social unrest

1. Introduction

City councils in Chile have taken on an increasingly prominent role in the political-economic and public-media spheres, especially after the emergence of the unexpected outbreak of the pandemic and the social unrest prior to Covid-19. The analysis of these institutions becomes relevant, as well as the need to establish interdisciplinary and econometric instruments, that can provide public policies with better data, in order to optimize the perspectives of local government efficiency in situations of high instability and global-local complexity.

In a country with a centralized administration system, the attributes of which intensified after the 1973 coup d'état and subsequent dictatorship of Augusto Pinochet, municipalities have since become bureaucratic units that are fundamental in the life and control of the population, due to a range of responsibilities assigned to them in their communal territories.

With the arrival of democracy in 1990, a number of political and participative adjustments were implemented that impacted the municipalities. However, the challenges continued to multiply as social and cultural transformations were taking place in these territorial areas, all of a different nature and stretching across more than 4000 km on the mainland and islands of Chile.

Nevertheless, the Chilean political system maintains its marked presidentialism and has not been able to move forward towards a decisive decentralization. High-ranking officials, such as regional and provincial governors, continue to be designated in accordance with criteria defined in the country's capital or by elite groups.

The OECD [1] points out that Chile has a long tradition of centralism, with an administration system associated with economic efficiency and political stability. However, there are discussions on the need to improve regional performance and competitiveness from a necessarily decentralizing role [2], capable of bringing the country, that received international recognition for its political and economic transition in the nineties, into line with the new challenges.

The objective of the following research is to select municipalities that are regional capitals with over 50,000 inhabitants, in order to determine the factors that influence the efficiency of these city councils in Chile, based on the quality of life index of the districts. To do so, an econometric model was developed to explain the specific factors of the efficiency of city councils in Chile, as well as the variables with the greatest impact on such efficiency.

We believe that this is a necessary yet seldom addressed dimension in Chile, in terms of the inputs that econometrics can provide, to move forward with better interdisciplinary perspectives in order to empower regional governments that promote human development in pursuit of sustainability and the best possible democratic and social conditions.

2. Theoretical framework

In 2019, Chile experienced an outbreak of social unrest that began in October 2019, and was only interrupted by the arrival of the Covid-19 pandemic, in March 2020. This period of mobilization prior to the coronavirus, marked by ongoing protests throughout the country, demanded a new social and political pact, substantiated on the lost credibility of government institutions, politicians, business people and the clergy.

The crisis was felt with unexpected force and presence in the streets and major public areas of the regional capitals, particularly in those with larger populations.

The citizenry demanded better conditions for old-age pensions, access to healthcare, protection against market abuse and gender-based violence, among other things. These social causes have tended to come together under feelings of indignation that have sparked off a demand to end the most urgent inequalities and to bring greater dignity to the population. This has led to articulating the need for a more systematic change, driven by the demand for a new Political Constitution.

During the most critical times of the social unrest, between October and December 2019, with episodes of public violence and obvious problems of governance at the central level, the city councils proved to be a strategic political space by building bridges to address the citizens' malaise. They showed a greater sensitivity and capacity for participation with different stakeholders and organizations of the local territories. The municipalities also made their resources available to help unblock the lack of social dialog and revert an increasing political polarization.

With the onset of the health emergency in Chile in March 2020, the city councils once again became important spheres for social and political-media leadership, requesting the central government to implement quarantine measures, for greater coordination with the public health system, and urgent economic support plans for Covid-19, in response to public concern about the quick propagation of the virus.

The city councils also focused their resources on meeting the people's most immediate and actual demands, complementing the efforts of the ministries involved in managing the crisis.

During both of the episodes described (social unrest and Covid-19), that is, within the scope of a political and a health crisis, various surveys and public opinion polls showed that the Chilean city councils were among the most valued government institutions by the people.

Indeed, the potential that this kind of municipal organization has for future political, health or economic challenges could be crucial for the efficiency of the State and the identity of the territories. Therefore, we stress the need for a more in-depth study of the context and the variables that could improve the living conditions of the communities located within the municipalities.

2.1 Political reality of the city councils

At present, there are 345 municipalities in Chile and they are defined in the Constitution as "autonomous public law corporations with legal status and their own assets. Their objective is to satisfy the needs of the local community and ensure their participation in the economic, cultural and social development" [3].

The Constitutional Organic Law of Municipalities N°18.695 specifically regulates the most important aspects of the communal administration. For instance, it establishes the existence of a mayor and a city council, along with their respective functions and powers. However, there are numerous laws that regulate other aspects.

According to political theory, Chile's municipalities constitute a public service that operate as a decentralized State body and are the State's closest visible face for its citizens [4]. However, the concentration of the Chilean political system is evident in the difference established between the government and the administration.

The government has the capacity for political decision-making, while the administration is a more limited concept and is further removed from political power. In fact, government powers in the territories are in the hands of the regional and provincial governors (chosen by the president in office) and those of the mayors are only for the municipal administration of their communes or cities [4].

A local government, as a political body of representation and not only of the administrative kind, is vested with the right of its municipalities to take certain decisions without the authorization or interference of the central government. In other words, [5] with its actions, a municipality can have independent effects on significant aspects of a specific community.

2.2 In search of decentralization

In 2009, a process began to implement territorial decentralization through a series of legal changes, in pursuit of the election of regional counselors (regulated in 2013) and governors (suspended due to Covid-19, although regulated in 2018), along with establishing a system to transfer competences to regional governments (formalized in 2018). For some authors, this has meant progress, from a model of deconcentrated transiting towards one of territorial decentralization, as these laws would allegedly favor the modification of regional administration and the relationship of vertical political power [2, 6].

However, the Regional Authority Index [7], which compares the degree of decentralization between different countries, ranks us in 52nd place out of 63. This position is similar to nations of a smaller scale and population such as Ireland and Lithuania. Explanations could argue that Chile is compared with countries of a very different size and institutional regime. But if we limit the comparison to OECD unitary states with more than 3 million inhabitants, the results do not improve [8].

Maintaining a tendency towards centralization may bring about negative effects. For example, it creates administrative inefficiencies when requesting permits that need to be approved at the central level, hindering the possibility of innovation in public policies, due to the lack of competences and economic resources. It also limits economic growth and productivity, generating territorial imbalances and inequalities, where some regions are winners and others lag behind [8].

One of the most specific aspects for true decentralization, that seeks to favor the power of municipalities, lies in transferring the competence and decision-making capacity, including, most notably, on budgetary matters, which "are fundamental and unavoidable" [9].

The efficiency of the Chilean State's resources should focus on a better connection with local spheres and study, in turn, what municipalities are doing with their administrations and how their decisions are impacting their respective communities. In fact, the OECD [1] pointed out that, in Chile, centralization hampers the development of the country.

2.3 Economic dimension

As for the economic situation, municipalities have several sources of income that can be differentiated between own funds and external funds [10]. While own funds consist of the Municipal Common Fund and Permanent Own-Source Income, external funds include those transferred to municipalities for programs or projects promoted by the central government and executed by local governments [11].

The Municipal Common Fund (FCM) is regulated by Law N°20.237, the abovementioned Constitutional Organic Law of Municipalities (LOCM) and Decree N°1293 of the Ministry of the Interior of 2009. Law N°20.033 established that, as of 2005, a fixed monetary contribution from the central government for 218.000 UTM (approximately 11 billion Chilean pesos, or US$13.5 million) would be made to the FCM [11].

It is worthwhile mentioning that the Municipal Common Fund is defined by the Political Constitution of the Republic (Article 122) as a "mechanism for the solidary redistribution of own incomes among the municipalities of the country" [11].

2.4 Political efficiency

The concept of efficiency applied to interdisciplinary dialog from the point of view of political and administrative theory, becomes especially important in times of crisis and empowerment of the people in their local setting.

Political efficiency is linked to "a government's capability, competence or potential to establish guidelines that lead to objectives considered to be valid by a society at a specific time" [12]. City councils, on this level, are an institutional and operational power that, within their areas of impact, enables to achieve socially accepted and legally enshrined objectives.

At the level of public management, administrative efficiency is legitimatized when it receives public recognition [13]. Citizen support of a State is largely the result of a performance that is perceived as efficient and effective, as for example, when it reduces poverty, unemployment or inequality. Hence, the democratic apparatus is strengthened and the people perceive that the performance of a municipality is coherent or fair. Public management creates a value [12], as long as there also is political communication that sets out these advances or achievements in a credible and plain way.

The discussion between efficiency and democracy, under the perspective of legitimacy [14], understood as the capacity of political systems to generate, on the one hand, citizen representation and political responsibility (input-oriented legitimacy), and on the other, satisfactory results of public policies (output-oriented legitimacy) [15], is still valid in the current contexts we are analyzing.

In fact, there is a third dimension of legitimacy that refers to the decision-making procedure (throughput legitimacy), given by transparency, the degree of openness and of inclusion [16]. The concept of representative democracy expands when examining in-depth analyses on how decisions are taken and whether they include deliberative democracy instruments that allow greater participation of all public and private stakeholders [17].

2.5 Efficiency model

This study determines the factors that influence the efficiency of city councils in Chile, in terms of the Quality of Life Index of the communities. To do so, an econometric model was developed to explain the determinants of the efficiency of city councils in Chile, and to identify the variables that have the greatest impact on such efficiency. Municipalities that are regional capitals, with over 50,000 inhabitants, were selected for this study.

The efficiency model of the city councils demonstrates that, as described earlier, there is a growing interest in these entities in search of decentralization in Chile, as a way of strengthening the regions and to stop holding back the country's development [18], which to a large extent could be carried out through efficient city councils. Therefore, arriving at the factors that determine the efficiency of the city council is of great importance, as it shows us the aspects that require special attention. New public policies focused on these aspects would increase the favorable perception of municipal management and, more importantly, the quality of life of the people.

For the purposes of this research, a series of variables that are linked to the efficiency of Chilean municipalities will be included. Within this selection, variables stand out that have been a priority concern of citizens and that have tried to be incorporated into the country's public policies. We refer, as shown in the final model (**Table 1**), to the Municipal Common Fund (FCM), Permanent Own-Source Income (IPP), rate of domestic violence, average University Selection Test (PSU) score, overcrowding and density.

Variable	Coefficient	Std. error	t-Statistic	p-Value
RateDomesticViolence	-0.013222	0.004051	-3.263793	0.0016
OwnIncomesIPP	1.12E-07	3.26E-08	3.433896	0.0009
FCM	-2.15E-07	7.71E-08	-2.789977	0.0065
Overcrowding	-79.50409	17.53457	-4.534135	0.0000
Average PSU	16.36778	4.456570	3.672732	0.0004
PopulationDensity	-0.000430	0.000117	-3.668260	0.0004
C	59.43797	4.688335	12.67784	0.0000

Source: Own creation.

Table 1.
Final model parameter estimation.

1. Municipal Common Fund (FCM):

The FCM is the solidarity redistribution mechanism of own income in the municipalities of all Chile. In this regard, there is debate in political sectors of the country, about whether costs that are in line with resources would mean greater efficiency, since it would not translate into better provision of public services [19]. This is known in the literature as the "flypaper effect" [20], which could have a negative effect in the city councils of Chile.

2. Permanent Own-Source Income (IPP) [21]:

This is the budget of a city council, composed of the following accounts of the budget classifier: territorial tax, municipal benefit vehicle permits, municipal benefit licenses, sanitation taxes, other duties, property rentals, driver's licenses and the like, fines and interests, concessions, aquaculture patents, mining patents and casinos. The probability that the inefficiency of public officials and local politicians increases, when there is a higher level of income that favors an increase in the fiscal capacity of the municipalities, is an aspect that the literature describes [22]. Meanwhile, the fiscal deficit could also have a negative impact on the efficiency of the city council as a variable of the IPP. If a municipality spends more than it can, it is exposed to financial vulnerability [23].

3. Overcrowding:

This variable is the result of the absence of urban development, both in infrastructure and housing. It affects the minimum conditions of people, integrated into a commune or political-administrative and territorial space. For the purposes of the study, it represents the average level of overcrowding in households, expressed as a percentage. It is a "different type of factor that influences the efficiency of the city council" [24], since it is associated with the characteristics of local residents and how these citizens coexist with their vital environments.

4. Population Density:

Population density considers, for these purposes, the number of inhabitants per km^2. It has been shown [25] that a smaller number of inhabitants per square kilometer can increase the average cost of supplying goods and services, so that a municipality could be more efficient if its population density were higher.

5. Rate of Domestic Violence:

This is the rate of complaints of domestic violence reported per 100,000 inhabitants. According to studies on the subject, such violence ultimately harms an individual's health and quality of life without distinction of gender, race or ethnicity around the world. This is supported by UNICEF's definition of domestic violence, which includes that it is an affront to the quality of life [26].

6. Average University Selection Test (PSU) Score:

This is defined as the percentage of PSU scores equal to or greater than 450 points in municipal establishments. This score was defined, for the purpose of this research, under the assumption that each citizen who takes the University Selection Test (PSU) has a certain level of education and that he or she could potentially choose to improve that level. According to [25], it determined that the citizen participation variable, in relation with the educational level of the adult population, has a positive impact on the degree of city council efficiency. Along this same line are [23, 25, 26], which reinforce these results.

2.6 Efficiency of Chilean city councils

The research that explain the efficiency of the city councils, usually focus and limit themselves on socioeconomic, demographic and fiscal factors. In this sense, the literature is not abundant and tends to be obsolete, above all, because the local dimension in countries like Chile has undergone various changes in the last decade, being culturally and productively diverse.

The models that are reiterated in the theme of the efficiency of city councils also present a special interest in resources. For example, there are authors [27] that maintain that the material well-being and the quality of life of a person do not have a direct correlation, varying this relationship by the level of income of citizens, the satisfaction or dissatisfaction of basic needs, as well as other factors [28]. According to [29] the interrelation between needs, satisfaction and economic goods, is of a permanent and dialectical nature. This can be explained, on the one hand, because economic goods can affect the efficiency of satisfaction; on the other, they are decisive in the generation and creation of these factors.

Therefore, taking into account that the municipalities are responsible for the administration of economic assets, obtained by the redistribution of resources, management has a direct impact on efficiency, as well as on factors that influence the quality of life in its set. Therefore, the planning and budget of each local reality is relevant.

Different authors point out that, as Chile is analyzed from North to South, the indicators improve [30]. However, the most prominent indicators are located in the central area of the country. Meanwhile, [19, 25, 31] consider that the higher the population density of the commune, the more efficient the city council will be.

These hypotheses will be tested by the proposed final model, to determine the behavior of the Chilean municipalities and if it is related to what is presented in the literature.

3. Methodology

The research and analysis of efficiency in city councils in Chile, evidenced in the literature, is usually carried out from microeconomic theory, which evaluates two aspects of municipal efficiency: inputs and output.

In fact, municipal efficiency is considered optimal when it reaches its maximum level of production, compared to certain inputs and the minimum level of inputs in a given product [24, 32].

In the case of Chile, the studies and methodology applied to the efficiency of the city councils are few and focused on resources, not addressing other aspects of importance and complexity for the economic reality.

In relation to the methodology, the analysis was applied to 93 communes in Chile, incorporating a diverse sample of the country, both in its political-administrative and geographical configuration. In other ways, the study integrates communes from the northern, central and southern macro-zones of the national territory. A cross-sectional econometric regression model was developed to explain and predict the effect over the municipal efficiency measured by Quality of Life Index (QLI) [33–36]. This is validated by the assumptions of the residual before proceeding with the second objective, which is the estimation and interpretation of results [36, 37].

In order to build the database to be used to forecast the efficiency of city councils in Chile [38], the National Municipal Information System was consulted, together with the Library of the National Congress of Chile (BCN), as well as an approximation based on the Urban Quality of Life Index (QLI) for the year 2018, while bearing in mind the different areas of the country. The model estimate specified in Eq. (1) is presented in the following **Table 2**.

$$\begin{aligned} QLI_i = \alpha + \beta_1 * AveragePSU_i + \beta_2 * PopulationDensity_i \\ + \beta_3 * Overcrowding_i + \beta_4 * RateDomesticViolence_i \\ + \beta_5 * FCM_i + \beta_6 * OwnIncomesIPP_i + \beta_7 * HealthBudget_i \\ + \beta_8 * Scholarship_i + \beta_9 * OtherIncomes_i + \beta_{10} * GreenAreas_i \\ + \beta_{11} * Poverty_i + \mu_i \end{aligned} \tag{1}$$

After estimating the tentative model using Stepwise Econometric Regression Models, and considering all of the variables studied to determine the quality of life of the inhabitants of a commune, the variables relevant to the determination of the study's approach, such as municipal efficiency, were selected (see **Table 1**). The variables that were greater than the minimum level of confidence (p-value ≤0.05)

Variable	Coefficient	Std. error	t-Statistic	p-Value
RateDomesticViolence	-0.012964	0.004200	-3.086408	0.0028
Health Budget	0.076376	0.053567	1.425805	0.1579
Scholarship	-0.000210	8.57E-05	-2.445162	0.0167
OwnIncomesIPP	2.89E-07	1.05E-07	2.752694	0.0073
Other Incomes	-3.70E-07	2.59E-07	-1.431423	0.1563
FCM	1.64E-07	2.15E-07	0.762711	0.4479
PopulationDensity	-0.000564	0.000130	-4.355540	0.0000
Green Areas	1.84E-06	1.15E-06	1.598367	0.1140
Average PSU	12.81732	4.457474	2.875466	0.0052
Overcrowding	-57.43565	18.52834	-3.099881	0.0027
Poverty	-22.91616	13.88977	-1.649859	0.1030
C	59.64198	4.667443	12.77830	0.0000

Table 2.
Estimation of general model parameters.

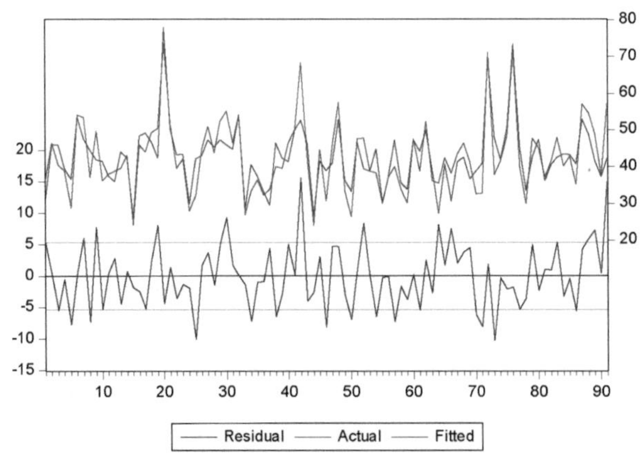

Figure 1.
Residual from the final model. Source: Own creation by means of EViews statistical program.

F-statistic	0.391564	Prob. F(2.82)	0.6773
Obs*R-squared	0.860859	Prob. Chi-Square(2)	0.6502

Source: Own creation by means of EViews statistical program.

Table 3.
Breusch-Godfrey serial correlation LM test.

F-statistic	0.462869	Prob. F(27.63)	0.9852
Obs*R-squared	15.06367	Prob. Chi-Square(27)	0.9685
Scaled explained SS	15.65709	Prob. Chi-Square(27)	0.9592

Source: Own creation by means of EViews statistical program.

Table 4.
Heteroscedasticity white test.

adopted for this study were eliminated from the model. In addition to this method, what was stated in the literature and determination of the endogenous variable was also considered.

Given the estimates of the variables described earlier in this chapter, a final econometric model was proposed that better and more up-to-date (**Table 1**) represents the factors that involve the efficiency of city councils in Chile.

According to the Quality of Life Index (QLI), the variability in the efficiency of Chilean municipalities is explained by 71% (R-squared) of the following variables: Municipal Common Fund (FCM), Permanent Income from own source (IPP), Overcrowding, PSU average, population density and rate of domestic violence. As for the hypotheses associated with the residues of the model, which can compare its behavior with **Figure 1**, they do not present problems of self-correlation of the residues, using the Breusch-Godfrey test[1] (**Table 3**), nor problems of normality of the residues,[2] nor problems of heteroscedasticity (**Table 4**) of the aforementioned.[3]

As illustrated by **Figure 1**, we can see the distribution of the residuals, considering the data obtained through QLI, as the estimation of efficiency through the final model proposed, with the difference shown on the graph explained by the R2 adjusted for the 71.29% model. By the way, the final model for the Urban Quality of Life Index (QLI) is [Eq. (2)].

$$\begin{aligned} QLI = 59.44 + 16.37 * AveragePSU - 0.00043 \\ * PopulationDensity - 79.51 * Overcrowding - 0.013 \\ * RateDpmesticViolence - 2.15 * 10^{-7} \\ * FCM + 1.12 * 10^{-7} * OwnIncomesIPP \end{aligned} \quad (2)$$

4. Conclusions

This study provides us with contrasts between different municipalities that allow us to reach conclusions on the current situation in northern, central, and southern Chile. It also allows us to find and tear down certain prejudices, such as the centralization of the country, showing the variables that are influential to a greater

1 Breusch-Godfrey F Test: 2.82; P-value = < 0.1.
2 Jarque-Bera Test: 4.4654; P-value = < 0.1.
3 White Test F-statistic: 27.63; P-value = < 0.1.

degree, according to our econometric model, and raises new aspects to consider in municipal management.

According to the literature reviewed, there are references that indicate that the quality of life can be interpreted from economic growth, which in various studies is considered a factor in determining the efficiency of city councils. The authors also indicate that the quality of life must be decoded by development, from a necessary environmental and social efficiency. For this, he points out [39] it is important to consider the factors that allow a "greening" of the economy, but also a closer relationship with politics. In this way, a set of criteria oriented to equity and distribution can be determined, which would reduce interterritorial imbalances, considered elements of high entropy. In sum, for a better quality of life for the citizens of a territory in which the city council manages resources, social variables, such as domestic violence in a given commune, should be considered, along with economic variables such as the Municipal Common Fund (FCM) and the Permanent Income from own source (IPP).

Therefore, although any variable, from economic matters to population density, can increase the efficiency of city councils, when linked closer to the quality of life of the inhabitants belonging to a certain commune, this factor tends to slightly decrease that efficiency, counteracting to some level what was raised by the literature. Indeed [37] rectifies the fact that the changes produced through economic development and well-being or the structural transformation in human development, in a study on the quality of life and how the environment and, ultimately, the changes that occur in it, can contribute positively or negatively in each individual, that is, how the administration and management of resources are implemented. This contributes to the efficiency of city councils in Chile, which in turn affects the quality of life of the inhabitants in each of the communes under study, concluding that, according to the data, findings and the existing literature, both factors mentioned are very closely related.

Regarding the assumptions made, it can be concluded that they are acceptable. In other words, there are better indexes in the central zone of Chile and the rates improve when advancing from North to South of the country, according to what is observed in the graphs and as predicted by the model.

Based on this study, it was concluded that the characteristics of the people who inhabit the communes cannot be excluded from this type of analysis, due to the cultural transformations and political demands that are taking place in countries like Chile. The efficiency levels of city councils cannot be limited by the information available only on a group of economic factors, but must integrate other aspects of social sensitivity.

The management of the social and economic crisis that the pandemic situation has generated, needs to integrate the reality of the territories, which is urgently demanded in Chile by civil society itself, which perceives imbalances in the responses provided by city councils. If the quality of life of individuals, as well as their characteristics, were taken into account, this would provide a more integrated and real result regarding the efficiency of city councils in Chile and their administration of resources. Therefore, based on the variables that make up the final model of this research, it can be shown that economic factors, typical of the management of resources that the network of city councils carries out throughout the country, as well as factors that characterize the population, are both a greater concern of those determinants that influence the quality of life of the inhabitants and their real impact on efficiency.

The results described above, obtained through econometrics and interdisciplinary dialog, can contribute towards the design and improvement of political-administrative models being demanded by the Chilean population, insofar as decentralizing power and managing the crises that are currently creating tension and polarization, the likes of which the country has not experienced for decades.

Acknowledgements

Claudio Elórtegui Gómez and Hanns de la Fuente-Mella are supported by Grant NUCLEO DE INVESTIGACION EN DATA ANALYTICS/PUCV VRIEA/039.432/2020.

Conflict of interest

The authors declare no conflict of interest.

Author details

Claudio Elórtegui-Gómez, Hanns de la Fuente-Mella*, Mauricio Alvarado and Matías Guajardo
Pontificia Universidad Católica de Valparaíso, Valparaíso, Chile

*Address all correspondence to: hanns.delafuente@pucv.cl

References

[1] OECD. Chile: Policy Priorities for Stronger and more Equitable Growth. Best Policies Series. Paris: OECD Publishing; 2015. p. 52. Available from: https://www.oecd.org/fr/chili/chile-prioridades-de-politicas-para-un-crecimiento-mas-fuerte-y-equitativo.pdf

[2] Henríquez O. Decentralization laws: Axis of change in territorial policy and intergovernmentality in Chile. RIEM. 2020;**21**:5-28. ISSN: 0719-1790. Available from: https://www.revistariem.cl/index.php/riem/article/view/252

[3] Dazarola G. Legal Framework of the Municipalities, Main Regulatory Provisions [Internet]. Biblioteca del Congreso Nacional; 2018. Available from: https://www.bcn.cl/obtienearchivo?id=repositorio/10221/25833/1/GRID_Marco_Juridico_Municipalidades_GD_Def.pdf [Accessed: 25 November 2019]

[4] Fernández R. The administration of the state and the municipalities in Chile. IUS. 2013;**32**:148-160. DOI: 10.35487/rius.v7i32.2013.37

[5] Cáceres P. Government, autonomy and local democracy. Notes for a normative theory. RIEM. 2015;**12**:197-215. ISSN: 0719-1790. Available from: https://www.revistariem.cl/index.php/riem/article/view/49

[6] Mardones R. Decentralization: A definition and evaluation of the Chilean legislative agenda (1990-2008). Eure. 2008;**102**:39-60. DOI: 10.4067/S0250-71612008000200003

[7] Hooghe L, Marks G, Schakel A, Osterkatz S, Niedzwiecki S, Shair-Rosenfield S. Measuring Regional Authority: A Postfunctionalist Theory of Governance. Vol. I. Oxford: Oxford University Press; 2016. p. 687. DOI: 10.1093/acprof:oso/9780198728870.001.0001

[8] Szmulewicz E, Saffirio I. Proposals for decentralization consistent with territorial equity. In: Cifuentes J, Pérez C, Rivera S, editors. ¿Qué políticas públicas para Chile?. Santiago: Centro de Estudios del Desarrollo. 2017. pp. 108-128. ISBN: 978-956-7815-14-2. Available from: http://www.ced.cl/cedcl/wp-content/uploads/2017/10/CED-2017-Qu%C3%A9-Pol%C3%ADticas-P%C3%BAblicas-para-Chile.pdf

[9] Thayer L. Decentralization and regional development in Chile. Polis. 2011;**30**:267-287. DOI: 10.4067/S0718-65682011000300013

[10] Bravo J. Municipal common fund and its disincentive to collection in Chile. Topics on the Public Agenda UC Public Policy Center. 2014;**68**:1-18. ISSN: 0718-9745

[11] Pérez M. Analysis of the Chilean municipalities: Income from management versus transfers from the Municipal Common Fund. Journal of Public Policy Studies. 2016;**2**:121-130. DOI: 10.5354/0719-6296.2016.44264

[12] Espejel J, Flores M, Rodríguez J. The facets of governance: Political and administrative efficiency of the state. Public Spaces. 2012;**35**:30-47. ISSN: 1665-8140. Available from: https://core.ac.uk/download/pdf/55530251.pdf

[13] Barzelay M. The new public management: Invitation to cosmopolitan dialogue. Management and Public Policy. 2003;**12**:241-252.ISSN: 1405-1079

[14] Easton D. A Systems Analysis of Political Life. New York: Wiley; 1965. p. 490

[15] Scharpf F. Introduction: The problem-solving capacity of multi-level governance. Journal of European Public Policy. 1997;**4**:520-538. DOI: 10.1080/135017697344046

[16] Papadopoulos Y. Cooperative forms of governance: Problems of democratic accountability in complex environments. European Journal of Political Research. 2003;**42**:473-501. DOI: 10.1111/1475-6765.00093

[17] Papadopoulos Y, Warin P. Major findings and paths for research: A concluding note. European Journal of Political Research. 2007;**46**:591-605. DOI: 10.1111/j.1475-6765.2007.00700.x

[18] National Congress Library. Law No. 18.695 Organic and Constitutional Municipalities. 2006. Available from: http://bcn.cl/1uuy [Accessed: 15 March 2018]

[19] Sampaio de Sousa M, Stosic B. Technical Efficiency of the Brazilian Municipalities: Correcting Non-Parametric Frontier Measurements for Outliers. Working Paper No. 294. Brasil: Department of Economics University of Brasilia; 2003

[20] Hamilton B. The flypaper effect and other anomalies. Journal of Public Economics. 1983;**22**:347-361

[21] National Municipal Information System. Budget Review [Internet]. 2016. Available from: http://www.sinim.gov.cl/archivos/home/597/Revista_Presupuestaria_SINIM_Junio_2016.pdf [Accessed: 01 August 2018]

[22] Silkman R, Young D. X-efficiency and state formula grants. National Tax Journal. 1982;**35**:383-397

[23] Balaguer-Coll M, Prior D, Tortosa-Ausina E. On the Determinants of Local Government Performance: A Two-Stage Nonparametric Approach. Working Paper No. 3. Centre for Applied Economic Research; 2003

[24] Pacheco F, Sánchez R, Villena M. Efficiency of Local Governments and their Determinants: An Analysis of Stochastic Borders in Panel Data for Chilean Municipalities, Directorate of Budgets of the Ministry of Finance. Vol. 9. 2013. p. 23

[25] De Borger B, Kerstens K. Cost efficiency of Belgian local governments: A comparative analysis of FDH, DEA, and econometric approaches. Regional Science and Urban Economics. 1996;**26**:145-170

[26] Loikkanen H, Susiluoto I. Cost efficiency of finnish municipalities in basic service provision 1994-2002. In: ERSA Conference Papers No. 5. European Regional Science Association; 2005

[27] Diener E, Rahtz D, editors. Advances in Quality of and Theory and Research. Dordrecht, Netherlands: Springer; 2000. p. 267. DOI: 10.1007/978-94-011-4291-5

[28] Ardila R. Quality of life: An integrative definition. Latin American Journal of Psychology. 2003;**35**:161-164

[29] Max-Neef M, Elizalde A, Hopenhayn M, Human scale development: an option for the future. Development Dialogue, special issue. 1989;1:7-81. ISSN: 0345-2328

[30] National Municipal Information System. Municipal Technological Reality [Internet]. 2018. Available from: http://www.sinim.gov.cl/archivos/home/649/Resultados_Encuesta_TIC_2018.pdf [Accessed: 08 December 2018]

[31] Alguacil J. Quality of life and urban praxis: New citizen management initiatives on the social periphery of Madrid [thesis]. Madrid: Faculty of Political Science and Sociology, Complutense University; 2000

[32] Herrera P, Francke P. Analysis of the efficiency of municipal expenditure and its determinants. Economia - PUC Lima. 2009;**63**:113-178. ISSN: 2304-4306 [Internet]. Available from: http://

revistas.pucp.edu.pe/index.php/economia/article/view/1031

[33] Coughenour C, De la Fuente H, Paz A. Analysis of self-reported walking for transit in a sprawling urban metropolitan area in the western U.S. Sustainability. 2019;**852**:2-16. DOI: 10.3390/su11030852

[34] Paz A, De la Fuente H, Singh A, Conover R, Monteiro H. Highway expenditures and associated customer satisfaction: A case study. Mathematical Problems in Engineering. 2016:1-9. DOI: 10.1155/2016/4630492

[35] De la Fuente H, Vallina A, Solis R. Stochastic analysis of the economic growth of OECD countries. Economic Research-Ekonomska Istraživanja. 2019:2-15. DOI: 10.1080/1331677X.2019.1685397

[36] De la Fuente H, Rojas J, Leiva V. Econometric modeling of productivity and technical efficiency in the Chilean manufacturing industry. Computers and Industrial Engineering. 2020;**139**:2-11. DOI: 10.1016/j.cie.2019.04.006

[37] Coughenour C, Paz A, De la Fuente H, Singh A. Multinomial logistic regression to estimate and predict perceptions of bicycle and transportation infrastructure in a sprawling metropolitan area. Journal of Public Health. 2016;**38**:401-408. DOI: 10.1093/pubmed/fdv179

[38] Library of the National Congress. Law No. 18.695 Organic and Constitution-al Municipalities [Internet]. 2006. Available from: http://bcn.cl/1uuy1 [Accessed: 23 September 2017]

[39] Daly H. For operational principles of sustainable development. Alfoz. 1990;**96**:27-30, Madrid. ISSN: 0212-5064

Chapter 16

Relationship between Economic Growth, Unemployment, Inflation and Current Account Balance: Theory and Case of Turkey

Tuğba Dayıoğlu and Yılmaz Aydın

Abstract

The relations between economic growth, unemployment, inflation and current account balance are analyzed theoretically and different comments on theoretical approaches are discussed in the study. Accordingly, while the unemployment-inflation relationship is considered with Phillips analysis and the scope of the growth-unemployment with Okun Law, the interaction between the current account balance and growth is shown with the equality of national income accounting. After the theoretical approaches described in detail with shared data and interpreted for Turkey. This study also examines the relation between the unemployment, inflation, economic growth, current account deficit with symmetric and asymmetric reserved causality tests were examined for the 2000Q1 – 2020Q4 period. The asymmetric hidden causality relationships between the series were researched with Hatemi-J (2012) method based on Toda-Yamamoto (1995) test in this study. When the relationship between the growth rate and the unemployment rate are examined between these years in Turkey it is observed that there is an inverse relationship between growth and unemployment, especially during crisis periods. After that to find this relationship we used symmetric and asymmetric causality. As a result of the estimates growth also has a one-way symmetrical causality relationship from negative shocks to negative inflation shocks. When the relationship between them is viewed only with one-way or two-way causality, there may be no relationship so the causality must be checked asymmetrically even to catch the assumption of the Okun's law correctly for Turkey.

Keywords: Phillips curve, Okoń law, growth, asymmetric and symmetric causality

1. Introduction

The economic growth, unemployment, inflation and current account balance are the most important variables that show the performance of an economy. The quality of the relationship between these variables is extremely important when the applying economic policies. Thus there may be harmony or contradiction between the policies to be implemented on the issues. In other words, unemployment policies for economic growth also lead to a decrease in unemployment, while trying to lower inflation could put negative pressure on unemployment. Therefore the

IntechOpen

alignment or contradictions between the intended objectives and the instruments to be implemented should be taken into account when making policy proposals. In this study, the relations between growth, unemployment, inflation and current account are first discussed in theoretical terms and it is examined whether these theories are valid or not in the case of Turkey.

Accordingly, the Phillip curve analysis, which explains the nature of the relationship between unemployment and inflation, was analyzed in detail by comparing interpretations of different economic approaches. In the case of inflation, the demand-side policies will have an effect on these variables. In contrast, according to the Monetarist and New Classical approach, demand-side policies are ineffective and therefore unnecessary. In more accurate terms, the relationship between unemployment and inflation is temporary in the short-term because both variables may change in the same direction in the long term. After this topic was discussed in the first part of the study after then the case of Turkey was examined and discussed.

Another theoretical approach that attempts to explain the relationship between macroeconomic variables analysis are known as Okun's law. The Okun's law suggests an inverse relationship between the growth rate and the unemployment rate. In the one study is determined by Okun with regression analysis between 1947 and 1960. This law that explained every %1 growth rate in the United States reduced the decreased the unemployment rate 0.5% points. However, the growth rate must exceed a certain level and average or trend growth rate in order to affect unemployment. Although the Okun's law is tested for different countries which are generally verified the nature of this relationship varies considerably from country to country.

The Okun's law was explained in details in the second section and its validity was tested for Turkey in the last section with symmetric and asymmetric causality. The another important indicator of a country's economic performance in macroeconomics is the current account balance. There is a very close relationship between the current account deficit and the growth rate which has become an important problem especially for developing countries.

In the many literature of econometric studies based on the relationships between economic growth, current account deficit, inflation and unemployment have also been conducted. In their study, [1] conducted the necessary econometric analyzes to determine the relationship between the variables using the monthly data 2007–2014 economic growth, unemployment and inflation. In the study under discussion, there is a causality analysis between the current account deficit, inflation problem and growth [2]. The study [3] Brazil, Russia, India, using annual data for the period 1993–2011 belong to China and Turkey, the panel analyzed the causal relationship between the current account deficit and inflation method. The relations between Azerbaijan, Kazakhstan, Kyrgyzstan, Macedonia and Turkey for the period 1996–2012 using data on inflation and unemployment with panel cointegration analyze and causality tests [4]. They are studied causality and vector error correction model between inflation, economic, growth and unemployment in North African Countries [5]. In the study the inflation and economic growth are taken for Nigeria with regression analysis. They studied the inflation, economic growth, unemployment relationship with Var analysis for Iraq. In this study, the relationship between the current account deficits, economic growth and the current account with certain explanations are wanted to examined [6].

The last part of our chapter we determined the relationship between the current account and the growth rate and they were explained with the national income inequality and the nature of this relationship was discussed in Turkey.

When we look at these relations in terms of causality, it is stated that the direction of the relationship in question will yield different results when viewed as asymmetric and symmetrical and should be adapted accordingly to their economic policies.

2. Unemployment and inflation relationship: Phillips curve

The relationships between macroeconomic variables in an economy and the reciprocal interactions of these variables are crucial to policy proposals. The intervention was deemed unnecessary because it was assumed that the economy would always reach the full employment balance thanks to its spontaneous, intrinsic mechanisms at the time of the classic-neoclassical paradigm. However, the Great Depression system in 1929 has shown that it is insufficient to solve many problems such as especially unemployment and furthermore problems become deeper than before. Keynes' masterpiece General Theory has been a turning point in terms of the government's intervention in the economy and the nature of this intervention [7].

It can be said that the Classic-Neoclassical paradigm is also in crisis with the publication of the General Theory which Keynes expressed his views about the crisis. Microeconomic analyses which examine the optimum distribution of resources in neoclassical theory were replaced by the analysis of macroeconomic variables such as employment, national product, total lack of demand in the post-Keynes period, and analysis of interactions between these variables. In this context, the study was published with the title "The Relation between Unemployment and the Rate of Change of Money Wage Rates in the United Kingdom, 1861-1957" [8]. This study led to a long discussion of the relationship between inflation and unemployment and the effectiveness of its policies to be implemented. Reflecting the views of neoclassical Synthesis Keynesian economists, the original version of the Phillips Curve shows the relationship between the rate of increase of nominal wages in the UK between 1861 and 1957, i.e. wage inflation and the unemployment rate [9]. Phillips said the hypothesis that the change in monetary wage rates (the rate of change of money wage rates) is determined by the level of unemployment and the rate of change of unemployment can be generally accepted. These conclusions are of course tentative. There is need for much more detailed research into the relations between unemployment, wage rates, prices and productivity [8].

Paul Samuelson and Robert Solow examined the relationship between inflation and unemployment by substituting the Consumer Price Index in the United States instead of the wage rate, and thus developed a new interpretation in 1960. In this study, it was concluded that if unemployment was held at 5–6% (if unemployment were held at 5 to 6 percent) the price index could be stable, whereas if unemployment was held at 4%, there could be a 2% increase in inflation [10].

This interpretation, also called the Phillips Curve, which has been modified and improved has gained great importance in the literature and has become meaningful in terms of economic policy in this way. The Philips Curve shows the inverse relationship between the unemployment rate with the inflation rate, compatible with the Keynesian approach, high inflation rate, low unemployment rate and low inflation with high unemployment rate means that a choice can be made between combinations of. The governments which can be called' Mitte-Rechts 'prefer the first combination, while the governments that are' left-of-Centre '('Mitte-Links') have adopted the second policy proposal. The stagflation process, called the combination of rising inflation and unemployment, was seen after the 1970 oil crisis. This situation has led to questioning and discussion of the stable relationship between prices and unemployment [9].

The fact that the stagflation phenomenon that emerged in the late 1960s could not be explained by Phillips Curve Analysis intensified the debate on the Phillips curve durin this period. Under the fine-tuning policy, for example, if the government wants to reduce unemployment, it must increase total demand. However, it is necessary to endure some inflation increase with increasing total demand.

According to Friedman and Phelps, the economy does not stabilize after the inflation rate rises. Because if the adaptive expectations approach is valid, when inflation rises, inflation-related expectations also rise. In other words, the Phillips curve shifts to the right and unemployment returns to its natural rate again. In such a case, it is possible to reduce unemployment below its natural level with ever-increasing inflation. In this context, Friedman suggests that the stable relationship between unemployment and inflation is due to differing expected inflation and realized inflation rates. When the expected and current inflation rates are the same, there will be no change in real wages and hence the level of employment. Because in this case, the expected inflation rate will be reflected in long-term wage contracts [11]. To sum up, according to Friedman's analysis, the negative-sloping Phillips curve, that is, the existence of an inverse relationship between inflation and unemployment is temporary. Friedman specifically emphasizes here that the temporary trade off relationship is due to false expectations about inflation that lead to rising inflation. In the long term, as a result of the revision of inflation expectations, the exchange relationship disappears and the curve becomes perpendicular to the horizontal axis [12].

According to neoclassical synthesis Keynesian economists the Phillips curve is negatively sloped that means there is an exchange between unemployment and inflation whereas the Monetarist economists argue that is only true in the short term. In contrast, the new classical approach suggests that the Phillips Curve is a right perpendicular to the horizontal axis both in the short run and long run. According to the new classical analysis, according to rational expectations, unemployment always remains at the level of natural unemployment, except for unforeseen shocks and random errors under the assumption that there will be no systematic error in the forecast of inflation. In other words, there is no relationship between unemployment and inflation. This situation is explained by the Lucas 'surprise' supply function is determined,

$$Y - Y_n = \alpha\,(P - P^e) \quad (1)$$

According to the current price level equation if the deviation (PPe) between the (P) with the expected price level (Pe) be more greater the differences between the actual production (Y) and the natural balance in the level of output (Yn) will be more as (Y − Yn). Since inflation is the same as expected inflation in rational expectations approach, current income is always at the level of natural income and unemployment is also at the level of natural and natural unemployment. It is possible to deviate from the natural level of unemployment if the inflation estimate is incorrect. Such a situation can only be explained by a "surprise" development [13], meaning that the actual inflation rate deviates from the expected inflation rate. The fact that the economy is always in balance at the natural level of unemployment means at demand-side policies are unnecessary. According to The New Classical Macroeconomics theory, which has Monetarist views at the point of origin, the conjuncture policy is ineffective. With monetary policies, it is not possible to increase production and employment levels even in the short term.

The existence of a relationship between unemployment and inflation, that is, tradeoff between these two variables or not is important for policy proposals. The Keynesian economists argue that if there is an exchange between unemployment and inflation, it is possible to achieve the desired result with the demand-side policies to be implemented. In this context, expansionary monetary and fiscal policies will lead to demand expansion, resulting in unemployment reduction, while demand-biased inflation increases will occur. On the contrary if it is necessary to lower inflation, the shrinking policies that will be implemented require some

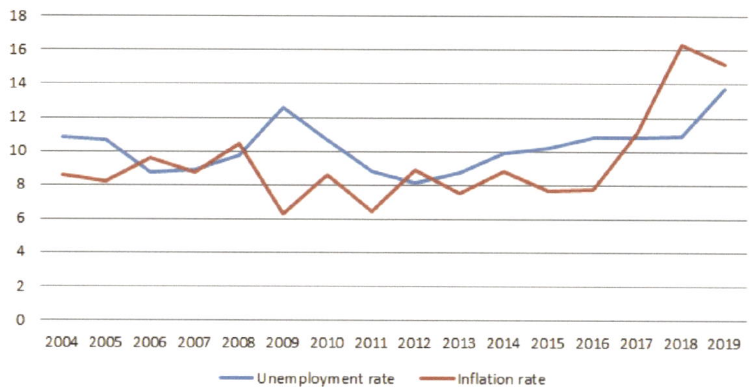

Figure 1.
Relationship between unemployment rate and inflation rate (2004–2019). Source: Turkish World Bank – TCMB.

amount of unemployment to be endured. In contrast, the Monetarist and new classical economists, who represent the orthodox approach, suggest that these two variables are independent of each other and that demand-side policies will have no effect on them. In this approach, which argues that inflation is always a monetary phenomenon the public intervention in the economy with cyclical policies will have unnecessary and negative consequences.

The below mentioned **Figure 1** shows the relationship between the unemployment rate and the inflation rate in Turkey. According to the chart, there is an inverse relationship between the unemployment rate and the inflation rate in general. In the period studied, the rate of increase in prices is low or vice versa during periods when unemployment rate is high in Turkey. In the post-2008 period when the global crisis occurred, unemployment decreased from 13 to 8% between 2009 and 2012, while the inflation rate remained unstable and rose from 6 to 9%. This can be seen as a result of expansionary monetary policies implemented in developed countries to counter the negative effects of the crisis on unemployment. As with other developing countries, capital inflows have accelerated with the increase in money supply in the global dimension. Intensive capital inflows can be said to have an effect that reduces unemployment by providing a high growth rate. The unemployment rate has started to rise after reaching its lowest level in 2012 and is nearing 14% in 2019. During this period, the inflation rate was bumpy but increased from 9 to 15%. This period occurs for the inflation and unemployment rising together and points to stagflationist developments.

Figure 1 shows that the rate of unemployment and inflation rose by 4 and 7 percentage points respectively in the period 2004–2019. Therefore, while it is possible to talk about the existence of a relationship between inflation and unemployment rate in the short term, it is observed that there is no exchange between the two variables in the long term. In other words, it is predictable that the expected impact of policies aimed at lowering the unemployment rate on inflation will be limited or short-term. Similarly, policies aimed at price stability should be expected to have a limited and short-term impact on unemployment.

3. Relationship between growth rate and unemployment: Okun's law

One of the highlights of the analysis on unemployment is the relationship between growth and unemployment. The main expectation of given the main determinants of economic growth is the unemployment rate decreasing in an economy where the growth is occurring or at the least the current unemployment rate does not increase.

In this context, the effects of economic growth on employment or unemployment rate are examined and whether growth creates employment is the subject of research both in the world literature and in Turkey [1]. Historically, it is observed that the relationship between economic growth and employment has weakened or, in other words, become more complex in recent periods. It is observed that there is neither a one-to-one nor a stable relationship between growth and employment, especially with the developments in countries 'economies after [14]. Economists who supported the structural adjustment policy predicted that employment would increase with the liberalization of foreign trade, which is the basis of the export-based growth strategy. What many developing countries have experienced in recent years is far from confirming these claims of neoclassical theory. In order to ensure adequate employment in an environment where the working age population is increasing at a high pace, growth must be sustained as well as high growth rates. The fact that the growth figures in Turkey have been below minus six percent three times since the 1990s shows that the growth has been extremely unstable. This indicates that the growth due to short-term foreign capital inflows is not permanent and its fragility is high with the liberalization of capital movements [15].

The view that economic growth will lead to increased employment and reduce unemployment is known as Okun's law in the literature. Arthur Okun examined the relationship between the unemployment rate and economic growth in the United States by regression analysis using quarterly data for the period 1947–1960. According to the developed regression equation, the difference between current income and full employment income varies in the opposite direction with the unemployment rate [16]. The law developed by Okun states that if the growth rate exceeds the trend or average growth rate measured at 2.25%, it will lead to a decrease in the unemployment rate. Exactly, the question of how much e ach percentage point of GDP growth that exceeds the growth trend will lower the unemployment rate is being sought. The Okun law can similarly be used to predict the growth rate needed to reduce the unemployment rate by %1 [17]. The study covering the above-mentioned period for the United States concluded that each % 1growth rate over the pre-growth rate reduced the unemployment rate by %0.5 points [18]. The Okun law can be expressed by the following equation;

$$\Delta u = k(y - y*) \tag{2}$$

Where Δu is the change in the unemployment rate, y is the growth rate of the product. Y* in the equation represents the growth trend of real GDP. This ratio varies from country to country. In the years in which the economy performs growth above the natural rate, there will be a change in the unemployment rate to k times the difference between the actual and natural growth rate. Accordingly, the relationship between growth and unemployment for the United States can be written as:

$$\Delta u = -0,5(y - 2,25) \tag{3}$$

Data covering the period 1975–1995 showed that unemployment decreased by 0.13 percentage points for every %1 point of growth exceeding % 4.3 in Turkey. In this context, the equation of Okun law for Turkey was found as follows:

$$\Delta u = -0,13(y - 4,3) \tag{4}$$

This study shows that the Okun law works very poorly for Turkey. The negative-directional regression line obtained in this study using regression analysis revealed the existence of an inverse relationship between the change in unemployment rate and the growth rate. However growth has an impact on unemployment it must be at least 4.3%. In other words, every %1 point increase after the growth rate reaches this level results in a reduction in the unemployment rate of only %0,13 [18]. It is seen that similar results have been reached in many different studies on Turkey. These calculations indicate that growth in the period of expansion of the conjuncture in particular had very low effects on employment, and hence the presence of non-employment growth. Another important finding obtained in these studies is that the relationship of Okun in the Turkish economy has an asymmetric structure, that is the effect of reducing unemployment during the expansion period of real output and the increasing unemployment during the contraction period are not same [3].

When the relationship between the growth rate and the unemployment rate are examined in 1999–2019 period in Turkey it is observed that there is an inverse relationship between growth and unemployment, especially during crisis periods. The unemployment rate reached high levels in 1999, 2001 and 2009, and in later years (in some periods) it began to decline, albeit lagging. Similarly, with the negative growth conditions caused by the foreign exchange crisis that took place in 2018, unemployment started to rise and reached its highest value in 2019 with 13.7%. On the other hand, the impact of the cyclical revival in the economy on unemployment remained relatively weak. Despite the growth rate approaching 10% in 2004 and 2005, the unemployment rate remained stable at high levels. It can be said that the decrease in the unemployment rate remained extremely limited in 2011, when the growth rate was the highest in the period studied. In the period of expansion that took place in 2013 and 2017, unemployment did not decrease, but rather started to increase (**Figure 2**).

Although growth statistics have increased over the years in the Turkish economy, unemployment rates have not decreased in the way predicted by Okun's law. In general accepted theory, when the growth rate of a country's economy increases, it is expected that employment will increase and the unemployment rate will decrease. Despite the high economic growth rates achieved in Turkey in recent years, this performance is not reflected in unemployment rates to the same extent, causing controversy. An economic growth model that depends on consumption-based foreign capital movements that do not provide employment is not sustainable. Considering the presence of rapid population growth and a demographic structure with a young population, it is of great importance to develop an economic

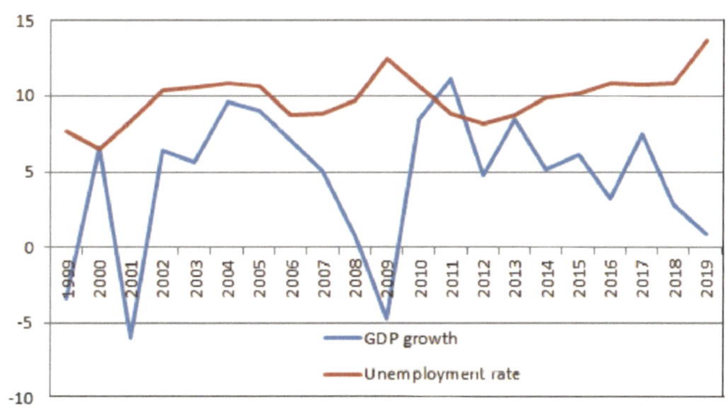

Figure 2.
Relationship between growth and unemployment rate (2004–2019). Source: Turkish World Bank – TCMB.

growth model with policies based on production, providing employment, focused on high value added products and reducing external dependence [17].

4. Growth and current account balance

The current account consists of two main items: the first is the foreign trade account showing the export and import of goods, and the second is the export and import of services, called "invisible trade" [19]. The current account deficit is less than the amount paid for goods produced and sold abroad to be consumed domestically, indicating that a country is making negative savings [20]. The relationship between the current account deficit and growth can be two-way relationship. Firstly the country with insufficient savings ratio or negative savings, the current account deficit can affect growth as investment spending is financed through the use of external savings. Second, as if income growth will increase demand for imported goods, the growth current account deficit may affect growth or may occur as a result of the growth rate itself.

The effect of the current account deficit on the growth rate is explained by providing investments with foreign savings if domestic savings are insufficient. It can be stated as follows if the savings are insufficient in an economy, investments are financed by borrowing of Foreign World Savings. In this context, as emphasized in both development economics and growth models, the source of growth is investment and the source of investment is savings ratio. If domestic savings are insufficient, it means that the difference can be met by using foreign sector savings and the current account deficit. The current account reflects the relationship between the financial markets and the goods and services markets in an economy. In the balance of payments, by definition, the current account deficit should be financed by capital account. In other words, the current account deficit may only be possible if necessary financing is provided in the capital account in the balance of payments.[1]

International flows of goods and capital are two sides of the coin and this can be explained by the national income accounting authority as follows [21]:

$$Y = C + I + X - M \tag{5}$$

This identification shows the components of National Income (Y), under the assumption of equivalence of public revenues and expenses. Total revenue equals household consumption expenditures (C), private sector investment expenditures and the difference between exports (X) and imports (M), i.e. net exports. When necessary adjustments are made here, it can be shown that net exports or the current account balance in a broad sense are equal to the domestic savings investment difference.:

$$S - I = X - M \tag{6}$$

This equality shows how the current account balance is achieved (If s = I and X = M) in an economy that finances domestic investments with domestic savings. Accordingly, if domestic savings are insufficient to meet the investments ($S < I$),

[1] The balance of payments, which is a current variable showing the sum of current account and capital account, is always in balance in ex post analysis. Current account deficit is possible by increasing the capital Account by the same amount. In other words, there can be no current account deficit that does not have a counterpart in the capital account, that is, it is not financed. Therefore, the view that the current account balance is a trivial problem as long as it is financed is an erroneous point of view, which has been put forward to emphasize that the current account deficit is not a major problem [10].

there will be current account deficit and the investments for finance to savings are provided from abroad [17]. Within the framework of this identification, for example, a study covering the 1980s for the United States concluded that the current account deficit could be explained by the lack of savings. In other words, the level of domestic investment is being supported by flows of foreign saving. The study also emphasizes that external savings flows are equal to the negative value of the current account balance [22]. The many studies similarly have found that the current account deficit affects the growth rate in Turkey as well. For example, changes in the current account deficit were shown to affect economic growth using the structured VAR method by evaluating the quarterly data in 2002–2014 [23]. The relationship between the current account deficit and growth in Turkey is closely related to the need for Energy (oil), investment goods and intermediate imports, as well as the insufficient savings rate. Turkey's dependence on exports in terms of oil and investment goods is an important factor affecting the reduction of the current account deficit. The realization of investments and therefore growth is linked to the current account deficit through the increase in imports. The consumption expenditures depend mainly on income in the Keynesian approach. Since income growth will affect demand for both domestic and imported goods, it will put a negative pressure on the current account. Thus, in this case, the rate of growth is the independent variable and the current account is the dependent variable, which varies accordingly. The relationship between these two variables is oriented from growth rate to current account balance. The import expenditure represented by M is an increasing function of income in the equality 6. The volume of imports consists of two components such as autonomous and revenue-dependent in the Keynesian model. Hence the total amount of imports varies in the right direction with income depending on the marginal import trend considered constant [24]. İt is observed that the mutual causality relationship is towards growth to current account deficit.

Figure 3 shows the ratio of the current account to GDP ratio and the growth rate in Turkey over the last 20 years. In the period examined, it is observed that the current account deficit increases during the expansion process and the current account deficit decreases during the contraction periods in Turkey. In addition, the current account balance has been continuously negative except the years 2001 and 2019. Especially when the economy experienced a contraction of close to 6% in 2002, the current account balance was realized at close to 2%. Similar to when the growth ratio reached its highest value (11.1%) the ratio growth to current account to GDP value reached % 8.9 in 2011, when the growth rate was a record it can be considered as an indication of how closely related the growth rate and the current account deficit are in Turkey.

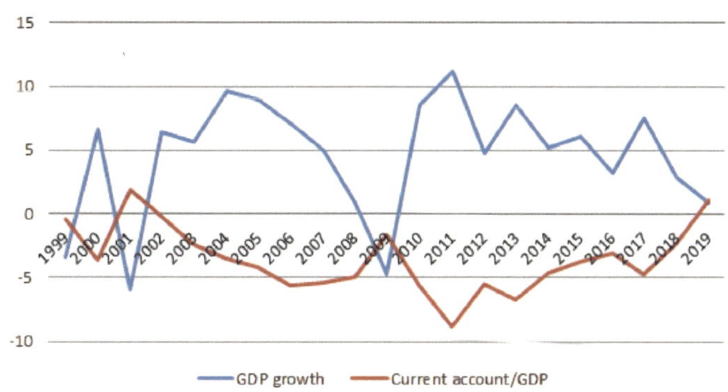

Figure 3.
Current account balance / GDP and growth rate (1999–2019). Source: OECD.

To summarize it is observed that while growth accelerated when the current account balance in Turkey gave a deficit. The growth slowed when the current account balance gave a surplus. In this context, the ratio of the current account deficit to GDP was 4.7% in 2017, while the same rate rose to 1.1% in 2019. In the same period, the growth rate started to decrease and reached 0.9% from 7.4%.

5. Data and variables

In this study we used Turkey's current account deficit (CAD), economic growth (G), inflation (INF) and unemployment rate (UR) data are used for the period 2000Q1-2020Q4. The data are taken from the Central Bank Electronic Data Distribution System (EVDS). Value of unemployment series from TUIK (Turkish Statistical Associatıon), others taken from EVDS.

6. Econometric methods

In this study, the degree of stationarity of series are found with Dickey Fuller and Ng -Perron methods. Between series interaction are measured with classic [25] causality test, [26] were analyzed by symmetric latent causality test and [27] asymmetric latent causality test methods. While [27] are developing symmetric and asymmetric implicit causality tests, [25] suggested the analysis which negative and positive shocks can be separated for the cointegration analysis with using the cumulative totals of these shocks. Firstly these series are divided into positive and negative shocks before these causality tests.

If causality relationships between two series such as y_{1t} and y_{2t} series,

$$y_{1t=Y_{1,0}} + \sum_{i=0}^{t} \varepsilon_{1i} \tag{7}$$

$$y_{2t=Y_{2,0}} + \sum_{i=0}^{t} \varepsilon_{2i} \tag{8}$$

And the positive shocks are showed,

$$\varepsilon_{1,i}^{+} = \max(\varepsilon_{1,i}, 0) \tag{9}$$

$$\varepsilon_{2,i^+} = max(\varepsilon_{2,i,}, 0) \tag{10}$$

The negative shocks are determined:

$$\varepsilon i1\text{-} = \min(\varepsilon_{1,i}, 0) \tag{11}$$

$$\varepsilon_{2,i^-} = min(\varepsilon_{2,i,}, 0) \tag{12}$$

The estimated equation will be held in the table with Toda- Yamamato causality;

$$\begin{aligned} cad_t = \gamma_0 + \sum_{i=1}^{k} \alpha_1\, cad_{t-i} + \sum_{j=k+1}^{k+dmax} \alpha_2 cad_{t-j} + \sum_{i=1}^{k} \alpha_3 G_{t-i} + \sum_{j=k+1}^{k+dmax} \alpha_4 G_{t-j} \\ + + \sum_{i=1}^{k} \alpha_5\, une_{t-i} + \sum_{j=k+1}^{k+dmax} \alpha_6 une_{t-j} + \sum_{i=1}^{k} \alpha_7\, \imath nf_{t-i} + \sum_{j=k+1}^{k+dmax} \alpha_2 \imath nf_{t-j} + \varepsilon_{1t} \end{aligned} \tag{13}$$

Other models will be helping one by one for each dependent variable with lagged independent other variables. When null hypothesis rejected that means there is causality for each taken dependent variable to independent variables. In the Todo yamamato causality test held the extra the lag value is expanded and taken dmax =1 and used the k levels with suitable lags levels.

They [26] refer to this causality analysis performed between the same types of shocks, [27] named this causality test asymmetric causality test performed between different types of shocks. In the study, Unit Root perron test [28] was performed and the findings were presented in **Table 1** below.

It was examined by the method of [28]. The MZa and MZt tests are developed from the type of ADF and PP type test whereas the null hypothesis says the variable is not stationary. MSB and MPT tests are KPSS group tests and the null hypothesis refers the series is stationary.

Table 1 was observed that all of the series were not stationary at level as I(0) but when the first differences were taken all variables became stationary as I (1).

After the determination of the degree of the level stationary of variables will be used for Granger causality test. In the analysis, causality relationships between the series were first examined by [29] method. The Akaike and Hannan-Quinn information criteria were determined based on VAR analysis. The first differences of the series were used for Granger causality and the results obtained are presented in **Table 2**.

Table 1 results show there is a strong one-way causality relationship between Inflation and Economic growth. The relationship is from inflation to growth ıt means that the inflation is cause of growth as the rejected null hypothesis shows it.

Inflation rates are also directly affects the higher economic growth rate in Turkey. The import of the raw materials and semi-finished materials are needed during the production effects the economy.

Variables	$I(0)$				$I(1)$			
	MZ_a	MZ_t	MSB	MPT	MZ_a	MZ_t	MSB	MPT
CAD +	−2,36 (18,15)	−1,34 (4,76)	0,46 (7,33)	5,54 (21,44)	−24,12 (−12,42)*	−4,54 (−3,11)*	0,45 (0,78)*	2,34 (3.34)*
CAD −	1,89 (18,1)	−1,67 (4,77)	1,42 (7,33)	34,55 (21,44)	−21,20 (−12,42)*	−4,33 (−3,11)*	0,34 (0,78)*	2,15 (3,34)*
UNE +	−4,33 (−18,7)	−2,44 (6,45)	1,56 (6,33)	22,13 (5,33)	−19,33 (−14,6)*	−3,43 (−2,44)*	0,64 (0,77)*	2,11 (3,21)*
UNE_	−4,21 (18,7)	−2,31 (6,46)	−1,57 (6,33)	25,45 (5,33)	−22,56 (−14,6)*	−3,66 (−2,44)*	0,67 (0,78)*	1,77 (3,21)*
INF+	−4,67 (20,3)	−2,44 (11,7)	0.55 (15,7)	27,56 (5,13)	−31,56 (−12,33)*	−3,89 (−2,67)*	0,22 (0,77)*	1,56 (1,88)*
INF-	−4,68 (20,4)	−1,66 (11,8)	0,34 (15,7)	31,42 (5,13)	27,45 (−12,33)*	−3,92 (−2,67)*	0,50 (0,78)*	1,42 (1,88)*
G+	−8,77 (4,22)	−3,77 (8,33)	0,21 (9,72)	8,55 (3,77)	−24,45 (−12,45)*	−2,44 (−1,16)*	0,33 (0,77)*	1,58 (2,33)*
G_	7,34 (4,24)	−3,59 (8,34)	0.22 (9,74)	9,88 (3,77)	−25,44 (−12,45)*	−2,56 (−1,16)*	0,34 (0.77)*	1,37 (2,33)*

The parenthesis shows the %1 significance level of asymptotic critical levels.
The stationary serial that has at %1 significance critical values. The I(1) all models have trend and constant.

Table 1.
Ng and Perron (2001) unit root test results [28].

Hypothesis	Opt.lag.	F statistics	Prob
G → INF	4	0,426	0.544
INF → G	4	0,210	0.021*
CAD → G	4	0,588	0.711
G → CAD	4	0,834	0.455
INF → UNE	4	0.615	0.233
UNE → INF	4	0,588	0.355
UNE → G	4	0,712	1.235
G → UNE	4	0,833	0.783

**The null hypothesis the caused to determined variables.*

Table 2.
Granger causality test.

Table 3 obtained the hidden causality test relationships results between the all variables which belong to [26]. We take the positive and negative shocks which refers different effect to causality between each other. The symmetric causality test shows the same shocks effect how affect the causality.

Table 3 shows the positive shocks on inflatıon causes the positive shocks on unemployment. The two way causality with unemployment and inflation under the positive shocks effect.

There is a mutual causal relationship between growth and unemployment under the positive shock situation. The inflation causes the growth when they are affected negative shock. There is a one way causality growth to inflation. In the symmetric causality we could not find any causality with other variables.

Hypothesis	Test statistic	Bootstrap Critical value
$G^{+} \rightarrow INF^{+}$	1231	4,87
$G^{-} \rightarrow INF^{-}$	4553*	2,31
$CAD^{+} \rightarrow G^{+}$	2237	4,55
$CAD^{-} \rightarrow G^{-}$	4674	5.22
$INF^{+} \rightarrow UNE^{+}$	8.232*	3,66
$INF^{-} \rightarrow UNE^{-}$	3478	4,21
$UNE^{+} \rightarrow G^{+}$	2361	5,67
$UNE^{-} \rightarrow G^{-}$	2456	7,34
$G^{+} \rightarrow CAD^{+}$	5346*	2,40
$G^{-} \rightarrow CAD^{-}$	5172	8,33
$UNE^{-} \rightarrow INF^{-}$	4164	6,22
$UNE^{+} \rightarrow INF^{+}$	4671*	1,67
$G^{+} \rightarrow UNE^{+}$	3477*	2,39
$G^{-} \rightarrow INF^{-}$	3782	6,33

**The causality with the %5 significance level.*

Table 3.
Symmetric causality test.

Hypothesis	Var lag (p + d)	Asymmetric causality test probe	ARCH-LM	White	J.B.
$G^+ \rightarrow INF^-$	4	0.867	0.645	0.788	0.001
$INF^- \rightarrow G^+$		0.563		0.231	
$CAD^+ \rightarrow G^-$	7	0.059	0.328	0.345	0.001
$G^- \rightarrow CAD^+$		**0.001***			
$INF^- \rightarrow UNE^+$	4	**0.003***	0.239	0.358	0.013
$UNE^+ \rightarrow INF^-$		0.548			
$UNE^- \rightarrow G^+$	6	0.458	0.234	0.127	0.022
$G^+ \rightarrow UNE^-$		**0.001***			
$G^+ \rightarrow CAD^-$	8	**0.002***	0.078	0.390	0.001
$CAD^- \rightarrow G^+$		**0.476**			
$UNE^- \rightarrow INF^{,+}$	5	**0.007***	0.084	0.56	0.002
$INF^+ \rightarrow UNE^{,-}$		**0.013***			
$G^+ \rightarrow UNE^+$	5	0.156	0.671	0.551	0.012
$UNE^+ \rightarrow G^+$		0.088			
$INF^+ \rightarrow G^-$	6	0.001	0.458	0.755	0.003
$G^- \rightarrow INF^+$		**0.002***			

*The **bold** numbers are statistically significant probabilities.*
**The asymmetric probability is statistically significant. The LM test for otocorrelation, White test for heteroscedasticity. The probability statistically significance levels for %5 confidence. Jarque bera test is for normality, the probability levels are statistically significant that eject the null hypothesis.*

Table 4.
Asymmetric causality test.

Table 4 shows the causality relationships between positive and negative shocks of series which they were investigated by [27] method which based on [23] test. The test of models are suitable for the analysis. There is no normal distribution because of asymmetric structure also there are no correlation and heteroscedasticity are found with Lm test and White test results under the null hypothesis accepted and not statistically significant probability levels [30–34].

According to these results the one way causality from negative growth shock to positive current deficit shocks. The negative growth shocks cause the positive unemployment shock. This means the positive effect on growth makes the negative effect on unemployment that makes the unemployment getting bigger.

The positive shock of growth causes the negative current account deficit shock. That means when the growth is becoming more well the current account deficit is continuing to increase. The negative shock on ınflation causes the positive shock on unemployment. Negative shock on growth causes the positive shock inflation. The negative shock on unemployment and positive shock on inflation have bidirectional causality.

7. Conclusion

In this study, economic growth for Turkey, the current account deficit, inflation and unemployment data in the period considered causality between these to show the differences in the relationship be followed when the shocks that affected both symmetric and was examined by asymmetric causality test.

When we look at the symmetrical causality test, one-way causality was determined from positive unemployment to positive inflation shock, positive growth shock to positive unemployment shock, positive growth to positive current account deficit. There is also causality from negative growth shock to negative inflation. The obtained from the study results the multiple causality between unemployment and inflation when the positive shocks are effective on one of them which another is not.

As a result of the asymmetric test, there is causality from positive growth shocks to negative unemployment shocks and causality towards negative current shocks and positive current account deficit shocks. The mutual causality was observed between positive growth shocks and negative current account deficit shocks. In this way, while studying the causing between them, this causality may not emerge, but causality relationship may arise from considering different responses to shocks.

In addition, the emergence of different relationship structures in response to these positive and negative shocks from an economic point of view also makes the situation and impact of different economic causes a matter to be considered.

According to these statements imports must increase in order to accelerate the economy since Turkey has a production structure dependent on imports. In this case, there is inevitably an external account deficit. This deficit, which means the use of foreign savings, has caused the foreign debt stock in Turkey to exceed the tolerable level. Increasing foreign debt and the consequent need for foreign currency means that the economy becomes more fragile and macroeconomic balances deteriorate rapidly. In order to grow without a current account deficit the significant changes in the production structure of the economy must be implemented immediately in Turkey. First of all the intermediate goods producing sectors must be developed and the dependence on imports must be decreased. Moreover, a competitive exchange rate policy in foreign trade should be expected to have positive results.

Author details

Tuğba Dayıoğlu* and Yılmaz Aydın
Nisantasi University Nisantasi University, Istanbul, Turkey

*Address all correspondence to: tugba.dayioglu@nisantasi.edu.tr

References

[1] Apaydın, Ş. ve C. Taşdoğan (2019). Yapısal ve Konjonktürel İşsizlik Çerçevesinde Okun Yasası Üzerine Bir Gözlem, Int. Journal of Management Economics and Business, Vol. 15, No. 1, pp. 61-76

[2] Gocer, I., Gerede, I., (2016). Cari Açık-Ekonomik Büyüme-Enflasyon ve İşsizlik Açmazında Türkiye: Yeni Nesil Bir Ekonometrik Analiz, Anadolu Unıversıtesı Sosyal Bilimler Dergisi , 16 ,35-46

[3] Akay, K.H., Aklan, N.A. ve M. Çınar (2016).Türkiye Ekonomisinde Ekonomik Büyüme ve İşsizlik, Yönetim ve Ekonomi Araştırmaları Dergisi - Cilt: 14 Sayı:1, ss. 209-226

[4] Gül, E., Kamacı A., Konya, S. (2012). Enflasyon ile İşsizlik Arasındaki Nedensellik İlişkisinin Test Edilmesi: Panel Eşbütünleşme ve Nedensellik Analizi. Internatıonal Conference on Eurasian Economies 2014. http://avekon.org/papers/861.pdf

[5] Sahnoun, M., Abdennadher, C. (2019). Causality Between Inflation, Economic Growth and Unemployment in North African Countries. Economic Alternatives, 2019, Issue 1, pp. 77-92

[6] Lucy, A., Tuama, A.S., Darko.S,. (2017). Inflation-Unemployment-and-Economic-Growth-Evidence-from-the-VAR-Model-Approach-for-the-Economy-of-Iraq. International Journal of Developing and Emerging Economies. Vol.5, No.1, pp.26-39

[7] Keynes, J. M. (1936 [2013]). The General Theory of Employment, Interest and Money, in: A. Robinson and D. Moggridge (ed.), The Collected Writings of John Maynard Keynes, vol. VII, Cambridge University Press, New York.

[8] Phillips, A. W. (1958). "The Relation Between Unemployment and the Rate of Change of Money Wage Rates in the United Kingdom, 1861–1957", Ec onomica, London School of Economics and Political Science, vol. 25(100), pages 283-299, November.

[9] Sesselmeier, W. , L. Funk und B. Waas (2010). Arbeitsmarkttheorien: Eine ökonomisch-juristische Einführung, Dritte, vollstaendige überarbeitete Auflage, Physica-Verlag, Springer-Verlag Berlin heidelberg.

[10] Pitchfold, J. (2003). The current account and foreign debt, Routledge, London and New York.

[11] Friedman, Milton: "The Role of Monetary Policy", The American Economic Review, Vol. 58, No. 1, (Mar., 1968), pp.1-17.

[12] Friedman, Milton: Nobel Lecture: Inflation and Unemployment, The Journal of Politcal Economy, Vol. 85, No. 3, (Jun., 1977), pp.451-472.

[13] Snowdon, B., H. Vane and P. Wynarczyk (1996). A Modern Guide to Macroeconomics: An Introduction to Competing Schools of Thought, Cambridge, Edward Elgar.

[14] Kara, M. ve M. Duruel (2005). Türkiye'de Ekonominin İstihdam Yaratamama Sorunu, İ.Ü. İktisat Fakültesi Sosyal Siyaset Konferansları 50. Kitap, (Prof. Dr. Nevzat Yalçıntaş'a Armağan – Özel Sayı), İstanbul, ss. 367-396.

[15] Onaran, Ö. (2006). Türkiye'de İhracat Yönelimli Büyüme Politikalarının İstihdam Üzerindeki Etkileri, İktisadi Kalkınma, Kriz ve İstikrar, (Oktar Türel'e Armağan), Ed., Ahmet Haşim Köse, Fikret Şenses, Erinç Yeldan, 3. bs., İstanbul, İletişim Yayınları, ss.579-601

[16] Ozcelık,O.,Uslu,N.(2017). Ekonomik Büyüme, İşsizlik Ve

Enflasyon Arasındaki İlişkinin Var Modeli İle Analizi: Türkiye Örneği (2007-2014), EKEV AKADEMİ DERGİSİ Yıl: 21 Sayı: 69,31-51

[17] Dornbusch, R. und S. Fischer (1992). Makroekonomik, Übers. U. K. Schittko, Oldenbourg Verlag, München.

[18] Yıldırım, K., Karaman, D. ve M. Taşdemir (2014). Makro Ekonomi, 12. bs., Seçkin Yayınları, Ankara.

[19] Rose, K. und K Sauernheimer (1995). Theorie der Aussenwirtschaft, 12. überarbeitete Auflage, Verlag Franz Vahlen, München.

[20] Duman, Y. K. (2017). Türkiye'de Cari İşlemler Dengesi ve Ekonomik Büyüme Arasındaki İlişki, Sakarya İktisat Dergisi, Cilt 6, Sayı 4, ss. 12-28.

[21] Mankiw, N. G. (2011). Makroökonomik, 6. Auflage, Übers. K. D. John, Stuttgart: Schäffer-Poeschel Verlag.

[22] Howard, D. H. (1989). Implications of the U.S. Current Account Deficit, The Journal of Economic Perspectives , Autumn, 1989, Vol. 3, No. 4 (Autumn), pp. 153-165.

[23] Şahin, İ. E. and M. Mucuk (2014). The Effect of Current Account on Economic Growth: The Case of Turkey, Conference Paper, 24 June 2014, 11th International Academic Conference, Reykjavik, https://www.researchgate.net/publication/337261389.

[24] Jarchow, H. J. und P. Rühmann (1994). Monetaere Aussenwirtschaft I: Monetaere Aussenwirtschaftstheorie, 4. überarbeitete und erweiterte Auflage, Vandenhoeck & Ruprecht, Göttingen.

[25] Granger, C.W., Yoon, G. (2002). Hidden cointegration , Department of Economics Working Paper. University of California, San Diego, http://www.escholarship.org/uc/item/9qn5f61j.pdf;origin=repeccitec

[26] Hacker, S., Hatemi-J, A. (2012). A Bootstrap Test for Causality with Endogenous Lag Length Choice: Theory and Application in Finance. Journal of Economic Studies, 39(2), 144-160 https://static.sys.kth. se/itm/wp/cesis/cesiswp223.pdf

[27] Hatemi-J, A. (2012). Asymmetric Causality Tests with an Application. Empir Econ 43, 447–456. http:// link.springer.com/article/10.1007%2Fs00181-0110484-x#page-1

[28] Ng, S. ve Perron, P. (2001), "Lag Length Selection and the Construction of Unit Root Tests with Good Size and Power", Econometrica, 69, ss. 1529–1554.

[29] Granger, C.W.J. (1969). Investigating Causal Relations by Econometric Models and Cross-Spectral Methods. Econometrica, 37, 424–438. http://webber.physik.uni-freiburg.de/~jeti/studenten _seminar/ stud_sem_SS_09/grangercausality.pdf

[30] Bağcı, E. ve M. K. Börü (2018). Ekonomik Büyüme ve Işsizlik Arasındaki İlişki: Türkiye'de Ekonometrik Bir Analiz", International Journal of Academic Value Studies, Vol: 4, Issue:22; pp. 890-897.

[31] TÜİK: http://www.tuik.gov.tr

[32] İLO: https://ilostat.ilo.org/data/

[33] EOECD: https://stats.oecd.org/

[34] Worldbank: https://data.worldbank.org/

Chapter 17

Determinants of Islamic Banks Distress in Gulf Council Countries (GCC)

Bakhita Hamdow Gad Elkreem Braima

Abstract

The study aims to investigate the relation between Z score and internal factors represented in Camel rating system ratios. To discover the best ratios that can be used as indicator. Also it aims to investigate the impact of external economic factors GDP, Inflation rate and currency exchange rate on the Islamic banks soundness.it follows quantitative method, simple random sample of five full-fledge Islamic banks in Gulf Council Countries is selected, parametric statistical analysis is used, especially linear multiple regression tool. The results of linear regression model showing that, there are some ratios affect positively and significantly on Z score, those are, Total equities to T. Asset; Total loan to Total Assets; market share price and Earning per share.; moreover the GDP and inflation rate do not effect on the Islamic banks soundness. Implication of the results in Islamic banks they should increase their Z score through increasing some ratios such as liabilities to Assets ratio, loan to Assets ratio, share market price, most important implication of the study result is a recommendation for amendment of Camel rating model. Further works are recommended with more statistical techniques. The relation between camel dimensions ratios and bankometer model should be conducted.

Keywords: Z score, bankometer, Camel, GDP, Islamic banks

1. Introduction

Islamic banks play major role as a financial intermediaries in the economy through mobilizing saving from surplus units, then handle them to deficit units which are need capital to produce goods and services in the economy. Thus they are contributing to wealth distribution by effective allocating of financial resources. The Literature Review have evaluated the efficiency of Islamic banks performance as compare their counterpart conventional banks performance .there are some studies investigate the impact of international financial crisis 2008 on Islamic banks, they had demonstrated that Islamic banks were stable and highly governance by local supervisory authorities, in order to avoid the same mistakes of American banks. Therefore, early identification of weak banks ranks is very important to monitory supervisors. As we know the majority of the Gulf Council Countries (GCC) nations are Muslims, so that Islamic finance is very important field in these countries should be study and develop as a result of this perception there are some studies have conducted in Islamic banks fields in GCC, such as [1, 2]

IntechOpen

(Vijaya Kumar and Hameedah Sayani, 2015), but they have used distress models like Z score, CAMEL, to evaluate the performances of Islamic banks as compare to conventional banks in GCC. So that there is no clear consensus about the relation between CAMEL dimensions ratios and Z score of Islamic bank,this gab is filled by this study There are twenty Full-fledge Islamic banks In Gulf Council Countries (GCC). The oldest one is Qatar International Islamic Bank (QIIB) in Qatar, which was establish in 1956, followed by Al Rajhi Bank established in 1957 in Saudi Arabia, the youngest one is Bank Nizwa in Oman established in 2013. See (**Tables 1** and **2**).

The researcher collects financial data from banks sites, and General Economic development indicators (GDP, Inflation rate, Exchange rate) for each country of GCC from World Bank site. Then all financial data with local currency was converted in to dollar, even exchange rate. After that Z score is calculated for each bank within the study period and it regressed with independent variables including CAMEL ratios as internal factors of the studied banks, and GDP, inflation rate and exchange rate as external factors. The results of multiple linear regression show the best ratios that can be used as indicators of CAMEL Dimensions ratio.

S	Country	Number of banks	Bank list	When bank has been established
1	Saudi Arabia kingdom	4	Al Rajhi Bank	1957
			Bank Albilad	2004
			Aljazeera Bank	1975
			Alinma Bank	2006
2	United Arab emirates	4	Dubai Islamic Bank (DIB) (1)	1975
			Abu Dhabi Islamic Bank (ADIB) (2)	1997
			Emirates Islamic bank (3)	1975
			Sharjah Islamic bank (4)	1976
3	Bahrain Kingdom	3	Bahrain Islamic Bank (BISB) (1)	1979
			Al Salam Bank (2)	2006
			Arabic Bank Corporation (Bank ABC) (3)	1980
4	Qatar	4	Qatar International Islamic Bank (QIIB) (1)	1956
			Qatar Islamic Bank(QIsB) (2)	1982
			Baraw Bank (3)	2007
			Masraf Al Rayan (4)	2006
5	Kuwaiti	3	Kuwait Finance house	1977
			Boubyan Bank	2004
			Warba Bank	2009
6	Oman	2	Alizz Bank	2012
			Bank Nizwa	2013
Total		20 banks		

Table 1.
Distribution of Islamic banks over six countries.

S	Bank name	Establishment date	Age
1	Qatar International Islamic Bank (QIIB)	1956	64
2	Al Rajhi Bank	1957	63
3	Aljazeera Bank	1975	45
4	Dubai Islamic Bank (DIB)	1975	45
5	Emirates Islamic bank	1975	45
6	Sharjah Islamic bank	1976	44
7	Kuwait Finance house	1977	43
8	Bahrain Islamic Bank (BISB)	1979	41
9	Arabic Bank Corporation (Bank ABC)	1980	40
10	Qatar Islamic Bank (QIsB)	1982	38
11	Abu Dhabi Islamic Bank (ADIB)	1997	23
12	Boubyan Bank	2004	16
13	Bank Albilad	2004	16
14	Alinma Bank	2006	14
15	Al Salam Bank	2006	14
16	Masraf Al Rayan	2006	14
17	Baraw Bank	2007	13
18	Warba Bank	2009	11
19	Alizz Islamic Bank	2012	8
20	Bank Nizwa	2013	7

Source the researcher from banks sites information.

Table 2.
Establishment date of Islamic banks in GCC.

2. Research design

2.1 Problem

There is no clear consensus in previous studies on GCC, which investigated the impact of the CMELS model ratios as internal factors of the bank on Z score as soundness indicator. Also there is no clear consensus in previous studies on GCC about impact of GDP, Inflation rate,exchange rate as external economic factors on Z score as a soundness of Islamic banks.

2.2 Objectives

The main objective of this study is to fill the gap in selecting the best ratios of CAMEL Dimensions indicators, that can measure bank's soundness.

2.3 Methodology

The research follows survey method to search sample consist of five full-fledge Islamic banks worked in GCC as population. But each a selected bank its age less than 10 years will excluded, because its experience cannot able it to achieve competitiveness. The total of full-fledge Islamic banks in GCC are 20 banks; they are distributed over 6 countries (see **Tables 1** and 2).

While population is homogenies (because the Islamic banks in GCC are homogenies) the researcher ranked these banks according to their establishment date (see **Table 2**), in order to use simple random sample with lottery method using serial number as assigned number to give equal chance for each bank, but each selected bank its age less than ten year should be excluded,because the period of study extend to fourteen years.Thus The age of selected bank Alizz bank is excluded because its age less than 10 years. Then start from the beginning and Al Salam Bank was chosen. After that the researcher examines normality distribution to ensure that this sample represents the population figures show histogram normality test results, are (**Figures 1–3**) moreover researcher employed one sample Kolmogorov–Smirnov test (K-S test) (**Table 3**) ensured that distribution of the sample is normal. Which allow researcher to used parametric test (linear regression).

Then secondary data were collected from annual reports of studied banks, and General Economic development indicators (GDP, Inflation rate, Exchange rate) for each country of GCC from World Bank site.

Multiple linear regressions is used to investigate causal relation between CAMEL ratios and Z score, also it used to discover the impact of economic factors (GDP, Inflation rate, exchange rate) on Z score of Islamic banks.

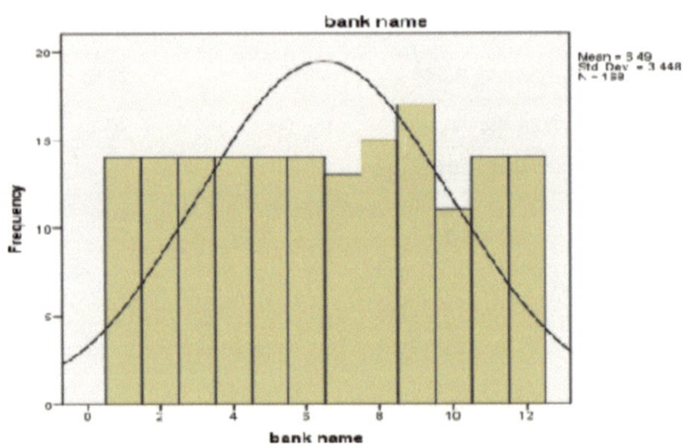

Figure 1.
Normality distribution of Islamic banks names.

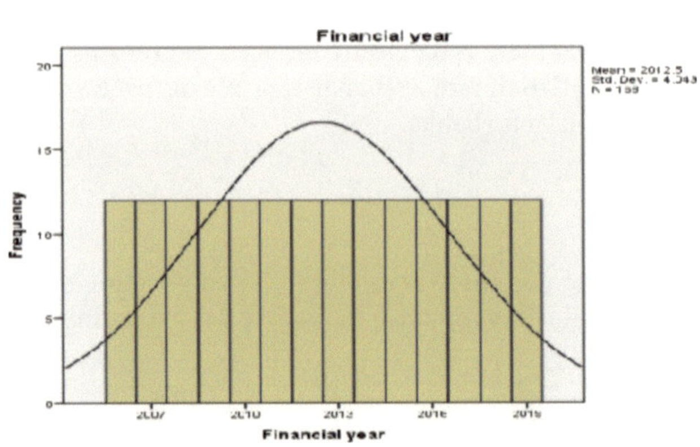

Figure 2.
Normality distribution of financial years.

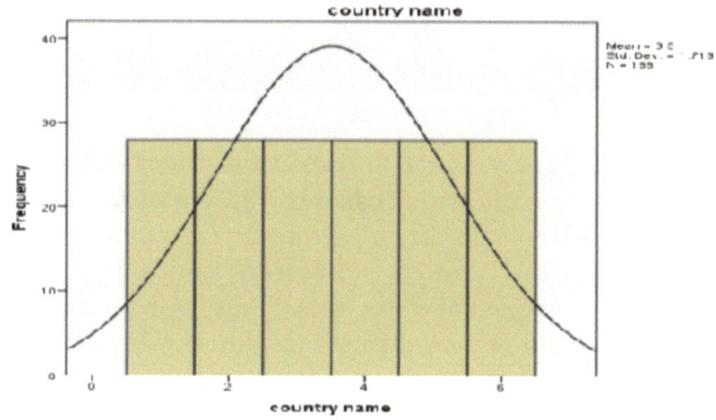

Figure 3.
Normality test of the country names.

One-Sample Kolmogorov–Smirnov Test					
		Bank name	**Country name**	**Currency name**	**Financial year**
N		168	168	168	168
Normal Parameters[a,b]	Mean	6.49	3.50	3.51	2012.50
	Std. Deviation	3.448	1.713	1.716	4.043
Most Extreme Differences	Absolute	.100	.143	.147	.092
	Positive	.098	.143	.143	.092
	Negative	−.100	−.143	−.147	−.092
Test Statistic		.100	.143	.147	.092
Asymp. Sig. (2-tailed)		.000[c]	.000[c]	.000[c]	.001[c]

Source the researcher from data analysis.
[a]*Test distribution is Normal.*
[b]*Calculated from data.*
[c]*Lilliefors Significance Correction.*

Table 3.
Normality test result.

2.4 The significant of the study

The structure of the paper as following: Section Two provides research design, Section Three briefly reviews the literature on the financial distress concept, measurement, and Section Four specifies the model and indicates the sources of data and setting up the statistical methodology used in the study. Section Five, contains the main findings of the study, their analyses and assessments. The final section contains conclusions and policy implications, recommendation, and limitations.

2.5 Organization

Contribution of this study representing in a recommendation for amendment of Camels rating model should be constructing as following:

Total liabilities to Total Assets ratio + Total loan to T. assets +Share market price+ net loan to Total Assets +Earning Per share+ provision Non-performing loan/Gross loan.

3. Theoretical background

3.1 Financial distress concept

There are several studies conducted in financial distress field, but there is no agreed of a formal definition of financial distress [3]. The absence of a formal definition of financial distress puts into questions on the validity of researches conducted within the domain. Different measures of standards would categorize non distressed firms as distressed and vice versa; thus, without a formal definition of financial distress, it would be very difficult to address this problem [3, 4]. Categorized financial distressed into three, namely: 1- event-oriented, 2- process-oriented, and [5] Technical.

In the first category (event oriented), financial distress is mostly associated with terms such as default, failure and bankruptcy [4, 5]. Explained that Four terms mostly used interchangeably are default, failure, insolvency and bankruptcy; even though these terms are often used interchangeably, formally each of them presents a different definition:

Failure, moreover, means that the realized rate of return on invested capital is significantly lower than prevailing rates on similar investments it should be noted that a company may have had an economic failure for many years, yet never failed to meet its obligations.

Insolvency, furthermore, is another term depicting negative firm performance, and is generally used in a more technical fashion; whereas technical insolvency may be a temporary condition although it is often the immediate cause of bankruptcy. [5] also defines that insolvency in bankruptcy sense is a condition where total liabilities exceed a fair value of total assets rendering the net worth of the firm negative.

Default distress can be technical and/or legal and always involve the debtor-creditor relationship [5]. Technical default takes place when the debtor violates a condition of an agreement with a creditor, and can be grounds for legal action [5]. Bankruptcy may be understood as a formal process where a firm announces in court that it has gone bankrupt followed by the petition to liquidate its assets or to undergo a recovery program [6]. As for the second category, financial distress is defined as a process; this definition helps in understanding financial distress as a phenomenon in constructing a comprehensive theory of financial distress [3, 4] stated that financial distress is a process situated between solvent and insolvent, and considered as a condition where the company experiences low cash flow and losses without being insolvent.

The third category defines financial distress through indicators used by various financial distress prediction models [3]. Though still criticized by many, the use of ratios in many financial distress prediction models is to produce results relating to the likelihood of financial distress and default within a company [3]. In general, ratios that measure profitability, liquidity and insolvency are commonly used in predicting financial distress, despite not knowing which one is the most significant [7]. Poor management has always been the core reason behind financial distress within companies [8]. Several non-internal factors, such as high interest rates, bad industrial performance, competition on the international level etc. may contribute to the occurrence of financial distress within a company [8]; conducted a research regarding the potential of financial distress within banks in UAE. In the research, [9] identifies several factors that are greatly relevant to financial distress, such as cost to income ratio as well as equity to asset ratio and non-performing loan ratio. Macroeconomic factors, on the other hand, do not play a significant role. [10] demonstrated that financial distress is considered as the financial problems faced by an entity that prevents it from independently meeting its obligations, thus resulting in the requirement for external aid to be able to continue operating either by means of a merger, acquisition, intervention by a consumer protection authority or public aid, with the most serious case of financial distress being bankruptcy.

3.2 Financial distress measurement

There are various detection models that have been constructed in CBs [11, 12] grouped the models into the following families of techniques: (i) statistical techniques, (ii) neural networks, (iii) case-based reasoning, (iv) decision trees, (iv) operational research, (v) evolutionary approaches, (vi) rough set based techniques, (vii) other techniques subsuming fuzzy logic, supporting vector machine and isotonic separation and (viii) soft computing subsuming seamless hybridization of all the above-mentioned techniques. Based on these methods, various authors came out with various research findings mentioned in the following section literature review.

3.3 Literature review

Found that stock market information can be used to estimate leading indicators of bank financial distress [13]. Had selected 64 European banks [13] pacified a logit early warning model, designed for European banks, which tests if market based indicators add predictive value to models relying on accounting data [14] also study the robustness of the link between market information and financial downgrading in the light of the safety net and asymmetric information hypotheses Other of their results show that the accuracy of the predictive power depends on the extent to which bank liabilities are market traded [15]. Conducted a research to use the financial data to identify changes in bank conditions. They used the call-report data to predict deterioration in condition as measured by changes in two main factors. The call report data could be used to construct non statistical early-warning models that mimic the examination process. The two main factors are the CAMEL ratings, and the role of off-site monitoring in the banking examination process. Off-site monitoring is an alternative method for on-site monitoring system in a bank using the financial ratios. There are twenty two commonly used financial ratios selected [16]. Each ratio is included because it provides insight into a dimension of the financial condition of the sample banks that is reflected in the actual composite CAMEL rating. The ratios generally are similar to those used in previous early-warning failure-prediction models. Fifty eight samples of banks in the US were chosen. They used logit regression and logit analysis ratio. They found five financial ratios that are significant as follows:

I. Asset quality indicators: defined as non-performing loans and leases divided by primary capital;

II. Liquidity-type ratios: loans plus securities/total sources of funds;

III. Liquidity-type ratios: volatile liabilities/total sources of funds;

IV. Primary capital/average assets;

V. Current-quarter ratio: nonperforming-loan ratio. For the Shari'ah compliance, the CAMEL ratings should be assessed. This CAMEL rating consists of elements from Capital adequacy, Asset quality, Management, Earnings and Liquidity [17].

[18] Stated that the CAMEL ratings generally assess overall soundness of the banks, and identify and/or predict different risk factors that may contribute to turn the banks into a problem or failed banks. These banks tend to perform the FFS. Bangladesh Banks have included an additional key point of "Sensitivity to market risk" to be the CAMELS. However, [18)] has recommended the CAMELS Rating Framework to be the CAMELSS in order to comprehend the Islamic Banking that is "Shari'ah Rating". In line with [18].

[18] Stated that Recommendation on the "Shari'ah Rating" is the Ethical Identity Index (EII) [18]. Said that EII is the Shari'ah compliance determination identified by the existence of discrepancy between the communicated (based on information disclosed in the annual reports) and ideal (disclosure of information deemed vital based on the Islamic ethical business framework), which was termed by [19] as Ethical Identities Index (EII) [19]. Examined seven Islamic Banks over a three-year period of longitudinal survey in the Arabian Gulf region [19]. Found that six out of seven Islamic Banks suffered from disparity between the "communicated" and "ideal" ethical identities. They demonstrated that: From both functions of the CAMELSS and EII, they could ensure the Shari'ah compliance in the IBs. They have Recommend that False Financial Statements (FFS) detection model in CBs could be applied similarly by adding this Shari'ah compliance control variable.

[20] used a simple stress test method, including three stress test areas: profitability stress test, capital stress test and liquidity stress test. His results showed that in term of profitability, Islamic banks in Indonesia are immune from losses if the default rate (Non-Performing Loan) is less than 8.5%. If the industry can improve the profit margin, the resistance will be higher. In term of capital position, by assuming loss given default (LGD) is constant at 40%, the industry will not go bankrupt if probability of default (PD) is less than 9%. If the PD is more than 9%, total expected loss is more than available capital.

[21] focused on cutting-edge FDP models and applied them to Islamic. They had employed three models: Altman Z-Score and Altman Z-Score for service firms, and Standardized Profits method, their results indicated that there is a need for a specific financial distress mechanism for Islamic banks, as variables that are indicative of a bank's status differ between the old Altman [7] standard and novel approaches. "Working Capital/Total Assets" was the most predictive variable for forecasting financial distress in Islamic banks. As for the Standardized Profits method, "Return On Revenue" was the most influential variable banks, they employed three models [22]. Examined, evaluated and compared the financial activities of selected Islamic and conventional banks of Pakistan for period (2003–2012.). Various parameters of CAMEL model were tested by employing simple t-test. His result showed that: there are significant differences between Islamic and conventional banks in risk-weighted credit exposures, regulatory capital, advances in proportion to asset portfolios, long-term debt paying abilities, management's control over expenses in proportion to income, return on assets, and liquidity.

[23], analyzed the financial performance of three selected Islamic Banks in Bangladesh over 8 years (2007–2014), he was using Camel Rating model to evaluate banks' performance, he demonstrated that all the selected Islamic Banks are in strong position on their composite rating system (CAMEL).

[24] Their study has conducted with the objective of comparing shariah compliance and traditional banks of Pakistan from performance perspective. The relative investigations were conducted by means of t.test, for the period 2010–2017. Ratios based on CAMELS approach are applied to identify the managerial and monetary performance of shariah compliance and traditional banks of Pakistan. They demonstrated that Shariah compliance banks are significantly better in managing capital adequacy, management adequacy/quality, earning ability, liquidity and sensitivity

to risk as compared to their traditional counterparts [23]. Aimed to analyze the financial performance of three selected Islamic Banks (Islami Bank Bangladesh Limited, Export Import Bank of Bangladesh Limited, Shahjalal Islami Bank Limited) over a period of eight years (2007–2014) in Bangladeshi banking sectors. For this reason, CAMEL Rating Analysis approach has been conducted and it is found that all the selected Islamic Banks are in strong position on their composite rating system. [1] aimed to analyze the performance of Islamic banks and conventional banks during the crisis and after the crisis, by comparing the performance of Islamic and conventional banks based in the Gulf Cooperation Council (GCC) during the period of 2008–2011 by deploying the CAMEL testing factors, his results showed that Islamic banks possessed adequate capital structure but have recorded lower ROAE and poor management efficiency. Asset quality and liquidity for both the modes of banking system have not recorded any significant difference. [2], Directed a study on the GCC for a period of 2002–2009, to assess the factors that affect the Islamic bank and conventional banks. The study included a sample of 38 conventional banks, and 13 Islamic banks. The factors that were studied were foreign ownership, bank specific variable and macroeconomic variables. Some interesting results were found. The cost-income was found to have a negative and significant impact on banks performance for Islamic and conventional banks. Equity was found out to be important factor in maximizing the profitability of Islamic banks. The size of the banks supported the economies of scale utilizing the ROE for Islamic banks. GDP was found to be positively related, while inflation negatively related to the banks performance [25]. Aimed to evaluate the soundness of Islamic banks in the GCC for the period 2008 to 2014. Methodology- The study involves 11 listed Islamic banks based in the GCC countries of Saudi Arabia, United Arab Emirates, Qatar, Bahrain, and Kuwait [25]. Applied the CAMEL parameters, which include Capital Adequacy, Asset quality, Management, Earning and liquidity. Multivariate Z- score model is also used to ensure robustness of the results. Findings-The findings suggest that although the Islamic banks in the GCC have adequate capital, their asset quality and earning ability have deteriorated over the period of study.

The applications of Altman Z score on banks have previously been researched by several researches like [26, 27], for banks in India and [28] suggested that Altman Z score is an analytical tool that may be applied in the banking industry. Additionally, [29] stated that Altman Z score has better predicting capabilities than CAEL model when predicting bankruptcy.

However, several studies indicated the inappropriateness of Altman Z score in predicting financial distress within banks. A study conducted [25] applied Altman Z score model, CAEL model and bankometer model altogether within the Bank of Papua in Indonesia. His results showed that the results of Altman Z score model in many occasions were contradicted with the results of CAEL model. Altman Z score model was initially formed from an empirical study of manufacturing companies which is very much different from banking institutions [30].

Z score indicator as follow: Altman, Edward (May, 2002) [31].

$$Z = 6.56\ X1 + 3.26\ X2 + 6.72\ X3 + 1.05\ X4 \tag{1}$$

Whereas
Z = a proxy variable of insolvency risk.
X1 = working capital to Total Assets [28].
X2 = retained earnings to Total Assets [28].
X3 = earnings before interest &tax to Total Assets.
X4 = Total book equity to Total liabilities [28].

A higher score indicates greater financial strength with a lower probability of default and vice versa.

The method examines liquidity, profitability, reinvested earnings and leverage which are integrated into a single composite score. It can be used with past, current or project data as it requires no external inputs such as GDP or market price.

	Symbol	**Calculation**	**References**
Capital Adequacy Requirement (CAR)	EQTA	Total Equities to Total Assets ratio.	
	D/E	Debt-to Equity ratio	Kaur Harsh Vineet [32]
Asset Quality (AQ)	TLTA	Total loans to total assets Ratio.	Muhammad Hussain &Rukhsana KALIM [24]
	LLR	Loan Loss Reserve	Ahsan Mohammad, 2014, Merchant [1],
	NPLR	Non-performing loan to Total loan	Kumar & Sayani, 2014,
Management Efficiency	COSR	cost to income ratio	Ahsan Mohammad, 2014, Merchant, [1], Zeitun [2]
	EPS	Earnings Per Share	
	IETA I	Interest expenses / total assets ratio.	Muhammad Hussain & Rukhsana KALIM [24], Vijaya Kumar & Hameedah Sayani (2014),
	PPE(Profit Per employ	Profit to employees number	Kaur Harsh Vineet [32]
	ROE	Net income/ net worth (T.Equities)	Kaur Harsh Vineet [32]
Earning Quality (EQ)	ROA	Net income to total assets	
	ROE	Net income to total equities	Merchant [1], Zeitun [2]
	NIITA	Net interest income To total assets ratio	Muhammad Hussain & Rukhsana KALIM [24], Vijaya Kumar & Hameedah Sayani (2014)
Liquidity (LQ)	LATCL	Liquid Assets to Current liabilities	
	CATCL	Current Assets to Current liabilities	
	NLTA	Net loan to total Assets	Ahsan Mohammad, 2014, Merchant [1]
	LA:TD	Liquid Asset/Total Deposit	Kaur Harsh Vineet [32]
Sensitivity (S)	PGL	Provision To Gross Loan	Muhammad Hussain & Rukhsana KALIM [24]

Source the researcher from literature review.

Table 4.
Camel dimensions ratios.

Zones of discriminations:
Z > 2.6 -"Safe" Zone
1.1 < Z < 2. 6 -"Grey" Zone
Z < 1.1 -"Distress" Zone
The concept of CAMELS'standard, It consists of six dimensions. Each dimension can be measured through different ratios. These ratios along with their measures are[1] grouped[2] in **Table 4**.

4. Data analysis

4.1 Capital adequacy requirement (CAR) test

Two ratios (total Equities to total Assets ratio and Debt-to Equity ratio)are Examined using step wise method **Table 5** shows the result, **Table 6** shows model Summary between Z score and liabilities to Assets ratio, **Table 7** shows significance for each individual studied ratio As a result of **Table 7**, the model between Z score and capital adequacy ratios is developed as following:

Z score = 8.9 Total liabilities to Total assets ratio + 6.6 Equities to Assets ratio. Thus lesson to be learned that T. Liabilities/T. Assets has more effects on Z score than T .equities to T. assets. See the following **Table 8**.

It shows exclude variables. **Table 8** indicates that the best ratio that can measure Capital Adequacy is debit to Equity ratio.

Model	Variables Entered	Variables Removed	Method
1	T.Liabilities/T. Assets	.	Stepwise (Criteria: Probability-of-F-to-enter <= .050, Probability-of-F-to-remove > = .100).
2	Equity/ total assets ratio	.	Stepwise (Criteria: Probability-of-F-to-enter <= .050, Probability-of-F-to-remove > = .100).

Source researcher from data analysis.
[a]*Dependent Variable: Z Score*
[b]*Linear Regression through the Origin*

Table 5.
Variables entered/Removed.[a,b]

Model	R	R Square[b]	Adjusted R Square	Std. Error of the Estimate
1	.888[a]	.789	.786	3.39385892
2	.896[c]	.803	.797	3.30345566

Source researcher from data analysis.
[a]*Predictors: T.Liabilities/T.Assets*
[b]*For regression through the origin (the no-intercept model), R Square measures the proportion of the variability in the dependent variable about the origin explained by regression. This CANNOT be compared to R Square for models which include an intercept.*
[c]*Predictors: T.Liabilities/T.Assets, Equity/ total assets ratio*

Table 6.
Model summary.

[1] In Shariah compliance banks it is the profit paid to total assets.
[2] 3 In Shariah compliance banks it is profit earned to total assets

Model		Unstandardized Coefficients		Standardized Coefficients	t	Sig.
		B	Std. Error	Beta		
1	T.Liabilities/T.Assets	8.898	.554	.888	16.051	.000
2	T.Liabilities/T.Assets	7.267	.918	.725	7.918	.000
	Equity/ total assets ratio	6.586	2.997	.201	2.197	.031

[a]Dependent Variable: Z Score
[b]Linear Regression through the Origin

Table 7.
Coefficients[a,b] of the test between Z score and capital adequacy dimension.

Model		Beta In	t	Sig.	Partial Correlation	Collinearity Statistics
						Tolerance
1	Equity/ total assets ratio	.201[c]	2.197	.031	.257	.346

Source the researcher from data analysis.
[a]Dependent Variable: Z Score
[b]Linear Regression through the Origin
[c]Predictors in the Model: T.Liabilities/T.Assets

Table 8.
Excluded Variables[a,b].

Variables Entered/Removed[a,b]

Model	Variables Entered	Variables Removed	Method
1	T.Loan /T.Assets	.	Stepwise (Criteria: Probability-of-F-to-enter < = .050, Probability-of-F-to-remove > = .100).

Source researcher from data analysis to Assets ratio interpret 88% of changes in Z score at significance level 0.0001.
[a]Dependent Variable: Z Score.
[b]Linear Regression through the Origin.

Table 9.
Test method.

4.2 Asset quality (AQ) dimension

Three ratios are examined: Total loans / total assets; Loan Loss Reserve; Non-performing loan to Total loan.

Table 9 shows test method (Variables Entered/Removed method).

Table 10 shows[3] model summary between Z score and Total Loan to Total Assets, it indicates that Loan to Assets ratio interpret 88% of changes in Z score by positive causal relation = 11.45 point, at significance level 0.0001, see **Tables 11–13** indicates that the best ratio can measure Assets Quality is Total Loan to Total Assets. However both provision of non-performing loan to net loans and Non-Performing Loan to Total Loan ratios are excluded because they have high multi collinearity statistics. (They are highly correlated with each other).

[3] Loan means Islamic finance portfolio in Assets side of the bank

Model	R	R Square[b]	Adjusted R Square	Std. Error of the Estimate
1	.886[a]	.786	.783	3.41686937

Source researcher from data analysis.
[a]Predictors: Total Loan /Total Assets
[b]For regression through the origin (the no-intercept model), R Square measures the proportion of the variability in the dependent variable about the origin explained by regression. This CANNOT be compared to R Square for models which include an intercept.

Table 10.
Model Summary between Z score and Assets Quality dimension.

ANOVA[a,b]						
Model		Sum of Squares	df	Mean Square	F	Sig.
1	Regression	2956.514	1	2956.514	253.235	.000[c]
	Residual	805.575	69	11.675		
	Total	3762.089[d]	70			

Source researcher from data analysis.
[a]Dependent Variable: Z Score
[b]Linear Regression through the Origin
[c]Predictors: T.Loan /T.Assets
[d]This total sum of squares is not corrected for the constant because the constant is zero for regression through the origin.

Table 11.
The significance of the model.

Model	Unstandardized Coefficients		Standardized Coefficients	t	Sig.
	B	Std. Error	Beta		
1 T.Loan /T.Assets	11.454	.720	.886	15.913	.000

Source researcher from data analysis.
***Table 12** shows that total loan to total assets positively on Z score.*
[a]Dependent Variable: Z Score.
[b]Linear Regression through the Origin.

Table 12.
Individual effect of independent variables: Coefficients.[a,b]

Model		Beta In	t	Sig.	Partial Correlation	Collinearity Statistics
						Tolerance
1	provision of non-performing loan /net loans	.030[c]	.536	.594	.065	.970
	Non-Performing Loan /T.Loan	.082[c]	1.226	.224	.147	.688

Source researcher from data analysis.
[a]Dependent Variable: Z Score
[b]Linear Regression through the Origin
[c]Predictors in the Model: T.Loan /T.Assets

Table 13.
Excluded Variables[a,b].

4.3 Management efficiency dimension

Four ratios are examined including: Cost to Income; Finance Cost /Total Assets; ROE. Market price (absolute value is used). The researcher could not find

Model	R	R Square	Adjusted R Square	Std. Error of the Estimate
1	.289[a]	.083	.078	4.86709490

Source researcher from data analysis.
[a]Predictors: (Constant), share Market Price
[b]Dependent Variable: Z Score

Table 14.
Model Summary[b] between Z score and management efficiency Dimension.

employees number, so that she excluded Profit per Employee (PPE) and replaced with Market Price, however it did not use before in previous reviewed studied as efficient management indicator.

Table 14 shows the model Summary which indicates that share market price plus constant interpret 28% of Z score changes (**Table 15**). And **Table 16** shows excluded variables (ratios) from the model between Z score and management efficiency Dimension (**Table 17**).

According to **Table 16**: Z score = 1.36 + 1.05 share market price.

Model		Sum of Squares	df	Mean Square	F	Sig.
1	Regression	358.058	1	358.058	15.115	.000[b]
	Residual	3932.310	166	23.689		
	Total	4290.368	167			

Source researcher from data analysis.
[a]Dependent Variable: Z Score
[b]Predictors: (Constant), Market Price

Table 15.
ANOVA.[a] test between Z score and management efficiency Dimension.

Model		Unstandardized Coefficients		Standardized Coefficients	t	Sig.
		B	Std. Error	Beta		
1	(Constant)	1.355	.683		1.985	.049
	Share Market Price	1.051	.270	.289	3.888	.000

Source researcher from data analysis.
[a]Dependent Variable: Z Score

Table 16.
Coefficients[a].

Model		Beta In	t	Sig.	Partial Correlation	Collinearity Statistics
						Tolerance
1	Finance Cost /Total Assets	-.025[b]	−.338	.736	−.026	.999
	Return on Equities	.061[b]	.820	.413	.064	.997
	Total Cost /Total Income	.086[b]	1.122	.264	.087	.941
	Earnings Per Share	-.082[b]	−1.093	.276	−.085	.976

Source researcher from data analysis.
[a]Dependent Variable: Z Score
[b]Predictors in the Model: (Constant), Market Price

Table 17.
Excluded Variables[a] from the model between Z score and management efficiency Dimension.

4.4 Liquidity dimension

Three ratios are examined using step wise method,they are: Quick Ratio,Net loan to Total Assets;Net Loan/total Deposits **Table 18** shows model Summary,it indicates that Net Loan to Total Assets ratio interpret 89% of changes in Z score. **Tables 19** and **20** show significance of the test at 0.0001 level.), and **Table 21** shows excluded variables(ratios) from the model between Z score and Liquidity dimension in camel model those are include Quick ratio,and current ratio. So that, these ratios should excluded from banks evaluation methods in the future.

4.5 Earnings dimension

Three ratios are used return on Equity (ROE), return on Assets (ROA), Earning Per share (EPS). **Table 22** shows the variables tested as indicators of Earning Dimension in Camel model, **Table 23** shows the model between Earning Dimension and Z score, and **Table 24** shows significant of the model between Z score and

Model	R	R Square[b]	Adjusted R Square	Std. Error of the Estimate
1	.896[a]	.803	.800	3.27566281

Source researcher from data analysis.
[a]*Predictors: Net Loan/Total Assets*
[b]*For regression through the origin (the no-intercept model), R Square measures the proportion of the variability in the dependent variable about the origin explained by regression. This CANNOT be compared to R Square for models which include an intercept.*

Table 18.
Model summary between Z score and Liquidity Dimension.

Model		Sum of Squares	df	Mean Square	F	Sig.
1	Regression	3021.721	1	3021.721	281.615	.000[c]
	Residual	740.368	69	10.730		
	Total	3762.089[d]	70			

Source researcher from data analysis.
***Table 19** shows significance of the test.*
[a]*Dependent Variable: Z Score*
[b]*Linear Regression through the Origin*
[c]*Predictors: Net Loan/Total Assets*
[d]*This total sum of squares is not corrected for the constant because the constant is zero for regression through the origin.*

Table 19.
ANOVA[a,b].

Model	Unstandardized Coefficients		Standardized Coefficients	t	Sig.
	B	Std. Error	Beta		
1 Net Loan/Total Assets	12.499	.745	.896	16.781	.000

Source researcher from analysis.
***Table 20** shows significant individual variable (net loan to Total assets ratio) effect on Z score.*
[a]*Dependent Variable: Z Score*
[b]*Linear Regression through the Origin*

Table 20.
Coefficients[a,b] of the test between Z score and Liquidity Dimension.

Model		Beta In	t	Sig.	Partial Correlation	Collinearity Statistics
						Tolerance
1	liquid assets / current liabilities	.012[c]	.193	.848	.023	.798
	Liquid Assets/Total Deposits	.119[c]	1.730	.088	.205	.585

Source the researcher from data analysis.
[a]Dependent Variable: Z Score
[b]Linear Regression through the Origin
[c]Predictors in the Model: Net Loan/Total Assets

Table 21.
Excluded Variables[a,b] from the model between Z score and Liquidity dimension in camel model.

Model	Variables Entered[a]	Variables Removed	Method
1	Earnings Per Share in dollar, Return on Assets, Return on Equity[b]	.	Enter

Source the researcher from data analysis.
[a]Dependent Variable: Z Score
[b]All requested variables entered.

Table 22.
Variables entered/Removed.

Model	R	R Square	Adjusted R Square	Std. Error of the Estimate
1	.372[a]	.138	.099	6.53448

Source the researcher from data analysis.
[a]Predictors: (Constant), Earning Per Share in dollar, Return on Assets, Return on Equity

Table 23.
Model summary between Z score and Earning Dimension ratios.

Model		Sum of Squares	df	Mean Square	F	Sig.
1	Regression	451.655	3	150.552	3.526	.020[b]
	Residual	2818.162	66	42.699		
	Total	3269.817	69			

Source the researcher from data analysis.
***Table 24** shows significant of the model between Z score and Earning Dimension ratios.*
[a]Dependent Variable: Z Score
[b]Predictors: (Constant), Earning Per Share in dollar, Return on Assets, Return on Equity

Table 24.
ANOVA[a] test between Z score and Earning Dimension ratios.

Earning Dimension ratios, but **Table 25** shows significance of individual variable, it indicate that only Earnings Per share (EPS) as Earning indicator affects positively and significantly on Z score. However EPS did not use previously as Earning indicator in reviewed studies. The results of **Tables 23** and **25** show that only Earning per share can affect negatively on Z score at 1% level, however there is no significant effect of ROE&ROA on Z score.

Model		Unstandardized Coefficients		Standardized Coefficients	t	Sig.
		B	Std. Error	Beta		
1	(Constant)	4.340	1.554		2.793	.007
	Return on Assets	121.732	132.351	.181	.920	.361
	Return on Equity	−5.350	22.077	−.052	−.242	.809
	Earnings Per Share in dollar	−2.860	.992	−.384	−2.883	.005

Source the researcher from data analysis.
***Table 25** shows significance of individual variable.*
[a]*Dependent Variable: Z Score*

Table 25.
Coefficients.[a] *of the test between Z score and Earning Dimension ratios.*

Model	R	R Square[b]	Adjusted R Square	Std. Error of the Estimate
1	.342[a]	.117	.104	6.93927225

Source the researcher from data analysis.
[a]*Predictors: provision /Gross loan (PGL)*
[b]*For regression through the origin (the no-intercept model), R Square measures the proportion of the variability in the dependent variable about the origin explained by regression. This CANNOT be compared to R Square for models which include an intercept.*

Table 26.
Model summary between Z score and Sensitivity Dimension.

Model		Sum of Squares	df	Mean Square	F	Sig.
1	Regression	439.498	1	439.498	9.127	.004[c]
	Residual	3322.591	69	48.153		
	Total	3762.089[d]	70			

***Table 27** shows significance of the test.*
[a]*Dependent Variable: Z Score*
[b]*Linear Regression through the Origin*
[c]*Predictors: provision/Gross loan (PGL)*
[d]*This total sum of squares is not corrected for the constant because the constant is zero for regression through the origin.*

Table 27.
ANOVA[a,b].

4.6 Sensitivity dimension

Only one ratio (provision/gross Loan) is used to measure sensitivity effect on Z score **Table 26** shows model summary, between Z score and sensitivity ratio which indicates that provision to Gross loan ratio interpret 34% of changes in Z score. **Table 27** shows significance of the test (0.004) (**Table 28**).

4.7 External factors analysis

The researcher used three economic factors as explanatory variables of Z score in Islamic banks, including gross domestic Product Growth rate (GDP), Inflation rate, and exchange rate in Dollar. **Table 29** indicates that exchange rate causes69% of changes in Z score, **Table 30** shows significance of the model, The result of **Table 31** shows that exchange rate affect negatively on Z score in Islamic banks at

Model	Unstandardized Coefficients		Standardized Coefficients	t	Sig.
	B	Std. Error	Beta		
1 provision/ Gross loan (PGL)	23.147	7.662	.342	3.021	.004

***Table 28** shows individual variable significance.*
Source researcher from data analysis.
[a]Dependent Variable: Z Score
[b]Linear Regression through the Origin

Table 28.
Coefficients[a,b] of the test between Z score and Sensitivity Dimension.

Model	R	R Square	Adjusted R Square	Std. Error of the Estimate
1	.699[a]	.489	.481	4.95918

Source the researcher from data analysis.
[a]Predictors: (Constant), exchange rate in Dollar

Table 29.
Model summary between Z score and economic factors.

Model		Sum of Squares[a]	df	Mean Square	F	Sig.
1	Regression	1597.460	1	1597.460	64.955	.000[b]
	Residual	1672.356	68	24.593		
	Total	3269.817	69			

Source the researcher from data analysis.
[a]Dependent Variable: Z Score
[b]Predictors: (Constant), exchange rate in Dollar

Table 30.
ANOVA[a] test between Z score and economic factors.

Model		Unstandardized Coefficients		Standardized Coefficients	t	Sig.
		B	Std. Error	Beta		
1	(Constant)	8.486	.837		10.138	.000
	exchange rate in Dollar	−3.442	.427	−.699	−8.059	.000

Source the researcher from data analysis.
[a]Dependent Variable: Z Score.

Table 31.
Coefficients[a] significance of the model between Z score and exchange rate.

significance level .1%, **Table 32** shows excluded variables (GDP & inflation rate) from the model. According to **Table 32** the study can demonstrate there is no causal relation between that inflation rate, GDP and Z score. This result go in contrast with Zeitun [2] he stated that GDP was found to be positively related to banks performance, while inflation negatively related to the banks performance.

Model		Beta In	t	Sig.	Partial Correlation	Collinearity Statistics
						Tolerance
1	Inflation rate (%)	.054[b]	.617	.539	.075	1.000
	Gross Domestic Product annual Rate (%)	-.050[b]	−.561	.577	−.068	.950

***Table 32** shows excluded external economic variables from Z score model.*
Source: the researcher from data analysis.
[a]*Dependent Variable: Z Score*
[b]*Predictors in the Model: (Constant), exchange rate in Dollar*

Table 32.
Excluded variables.

5. Conclusion

5.1 Results assessment

1. T. equities to T. Asset ratio affects positively with significance level 0.03 on Z score for Islamic banks,it represent 6.6 of changes in Z score.

2. The best ratio that can measure Capital Adequacy is debit to assets ratio, because it interprets 8.9 of changes in Z score with significance level 0.0001 as compare to Equities to T. Assets ratio which represents 6.6 of changes in Z score of the Islamic banks. so that it can be used as indicator of Capital adequacy in Camel rating system.

3. Islamic finance portfolio (T. loan) to Total Assets interprets 88% of changes in Z score with positive causal relation at significance level = 0.00001.

4. Provision of non-performing loan to net loans ratio does not effect on Z score of the bank.

5. Non-Performing Loan to Total Loan ratio does not effect on Z score of the bank.

6. Provision of non-performing loan to net loans and Non-Performing Loan toT. Loan ratios are highly correlated, so these ratios can be used as indicators of credit risk in Islamic banks. But they did not affect significantly on Z score.

7. There are some ratios commonly used in Camel rating system as indicators of management Quality, but they are not Effect on Z score of Islamic banks, those are include cost to income, Return on Equities, Finance Cost to Total Assets, this result is contradicted to the results of Ahsan Mohammad, 2014, Merchant, [1], Zeitun [2].

8. Market share price represents 28% of changes in Z score in Islamic banks with significant level = 0.0001 with the model (Z score = 1.36 + 1.05 share market price).

9. Net Loan to Total Assets represent 89% of changes in Z score of Islamic banks, it affect positively by 12.499 times at significance level = 0.0001.

10. Liquid Assets to Total Deposit commonly used in camel rating system as indicator of liquidity sufficient, but it does not effect on Z score according to the results of this study see **Tables 18** and **21**.

11. Earnings per Share effect positively on Z score with significant level = 0.005.

12. There are some ratios commonly used in Camel rating system as Earning Quality (EQ) indicators, but they are not effect on Z score according to the results of this study see **Tables 23–25**, those are include return on assets (ROA) and return on Equity (ROE), this result is contradicted to Merchant [1], Zeitun [2]

13. Provision for non-performing loan /Gross loan ratio effect positively on Z score with significant level = 0.004, it interpret 34% of changes in Z score.

14. Gross Demotic product (GDP) does not affect significantly on z score of Islamic banks

15. Inflation rate does not affect significantly on Z score. The results number 15 and 15 are contradicted to the results of Zeitun [2] he stated that GDP was found to be positively related to banks performance, while inflation negatively related to the banks performance.

16. Exchange rate in foreign currency effect negatively on Z score, it represents 69% of negative changes in Z score.

5.2 Results implication

The results of this study will imply with two groups as following:

5.2.1 Results implication for Islamic banks

1. If Islamic Banks need to increase their Z score with one unit, they should increase liabilities to Assets ratio by 8.9 times

2. If Islamic Banks need to increase their Z score with one unit, they should increase loan to Assets ratio by 11.5 times.

3. If Islamic Banks need to increase their Z score with one unit, they should work to increase their share market price with one unit of the currency which is used in the market exchanging plus absolute value = 1.36.

4. If local currency of the Islamic bank home decrease in front of foreign currencies,Islamic bank should understand that its z score will decrease by 3.4 times

5.2.2 Results implication for supervisory and regulatory bodies

Amendment of Camel rating system should be applied as following:

1. The important performance indicator of Capital adequacy is Total liabilities to Total assets Ratio, this results is going in consistence with [33–35] their results

have revealed that capital adequacy (ratio of total equity to total assets) is the important performance indicator in the classification of banks

2. The best ratio can measure Assets Quality is Total Loan to Total Assets.

3. The best indicator that can measure management efficiency in Camel rating system is Share Market Price

4. The best indicators of liquidity availability is Net Loan to Total Assets ratio

5. The important performance indicator of profitability in Camel rating system is earning per share

6. Provision for non-performing loan to Gross loan ratio should be used as indicators of sensitivity to market risk for Islamic finance.

5.3 Recommendations

Some further studies are recommended to conduct such as:

1. Impact of external economic factors on Islamic banks financial soundness.

2. The relation between camel dimensions ratios and bank meter model.

3. The relation between bank age and Z score model.

4. More techniques should be employed by further studied in Islamic banks field such as neural networks, decision trees,used logit regression and logit analysis ratio, call-report data,and soft computing subsuming seamless hybridization of all the above-mentioned techniques.

5.4 Limitations

1. The study does not use probability model like log-linear model, because there is no time.

2. The study focuses on few samples with homogenized characteristics.

3. Researcher has worked under pressure, because she has huge tasks and responsibility as a result of Covid 19 condition which effects on professors time.

The age of selected bank Alizz bank is excluded because its age less than 10 years. Then start from the beginning and Al Salam Bank was chosen.

Table 12 shows that total loan to total assets positively on Z score.
Table 13 shows excluded variables.
Table 19 shows significance of the test.
Table 20 shows significant individual variable (net loan to Total assets ratio) effect on Z score.
Table 25 shows significance of individual variable.
Table 27 shows significance of the test.
Table 28 shows individual variable significance.
Table 32 shows excluded external economic variables from Z score model.

A. Appendixes

A.1 The Sample description

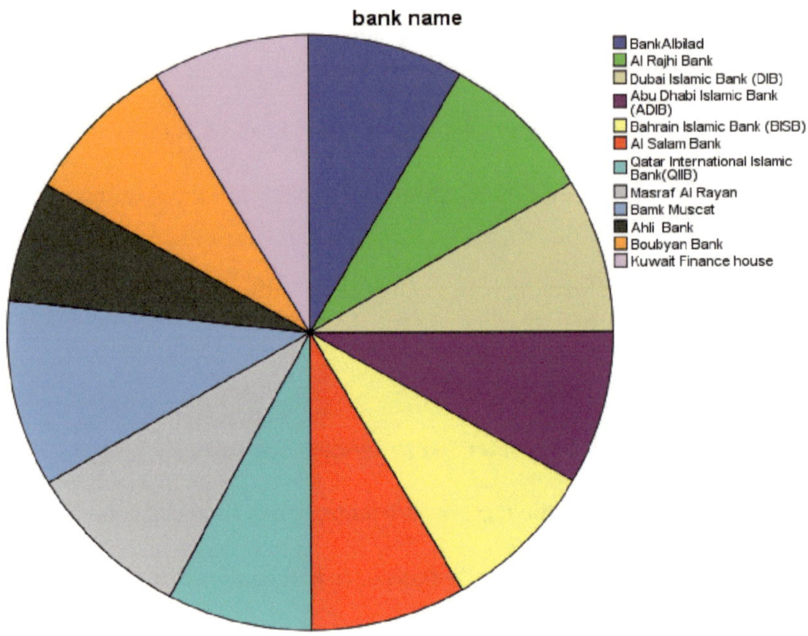

A.2 The period of the study

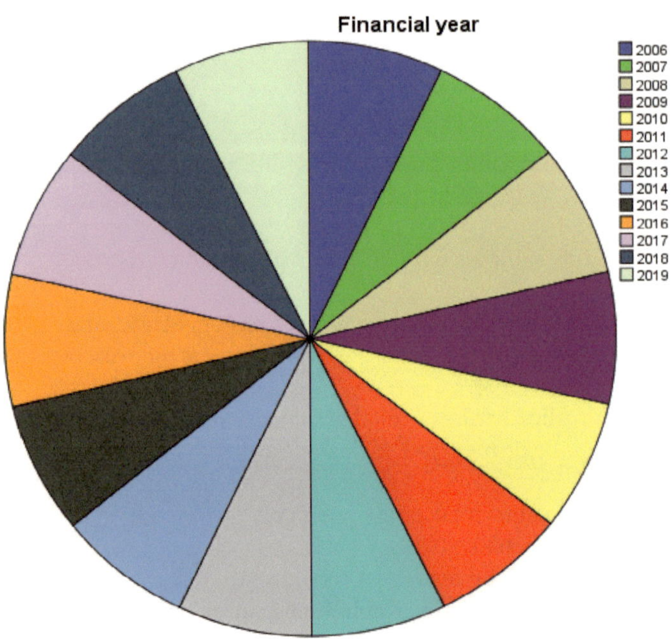

Source the researcher from the data.

A.3 Gulf Council Countries name(GCC)

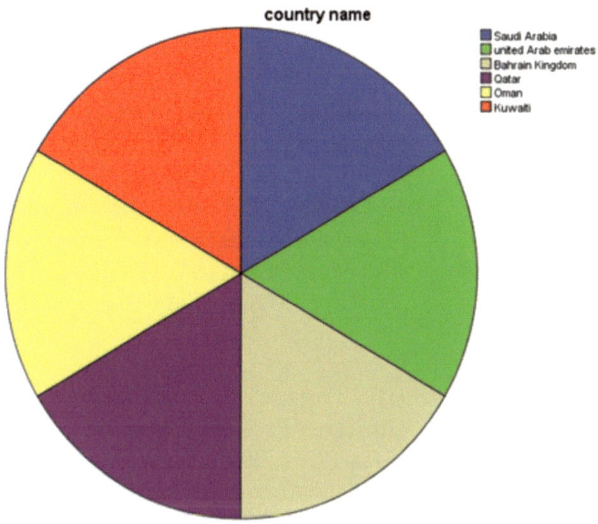

Source the researcher from the data.

Author details

Bakhita Hamdow Gad Elkreem Braima[1,2]

1 Finance and Investment Department, Faculty of Business Administration, University of Tabuk, Saudi Arabia

2 University of Kordofan, AlObied, Sudan

*Address all correspondence to: bgadkreem@yahoo.com

References

[1] Merchant, I. P. (2012). Performance analysis of banks using CAMEL approach, An Empirical study of Islamic Banks Versus Conventional Banks of GCC, Global Journal of Management and Business Research Volume 12 Issue 20 Version 1.0 pp.32–42

[2] Zeitun, R. (2012) "Determinants of Islamic and Conventional Banks Performance in GCC Countries Using Panel Data Analysis", Global Economy and Finance Journal, 5 (1), pp. 53–72. Available at: https://brightinvisiblegreen.com/research-proposal-on-analyzing-performance-of-banking-sector-in-pakistan

[3] Platt, H. D. & Marjorie B. P. (2006). "Understanding Differences Between Financial Distress and Bankruptcy." Review of Applied Economics, Vol. 2 No. 2, pp. 141–157.

[4] Outecheva, N. (2007). Corporate financial distress: An empirical analysis of distress risk (Doctoral dissertation, University of St. Gallen).

[5] Altman, E. I., & Hotchkiss, E. (2010). Corporate financial distress and bankruptcy: Predict and avoid bankruptcy, analyze and invest in distressed debt (Vol. 289). John Wiley & Sons, Inc.

[6] Wertheim, P., & Robinson, M. (2011). "Evidence On The Effect Of Financial Distress On Type II AuditErrors." Journal of Applied Business Research (JABR), Vol. 27 No. 6, pp. 135–150.

[7] Altman, Edward. I. 1968. Financial Ratio, Discriminant Analysis and the Prediction of Corporate Bankcruptcy. The Journal of Finance, 23(4): 509–609.

[8] Purnanandam, A. (2008). "Financial distress and corporate risk management: Theory and evidence." Journal of Financial Economics, 87(3), pp.706–739

[9] Altman, Edward, and Edith Hotchkiss, 2006, Corporate Financial Distress and Bankruptcy, 3rd edition (Hoboken), New Jersey: John Wiley and Sons Inc.

[10] Zaki, E., Bah, R., & Rao, A. (2011). "Assessing probabilities of financial distress of banks in UAE." International Journal of Managerial Finance, Vol. 7 No. 3, pp. 304–320.

[11] Vianez,Jessica Paule, Milagros Gutiérrez-Fernandez and José Luis Coca-Pérez, 2020, Prediction of financial distress in the Spanish banking system, Applied Economic Analysis, Vol. 28 No. 82, 2020, pp. 69–87

[12] H. Nurul Husna and R. Abdul Rahman, 2012, Financial Distress–Detection Model for Islamic Banks, International Journal of Trade, Economics and Finance, Vol. 3, No. 3, pp.158–163

[13] P. R. Kumar and V. Ravi, 2007, "Bankruptcy Prediction in Banks and Firms via Statistical and Intelligent Techniques – A Review," European Journal of Operation Research, vol. 180, pp. 1–28.

[14] Isabelle. Distinguin, P. Rous, and A. Tarazi, "Market Discipline and the Use of Stock Market Data to Predict Bank Financial Distress," Journal of Financial Services Research, vol. 30, pp. 151–176.

[15] G. Whalen and J. B. Thomson, may m2011,"Using Financial Data to Identify Changes in Bank Condition," 1988, pp. 17–26. http://clevelandfed.org/research/review/ retrieved on 18 May 2011

[16] S. S. Ali, 2007,"Financial Distress and Bank Failure: Lessons from Closure of Ihlas Finans in Turkey," Islamic Economic Studies, vol. 14, no. 1 & 2, pp. 1–52

[17] Tesfaye Boru Lelissa & Abdurezak Mohammed Kuhil. 2018, Empirical Evidence on the Impact of Bank Specific Factors on the Commercial Banks Performance: The Camel Model and Case of Ethiopian Banks, Global Journal of Management and Business Research: C Finance V. 18 Issue 5 Version 1.0 Year 2018. P.18–30.

[18] A. A. Sarker,2006,CAMELS Rating System in the Context of Islamic Banking: A Proposed 'S' for Shariah Framework," Journal of Islamic Economics and Finance, vol. 2, no. 2. pp. 1–26

[19] R. Haniffa and M. Hudaib,2007, "Exploring the Ethical Identity of Islamic Banks via Communication in Annual Reports," Journal of Business Ethics, vol. 76, pp. 97–116,

[20] Dece Kurniadi, Abdul Mongi, and Sutan Emir Hidayat, 2018, A Simple Stress Test on Indonesian IslamicBanking Industry, Jurnal Keuangan dan Perbankan, 22(1), pp. 148–161

[21] Khaled Halteh, Kuldeep Kumar, Adrian Gepp, 2018, Financial distress prediction of Islamic banks using tree-based stochastic techniques, Managerial Finance Vol. 44 No. 6, pp. 759–773.

[22] Pir Qasim Shah (2014) Performance Analysis of Selected Islamic and Conventional Banks of Pakistan through CAMEL Framework, Business & Economic Review: Vol. 6, Issue 1, pp. 19–39 available at: https https://imsciences.edu.pk/files/journals/vol6-issue1

[23] Mohammad Kamrul Ahsan,(2016) Measuring Financial Performance Based on CAMEL: A Study on Selected Islamic Banks in Bangladesh, Asin Business Review, V6, No(1) issue 3, pp.:47–56

[24] Muhammad Hussain & Rukhsana KALIM (2018), How Shariah Compliance and Traditional Banks are Performing? A Case of Pakistan, INTERNATIONAL JOURNAL OF ISLAMIC ECONOMICS AND FINANCE STUDIES,Vol:4, Issue:3, pp.6–20

[25] Erari, A. D. (2013). "Financial Performance Analysis of PT. Bank Papua: Application of CAEL, Z-Scoreand Bankometer." IOSR Journal of Business and Management. Vol. 7 No. 5. pp. 08–16 available at: - https://www.pen2print.org/2016/12/pred

[26] Chotalia, P. (2014). Evaluation of financial health of sampled private sector banks with Altman Z-score model.International Journal of Research in Management, Science & Technology, 2(3), pp. 42–46.

[27] Pradhan, R. P., et al. (2014). Causal nexus between economic growth, banking sector development, stock market development, and other macroeconomic variables. The Review of Financial Economics. http://dx.doi.org/10.1016/j.rfe.2014.07.002

[28] Obaid Saif H. Al Zaabi, 2011. "Potential for the application of emerging market Z-score in UAE Islamic banks," International Journal of Islamic and Middle Eas, tern Finance and Management, Emerald Group Publishing, vol. 4(2), pages 158–173, June.

[29] Kusdiana. 2014. Analisis Model CAMEL dan Altman's Z-Score,dalam Memprediksi Kebangkrutan Bank Umum di Indonesia. Jurnal Tepak Manajemen Bisnis, 6(1): pp. 85–94.

[30] Endri. (2009). Prediksi Kebangkrutan Bank untuk Menghadapi dan Mengelola Perubahan LingkunganBisnis: Analisis Model Altman Z-Score. Perbanas Quaterly Review. Vol. 2. No 1. Pp.34–50

[31] Altman EI (2002) Revisiting Credit Scoring Models in a Basel II Environment.

[32] Kaur Harsh Vineet 2010,Analysis of Banks in India—A CAMEL Approach, GLOBAL BUSINESS REVIEW, 11: 2 pp. 257–280

[33] Ehab Zaki, Rahim Bah, Ananth Rao 28 June 2011, Assessing probabilities of financial distress of banks in UAE, International Journal of Managerial Finance, V. 7 Issue 3, pp.301–320.

[34] Endri. 2008. Prediksi Kebangkrutan Bank untuk Menghadapidan Mengelola Perubahan Lingkungan Bisnis Analisa Model Altman's Z-Score. Jurnal Perbanas Quarterly Review, 2(1), pp. 34–50.

[35] Nataraja NS, Nagaraja Rao Chilale, Ganesh L, 2018, Financial Performance of Private Commercial Banks in India: Multiple Regression Analysis, Academy of Accounting and Financial Studies Journal,V. 22 Issue: 2, pp.1–12.